"One of these two people should be president. . . . Looking over rosters from both parties, two stand out. They've won big elections, held major government posts, and have strong credentials. They are Gina Raimondo, a Democrat, and Mitch Daniels, a Republican."

—RON FAUCHEUX, nonpartisan political analyst, polling expert, and writer based in Louisiana; *The Times-Picayune*/NOLA.com, March 2023

". . . Daniels, he is revered among conservative intellectuals as a principled thought leader within the Republican Party."

—BLAKE HOUNSHELL, editor of the *On Politics* newsletter and frequent contributor to the *New York Times*; *New York Times*, December 2022

"Purdue has the president the nation needs."

—GEORGE F. WILL, *Washington Post*, June 2016

". . . Daniels has refashioned himself into a national leader on higher education reform."

—ADAM WREN, *Politico*, August 2022

"Mitch Daniels for president? We never seem to get the chance to vote for somebody reasonable."

—JAMES SPIRO, *Wall Street Journal*, September 2022

"Daniels will leave behind a legacy of principled leadership, moral vision, and prudent fiscal management that would be remarkable in any era—but especially one in which college presidents are often unwilling to make tough decisions or take principled stands."

—FREDERICK HESS, senior fellow and director, education policy studies, American Enterprise Institute, June 2022

"To me, the top award for American higher education innovation must go to Mitch Daniels."

—RICHARD K. VEDDER, author of *Restoring the Promise: Higher Education in America*

"An adult on campus: Mitch Daniels offers a lesson to college administrators."
—*WALL STREET JOURNAL* OPINION, November 2015

"His parsimonious nature, when applied to public matters, is one reason he received more votes than any other officeholder in Indiana history in 2008, when he won reelection as governor, and it's why he and his university—a 150-year-old land-grant school in West Lafayette, Indiana—are objects of curiosity and even wonderment in the world of higher education."
—ANDREW FERGUSON, *The Atlantic*, April 2020

"Though much has been made of the last few years of his [Purdue] administration and Daniels's choice not to run for president, the former governor's two terms in Indianapolis are widely considered to be among the best in the state's history."
—DANIEL SUDDEATH, *News and Tribune*, Jeffersonville, Indiana, July 2022

"Daniels is trying—and succeeding—at lowering universities' costs, rather than merely passing along the (ever-larger) bill to already-cash-strapped state legislatures and the taxpayers they represent."
—TOM LINDSAY, *Forbes*, October 2017

BOILER UP

THE FOUNDERS SERIES

The Founders Series publishes books on and about Purdue University, whether the physical campus, the University's impact on the region and world, or the many visionaries who attended or worked at the University.

A UNIVERSITY PRESIDENT IN THE PUBLIC SQUARE

Mitch Daniels

Foreword by Former U.S. Secretary of State Condoleezza Rice

Purdue University Press · West Lafayette, Indiana

Cataloging-in-Publication Data is available from the Library of Congress.
978-1-61249-936-9 (hardcover)
978-1-61249-937-6 (epub)
978-1-61249-938-3 (epdf)

Except where noted, all columns appeared in the *Washington Post*.

Cover: *Purdue Gateway Arch*. Photo by Rebecca Robiños / Purdue University.

For the students of Purdue University

Contents

Foreword

O VER MY MANY YEARS IN PUBLIC SERVICE AND IN THE ACADEMY, I HAVE COME TO BE-
lieve that the best leaders are those who don't actually seek the positions for which they are most needed—and in which they turn out to
be consequential.

This was the case with my friend Mitch Daniels. He had concluded two terms
as arguably not only Indiana's most effective governor but one of the most highly
regarded leaders in the country. Everyone—including yours truly—thought
that he should run for president of the United States. Instead, fate would lead
him to another kind of presidency in a field in which he was an outsider: higher
education.

I will admit that when Mitch's appointment was announced, there was some
eye-rolling in university circles. The academy is a guild with merit measured in
forty-year careers spent writing articles and teaching students. Could this man,
this politician, really lead Purdue academically and without partisan intent?

A decade later, no one asks that question. Rather they ask, How did he do it?
How did Mitch Daniels lead Purdue to record investments in research programs
across countless academic departments, vastly elevating its reputation and prestige? How did Mitch Daniels put a stake in the ground concerning the affordability of higher education, rejecting tuition increases at a time when inflation
in the cost of college was nationally at 7%?

How did Mitch Daniels lead Purdue to build on its considerable strengths in
engineering and the sciences and yet broaden the university's reach into the social sciences and the humanities? And how did he encourage an environment at
Purdue that valued spirited debate and mutual respect for diverse points of view?
No democracy can last if these principles are not upheld. Mitch was determined
that Purdue would be a place that took that stand.

Moreover, his own vow of "political celibacy" was the perfect perch from
which to demand civility rather than partisanship. And it also answered allega-
tions that he had taken the job as a way station on the way back into politics and

possibly to the White House. Mitch Daniels, it turns out, was totally and completely dedicated to the transformation of Purdue and changing how we think about higher education.

I saw this firsthand when I visited Purdue in the fall of 2019. I had asked to meet with faculty who were innovators. I expected the usual collection of engineers and scientists and maybe the occasional economist. But much to my surprise, my conversation was with faculty from a diverse set of fields; the arts and humanities were robustly represented. I was treated to a stimulating discussion of how data science is infusing the teaching and research in every academic corner of Purdue. And we talked about how, in the age of computing, interdisciplinary exploration of the new world of knowledge was essential. Purdue, like its president, is not wedded to the old ways of doing things. It is a refreshing challenger to the academic enterprise, which is much in need of new ideas and ways of carrying out its critically important mission.

Mitch's tenure as president of Purdue is a tale of steadfastness and persistence. He has shown how to lead with authority and direction, but also how to encourage collaboration and innovation from across the university. Mitch would be the first to say that he did not know the answer to every challenge he found. But what he has done is to empower people—faculty, students, and staff—to lead as well. Purdue is the better for it and so is higher education. I hope that others will follow and that Mitch's next chapter—and there must be a next chapter—can bring life to other important American institutions in the future.

Dr. Condoleezza Rice
Sixty-Sixth U.S. Secretary of State, Nineteenth U.S. National Security Advisor, and the Hoover Institution's Tad and Dianne Taube Director and Thomas and Barbara Stephenson Senior Fellow on Public Policy

Introduction

THE INVITATION CAME, AS SEVERAL OTHER PROFESSIONAL OPPORTUNITIES HAVE, OUT of the blue. At first, and second, and at least third blush, the notion of serving as president of a university, let alone one the size and renown of Purdue, seemed improbable at both ends, mine and the school's.

It wasn't the return to private life I had in mind at the time. My standard answer back then to the "What's next?" question was, "I don't know, but it will be somewhere in the NDB (none of your damned business) zone," meaning someplace where people wouldn't feel entitled to read my emails, scan my visitors logs, and know my daily whereabouts.

And it was far from assured that I, a total rookie in the world of higher education, could do the job justice; those who doubted and questioned the search committee and trustees' judgment had ample reason to do so.

But a persuasive board, and a positive vote from a persuasive wife, convinced me to give the job a try, and I'll always be grateful to those who helped me decide to do so. Purdue quickly became the institution closest to my heart, and working for Purdue the most fulfilling assignment I could have hoped for.

Having made the, as we say around here, giant leap, I asked myself the question any new employee should start with: "Where might I add value to this place? What if anything could I do that might augment or add a new dimension to the success it is already enjoying?"

I would like to believe that over the past decade, along with an extraordinarily talented team of co-workers, we delivered several answers to that question. I hope future Boilermakers will look back and find the era one marked by generally wise strategic decisions, well-chosen investments, effective management of Purdue's day-to-day affairs, and the upholding of the highest professional and academic values. All with the best interests of our students, present and future, at the center of our bull's eye.

But whatever history's judgment of those matters, I am reasonably sure that it will be remembered as a decade in which Purdue's reputation, and recognition among the very top tier of the world's universities, advanced substantially.

A variety of market research findings attest to it; a growing list of awards and high rankings reinforce those data. When *Fast Company* magazine inaugurated its "Brands That Matter" list in 2021, it identified only one university to place along-side McDonald's, IBM, and IKEA in that category, and it was ours.

That was a primary goal from the outset. It seemed obvious to me that, blessed with an abundance of contacts and relationships from past lives, with important business, media, intellectual, and political figures, I could and should work to utilize those assets on Purdue's behalf.

I thought Purdue deserved it. It's frequently observed that a tradition of humility—a highly admirable trait I hope we never lose—has often prevented Purdue or many of its star performers from receiving the attention their achievements warranted.

I also thought Purdue could use some more visibility. Shortly after the announcement of my appointment, I heard from a good friend in New York City, a top-level marketing executive married to a tremendously talented and renowned leader in the publishing industry. He said that when he asked his wife if she had heard the news about my new role and told her, "He's going to be president of Purdue," she replied, "I think that is just terrible." When my friend then said, "Gee, I think it's pretty cool," his wife sniffed, "His talents will be totally wasted in the chicken business."

We had a good laugh about it, but it did suggest that Purdue wasn't getting all the recognition, even simple name recognition, that its wonderful history and present contributions merited. With half of our modern student body coming from outside Indiana, greater visibility is a key element in attracting both the excellent students and faculty we need for true greatness. If I could play some part in moving the recognition needle, I ought to do so. My motto became "If it (publicity) is neutral to positive and they spell it with two *u*'s, it's a win."

Over the years, I had a host of speaking opportunities, national media interviews, and invitations to contribute written work in venues that would not ordinarily present themselves to someone in my current role. So, I hope selectively but not indiscriminately, I tried to take advantage of these opportunities as one way of adding some unique value to our institution.

The nature of the likely opportunities was pretty evident. I knew and was known by a host of journalists on the national and, of course, the state scene, and could expect to be called on for comments on a range of topics well beyond my new world of higher education. The proliferation of broadcast channels had afforded me scores of appearances, especially over the past twelve years, that provided me a wide range of contacts (not to mention valuable practice) and was likely to add invitations to be heard.

I had recently written a book, promoted during a national tour. I had published columns in the op-ed pages of most of the national newspapers over the years, and could hope that an occasional submission might find favor with a familiar editor.

And the variety of my previous vocational experiences had produced a "rolodex" of past associates from a wide array of places and backgrounds. Two tours in D.C., separated by fifteen years and two presidencies; several years in the contract research business and think tank world; the longest single stretch, a decade plus in a global pharmaceutical and biotech company, which had taken me all over the world. And, of course, the most recent pre-Purdue job, in which Indiana's policy innovations and overall success had drawn an unusual degree of national attention.

So, if I had the imagination and initiative to recruit them, there would be no shortage of interesting men and women I should be able to enlist them to bring their experiences and insights to our campus. As I often put it, part of my new job should be to ramp up the intellectual traffic flow at Purdue.

So the why, the who, and the how of generating more attention to our institution were fairly obvious. The harder questions centered on the what, as in, "With what subjects should I deal in public forums, and which ones if any should I decline to address?"

The biggest set of opportunities was the one I most obviously had to avoid. Had I been willing, I could constantly have been giving speeches, and all over television and other media, pontificating about politics and all the state and national issues of the day. And, to be sure, over the years we turned down hundreds of requests to do so, and many other times I ducked a question slipped into an interview ostensibly on nonpolitical subject matter.

But I had forsworn exactly that activity, in fact six months before commencing Purdue's presidency. At the announcement of my selection, on June 21, 2012, I said, "Effective immediately, I will recuse myself from any partisan political activities or commentary."

Although some seemed surprised at that position, there was never any question in my mind. It's true that, at many points in the past, private university presidents have been highly active in public controversies of the day. But, as a public institution, supported by taxpayers of all political views, I believe Purdue must stand aside from partisanship of any kind.

Second, in a wise decision some four decades before, Purdue's trustees had laid down the principle that the university would take no stance on any matter of public debate unless the institution's own interests were involved. No president, let alone one just arrived from the realm of politics, could plausibly claim to be speaking "just for himself" without implicating the university in his statements.

But I had one additional reason, maybe an overriding one, to take what I have always called my "vow of political celibacy." I understood and accepted the suspicion of many people that I saw my new role as a sinecure, or a temporary launching pad back into political life. Clearly others have used college presidencies in that way.

But I would never have accepted Purdue's offer with any such intent. No one should take a job, at least not one with broad responsibility, without putting the enterprise, and its people, ahead of any personal agenda. As the Marine Corps has long taught its officers, "My mission, my men, myself." The order, of course, is the point of the maxim.

So I wanted it to be plain from Day One—in fact, from Day One minus six months—that Purdue's success was my only agenda, and that I would not risk tainting it even if it resulted in wider exposure. That eliminated countless opportunities to be seen and heard, but those that remained were those that reflected best on our institution and the ways in which it has separated and distinguished itself from its competitors.

The material that follows could have been organized thematically, because looking back there are several topics to which I found myself returning frequently: the likelihood (and the need for) disruption and reform in higher education, the new tribalism in society, the parallel erosion of civility and constructive compromise, the risk of our graduates losing touch with those less intellectually gifted or academically prepared, the emotional fragility of too many young people and the need to build and encourage the grit necessary to success, and others.

Instead, we have chosen to group the selections by medium: speeches, interviews, and written material. One hopes that here and there they contributed constructively to various public debates, while playing a meaningful role in elevating Purdue's name and reputation. A wealth of evidence and market research says that has happened, that Purdue is better known and more highly regarded than a decade ago.[1]

I trust the data, of course, but I also have my own markers of success: No one these days thinks we're in the chicken business. And no one spells Purdue with two *e*'s.

PART I

Speeches, Interviews, and Messages

PEECHES AND INTERVIEWS PRESENTED ABUNDANT OPPORTUNITIES TO DELIVER WHAT
I called "Purdue commercials," but with them came a particular dilemma
when I was asked to talk about Purdue's own sector of higher education.
Once nearly immune from criticism, higher ed had already become a subject
of debate when I changed jobs in 2013. Both its value (Is it worth the ever-
escalating price?) and its values (Is it teaching students how to think, or telling
them what to think?) were under increasingly sharp criticism, which only inten-
sified over the ensuing decade.

Like any attentive citizen, and as a tuition-paying parent, I had been well
aware of these issues for years. As an elected official, I had had the responsibility
to examine the performance and the budgets of our state universities. I arrived
at Purdue with a conviction that all was not well in higher ed, and a strong view
that our state and nation needed its universities to succeed. The chance to help
one great institution, one which I viewed as already meeting its mission better
than most, was a powerful attraction in persuading myself to take on the new role.

Both to force myself to study and think through the questions I would face in
my new life, and to introduce myself to a campus and alumni community rightly
curious about what such a rank outsider might be about, I wrote the first of what
became an annual open letter, released at New Year's. In each of these epistles,
I tried to report candidly on both the broad environment of higher ed and developments at Purdue during the year past. While there were always people to
praise and things to brag about, I tried to avoid the cheerleading and propagan-
dizing that usually dominates such accounts.

Much like the commencements, I was surprised by the extent to which these yearly missives, written explicitly for a Purdue audience, circulated around the country. Every year brought requests for copies, and reports that people had shared them with their mailing lists, or sent them to their own school's trustees, or otherwise handed them around. Many were quoted in articles far from Purdue, and I began inserting small disclaimers that we were not recommending steps we were taking to any other school, only making moves that we thought fit our institution, its students, and its mission.

I had been taking that same stance in speeches from the very outset, in public appearances. Almost every such venue brought the invitation, explicit or implied, to prescribe to other colleges how they ought to run their affairs. I deflected these questions on virtually every occasion, although when the issue involved an overarching value like freedom of inquiry or freedom of expression, I suppose I did become prescriptive.

As Purdue embarked on a host of new initiatives and departed further from the practices typical at most American universities, the invitations to speak, and to criticize other schools, came even faster. I tried to avoid any such deprecation and to let Purdue's innovations and results speak for themselves.

My goal always has been to serve one institution as well as I could, while perhaps here and there creating examples for others to emulate if they thought it fit their own situation. With all its obvious flaws, America's network of higher ed institutions is and must remain an essential national asset, and source of competitive advantage. If, while pursuing my personal task of building regard for our university around the country, I could encourage others to take reformist action at their own schools, that would be a fine outcome. I hope time will reveal that some of that occurred.

SPEECHES AND INTERVIEWS

**U.S. Department of Energy
Advanced Research Projects Agency–Energy
Fourth Annual ARPA-E Energy Innovation Summit
February 2013**

I have been asked by the organizers to say a few words about, or at least use as a point of departure, the state of science, technology, engineering, and mathematics education in America—STEM education as we are now all fond of calling it. And obedient to that charge I will say a few words about it, but then I hope to broaden the subject just briefly before turning you over to someone better known and more erudite who will follow me.

I doubt I need to document the woeful state of numeracy, of scientific and technical learning among our citizens at all levels, but most important and tellingly among our younger citizens. I will not burden you, as I could have, with a slide show or a realm of statistics. But maybe I'll just mention a few numbers that will remind you of what you already know. Namely, we've got a long way to go.

At the most recent measurement, fewer than a third of American eighth graders had what is called a "basic" command of math—that is, the lowest tier or lowest categorization on the international test that is given. What is "basic," you ask? Examples are to use an average to solve a problem; to use a measuring cup to describe a given fraction; or to solve a simple story involving computing with money, even with the benefit of the calculator. Fewer than a third of our eighth graders could manage tasks like that. At the other end of the spectrum, fewer than a fourth of our twelfth graders have achieved what is called "proficiency," the highest standard. And it is no surprise when you consider that nationally fewer than 30% of our high school physics and chemistry teachers majored in either of those subjects.

In my home state we have attempted to deal with this in a variety of ways. You will no longer get a license to teach those subjects in Indiana if you *didn't* major in one of those subjects. It's acceptable to have taken pedagogical courses up to a certain level, but we have embraced the radical notion that if you are going to teach math, you ought to know a little math.

We were the first state, fortunately, chosen by the Woodrow Wilson Foundation to welcome to the teaching ranks mid-career physicists, chemists, biologists, and other skilled technical people, and people with scientific backgrounds from business, from the military, from every walk of life you can imagine whose hearts have called them to teaching. We have opened the door for them to get a master's in one year and go straight to the classroom, as long as they will commit to teach our young people for a while longer. We have done things large and small. I raised some money to offer $10,000, the largest science fair winner prize in America, as far as I know.

In my new endeavor at Purdue University we hope to pursue our contributions to this national need as aggressively as we can. It is in keeping with Purdue's tradition as a land-grant school, but with special emphasis these days.

I want to teach you a new acronym, by the way. We don't say STEM at Purdue. We say STEAM. We insert an *A* for agriculture, which many of you know is as technology-intensive a realm of endeavor as we have these days and, I would submit, takes every bit as much energy. At Purdue we are proud to be home to two of the last World Food Prize winners—loosely termed the Nobel Prize of Agriculture.

My new colleagues at Purdue see in the not distant future corn half as tall as today, but with twice the kernels per ear, and therefore with a much-reduced environmental footprint. They see self-driving tractors that, row-by-row in real time, will plant the right seed, biologically speaking, for the nutrients and the condition of the soil; will fertilize it appropriately and only appropriately; and later in the season will spray with the same limited, only necessary quantity.

But our focus at Purdue is equally and always has been on the rest of the acronym. We graduate more engineers and students in technical fields each year right now than any other school in the country. Fifty-three percent of the degrees we conferred last year went to engineering, science, and technology students. I looked at the list of the top ten degrees as measured by the marketplace. We offer them all. If you take out airline pilots and actuaries (we are also pretty good at those two things), all the rest are in disciplines you would recognize, and we think Purdue excels at them. We will add over a hundred new engineering faculty in the next five years because we think this is where our greatest contribution to society can be. (We're happy to take applications in the lobby afterward if any of this excites somebody here.)

Most of all we are trying to build a culture of invention, impact, and entrepreneurism at our school. Just last week in what I thought was a small deal, but may actually be somewhat larger than I imagined, we told all of our undergrads that any intellectual property or any potentially patentable discovery that comes out of their work is theirs, not the university's. We want to encourage everybody, from the youngest undergrad to the most senior researcher to invest themselves and commit themselves to the job of transferring the learning and the brilliance that is abundant on that campus, as on so many, into the betterment of society. We are going to worry a lot less about what the university owns and a lot more about moving into commerce, into the world around us, the genius that abides at Purdue. We imagine that the university will come out all right in the long run if we do that.

It is not enough simply to prepare students who are expert in the STEM or STEAM disciplines. We want to produce for society STEM citizens. People who lift their head up from the research bench or stick it out of the lab long enough to participate in, and to help their fellow citizens understand, the issues of our time. Every student at Purdue is now encouraged, virtually required, to have a leadership experience every year. It could be a service club, it could be a student activity, but we virtually insist that they do that.

We want to make sure they know enough economics to know that nations whose private sectors do not grow vigorously ultimately condemn themselves to second-rate status; enough history to know that nations who borrow and borrow and ultimately cheapen their currency in an attempt to evade paying their debts always run on the rocks; certainly enough sense of risk and benefit to judge for themselves, and help their fellow citizens judge, the trade-offs that are part of a life in a democracy; and to see the technologies and the disciplines in which they are expert in the broader context of society. Humanity has never lived in an era that needed technologically credible civic leadership more than today. And in one other potentially useful statistic you probably know, my last tally shows the U.S. Senate with 45 lawyers and 1 engineer; the U.S. House with 128 lawyers and 2 engineers.

I'll just give you two examples that for my money are important for people like our students and people like this audience to be heard on. The best break, as far as I can tell, the American and even the world economy has gotten, perhaps since the invention of the silicon chip, is the breakthroughs in extraction technology that I know people in this audience contributed to. Thank you very much. You have once again exposed the fallacy of extrapolation, once again embarrassed the sort of Malthusian thinking that we are going to run out of this and run out of that. Human ingenuity has won again, at least potentially.

The upside is huge. Every time I see it quantified somebody is bumping it up a little, but we are talking cautiously on the order of 1% to 2% of GDP, the jobs, the change in the trade balance, and in our part of America, the resurgence of manufacturing this is likely to make possible. Very important is the government revenue so desperately needed that could come from that kind of incremental growth and the benefits for our national security. This should be the easiest call—the optimization, maximization of this possibility, supported by public policy at all levels—since, oh, the Keystone Pipeline. Oh, wait a minute . . . we got that wrong too.

I've talked at great length to the people at Purdue, and I feel confident in saying to lay audiences that this is a great course for our country. The problems, where they exist at all, are mitigatable or easily addressable. Let's get on with it. And when the "University of Hollywood" produces a product that is full of bunk, somebody in a crowd like this ought to accept the responsibility to speak up and debunk it.

The second example I would give has to do with Topic A of the day, the federal budget. I get an email a day right now from people in higher ed associations to which we belong. We read horror stories every morning in the paper about this dreaded sequester business. I hope you will pardon me if I decline to join the hysteria. A 2% reduction in a federal budget that has been growing by double digits year on year on year is not an unmanageable thing. A reduction in the upward trend, *upward* trend, from 14% to 12% over the next few years is simply not draconian, certainly not in the context of the danger we face for the debts we've piled up and those we've scheduled for ourselves. We are talking about funding the National Science Foundation at 2010 levels, and we were not starving in 2010.

Is this a smart way to begin the process of fiscal integrity in this country? Of course not, but we have to start somewhere. And I'll just say that debt and slow growth—debt and a national economy barely moving along at a point and a half or so, which we did last year—is a lot bigger threat to the R&D that needs to happen in energy and in these other research areas. It's a lot bigger threat, honestly, than this ham-handed sequester that may well happen.

The biggest threat to the budgets that support a lot of the work going on in the places represented in this room is not this sequester. It's Medicare growing at more than 60% year on year, already part of a complex of entitlement spending that is close to two-thirds of the budget. The biggest threat to the graduates who will pick up a diploma, coming across the stage at Purdue in a few months, is not the $27,000 a year they may owe in student loans. It's the three-quarters of a million dollars they already owe *each* for the debts their elders have racked up for them.

On behalf of our university, and I hope we are typical of many, we are proud to try to prepare the leaders of tomorrow—the engineers, the scientists, the chemists and physicists, and the mathematicians—on whom our human progress depends. We will work hard to prepare those leaders, and we simply implore those who are already leaders—I'll never see a room with a heavier concentration than right here—just make sure there is a great country worth their leading when their time comes. Thank you very, very much.

National Academy of Engineering
Washington, D.C.
October 2013

Mr. President, members of the Academy. It is conventional to the point of banality for a speaker on an occasion like this to proclaim what a privilege it is to be invited. In my case today, the honor is so literal and so profound that I cannot fail to note and thank you for it. The opportunity for a nonmember, in fact a non-engineer like me, to be afforded the privilege of this podium is so unlikely that I am tempted to ask, "Who canceled?"

But the invitation came many months ago, and thus I know was sincere. And if such an improbable choice of speakers makes any logical sense, it must be because your organizers saw a chance to bring variety, and perhaps a complementary perspective, to those magnificent scholarly presentations that always characterize your meetings. If I can add any value today, it will come through the reflections of someone who was neither wise nor fortunate enough to pursue a life in engineering, but who has worked in close proximity, in several different settings, to superb engineers, and who has studied the dramatic and essential contributions that your profession makes daily to the prosperity, happiness, and literally the future survival of us all.

Among my most educational exposures to engineers and their thought processes were the days I spent at the Hudson Institute, the RAND Corporation spinoff that, at that time, was a contract research organization known for its often surprising, contrarian findings. To capture the spirit of the place, our research fellows made up the following fable.

When the anti-intellectual revolution came, Hudson's founder, the legendary Herman Kahn, was among those imprisoned and sentenced to the guillotine.

As he awaited his turn on the execution platform, the blade failed to drop on another victim, who by custom was then released. The next defendant was brought forward but again the blade malfunctioned, and he too was let go. As Herman's head was placed on the block, he looked up at the mechanism above and said, "I think I see your problem."

My appreciation for unbiased thinking, for unconventional viewpoints, and for the problem-solving mindset we associate with excellent engineering has grown steadily over the years, as I have been lucky enough to see great engineers at work in the pharmaceutical industry, and in the more excellent of our public sector activities. The most recent of those exposures I also owe to this Academy, whose past president Charles Vest asked me to co-chair the National Research Council's current commission on the future of human spaceflight.

The chance to promote engineering was a major reason that I accepted Purdue University's invitation to service. I can say honestly that I had never aspired to a role in higher education, or imagined myself occupying one, prior to Purdue's overture. But as I contemplated the offer, I found myself drawn to the "sound of the guns": first, to try to contribute to the support of higher education and, specifically, research universities, at a time of unprecedented stress and threat; and second, to help meet the well-documented national need for more STEM graduates and, specifically, engineers.

A few days ago, Purdue was excited to welcome to campus GE CEO Jeff Immelt. Mr. Immelt was one of the few people to whom I had confided my potential new role in advance of accepting it. His strong encouragement was one important factor in my saying yes. "Absolutely you should do it," he told me. "You can be the patron saint of engineering." Well, I will never be a candidate for sainthood, of engineering or anything else. The very idea calls to mind St. Augustine's confession that, in his younger days, he had prayed, "Lord, make me chaste. But not just yet." Unlike Augustine, I failed to progress much past that stage.

Nonetheless, knowing how purely metaphorical Jeff's comment was, I understood the seriousness of the objective to which he was alluding. For years, report after report, commission upon commission has pointed to the severe shortfall in new engineers and scientists that our nation faces. The dimension of the problem is familiar to everyone here, and the alarming numbers need no repetition. While China, India, and other nations forge ahead in attracting or steering their best young minds into STEM disciplines and careers, the U.S. is falling woefully short of producing the new talent, in particular engineering talent, our economy and national interest require. Jeff Immelt is fond of pointing out that we routinely turn out more sports exercise majors than electrical engineering majors. As he puts it, "If you want to become the massage capital of the world, you're well on your way."

So, to me, Purdue was not just another prestigious major university. It was already home to one of the finest engineering colleges, one which produces each year more undergraduate engineers and technology graduates than any other American institution. Moreover, I learned to my great excitement, Purdue's board was considering a significant expansion of that school. In fact, late last year, we made official our intention to expand our engineering faculty by more than 100 and our student population by more than 700 undergraduate and 700 graduate students over a five-year period.

I am pleased to report to you that last month our Board of Trustees endorsed my suggestion that we already begin planning a further expansion of the college, either to follow immediately or to overlap the current plan. At the same time, we committed to a 25% growth of our Department of Computer Science and a transformation of our College of Technology, featuring a revamped, more experiential and project-based curriculum aimed at cultivating an aptitude for innovation among its students. When these actions are complete, we believe we will be the second most STEM-centric public university in the nation, behind only Georgia Tech, a school barely half our size. Against the commonly expressed national goal of graduating an additional ten thousand engineers per year, our university alone will contribute between 5% and 10%.

I would also like to stress that at Purdue we remain fully committed to our land-grant heritage, and to the mission of providing a first-rate education to all who meet our standards at a price affordable to families of any income level. This spring, we announced a two-year freeze on tuition, as well as a 5% reduction in the cost of meals and a larger cut in the fees charged to engineering students participating in our work-study, or co-op, program. It is our intention to furnish the best engineering program, dollar for dollar, available anywhere.

We have also set out to improve the rate at which Purdue discovery and technology transfers to the market for the benefit of society. Many of our engineers and scientific faculty had told me of the obstacles and burdens our historic practices often placed in the path of inventors and would-be entrepreneurs, and beginning immediately in January we initiated changes to ease and encourage tech transfer activities.

We have centralized tech transfer promotion in our Purdue Research Foundation and created new facilities, available to all, for prototype development and new company formation. We have revised a host of contract and intellectual property rules. A standard ten-page minimal royalty contract is now available and can be signed in minutes, vs. the lengthy negotiations to which we used to subject our faculty innovators. We now return all IP rights to the discoverer in no longer than six months if the university decides not to proceed with patent filing. And, in a step I took the morning after a student alerted me to the topic at dinner, we now treat intellectual property arising from undergraduate research or engineering projects as the student's IP, not the university's.

So at Purdue we are consumed with the mission to address America's engineering, STEM, and innovation deficits. Count on us to do our part.

But led, it is important to say, by our engineering faculty, we believe that building scientific and technical excellence alone does not constitute the entirety of the job we have in preparing tomorrow's leaders of your profession. A firm grounding in the liberal arts, and in the skills of teamwork and communication, must also be part of the package.

In the same week that we unveiled our STEM expansion plans, we also were thrilled to announce the endowment of two new chairs in our History Department—one in the history of science, the other in the history of medicine. We want our STEM students to understand where their disciplines have come from just as well as they understand where they may be headed.

Similarly, we want them to depart Purdue with all the tools necessary for effective citizenship. Among these are the ability to write clearly, to speak clearly, and to work collaboratively with others. There may have been a time when engineers and technological experts could afford to stand aside from important public debates, talking only to each other, but that time has passed.

We live in an age of scientific complexity far beyond the comprehension of most citizens. It is easier than it has ever been for opponents of innovation to alarm others about even the most promising and important of scientific breakthroughs. Substances now measured in parts per billion sound no less scary to people who cannot put such infinitesimal risks in perspective. The trade-offs inevitable in new medical therapies or energy production or genetic modification can be misrepresented to either overstate or understate the net societal benefits, and too often those most audible in the discussion are not those scientifically best equipped to make such judgments.

Moreover, issues of direct consequence to science and technological progress increasingly depend on public decisions on far broader, nonscientific questions. It is regrettably true that public support for investments in research and the quest for new and unpredictable knowledge is lower than it should be. We have seen this all too clearly in our work for the National Academies' human spaceflight commission. We must all speak on every possible occasion about the centrality of research, particularly basic research, to the nation's future prospects.

But we face far greater threats than public indifference, and our greatest engineers and scientists must somehow find the time to make themselves heard on these broader issues. I will cite three, each of which menaces our innovation engine in a fundamental way. They are the runaway growth of the so-called entitlement programs, the host of ways in which public choices limit economic growth, and the continued failures of our K–12 education system.

On the last item, there is nothing new I can say, except that not enough is new. Three full decades ago, a national commission report labeled us a "nation at risk" and asserted that if a foreign power had sought to undermine the United States, it would have started by giving us the K–12 public school system we have. Thirty years later, we have only just begun to take the steps necessary to produce literate, numerate, scientifically capable young people with some true sense of the history and the values necessary to a successful free society. Meanwhile, the job has gotten much tougher; other societies now far surpass us in the cultural underpinnings conducive to a well-educated, technically proficient population. At every opportunity, we must insist that our children be taught rigorously, to high standards, in an environment of genuine competition and accountability.

The other two topics bear a bit more discussion. In my view, the nation's transcendent problem, the one that endangers our entire position as the leading country of the world, is also the single biggest danger to the future of our historically dominant scientific research enterprise. I refer to our national debt, which I have elsewhere labeled the new "red menace," this time consisting not of a militarily aggressive Soviet imperialism, but in the perhaps more dangerous red ink in which our national finances are drowning.

The terrible inequity through which massive national borrowing will penalize future economic growth and plunder the same young people we are now striving to educate at Purdue and your universities is a sermon for another Sunday. For today, allow me to focus on the direct hit our federal deficit and so-called entitlement spending in specific increasingly impose on the National Science Foundation, the National Institutes of Health, and federal departments like Defense, Homeland Security, Agriculture, and others. These vital research budgets are being brutally squeezed by the way in which Social Security, Medicare, Medicaid, food stamp, and other automatic spending programs are devouring all the dollars American taxpayers can produce. Within a decade or so, autopilot spending and debt service will consume every dollar Americans pay in taxes, meaning that every dollar for the discretionary core of government would have to be borrowed money.

Much of the research community's advocacy in recent days has concentrated on making the case for the value of scientific inquiry and its huge and often unforeseen contributions to national wealth and well-being. We can never make this point too frequently.

But in large measure, this is pushing on an open door. Ironically, the importance of basic research and public support of it is one of the few things on which I find that decision-makers who differ on other questions generally agree. The real problem is that there isn't any money; more each year, it flows out the Treasury door in the form of checks and payments for medical bills. And, unjustifiably, it flows not just to poor or middle-income people, but also to the wealthiest among us, in systems 50 to 80 years old, designed for bygone eras.

Our approach to public policy has become, without anyone intending such a perverse result, to indulge in current consumption at the expense of the investment needed for a better tomorrow. Reversing this mis-priority will be the test of this generation; failure to act on it will properly lead to our condemnation in the eyes of history.

Friends of the research enterprise should be out front in demanding bold action to reform entitlement spending and again liberate resources for the investments in new knowledge that, without public dollars, are unlikely to come any other way.

In the same way, we must advocate any reasonable action that is likely to generate faster economic growth. An economy limping along at less than 2% annual growth cannot possibly produce the public revenue needed to sustain the research and other investment spending we need. And quite often, the senseless decisions we make are the product of unscientific or even anti-scientific arguments.

Consider just one, in my estimation the most important current example: the new energy extraction technique referred to as fracking. This triumph, not of basic science and certainly not of public policy, but of engineering, is the single most positive development for the American economy since the silicon chip. Like so many breakthrough technologies of the past, it has suddenly rendered all the existing models and projections obsolete, and given birth to a new world of possibilities.

The vast new amounts of domestic oil and natural gas now in prospect can be a boon to poor people through lower energy costs, and to unemployed people as new jobs are created both directly in the extraction and transportation of these new resources and indirectly as dramatically lower natural gas prices make onshore manufacturing attractive once again. No new fertilizer plant has been built in the U.S. in more than twenty years; fourteen are now proposed, and in my home state alone, two new plants, with a combined capital investment of over $2 billion, are now headed for construction.

And that's just the beginning of the possibilities. Our long-standing balance of payments problem could soon look entirely different, as we import less oil and perhaps become a significant exporter of natural gas. The economic benefits could be matched by a new and healthier geopolitical environment in which the Middle East is no longer nearly so important to us. And then there's CO_2, where we have already seen reductions well beyond those envisioned by the various command and control schemes that have caused such heated debates in our country.

A nation led by engineers would leap to maximize this set of massive opportunities. It would see the risks and unknowns around fracking as problems to be tackled, as surely they can be, and would get about addressing them. Let's hope this is the course we adopt as a nation, but it is troubling how mixed our response has been in some states and at the federal level, where the first instinct in many cases was to throw up obstacles and delays and to rush to regulate and control this new growth sector. One hopes that some of the matchless credibility and prestige in this room can be brought to bear on this and similar debates.

Just as some dispute or dismiss the value of the new energy era, there are those who do not share Purdue's urgency about the need for more engineering education and research. There are analysts who believe the need for more STEM graduates has been greatly overstated and is merely an obsession and a myth. At least one of the corporate recruiters visiting our campus recently asserted that we are headed for a glut of engineers in a few years.

My attitude is, let's try to cause such a problem. For one thing, the data as I read them seem squarely on the side of Norm Augustine's 2010 *Gathering Storm* report and its kin. But even if the skeptics prove to have a point, we will be a stronger nation with a lot more engineers around.

Engineers, unlike, for instance, lawyers or financial experts, frequently generate through their innovation new work for themselves and others. Somewhere in any potential glut will be new Watts and Edisons and Noyces who give birth to entire new industries that require the services of engineers and non-engineers alike.

But even if we were to somehow outrun the market's need for engineering talent, we will be a far stronger country if the engineering mindset takes a more prominent place in our national conversations. Too often today it is a fearful, risk-averse, regulatory impulse that dominates our debates, rather than the problem-solving, can-do attitude one associates with engineering and related professions. A competitive, successful twenty-first-century society will constantly ask not, "What if something goes wrong?" but the engineers' questions: "Why not?" "What's next?" and "Let's figure it out."

On behalf of one university that reveres this Academy and the indispensable profession whose pinnacle it represents, I pledge Purdue's best efforts to train the next generation of great engineers, and to help launch them on careers of world-changing research and invention.

As an appreciative and grateful citizen of a nation made great largely through the brilliance of people in this room and your predecessors in engineering excellence, thank you for the better life you have made possible for millions, and for the ongoing national success I know your continued leadership will ensure.

Thank you very much.

National Association of Manufacturers
Santa Ana, California
March 2014

I have been an optimist about manufacturing for a long time, and now I think there are all kinds of good reasons to be optimistic, if we make a few of the right commonsense moves in this country. One of the things we need to do to ensure a strong future, of course, is to produce the kind of people who can work in and lead businesses like those represented in this room. For the first time in recent years, that has come under more scrutiny and more questioning. I was trying to decide coming out here if this is a business talk or an education talk. Really, it's both because the two are convergent. So let me just offer a few observations and tell you a little bit about how I think things can be done a little better.

If I had brought a slide show, the first one would have been a grainy picture of a nerdy looking guy. It is Joseph Schumpeter, the Austrian economist who gave the world the term "creative destruction." He was the first one who really explicated how the force of capitalist competition creates progress, but as it does, it disrupts the incumbent—the new business, the new theory, the new industry, the new disruptive technology—and quite often threatens and displaces the old.

A colleague spent his career at Eastman Kodak, and there is no more graphic example of a company that owned a market for a long time. It wasn't that people in the company didn't catch on that maybe there was something different coming. They owned patents on digital cameras, but the leadership of that business just couldn't bring themselves to make any of the changes necessary and, of course, at the end there was nothing left in bankruptcy but the royalties from those patents. What a point in history. It was very interesting to hear it told from the inside.

As everybody here knows, that process has sped up, and sped up, and sped up. If you look back at the Fortune 500 of 1955, in twenty-five years half of them were gone. Some were acquired, some just disappeared, some were still around but they slipped out of the top position. It took twenty-five years. The Class of '75 took thirteen years. The Class of '95—we've got another year or something to go, but the turnover is happening even faster. Somebody pointed out to me a very popular movie about thirteen or fourteen years ago called *You've Got Mail*. The villain was the big bookstores. Now, Borders is gone—from villain to victim in a decade.

For leaders of successful businesses, it means you are looking over your shoulder. You are trying to be the disrupter if you can, but you certainly are aware that your responsibility is to make necessary changes. Well, there is a sector that has changed, some would say, not at all in the last millennium—and that's higher education, where I live professionally now.

It is perfectly plausible, in fact, that there are people asking this question: Is higher education going the way of Borders Books? It's an information distribution business after all, like newspapers, which are suffering severely. It's easy to draw lots and lots of analogies, and people are asking questions. You are asking questions, I'll bet, that were never heard until the last several years. Are too many kids going to college? Are they learning anything meaningful while they are there? Whatever they are learning and studying, is any of it useful? Something they can really apply in the world of work? What's a diploma mean? If everybody shows up with a 3.6 GPA, how do I tell who really has it and who doesn't? And then perhaps most persuasively, why does it cost so darned much? And if it costs so much why aren't these young people really ready when they show up at my HR Department? These questions are absolutely appropriate, legitimate. I was asking them myself before I found myself parachuting into this new environment.

It's a darned shame if Kodak loses out first to Fuji and then to all the people building digital cameras. But life will go on, and it has. But the higher education complex in this country is one sector, if it's fair to call it that, where we do not want to lose world leadership. We may have slipped in different ways as a country, but most people would still say, and the world says, voting with young feet, that American universities and colleges are still the finest around. This is incredibly important to preserve if we can. But it has all the hallmarks of an industry or a business that could quickly be taken down.

Everybody here would love to be in the situation they've been in—terrific pricing power. In fact, not only was the demand elastic, but when you raised your prices, most people assumed it meant higher quality. It's pretty rare—talk about a catbird seat—and no validation of the product. Who wouldn't like to be in a business like that?

Meanwhile, here come a lot of new competitors. In another slide you would have seen in the full version—a slovenly guy, unshaven, in his pajamas, with a Coke and Cheetos, and a laptop. This is the new competition. People are asking why would you move somewhere, spend all that money, live four years or more, when we can bring the best professors and the best education in the world right into your living room, sitting around in your pajamas? So, I talk about the pajamas test.

In the face of all this, there is still a lot of denial. I can only speak for one university and am going to give you a few thoughts about how we intend to try to answer this call and answer these questions.

First is what we teach at Purdue University. We are already one of the most STEM-centric universities around. A higher percentage of our students are studying science, technology, engineering, math, or something related than in all but a very few schools. We are going all out in that direction. It is what we do best, and a pretty good principle is to do more of what you are really good at.

Second, it's what this nation and what our state really needs. After expanding our Engineering College and Computer Science program, our current College of Technology will be transformed. We are going to call it the Purdue Polytechnic Institute. Think applied engineering. These students will study almost entirely on project-based teams, most of them business-sponsored or business-initiated. Norm Augustine and the commission he led[2] said the nation needs 10,000 new engineers a year, and it is our intention to supply 6% to 8% of them as one university and send them out to work for great companies like the ones represented in this room.

How we teach is going to change, too. Project-based learning, already a big part of education at Purdue, will be even more prevalent. No one will graduate from any of our colleges, even our liberal arts college, without having approached problems in teams. A vast majority of our students will have had at least one undergraduate research assignment, working on genuine research under the leadership of a professor. Most will have studied internationally for at least one semester, and all will have been encouraged to think entrepreneurially.

I have dinner once or twice a week with students, and after one such occasion last year, three or four young folks were talking about the engineering course they just finished. One mentioned that their professor liked their project so much he thought it might be patentable. When I asked if they had patented it, he said he didn't know—the university had the rights to it. The next morning, I changed the policy. A Purdue undergraduate who invents something that is eligible for intellectual property protection will own it. We want to encourage our young people to think that way even while they are with us.

We are going to do all this while maintaining rigor in the curriculum. Another slide you've been spared describes the phenomenon called grade inflation. You've probably seen it, but over the last thirty or forty years, the average grade at almost every American college has drifted up and up and up. There are some places where it's not clear what you've got to do to get a B. But when they show up at your office looking for a job, how do you know? It's still really hard to get a high grade point average at Purdue University. I tell our students, "I hope you know you've come to a tough school. Congratulations. When you get out of here with a solid grade point average the world is going to know you learned something."

Finally, who do we teach? The answer is everybody. Everybody who can meet our standards, which are getting higher all the time. By everybody I mean we are a land-grant school, and I'm proud of it. We are very imbued with the mission to teach, as Abe Lincoln said, "the agricultural and the mechanic arts." We do and will even more so, but the other point of the famous Morrill Act was to open the doors of education to the masses, so it wouldn't be just the privilege of the elite and wealthy anymore. And we believe that. This country is headed the wrong direction in that respect.

After I was at Purdue only two or three months, on instinct I said, "I'll tell you what, let's hold tuition flat." Tuition had gone up thirty-six years in a row. Not unusual. At the schools you are trustees of, or that you attended, I'll bet it's about the same. I said, "Let's try something different and just get off that escalator. I'll bet you we can freeze tuition and make ends meet. Let's try to solve the equation the other way around—instead of again asking our students' families to adjust their budgets to our spending, let's adjust our spending to their budgets." It turned out not to be too hard to do. We've done it and now we've extended it for two more years and I'm working on year four.[3]

The point we want to make—one so elementary that I almost hesitate to say it—is that the simplest equation in all of life needs to start operating in higher education. That, of course, being quality over price equals value. We will be presenting ourselves as delivering value, and I predict that successful other universities and colleges will start doing the same. Our students deserve it. Their potential employers deserve it.

We will try to prove that quality in new ways. In early May, you will probably hear something about a new measuring stick. It's called the Gallup-Purdue Index. I was looking around for somebody who seemed to know something about how we could prove what we suspect strongly. When we survey CEOs or HR managers, or somebody else does, there is fragmentary but consistent evidence that says graduates of our school, and frankly a lot of schools like ours, are highly valued and valuable when they come to work in your companies. But nobody knows for sure. It's time that higher ed had to prove, as we say in business, the efficacy of its product. Just as each of you does every single day . . . or else.

The Gallup-Purdue Index is drawn from thirty years of what Gallup has done for your companies. I guarantee that many in this room have worked with Gallup, because they work for almost everybody, and they have learned what makes a highly valuable employee. Yes, content mastery for sure. If somebody is an electrical engineer, you want to know how much of that he or she knows. But so much has been learned about what makes a productive, or as they would say "engaged," employee—the kind of employee that makes people around them better, not brings them down and maybe even makes them worse.

We intend to find out what we can about our graduates. It will be the largest survey of college graduates and a comparison group who didn't finish. We'll look at what qualities, what sorts of experiences on campus are associated with that kind of employee, and by the way, that kind of citizen. We will see what we find out, but I'm sure it won't be perfect. It will need to be refined, but the principle of accountability has to be established, and we want to be some small part of doing so.

So, the great gurus from Schumpeter on . . . there was Clayton Christensen . . . tend to say it is the incumbent company in a business sector that usually can't make the necessary changes. Too stuck in the old ways, too slow. That may be true. I don't know. But at Purdue we intend to see, and other schools are starting to move the same way.

A line I first heard from some of the central nervous system scientists at Lilly is, "How many psychiatrists does it take to change a light bulb?" The answer is, "Just one, but the bulb has to really want to change." At our school, and certainly at the schools many of you are so closely associated with and helping to lead and direct, I hope you see the need for change. I hope you see the incredible upside, if we get it right, if America continues to have the finest research universities, the finest producers of new talent anywhere. And speaking for one such school, we intend to, as they used to say, "give it the old college try."

Thank you very much.

Mackinac Public Policy Conference
Excerpts from keynote address
Mackinac, Michigan
May 2014

My sense is that public leadership starts with some very, very basic down payments. The first is honesty. The first thing we did in Indiana, among many first things on arrival, was to rewrite by executive order, and then as fast as we could sign into statute, all the ethics laws of state government. Make them as pristine, as unimpeachable, as unequivocal, as tough as any we could find anywhere—a zero tolerance attitude. Mercifully in eight years, very few people, even at low levels, tried to color outside the lines. But we took an attitude of absolutism about it. The public needs to know that the people entrusted with its money and with public responsibilities are in it for only the highest of motives.

Second is simple competence. I say simple, but this is really a paradoxical thing to me. If there is anything that people who differ honestly about other subjects ought to agree on, it is that government has a solemn duty to perform well. But how rarely this is an area of genuine focus and concentration. Some people who believe in very limited government think the job is done when they've trimmed it some, or limited it, and confined it in some way. Others who believe in a more active, more involved, and expansive government think their job is done when they've got more money for whatever purpose. They are very uninterested in whether that money is well spent or whether we get real results for the government we have.

One thing we ought to agree on is whether I may believe the government should be careful not to get outside a certain sphere of activity, and you may believe in a much larger sphere, but whatever it does, it ought to do very, very well. I used to tell people, "You know, you would be amazed how much government you'll never miss." Even if you are one of those people who might miss more than I would, we ought to share a commitment to do things right.

On things as fundamental as child welfare, we in Indiana literally went from the worst in the penalty box of the federal government, for good reason, to winning national awards. It takes a relentless and almost tedious commitment to measurement and to reward people for good performance.

Many people misconstrued some of the actions we took. Sometimes we decided to work with the private sector to deliver a necessary and important public service, and they thought it was something theological to talk about privatization. I never once used that p-word; I said the only p-word we use is pragmatic.

Question one is whether a given service should be delivered. It really should be if it's a proper expenditure of a dollar we took from a free citizen in taxation. The next question is, What's the best way to do it? Sometimes that led us to add to the government we had, like child welfare workers, or state police. Sometimes it led us to hire somebody who did it for a living all day, every day. I used to say to people, "If it's in the Yellow Pages, maybe somebody can do it better than we do."

I hadn't been in office a month when I got a call from a bright young guy who ultimately turned our whole Corrections Department into one of the best in America. He said, "Do you know you are paying $1.43 a meal for food?" I said, "Well, no, is that a lot?" And he said, "Yeah, it's a lot. I worked in another state, and it was $0.95, and I think the food was better. Do you mind if I look around?" I said, "No, go see what you can do."

He came back after a rather swift process, having hired a well-known firm which probably feeds you at the football stadium. I think the bid was $0.98—a savings of $0.45, times 22,000 inmates, times 3 squares a day, times 365 days a year. I know you are doing the mental math as I say this. It came out to a savings of $14 million or $15 million a year, with higher standards for nutrition and quality.

The example of competence that every Hoosier will remember, when they can no longer remember who the governor was, is our Bureau of Motor Vehicles. I don't know a state populace that doesn't hate theirs. But I guarantee there couldn't be any place that was much worse than Indiana, until a few years ago. I used to say, "People go to the Indiana License Branch with a box lunch and a copy of *War and Peace* and hope they don't finish them both before somebody notices they are there." Now, even if you have to go to an Indiana License Branch, which you can skip 70% to 80% of the time, you can make an appointment. You can go online and see where the lines are shortest; but they are all short. You will be finished, on average, in nine and a half minutes, and 98% of the time you will be satisfied.

Why were we so fixated on the BMV? Because it was the agency that every citizen visits and every citizen encounters. There are only so many of those, like the Department of Revenue. But with the BMV in particular, I was determined that we would do whatever it took to make it work right, because public confidence is important.

Referring to the down payment referenced earlier, the third thing is just pay your bills. Don't go broke—pretty simple.

If you display honesty and a total commitment to integrity, if you are very serious about delivering basic public service as well, and you are careful about the public's money, that's the price of admission. That's the entry price for asking the public to join you, and join together, in doing big things.

It doesn't happen just as an act of the will—we had to put some things in place by executive order. We made unionism in public and state public employment voluntary. (Incidentally, within eight months, 92% of state workers had voluntarily stopped paying the dues.) It had nothing to do with unions per se and wasn't really to save money, although indirectly we wound up saving boatloads of money. It was about 160 pages of dos and don'ts that basically said you couldn't do the simplest thing without a sixty- or ninety-day consultation with somebody. You couldn't combine departments, you couldn't divide departments, you couldn't reassign people, you couldn't get rid of people who weren't upholding the public trust.

One year later, we had put in place across Indiana state government what, as far as I know, is still the only system of true performance pay. This won't seem strange to most people in this room, but in government it is very strange that the best performers get paid a lot more—paid on a bell curve. Those at the bottom, who get a second chance, are placed on probation but are out if they don't improve. Eight years later, we had an important culture of performance.

How do you do the really big things if you've made the down payment, and if people are willing to listen to ideas for big change? You know the old saying "I've been rich, I've been poor, and rich is better." Well, I've operated with a friendly legislature and a divided legislature, and I can tell you which is better. Churchill said, "There is only one thing worse than fighting with allies, and that is fighting without them," and I know what he means now. There were times even with divided government when we were able to make big things happen. Sometimes it was because there was a genuine alignment of interest.

In 2008, we decided that Indiana's biggest problem in taxation was property taxes, which were too high, or at least too unpredictable. We were a little too lop-sided in the composition of our revenues and decided to pursue reform. In that case, our opponents really didn't like what we wanted to do and probably disliked it intensely, but they didn't want to get in the way of a public that had united around the issue. We made certain, despite knowing their private views, to include them in the credit. They weren't smiling much, but they were right there at the signing ceremony as I thanked them for their indispensable help.

This attitude of amity, comity, and trying to get people together has its limits, of course, and politics can get in the way even of a shared goal and a good idea. I will give you the example of infrastructure. It's not hard to list the areas in which this divided nation of ours ought to find agreement, but one of them is certainly public infrastructure. Regardless of your view of economics, or the size or shape of government, having a first-rate infrastructure to enable business and enterprise to thrive and be more efficient surely is a responsibility of government. As always, how you do it is open to debate.

We were very fortunate to see an opportunity and seized it. In 2006, the markets were right, the climate seemed right, and we had a huge infrastructure gap—I don't know a state that doesn't. Having looked at thirty-one options, the only one that had a prayer of generating the necessary billions was to see if anyone wanted to lease our Toll Road, which was losing money as a patronage operation. We received an enormous bid and took it to our legislature, which I naively thought would rush to embrace the idea. With $4 billion in cash, we could build projects all over the state that people had dreamed of and been promised for decades—ones that we didn't have a prayer of building or rebuilding otherwise. But because the winning bidder included some international investors, some saw a political opening, and what should have been a consensus love-in turned into a Donnybrook.

I became interested in the Toll Road while driving relentlessly across the state of Indiana as a no-name, first-time gubernatorial candidate. At the last tollbooth before Chicago, the fee was $0.15—one-five. These days, who has a nickel? Once elected I asked, "What's with that $0.15? How much does it cost us to collect a toll?" Government being government, they didn't know, but they returned in a couple of weeks with an answer: "We think it's $0.34." Great business model. I suggested a better plan. "Fire the patronage workers, close the tollbooth, put out a goldfish bowl or cigar box, and go to the honor system; we would be $0.19 ahead. Occasionally some nice person will toss in a quarter, just to be a good citizen." That's when I first had the idea that perhaps there was some trapped value in the Toll Road.

You may be wondering why the road was losing money. Well, they hadn't raised the tolls in twenty-five years because somebody might get upset.

We valued the road at $1.3 billion, perhaps higher if you pushed it. The highest bid was about $4 billion, plus huge investments in the road itself. It's better than it has ever been. I tell all my business friends, if anybody ever walks into your office and says, "I would like to offer you 61-times EBITDA for this business," don't say, "Let me sleep on it." Don't even call the board, they are going to forgive you. Before the guy comes to his senses, sign. It was like walking on coals to get the lease done, but we saw it through, and thank goodness we acted when we did. If we had heeded the abundant counsel—maybe we ought to wait, let's study it for a year—the deal would never have happened. But there is a basic principle: If you've got a good idea, move fast. The results are what matter in the end.

Abe Lincoln said, "Some stumps you can dig up, some stumps you have to blast out, some stumps you just have to plow around." We plowed around stumps on a lot of issues. And although we were not always successful, we always tried to see if we could bring people together so that the changes we made had staying power. If somebody on the other side felt some investment, they might not undo it the first chance they got. But there were a lot of other stumps that had to wait dynamiting—things like sweeping education reform, unemployment insurance reform, making permanent the Civil Service changes that I mentioned, and of course Right to Work.

I'll wrap up with a few thoughts that are a little broader. The single consensus we need most in this country, and I hope one day we will achieve it, is the issue of a private economy that grows much faster, and doing all we can do to make it happen. Whatever size government you think is appropriate and necessary, we are never going to deliver it with an economy staggering along at 1% growth. It just won't work. In fact, ironically, those who favor a big, very active and expensive government have a deeper stake in a faster growing economy. Otherwise, the revenues to pay for it cannot possibly be there.

I want to speak specifically on behalf of the young people on the Purdue campus, on campuses everywhere else, and all those who are not on campus at all. The debt we are about to dump on the next generation is an economic problem. It will stunt growth over the long term and it is squeezing the life out of necessary government programs, including higher education. It is a moral problem. It is an indefensible position morally to borrow money in gigantic quantities and spend it—not investing it in roads, bridges, and the kinds of things that our Major Moves Program did in Indiana but to spend it on consumption today and on the oldest generation—at the ultimate and inevitable expense of the next generation. We cannot tackle it at at 2% year-on-year growth in this economy.

At least as large a question is what a prolonged period of economic stagnation will do to social cohesion in this country. To the sense of opportunity, promise, and upward mobility that has brought people to this nation and has kept us together as a nation not bound by any other tie of ethnicity, religion, or anything else. Fewer people are participating in the workforce now than since the days of the stay-at-home mom. Why aren't they working? They have given up, and it's unacceptable. It's not just displaced older workers. The unemployment rate among those under 30 is as high as it has ever been. High percentages of young people are living at home, and high percentages of people who have been to college are in occupations that really don't require a college degree. We can disagree later about how to spend the money. First let's generate some for government. Let's pay our debts, or at least stop incurring them at a staggering, mathematically unsustainable rate.

When I was first elected, I said to our team, "Listen, every great enterprise I ever saw—private, public, nonprofit—had a very clear purpose. It was on the wall, the annual report, or the laminated ID card. It was their mission, their vision. It was a clear statement of why they were there, and everybody knew what it was. Everybody and every unit knew what their role was in trying to produce that outcome, and if they had their act together, there would be a measure to see if they were delivering or not."

I used to do a lot of business with Walmart, and they used to say, "If you're not keeping score, you are just practicing." So, we measured everything. I said, "Okay, here is our purpose. We are here to raise the net disposable income of Hoosiers. That's it. I don't know if we are here for four years or eight years, but every day we are here that's what we are working on. If we do that, if we have more jobs, if on average the jobs over time pay more than the jobs of today, if we find ways to leave a few more of those earned dollars in the pockets of those who work for them, other problems start to get smaller. We will have the revenue for great schools, roads, parks, universities, and everything we want. We will have a place that people want to move to, not move out of, because they see the opportunity there."

I urged everyone to find a way they could contribute. How long it takes to turn around a permit; how fast somebody gets their tax return back and has the cash returned to their own hands. Maybe it's how few minutes they spend in the license branch when they could be out doing something productive. What could we either do, do better, do faster, or maybe stop doing that would make it more likely that next job came to Indiana, not Illinois, not Michigan, not California … and when it gets here, it pays a little better and all the rest of that. Whatever it was, we were going to figure it out.

I only tell you that because I really hope that our nation will make a similar focused commitment to break all the ties and close calls, until further notice, in favor of growing the private economy from which all good things must ultimately come. That doesn't mean other priorities aren't important. Of course they are. But nothing should displace that.

On behalf of our students and young people everywhere, I hope this makes some sense to you and that the important voices in this room will be heard on those subjects.

Thank you very much.

**University of Chicago Institute for Politics
Excerpts from on-stage interview
Chicago, Illinois
January 2015**

Jodi Cohen was an investigative reporter and editor at the *Chicago Tribune* for fourteen years. Subsequent to this interview at the University of Chicago, she joined ProPublica as a reporter.

David Axelrod is a distinguished senior fellow at the University of Chicago Harris School of Public Policy. He served as senior advisor to President Barack Obama.

MS. COHEN: Purdue has been making news since you became president with headlines that praise you for "reinventing the public university." Perhaps most notably Purdue has frozen the cost of tuition for several years. What do you see as your biggest successes from the past two years and how, in particular, is freezing tuition working out?

MITCH: First of all, I reject the notion that we are reinventing anything. It's a nice aspiration, but I think that would be an overclaim for anything we've done so far. Many of the things we've done, which to me seem fairly modest and obvious, are still a little unusual in higher ed, and so I guess I know why they occasionally excite some attention. Yes, our tuition freeze has gotten a lot of notice. In our university the tuition had gone up thirty-six consecutive years, and that is not unusual. As David and I were discussing earlier, it's the only thing you can find that has gone up faster than health care costs in America.

More on instinct than anything else, I suggested to our trustees that we ought to freeze tuition. I suspected, and it turned out to be accurate, that we could do that and still run a first-class university. Second, I believed it was the right thing to do. We are a land-grant school and, remember why those were created—to open the gates of higher education beyond the elites and beyond the wealthy. And that, to me, is as profound a responsibility today as it was when Abe Lincoln and his allies created such schools.

And third, my business life gave me the intuition that the whole business model was about to change. The first principle of marketing is to differentiate the product. I thought that by getting off the tuition escalator we could differentiate Purdue and possibly catch the attention of even more students and families. I think that has happened. Our applications skyrocketed last year and are up more than 10% this year, which is counter to the national trend. As a matter of principle and as a matter of the business of the school it has worked out. And as a matter of future differentiation, I think it has proven so far to work. I guess you would say that's the most noteworthy thing we have done. We've extended the one-year freeze for two more, so the students I welcomed in my first year, if they graduate in four years, will never see a tuition increase. It's not an answer to the affordability question, but it's a start.

MS. COHEN: You are now, of course, getting copycats to your tuition freeze. The University of Illinois this week decided to freeze tuition, so in terms of differentiation . . .

MITCH: Sort of. For new students only, in-state students only, but it's a start. There is no patent or trademark on anything.

MS. COHEN: What is the right balance between in-state and out-of-state students?

MITCH: Balance is the right question, and it's not new. It hasn't changed too much in the two years I've been at Purdue, maybe just by a percentage or two. At Purdue 45% of our students are from elsewhere.

I meet hundreds of Chicago area kids who attend Purdue, and I always tell them, "I know why you are here. It's a really good school and it is close enough to home—you can take your laundry home when you want, but it is too far for mom to come down by surprise." They agree completely.

We look at the balance question all the time. Number one, there is no shortage of capacity. If anything, Indiana has an overcapacity of higher ed slots. We are a state of 6.6 million people, we have two Big Ten universities, two other large public universities, a host of smaller schools, and other regional campuses—mathematically there are lots of places.

Second, a Hoosier kid who applies has an 87% chance of being accepted into our system. To some of them we say, "You can come, but you've got to start at Purdue Calumet, or you have to start at Purdue Fort Wayne," but they are accepted at a very high rate. And 72% of those who apply to West Lafayette do get in.

Third, it is a lot harder to be admitted from Chicago, California, or Beijing than it is from Indiana. The profile of the in-state student is better than it has ever been, but it is easier to get in, and that's the way we think it ought to be.

Finally, there's no reason not to say it directly: we charge the out-of-state students three times the in-state tuition. We think we are a great value. I guess they do too. We are out to prove that. We are still a lot more affordable for many of them than the schools in their own state. The cross-subsidy is how we keep the tuition under $10,000 for Hoosier students, and I have no problem with it. Hoosier students' parents have been paying taxes for eighteen years to support schools like ours, and balance is exactly the right question. I hope we have these things in rough balance.

MS. COHEN: The number of Chinese students has been skyrocketing at Purdue and other places. Do you think this increase in population has been wise, particularly when so many Americans are seeking a college education, and also because most of those students from China end up returning to China?

MITCH: I am not unhappy with the number of international students we have. I have said I think we are a little lopsided. Seventy percent of our international students are from three Asian countries—Korea and India are the others. By the way, it is not new. Purdue has a long history of attracting Asian students—there are octogenarians I've met in China who came to Purdue University a long time ago—so this is not some recent phenomenon, but it has grown. I would like to see, and we are working to encourage, one in six students coming from somewhere else.

I tell our students that we want them to study abroad if they can, and we are going to help them do it. But if they make the effort to know their classmates, they can get a study abroad experience without ever leaving campus, or before they do. We would like to have more students from Latin American, from Africa. We would like to spread the demographic footprint a little bit.

The real problem we have is the self-segregation of Chinese and other students. We work at it, but we have not yet cracked the code of how to maximize the value of students from elsewhere, for their sake and for the sake of the domestic students. We want them to know each other well enough and to learn as much as they can from each other. We are not getting that done to my satisfaction yet.

MS. COHEN: Nationwide, leading public universities have lost roughly 30% of their state support on a per student basis, which is one factor why tuition for years was going up. How do you propose to deal with this, and how do the state universities maintain the quality of education when there is decreasing state funding and at the same time pressure to lower tuition?

MITCH: First of all, by the last measure I saw, Indiana was third in America in terms of maintaining spending for public education. A couple of oil states were first and second, perhaps North Dakota and Wyoming. So, somebody paid attention to this even during the recession.

I've seen this from the other side of the table, and what I saw was the same thing that people see when they look at student loans—Pell Grants and other forms of financial aid. For a long time, more and more money flooded in—public dollars—and universities pocketed the money, and it didn't do the students much good. Tuition just went up to match.

I don't consider it our biggest problem. We said when we froze tuition in the first year that it was not conditional on the state providing some significant funding increase. We would find a way. My little formulation has been "let's see if we can adapt our spending to our students' budgets as opposed requiring them to adapt their family budget to our spending."

There are some states, particularly since the recession hit, where the cuts have been so swift and so huge that I sympathize with the people who are running institutions there. But in general—it's all very well-documented—schools vastly expanded spending on things that aren't directly related to a better education. Amenities like climbing walls, and a lot of other examples that we've all seen.

I always say to people remember, even as the cost went up there was no validation that the value of the education was going up. In fact, it worked the other way around. It's an interesting economic phenomenon—quite the business to be in—there is no elasticity. Usually, if you raise the price, customers start to go elsewhere. But in this case, not only didn't universities lose customers, folks assumed that if it cost more, it must be worth more. I've asked, Who gets to do that? My wife said, "Well, Tiffany's." But who else? I think that game is over. A lot of scholars, public officials, and others are starting to ask the right question: prove it is worth it.

MS. COHEN: And how do you propose that colleges prove that it is worth it?

MITCH: Yes, accountability. What a novel idea. Just as it finally came to the K–12 world, it is coming to higher ed, and none too soon.

We are doing two things. Starting this fall, we will be measuring, using a well-validated instrument, the critical learning capability of our incoming freshmen; and we will measure them again at graduation. There has been some very interesting scholarship that shows, in many places where it is done, there aren't very many gains in critical thinking.

We struck a deal with the Gallup research organization, and this year the first Gallup-Purdue Index will be conducted—a measurement of how college graduates are doing afterward, in their adult lives. In the benchmark survey, more than 30,000 people were surveyed, and for the first time we can look in statistically significant ways at how these alumni are doing—graduates of public schools vs. private, by geography, sliced and diced any way you like. And it's not just economically, although that is a factor, but what Gallup calls the "domains of well-being." Twenty other schools have signed up to do this, too.

Contemporaneously, we studied our own alums so we could compare them to this first-ever benchmark. In general, we were happy to find that Boilermakers are doing really well compared to the typical college grad. But it also showed us a couple of things we could do better. When we asked what correlates with financial and societal success, it showed us a couple of places where we can improve.

MS. COHEN: President Obama announced a plan that would provide free community college to most high school graduates. What is your reaction to the president's proposal, and can you handicap for us the chances of it actually happening?

MITCH: Well, I like the direction. As it happens, I proposed this in Indiana. It was one of the few things in eight years we didn't get done. It was the same idea but would have been self-financing. We thought we saw a way to endow a program in which we could give every Indiana student two years at a community college, or they could take the equivalent to any other Indiana school, Purdue, for instance.

We've got to find ways to broaden or maintain access and raise quality in higher ed. I'm a little skeptical of another massive government entitlement program. This would be Medicaid on the higher ed front.

When I'm not worrying about student debt—which we spend a lot of time on, and which I am happy to tell you is coming down at Purdue—there is another consideration. I point out to students that even with an average debt of $33,000, which I'm not telling them not to sweat, they are already on the hook for ten or twenty times that amount in terms of the national debt that they didn't accumulate. My generation and the one before it did.

I worry about anything that adds to that burden. By the way, entitlement spending is not just a tomorrow problem, it's a today problem. I think it is hurting economic growth right now and would be much worse if we didn't have artificially low interest rates. If interest rates were anything near their normal level, the national debt would be dramatically more than it appears to be.

The challenge to higher ed is that autopilot spending—Medicare, Social Security, veterans' pensions, government pensions, and all others—is crowding out the ability of government to do discretionary things. As circumstances change and new problems emerge, the federal government has painted itself into a corner where less than a third of the money is available for things like academic research. It is squeezing the life out of our hopes for growth at the National Institutes of Health, the National Science Foundation, and other research funders.

So, those are reasons that I like the goal, but I'm not sure about the means. And as to the probabilities, I don't think they are high, but I'm often wrong about those things.

MS. COHEN: A Gallup survey in October found the percentage of people who believe a college degree is important has dropped to 44%, down from 75% just five years ago. Do you believe a college degree has the same relevance and importance as it did a generation ago? To what do you attribute the feelings reflected in the poll? What do colleges and universities need to do to change the public's perception?

MITCH: It is an alarming statistic. I've made it a practice of sending an annual open letter to our campus community after New Year's. In this year's letter, I cite the Gallup number, as well as some other very troublesome figures about declining enrollments, costs, and other issues. But the most troublesome one I've seen is this very data point, and it is stunning. To see a move of 20% to 30% in just two or three years in anything is eye-catching, but especially on so central an issue as this one.

Higher education or some form of postsecondary education has never been as necessary as it is today. That's a commonplace. But there is the issue of relevance. For a long, long time the credential alone was a kind of passport, and that notion is coming under scrutiny now, because along with many other questions, people are wondering if students are really learning anything on campus, if they are studying things that have any meaning later in life, and why it costs so darn much. A lot of employers and others are beginning to wonder whether these pieces of parchment really tell them anything.

So, the diploma may no longer have the same relevance. Some think that the big earthquake will be when people really begin to solve the online issue. I think that is going to have a big effect, but I think an even bigger one would be if large sectors of the economy—whole industries—start saying they can't trust those diplomas anymore. When everybody gets an A for studying things of suspect value, and it's unclear whether students learn much, then they show up in the workplace feeling entitled and not really ready for work, companies are saying, "We'll create our own tests."

This already is going on in the software industry. We have a CPA exam, and there are plenty of other examples. But what happens if large sectors of the economy say, "Keep your diploma, we just want to know whether you can pass this test that we've created, and if you can we will hire you, whether you dallied around college for four years or not." Now that would be a change, wouldn't it?

MS. COHEN: How much of a threat, if that is the right word, do you think online learning is and what do you think will be the impact of MOOCs, the massive online open courses, in particular?

MITCH: I remember someone in business saying that the most common strategic mistake is to correctly spot a trend and overestimate the near-term impact but underestimate the long-term. This might be one of those mistakes. A lot of people have said that online learning is going to sweep the decks clear right away. I don't think so. But it is already having an effect, and I think it may be a mortal threat to some institutions, depending on what they are doing and how they react to it.

Some foresee online education as getting the best philosophy professor from Harvard and the best computer science professor from MIT, and nobody will go to the University of Chicago anymore. Why? Because students can stay home and receive education on the cheap that way.

I don't want to be an ostrich about this, and history is littered with people who claimed their business is impervious to massive disruption. I can't tell you that it's not possible, but I think it would be a terrible thing if it did happen. We've slipped in a lot of ways, at least relatively as a nation, but we still have the finest universities on the planet, and I think everybody involved in one should feel a real duty to make sure that stays the case.

I think with the right changes the residential experience will still provide a value that is going to be very hard to fully replicate in a purely distributed way. For instance, our Gallup-Purdue Index shows a huge advantage if you had an undergraduate research experience; if you had any team-based learning where you worked on projects for a whole semester or longer; or if you had even one truly meaningful mentor relationship with a faculty member. If you make sure you deliver that kind of experience, keep the cost reasonable, prove that it is working—all those things you have to do for every other good or service you sell—then I have to believe that residential education will still be a very, very attractive and additive experience that won't fully be displaced by whatever technology comes next. But that's what they said at Eastman Kodak, too.

MS. COHEN: You taught a class on World War I this academic year at Purdue. I'm sure the students learned a lot and I'm wondering, What did you learn from teaching the class?

MITCH: That it is hard work, at least the first time around. If I had been teaching the same course for forty years, it probably wouldn't be so hard. But last year when people asked what I did over the summer, I said, "I studied for my class." But I enjoyed it. I really begged my students to complete an evaluation of the course—I'm a rookie, and if anybody needs evaluations it's me—and I tried to make it easy for them. They were very, very encouraging, but based on their feedback, I changed some things for this semester. The course was already somewhat interactive, but I'm going to give them an extra project or two. I probably assigned too much reading for a one-hour seminar course, so I made some adjustments. But I learned that I liked it and that you can do it if you put the effort in.

MR. AXELROD: Talk about the implications of a college education on long-term earnings potential, making college affordable, and making college relevant to the opportunities of the twenty-first century.

MITCH: I don't accept as a total answer these data—and we have plenty of them that say that people with college diplomas earn more—because that is looking in the rearview mirror. Those are the diplomas that were earned last year, or five, ten, twenty, and thirty years ago, so it doesn't necessarily tell us what the case will be when current students are in the workforce in ten years. But I suspect it won't be too different.

The nature of that postsecondary certificate, diploma, or credential may change a lot. Students may get it from all kinds of different places, and they may be just as valuable. Initiatives on community college, adult education, and for that matter vocational training have never been as important as they are today, but that can't be used as an argument for saying that people should go to the kind of schools we have always gone to and in the way we've always gone.

The person I've learned the most from, Michael Crow at Arizona State University, has really changed my thinking about certain things. Let me give you an example. Purdue is an extremely strong STEM school, and standards for admission having been going up, which was probably necessary. When I got there, I was imbued with the thought that we'll just keep doing that—keep raising the standards and more students will graduate. That is not a bad ambition, but it is in some tension with our land-grant heritage. Michael Crow likes to say our universities should be known, not by how many students they turn away—how selective they are—but by how many they graduate, and he's right.

Our philosophy now is to try to grow our school. We can grow by at least another couple of thousand students without big implications for capital spending—another big issue in the college business model. And I am ready to do that even if our academic profile of entering freshmen flattens out. We'll just take the assignment to use new tools in what is called "student success" to continue improving the graduation rate. That ought to be our goal and it will be.

Purdue alumni, especially in our Engineering School, all heard the same thing when they got there: "Look left and right, and you won't all be here for graduation." There was a weed-out mentality. Now we've said no, not anymore. It is primarily the student's job to succeed, but we have to accept the assignment to give them every chance to do so and help them where we can.

MS. COHEN: What is the answer to what you have called the "cocooning" of highly educated people in society?

MITCH: Because higher ed done properly does confer more advantages than it ever has on those who succeed at it and do well, there is a very high likelihood that the students here and their schoolmates are going to get a first-rate education. You are very likely to do well in life, and you are also very likely to associate with people, probably in marriage, but certainly professionally, socially, and otherwise, who are a lot like you. We are seeing not just an economic gap, but also a social distance in our society. One of our great scholars said that it is not a problem if truck drivers cannot empathize with the problems of Yale professors. It is a problem if Yale professors, CEOs, and producers of network television shows—various elites—cannot empathize with the problems of truck drivers.

That's an issue I don't think is yet getting quite as much attention as it deserves. It bothers me a lot and I hope will bother you. I've encouraged students that life will enable them to settle happily into the world of success, but if they really want to be successful citizens and contributing citizens, then they must push themselves into a discomfort zone—through volunteer activities, through political activities, by joining a bowling league or a softball league, by attending a church across town . . . something that gets them out of their comfort zone. They may not even notice it, but if they're not careful, they could easily wind up, to use the metaphor, in a "gated community" in all of life. Don't let it happen.

U.S. Department of Agriculture
2016 Agricultural Outlook Forum
February 25, 2016
Arlington, Virginia

I just want to say how much Purdue, not to mention me personally, values this opportunity to be with this particular crowd. I know you enjoyed your meal—it was quite excellent. But did you stop to consider how astounding an event that was? Because aside from the youngest in the room, you should all remember that two or three decades ago we were all told that we would have starved by now. That the world was going to run out of food and there wasn't anything anyone could do about it.

People standing in the not-so-proud tradition of Thomas Malthus and the Club of Rome wrote pompous books, gave goodness knows how many speeches for goodness knows what honoraria, to tell us all that disaster was dead ahead. You know, Jeremy Rifkin; Paul Ehrlich who wrote, "The battle to feed humanity is over"—that hundreds of millions of people will die, and nothing can prevent an enormous increase in the human death rate. For this, somebody—we will leave the foundation unnamed—declared him a genius. If that is genius, what would foolishness look like?

Everyone in this room knows that instead, the intervening decades have seen the greatest upward surge for the good of humanity in the history of the planet Earth. That the combination of greater freedom in important countries and technology, instead of worldwide famine and the certain disaster that was so confidently predicted, has brought down by hundreds of millions the number of our undernourished brothers and sisters, even as the population grew by billions. Life expectancy worldwide has grown by fifteen years in a quarter of a century. There has never been anything remotely like it in the history of the species we call *Homo sapiens*.

A lot of fabulous people contributed to this. Oh, Deng Xiaoping should get a lot of credit, but to a large extent this is the triumph of people in this room, or by extension the organizations you represent, the companies you represent, the academies you represent. If you don't feel proud, at least by association with those entities and endeavors, you really should. It has been a spectacular accomplishment and refutation of what so many believed was coming.

Now, of course, having climbed a mountain that people said was insurmountable, we all face the next one. Nine billion people in a historical blink from now, maybe three decades. I don't know how you feel about it, but I believe there is every reason for optimism. Once again, we face this "grand challenge," to use a phrase people like these days. If there ever was a grand challenge, this one deserves the term. But I think we know what to do.

We can start by disseminating the technology we already have. In many places the lessons that have been learned have yet to be applied even in their most elementary form. I asked Mr. Howard Buffett, who you hosted here this morning, to come to Purdue a few months ago, and it was terrific to hear his passion for spreading technology and self-sufficiency through Africa and the developing world. I was thrilled to hear him talk about the places where the land-grant university model, of which Purdue is one example, might be planted and might lead not only to the preparation of new leaders for agriculture and related fields, but to the more rapid distribution of much of what we already know how to do.

We all know that if we could simply use the food we already produce—the one-third of the food grown on the planet that doesn't make it to someone's table—there would be enormous upside opportunities. At Purdue University, some of our most successful scholarly endeavors have involved not the production of more food, but its more effective storage and preservation against insects and against spoilage of other kinds.

Then the essential item, of course, the sine qua non, will be the continued progress of agricultural research, scientific research. The advance of new technologies has so much incredible promise, not only for increasing supplies, as essential as that will be, but to do so in ways far friendlier than today's to Mother Nature: moderation of the use of pesticides and herbicides, more effective use of water, more effective conservation of the land, and the use of less land, most importantly, to produce the food we need.

Even, we are now learning, the reduction of CO_2. Last week I stumbled across one of my Purdue colleagues, Professor Wally Tyner, and asked him what he was working on. He and his colleagues have a paper coming out in which they have calculated that a ban on genetically modified organisms in the United States, in addition to many other catastrophic consequences, would produce an enormous increase in food costs. But the more interesting finding was a 7% to 17% increase in agriculturally based CO_2 emissions, which equates to a 1% to 2% increase in global CO_2 emissions.

Of course there are huge threats and impediments to our ability to feed a world of 9 billion fellow humans, but they are not the ones we've known in the past. By the way, my personal prediction is, with the emancipation of women in countries yet to experience that important phenomenon, with the advance of education, very probably the population estimates are too high, as they have often been. But let's just say they are right. The threat is not that we will have too many people. The threat is not that we can't produce enough food and new forms of food with higher protein content for that many people.

The threat this time is internal—a potential ban on genetically modified organisms in the United States. It will be a self-inflicted wound. And of course what is troubling me, and I hope troubles you, is that there is a shockingly broad, and so far shockingly successful, movement that threatens this important ascent of humankind out of the condition that has plagued us since we first walked upright—of enough food to meet the most basic, the most elementary need of any living species. It threatens our ascent by choking off the very technologies that could make that next great triumph possible.

It is the sort of practice that leads to a twenty-year delay in the availability of genetically modified salmon. Like everybody, I've learned salmon is awfully good for you and I eat it every chance I get. The idea that for no good reason we have taken twenty years to make salmon more affordable and plentiful is one example among so many that I hope we will stop repeating.

I guarantee you I am the least expert person in this room to discuss the technical aspects of the subject I am discussing. Anything I can tell you, you already know. What I want to submit to this audience is that too many of you are keeping what you know to yourselves, with the consequence that too many people outside this room and rooms like it don't know what you know, and have been actively misled in a way that is very dangerous—perhaps not to them, but to the poor and hungry people of this world.

It is attributed to Mark Twain—he probably wasn't its author or at least the first, but you know the saying: "It ain't what you don't know that gets you in trouble. It is what you know for sure that ain't true." There are a lot of people who have been told something, a lot of things, about modern agricultural technology that ain't true. If this were almost any other subject, I would say that's too bad, do your best, maybe the facts will eventually come out. But the stakes are too high here. We are talking about not merely the happiness and fulfillment of potential, but the survival of millions of people.

So, when I get a chance to talk to an audience this influential and this knowledgeable, I cannot resist suggesting to them, as I suggest to you, that you have a positive duty to do things that probably do not come naturally—to contest and refute junk science and false claims against the technologies that offer so much promise to the world. And not solely on the polite objective grounds that come most naturally to folks in the pursuits represented here—to people who work in the regulation of agriculture and its products, to those who study academically these subjects and work on the new technologies and the policies around them, or to the businesses that produce these products as the technologies become available. We are used to and only comfortable with polite and civil PowerPoints, facts, data at meetings where people have agreed, at least tacitly, to follow the facts where they lead.

That is not this argument. We are dealing here, yes, with the most blatant anti-science of the age. But it is worse than that. It is inhumane and it must be countered on that basis. Those who would deny with zero scientific validity

the fruits of modern agricultural research to starving or undernourished people need to be addressed for what they are, which is callous, which is heartless,
which is cruel.

Marie Antoinette, I didn't know her personally, but she may have at least had
the excuse of naivete and ignorance. That excuse cannot be made for the people
who are attacking GMOs and other technologies like it today. When starvation
was imposed knowingly, in cases and instances we can all think of from the past,
we knew what to call it. And I can't for the life of me see a moral distinction between those instances and these.

I realize that some of the experiences which have taught me the rough and
tumble of public debates, like the one I am discussing here, have not come naturally to good people like you. Scientists, God bless them, operate in a world
where one assumes that the facts will prevail and that good science will win out.
Regulators are naturally cautious. That's a good thing. They are very careful, lest
they make a mistake with serious consequences. Folks in business aren't in business to have arguments and to deal in controversy, and certainly not to argue with
their customers. And so they very naturally shy away, I know that.

I didn't think of this until literally last weekend as I was mulling about what
to talk to you about tonight, but I want to tell you a little story. In 1990 I entered
the pharmaceutical business—something I had not anticipated doing but was
one of those surprises that comes along in life—and the timing was extraordinarily memorable to me. At the company I was working for, a fantastic team of
three scientists had come up with a molecule called fluoxetine that offered enormous promise. This was a technological innovation like the ones that many of you
work on that literally could change lives and save the lives of millions.

This molecule addressed depression in a very effective way. In fact, it worked
so effectively and so safely that the treatment of depression could spread beyond
the small subset of psychiatrists into the broader medical population and thereby
reach many more people. You could take a bottle of the pills and it wouldn't hurt
you. That is not true of the predecessor molecules. This is the drug the world
came to know as Prozac.

Early after its launch it was attacked violently, viciously, and anti-scientifically
with a vengeance by an organization with its own agenda and its own motives.
That organization calls itself Scientology. Like many of today's anti-GMO zealots,
with that organization there were many parallels. The longer I thought about it,
the closer the fit. They had no regard for scientific facts, that was just a given. They
were well funded, and they were accorded generous attention by a very credulous

media. And they were aggressive and ruthless in their tactics—full-page ads and cooked-up news conferences with alleged victims.

I will never forget. It happened to be my first day on the job and they said, "Come along to this meeting. We think we've got a little problem," because the first news conference and bogus lawsuit had just happened. Being good scientists, the first half hour was a review of what we thought we knew about the contention that this drug, which actually treats depression, might be inducing suicide or self-harming behavior. There was a presentation, but that information was not in there anywhere. "But," the scientists said, "we know what to do about this. We will run some further studies. We think we can do a meta-analysis of all the data that are out there now. We will publish it. It will all take about eighteen months, but it will be in the *New England Journal of Medicine*, and that will take care of it."

I kept my mouth shut because, what did I know? I was thinking then, and I really thought later, I don't know how to spell fluoxetine but I know one thing—if you let people lie about your product relentlessly without direct contradiction, people are going to believe it. It was very contrary to the culture of that company, the whole industry, and really business in general, but at the end of the day we decided that we did not have an option. As some of you may remember, it touched off a hand-to-hand, dollar-for-dollar tug-of-war until ultimately the situation was resolved.

I know Purdue, our sister universities, and our colleagues everywhere will do our part to educate about the tremendous importance of GMOs. Perhaps one of the best things schools like ours do is train young people. I love our Ag Day in the spring when people come from great distances, especially young school children. We are trying to interest them in agriculture and related fields, and I love to wander around and listen to our undergrads explain the wonders of the technologies that they are seeing and working on in company with our faculty. They explain that there is nothing new about this—we've been doing it since the Egyptians or before. The only thing that is new is the techniques of today are so much more precise, so much more narrow, so much safer than the hit-and-miss, broad swath genetic manipulations of the past. So that is contribution number one.

Second is to continue producing our share of the new research. Purdue's latest World Food Prize winner received the award for new strains of drought resistant sorghum which have saved countless people in his native Ethiopia and other places. If you go to Ethiopia with Dr. Gebisa Ejeta,[4] you are not going to find anybody carrying an anti-GMO placard. You are going to run into people who know him as a celebrity. People know Gebisa there in the way the world knows Norman Borlaug.[5]

At Purdue, we are making deep investments in precision agriculture. This spring, the world's most advanced automated phenotyping lab will open on hundreds of acres near our campus, and our researchers, and any of you who want to come and use it, will be able to study in real time the exact phenotypical expression of genetic variations in the real environment.

We know how much good can come from all this. The last time I checked with my poultry friends, research had gotten the feed-to-meat ratio down to 1.2 pounds in for 1 pound out. This is magic. What a boon to a world that not only wants to eat enough to survive, but wants to eat protein, wants to eat the way we all just did.

I see some hopeful signs. Maybe I am just bred to try to be optimistic, but I do. I'm told there is legislation under serious consideration that would try to stop the pernicious tactic of state-by-state, death-by-a-thousand-cuts regulation in the area of GMOs. And I think we've come a little way from Cheerios to Chipotle.[6] In fairness to General Mills, or maybe in tribute to the 98% of their shareholders who voted against an anti-GMO proposal, that company now seems a little bolder. With the Chipotle incident, I am struggling. My preacher would remind me not to engage in that four-syllable German word that is hard to pronounce, where you take satisfaction in the misery of others. I am struggling not to engage in it, but that's not really the point.

The point is, we've seen here an object lesson for those who had been misled. You know, it turns out *E.coli* is all-natural. But any of this activity, any of these object lessons that might come along, are likely to be inadequate unless they are accompanied by a vigorous and unapologetic calling to account. Not merely reacting, not merely defending these breakthroughs and these essential steps forward. But calling to account those who would, for reasons I cannot fathom, deny the world these essential advances.

I am prepared to believe, I choose to believe, that this is a problem of cognitive dissonance on the part of those who surely know the falsity of what they are saying. There have been some recantations. There have been some high-profile people who have stepped forward and said, "I was wrong. There is nothing wrong with these technologies. In fact, we need them badly." There will be General Mills moments that happen here and there, but it won't be enough.

No, folks who have taken that point of view have got to be called to account. How can they say to the hungry of this Earth—to those who don't enjoy the luxury that we all do and that the developed world in general does—how can they tell those folks, "Sorry about your luck." You know this is an indulgence of the rich and it is, as I said before, not just scientifically indefensible, it is morally indefensible. And as much as we would like not to have to engage in arguments like that, somebody had better, and no one is more credible than the people in this room, people like you, the folks you know, the folks you influence, the folks you work with every day.

Paul Harvey, if anybody still remembers him, used to end his radio show with "the rest of the story." So, the rest of the Prozac story is, in the end the innovation survived. In the end, anti-science was countered. Not just the falsity of the charges, but the unacceptable motives of those making the charges were exposed sufficiently that the molecule survived, was eventually joined by others like it, and countless people were helped. Suicide rates are down. Depression is no longer stigmatized—it is widely treated and understood, not as a fault in one's soul, but as a chemical imbalance in almost every case. And we are in a better world.

We are going to have to have some sort of a victory like that in the area of GMOs. I take your time tonight on this because I just don't know a more important quest that any of us could pick up, if you are willing. The GMO debate is even bigger and even more imperative than the one I described about depression. We will need all the voices in this room to prevail. But what a great assignment. If we can achieve it, then we can get on with the thrilling humanitarian assignment of saving lives and feeding 9 billion people on a planet cleaner and safer than the one we inhabit today. Thank you so very much.

Invited remarks
San Francisco, California
July 2016

There are certain speaking invitations that are simultaneously gratifying and fearsome. Eulogies of dear friends, responses to presidential State of the Unions. They come with an equal measure of privilege and apprehension—you have to say yes, but you'd better be good. I can relate at this moment to the tar-and-feather victim in Lincoln's famous story: "But for the honor of it all, I'd just as soon it happened to someone else."

My assigned topic today adds another layer of risk. Higher education, especially in a gathering like this one, is a subject with which everyone has some direct experience and probably some strong viewpoints. Everyone's an expert. So, heat up the tar while I endeavor to add to what you already know.

I try to avoid titling speeches, because usually I don't know quite what's coming until I hear myself say it. But this occasion demanded a title, so I plagiarized one from George Will, who ended a scathing column on today's higher ed this past year with the question "Higher than what?"

There are bookshelves of recent criticism of higher education that until recently had seemed sacrosanct and immune to rebuke, asking a host of tough, new questions: Are too many young people going to college? Are they learning anything useful or meaningful while there? How can one tell who the best talents are when it seems everyone gets straight As? Are students being taught to think for themselves, or told what to think? And underneath it all, why does it cost so darned much?

Consider the question, What percentage of today's postsecondary students graduated from high school and within one year entered a four-year, residential college or university? The answer is about 22%. Addressing America's looming talent challenge in a knowledge economy is really more about better community colleges, vocational training, and adult remediation than about improvements at the four-year residential institutions.

But what happens at those colleges and universities still matters, maybe more than ever. Because this is where the career readiness, social attitudes, and fitness for citizenship in a free society either are or aren't developed in the stratum of talent destined to drive our economy and lead our institutions. The news isn't good. Our higher ed institutions, which we need to be the world's finest, are seriously challenged by threats external and internal, which in turn threatens our nation's prosperity and, even more important, our civic life as a free and self-governing people.

The U.S. may have slipped in some dimensions of international influence and competitiveness, but at least until recently no one quarreled with the notion that we lead the world in the quality of our higher educational institutions. Globally, families who can do so send their children here to study, some 1 million of them this past academic year. Think of it as a $31 billion export industry. This has come in the face of a run-up in price that after years of observation still astonishes.

I tell old business colleagues, "Here's the racket we should have gone into." You're selling a product deemed a necessity; just can't make it in life without that diploma. No one has devised a method of determining quality, so accountability for results is near zero. Your market is lavishly subsidized by government, desensitizing your customers to price increases. In fact, it's better than that: You have complete pricing power. You can raise prices at will and never lose customers. In the absence of any objective measurements of what kids are learning, buyers have associated sticker price with quality. If it costs more, it must be better.

By now, most people know the outcome. The only three consumption items in the entire economy that have risen in price faster than health care are college tuitions, college fees, and college textbooks. And we all know how student debt has exploded to meet these charges, almost tripling over the last decade, to a total of $1.3 trillion,[7] outstripping auto loans, credit card debt—every form of borrowing except home mortgages—with documented negative impact on rates of household formation, childbearing, income independence, business startups, and more.

There are multiple analyses of what caused this escalation. The party line on the public school side is, "The state made us do it." It's true that the share of university budgets funded by state governments has fallen by almost half over the last few decades. It is now below 10% at places like Michigan and Virginia. But I sat for eight years on the other side of that table. Given the rate of spending increases at most such schools, it would have been impossible for a prudent state government to keep up. And, even if persuasive, this excuse would not explain the escalation on the private school front, up 70% after inflation the last twenty years.

There is the Baumol-Bowen theory of service productivity, which holds that in certain service occupations, productivity increases cannot keep pace with those in other sectors, but to remain competitive for talent, salaries must do so. Centuries later, it still takes four musicians to play a Beethoven quartet. Fine, but it's not clear that, in a wired age, we should still need as many professors per student as we once did.

A more persuasive case was made by Bill Bennett, who hypothesized as early as the 1980s that the flood of government grants and loans would be pocketed by the higher ed sector in steadily higher prices, leaving the student no better off, in fact worse. Commonsense observation, and a parade of studies, confirm Bennett's conjecture. Last year the New York Fed found that, for every dollar of additional student aid, college costs rise at least 60%. It's one of many reasons that notions of so-called free college tuition are nonsense. As P. J. O'Rourke said of health care, "If you think it's expensive now, just wait 'til it's free."

Each of these explanations has validity, but as usual a quick cut with Occam's razor produces the clearest answer: They raise the price because they can. And because at least some parents accept a stratospheric sticker price as a proxy for excellence. And, it has allowed schools enormous margins with which to dress up their class demographics, through hidden cross-subsidies and backdoor discounting. Generous, ego-flattering scholarships, many of them to wealthy students, this year totaled 49% of the surface price.

A friend of mine attended a symposium at which one speaker was the president of a small, very pricey Eastern college. An astute member of the audience posed a question all such officials should be asked annually: "How many of this year's freshmen paid the full tuition?" The speaker hemmed and hawed before answering, "Uh, one." It so happened that my friend had a niece in that class. He went out to the hallway and called his sister to ask what percentage of the stated price she was paying. When she said all of it and he told her what he'd just learned, her reply was justifiably unprintable. As the poker players say, if you can't tell who the sucker is, it's you.

At Purdue, we have opted for a different approach. During my first month on campus, I suggested that we call a one-year time-out from the yearly tuition hike. There had been one for thirty-six straight years. I argued that particularly for a land-grant school like ours, created by Abe Lincoln and his allies to throw open the doors of higher education beyond the wealthy and the elite, it would be appropriate to signal that we were listening to the growing concern about cost. I said to my new colleagues, "Rather than demand that our students' families adapt their budgets to our spending, why don't we try adapting our spending to their budgets?"

Well, there were those who warned that we'd never make ends meet, we'd have to turn out the lights—the usual bureaucratic response to any proposed economy. I knew better than to listen to that. But the more interesting reaction came from the enrollment staff, who said, "If we stand pat while all our competitors go up, people will think there's something wrong with our product." Yes, really.

Three years later, we still have not raised tuition, and we have pledged to extend the freeze for at least the next two years. By then three classes will have entered and graduated from Purdue without ever seeing a tuition increase. In fact, because we have also reduced the cost of room, board, and books, it is less expensive in nominal dollars to attend our university today than it was in 2013. Incidentally, total student debt is down 28%, mainly because of the tens of additional millions we didn't charge them.

And the customer reaction? It turns out a reputation for affordability sells. Applications have surged to a record 48,000 this year.[8] This spring, those same enrollment people were clamoring for an early announcement of the freeze extension, because they knew it would boost acceptance decisions. And it did. We will welcome the biggest Purdue class in a decade. Despite their size they arrive with yet another record academic profile. Sometimes one truly can make it up on the volume.

But no other school I know of has chosen quite the same path. There has been some deceleration of tuition growth, and here and there state governments have mandated some restraint. But prices overall have continued their upward climb, up 3% per year over the last five years. A new trend is to make moderate tuition increases while adding so-called fees for athletics or various student activities. All this leaves many institutions as classic candidates for the disruption to which businesses in the real world of the economy have long been accustomed.

For presentations when I bring a slide show, I sometimes start with a grainy black-and-white photograph of a tweedy, obviously academic gentleman in front of an ivy-covered wall. Most audiences need me to tell them that it is Joseph Schumpeter, the Austrian economist who taught the world about creative destruction.

It's easy to see the potential disrupters of a sector so pampered and complacent as today's higher ed. No business is more easily disintermediated in our wired age than one that sells information. Ask newspapers, record companies, or big-box bookstores. Predictably, a host of new entrants has arisen, offering to deliver the information we call education in far less expensive ways.

Companies with names like edX, Coursera, and Udacity, based at places like MIT and Stanford, are offering free, high-quality content for credit, through the vehicle now known as MOOCs—massive open online courses.

I tell my co-workers that our biggest assignment is to pass the pajamas test. Some very smart people, backed by some very big money—undoubtedly many of them sitting here—are telling our potential students, "Whaddya wanna do that for? Move somewhere, spend four or five years and a ton of money? I'll bring the best professors in the world right into your living room. Just sit there on your couch in your pajamas and take it all in." I always say that the stay-awake issue for a person in my job is how we are going to add value so clear and unquestionable that, twenty years from now, bright young people will continue to make the decision to get off that couch.

Some scholars in the field of economic dynamism assert that an incumbent business is simply incapable of transforming itself sufficiently to ward off a genuine disrupter. The danger rises with the incumbent's level of dominance; it's hard to believe that what has worked well over time won't keep on working. Surely those foreign economy cars, or digital photography, or Internet book sales, is just a fad. Just wait 'til those customers discover all the shortcomings. They'll be back. Higher ed's ability to respond to its looming disruptive challenges is hampered by its antique, ponderous decision processes. General Motors or Eastman Kodak were gazelles of nimbleness compared to today's university, handcuffed by practices like lifetime tenure and "shared governance," a cherished anachronism through which faculty feel entitled to take an active hand in not just academic but often administrative, financial, or strategic decisions. Process is sacred, committees are rampant, action when it happens at all is tediously slow.

The chances of establishment higher education responding in time to its new challenges are further reduced by the thick layer of self-righteousness that pervades its careerist leadership. "That'll never happen" is reinforced by "How dare they?" Roll these factors together and you have a classic portrait of a sitting duck.

Most of the attention in terms of threats to traditional higher ed has been captured by tech-savvy upstarts like edX. But a different menace may cause even greater trouble, and sooner. That is the growing awareness among employers that many college diplomas tell very little about the bearer's readiness for either work or life.

Widely publicized research has found that today's college students demonstrate little or no growth in critical thinking skills between their freshman and senior years. In one major study, 36% of students demonstrated no intellectual growth after four years of college. Employers increasingly report that new hires show up with credentials from well-regarded universities but without basic skills or work habits. Companies have learned that the diploma may be a proxy for the intelligence to get admitted to college in the first place, but that it often proves nothing about a student's degree of growth while there.

High grades are equally deceptive. The phenomenon called grade inflation has debauched the currency of a high GPA. The average grade at Florida is 3.35; at Middlebury, 3.53; at Brown, 3.64. One wonders, How bad do you have to be to get a B?

A startling 45% of recent college graduates are now in jobs that do not require a college degree. And that is when they have found work at all. You will have heard that a record percentage, almost half, of recent graduates are back living with their families. When I tell parents of prospective students, "If you send your child to Purdue, I promise you he won't move back in the basement," it's my most popular and probably persuasive line.

Meanwhile, other paths to family-supporting incomes are increasingly apparent. Twenty-eight percent of two-year associate degrees lead to starting salaries higher than the median four-year liberal arts grad's. Certificates in fields like emergency medical technician, auto mechanics, and computer specialist recover their cost twice as quickly as four-year degrees in psychology or women's studies.

So, the single greatest disruption to which the system is exposed is that large businesses and business sectors will decide to seek out or devise their own alternative credentialing or qualification processes. Today's CPA, CFA, and bar exams could soon be joined by a host of others as the gating mechanism for various occupations. Already, some units of Ernst and Young blind their recruiters to applicants' college history, using an online test instead. Amazon has refused to give specifics, but the company has recruited high-profile academics to "scale and innovate workplace learning." What happens when other companies begin accepting Amazon credentials as qualifications? If the time comes when young Americans conclude that quality careers no longer require the time and expense of college, our institutions may shrink to quaint finishing schools where the children of the most privileged go to extend their adolescence. Or, as someone recently put it, "the debutante cotillions of the twenty-first century."

Reviewing this array of threats—a smug, complacent incumbent industry with little inclination or ability to reform itself; a product of dubious and seemingly declining quality; prices that have soared beyond the bounds of reasonableness; ingenious new technologies that promise better for less; innovative business models unencumbered by the ossified practices of a millennium-old establishment—it is tempting to conclude, as many have, that higher ed is on borrowed time. That a shakeout of massive proportions is in the offing. Some analysts are estimating that as many as half of today's colleges will be bankrupt and defunct within fifteen years.

Though one should never doubt the power or the swiftness with which creative destruction can visit its effects on its victims, I think these forecasts are only directionally correct. A wave of closings and consolidations is likely and indeed has already begun, and the pressure of competition is the only impetus sufficient to jar most institutions into motion and a concern for delivering value.

The inertia in the system, plus the luxury a rich society enjoys of subsidizing inefficiency, I am guessing will enable most of today's universities to survive and lumber on indefinitely. That leaves the question, Do they deserve to? Because all the external challenges are matched by internal failings that call into question the self-justifications and the claims of higher ed to a place of honor among our nation's institutions.

A standard academy response to criticism is that college is not vocational school. That it is not about the acquisition of skills, which will have limited shelf life in today's world, but about how to think critically, and "learning how to learn." Additionally, we are told, our universities are there to prepare citizens for leadership in a free society.

Leave aside that some 85% of applicants say that getting a good job is their primary motive for going to college and accept the validity of these defenses. It is hard for the apologists to assert that they are being delivered on.

We have already dealt with the scarcity of evidence that critical thinking and intellectual growth are occurring at many of our schools. How about citizenship, and the ability to evaluate and compare judgments on the important public questions which a free people must contemplate and decide?

In study after study, young people (and, by now, those not so young) cannot answer the simplest questions about our system of government. On a truly basic civics test, asking stumpers like "Who has the power to declare war?" and "Name a right guaranteed by the First Amendment," college grads average 54%. Ivy Leaguers scored a whopping 64%. At many schools, freshmen did better than seniors; researchers call this "negative learning."

On most campuses, so-called diversity reigns as the cardinal virtue, except for the form that should matter most: diversity of thought. A survey this year could uncover only 49 self-declared Republicans in a University of North Carolina faculty of 1,300. Seventeen entire departments, including Public Policy, had zero.

A self-perpetuating guild of tenured faculty, selecting its own successors through two or three generations now, guarantees, many believe, that no return to balance can be expected. In the places where the free exchange and collision of ideas should be most prized and prevalent, too often an enforced, dreary conformity has descended. Students—not often at Purdue, I should mention—report the need to regurgitate an ideological catechism to satisfy their professors, and sometimes to avoid academic punishment.

Worse still, students are being encouraged to see the silencing of disapproved viewpoints as legitimate. Many are seizing the opportunity to do the silencing themselves.

Each recent school year has brought its ration of outrages. You've read about them, but they're hard to keep up with. Dangerous radicals like Condi Rice, Christine Lagarde, and George Will disinvited from campuses. Michael

Bloomberg, Israeli ambassador Michael Oren, and NYPD commissioner Ray Kelly shouted down when they do show up. Presidents' offices and other campus spaces "occupied" and defaced. A startup company called Crowds on Demand now offers to organize protests for profit. Like acts of physical terrorism, these incidents eventually can leave us desensitized and resigned. But we should never just shrug off violations of the free expression on which our entire edifice of self-government depends.

If universities are willing to disgrace and embarrass themselves by permitting or even encouraging trespasses of basic American freedoms, that's their problem. But if they are spawning a generation of little authoritarians, drilled in one ideological philosophy and socialized to trample on the freedom of those who disagree, that's everybody's problem. This pattern has led some observers to decide that the situation is beyond repair, and to root for the disrupters to take down the whole structure.

I for one hope not. With all its flaws, our complex of higher ed institutions remains the world's finest, and we need it to be. And there are some positive signs.

Assaults on free expression have now begun to affect not just outside speakers and administrators but faculty in their classrooms. One professor, writing last summer in an avowedly left-wing publication, said, "I'm a liberal, and my liberal students terrify me." A *Lord of the Flies* environment no longer seems so amusing when it's you at the stake.

In 2015, the University of Chicago promulgated a statement reaffirming its commitment to free inquiry and free expression. It contains provisions like "debate or deliberation may not be suppressed because the ideas put forth are thought by some or even by most members of the University community to be offensive, unwise, immoral, or wrong-headed." Purdue and several other schools have adopted what we call the Chicago Principles, hoping to generate a movement back toward a climate of genuine intellectual openness. It is too early to throw in the towel and join those who hope for the complete dismantling of institutions on whose performance our national success depends, perhaps more than ever.

Few audiences anywhere could do more to help. Virtually every alumnus here has or could have influence at his or her institution. Please use it. But I notice that people who are relentless and tough-minded in their business and professional lives go all weak in the knees where Dear Old Alma Mater is concerned.

Before you write that next big check, ask your college trustees to endorse the Chicago Principles, and to repeal any limits on free inquiry or free speech.

Ask your president what this year's net tuition is and what percentage of the students are actually paying the stated price. Ask questions not just about tuition but about student fees and the total cost of attendance, and what plans there are for containing it. Ask what tests or other mechanisms are in place to measure intellectual growth of the students on your campus. Ask what courses are taken by fewer than fifteen or twenty students, and why they aren't being discontinued. If you are a trustee, and not prepared to delve into matters like this, please stand down and let someone more aggressive have a turn. They'll let you keep the fifty-yard-line seats.

I've probably painted too grim a picture in some respects, and obviously I've not taken time to praise all the remarkable teaching and research that happens to some degree on almost every American campus. But the national importance of primacy in this realm mandates urgency. As a society we must resolve that higher ed won't cut it; only the *highest* ed will do. If you're in a position to help, I earnestly hope you will.

The 2017 Ian Rolland Lecture
Allen County, Indiana
October 2017

> This annual lecture is given in memory of Ian Rolland, who chaired the capital campaign to endow the Lincoln Financial Foundation Collection and served as vice president of Friends of the Lincoln Collection of Indiana, Inc., until his passing in 2017.

In the latter couple years of my last job, some misguided souls (not to incriminate him, but Ian was actually one) suggested that I ought to seek higher office, nationally. And I gave it a thought. As I tell my co-workers at Purdue when they bring it up these days, I held out and got a better job. So instead of that, my common sense and the good luck of the republic prevailed, and I didn't run. But instead, I wrote a book.

The book talked about what I saw as a looming threat to our free institutions and to our democracy. I somewhat flippantly called it the "red menace," this time referring not to military threat of a foreign power, the Soviet Union we once knew, but the red ink of debts that we have and continue to pile up for the nation's future and are going to inflict, very unjustly, on following generations. I wrote about it as a test of our maturity as a democracy.

Could we act, as adults must ultimately, and forgo immediate gratification in order to protect for the future? When we spend money, spend it more often in investments for the future of our children and their children, not simply on current consumption, which has been what we've done? I thought of the book as something of a love letter to the American people because it took the obstinately optimistic viewpoint that, yes, we can do this. We can speak to ourselves politically in a way that will lead us to do those prudent things, those fair things that will ensure the nation's long-term success. Even as I wrote, however, a new threat, a new test of our democracy, was somehow bubbling up, and I confess I really didn't see it. And that's just a few years ago.

It's the subject I want to talk about tonight. I had an argument with the publishers of that book that went on for quite a while, and it was about chapter 2. Having set the stage for the subjects I wanted to discuss, I was fixed on the idea that I wanted to write a short chapter about the fragility of our democracy, a little tour through history. I promised them—because I'm not really competent to do it—that it wasn't going to be exhaustive, it wasn't going to be too long, it wasn't going to pretend to be profound. I just wanted to make the simple point, because not all our fellow citizens have thought of about it, that democracy as we've known it—government of, by, and for the people—is not the natural state of affairs in world history. In fact, the United States and now a few other modern nations are anomalies.

World history is populated overwhelmingly by tyrants and militarists and warlords and dictators. Totalitarian states dominate the lives of their citizens and have little or no regard for their welfare, let alone their viewpoint. We Americans have only been accustomed to freedom and free institutions. The founders were painfully aware of this. They were trying to give birth to a new system and a new nation coming out of a history that they knew full well was unfriendly to the aspirations of common people to have control of their own lives. They expressed the doubt repeatedly for multiple reasons, even as they risked their lives, liberties, and all their possessions and their "sacred honor," that this experiment could last for long. John Adams said maybe two generations.

Their fears were in various categories. One was that, like many previous attempts at democratic government, we would spend ourselves broke. It would be too easy for a set of demagogues to promise attractive things to people, and when

51% found out they could plunder the other 49%, school would be out. Sometimes they thought the very success of free institutions might have within it the seeds of their undoing—that in general the economic success of such a society would lead to opulence, indolence, and ultimately a collapse of the very character which had made the success possible in the first place.

Maybe their biggest fear, expressed over and over, was that the underpinnings that they thought were essential to this experiment in freedom—morality and religion—would fade. It's in all their speeches and writings, from George Washington to our Constitution, that our system is only fit for a moral and religious people. Adams observed that if morality and religion ever fade, with it will fade the freedoms they have given birth to.

I just recently read a book about a much less well-known founder, Oliver Ellsworth. He wrote anonymous tracts called *A Landholder*. Think of them as Federalist Papers for his State of Connecticut, arguing for the Constitution. There was a line that stopped me cold because it sounded just a little too reminiscent of the situation which we seem to find ourselves in today. He said if we should ever become "ignorant, idle and vicious," then we would be fit for slavery, and that "it will be an easy business to reduce us to obey tyrants."

If you only read one recent article or essay, I would encourage you to read Andrew Sullivan's piece in *New York Magazine* earlier this month.[9] He writes about this subject and uses much of the same language that I have been ruminating over recently. Sullivan writes that the project of democracy was always an extremely precarious endeavor. It rested on the eighteenth-century hope that deep divides could be bridged by a culture of compromise and that emotion can be defeated by reason.

He observes in the article, as you will have observed I'm sure, that one way or another we have come to a point of very deep divisions in our country that go beyond disagreements about what is wise and what is not, and what is even right and what is wrong. That we have, it seems, come to a point of what could be called a "new tribalism," and he works that concept out more thoroughly than anybody I've seen until now.

He points out, much as I just attempted to, that tribalism is not one possible feature of the human existence—it is, as he calls it, "the default human experience." It is the natural way of things for people to clump together—like with like—and to fear and even come to despise the other, trusting only those in the tribe. We can look around the world and feel superior or feel fortunate that we are not Iraq, or Lebanon, or Syria, or Rwanda, or the Balkans, or more recently Myanmar, or in past days Northern Ireland.

We have seen all too often both the phenomenon and the consequences of tribalism, of situations where, as Sullivan says, people may be nominally citizens of the same place, but their deepest loyalty is to something else. Looking at the American situation today, he sums up, when race, religion—here we could say religion or the lack of—and geography define your political parties, you are deep in trouble.

Well, how did we get here, and am I the only one that found that it happened rather suddenly? I confess that just a few years ago I spent a lot of time writing an entire book about a different threat to our democracy, and I don't recall mentioning a word about this problem, except maybe in its incipient phase of an eroding civility in our discourse, which I did see.

Again, how did we get here? I think there were some natural causes and some societal changes that have simply led to Americans being more divided, more suspicious, even hostile to each other. There is the phenomenon called the Big Sort—the fact that in a knowledge-driven economy, increasingly wealth and influence go to people who are able to manipulate symbols and information. That there has been some division based along those lines is reflected in the fact that people who have those skills tend to work together and eventually live together. Then there is one of those sociological terms, "assortative mating," a $25 term for people who marry people like themselves.

More recently we've seen geographic clustering. It's very curious and very different. In the 2012 election, only 5% of the more than 3,000 counties in America had an outcome in the presidential vote within 5%, plus or minus. Only 15% were within 10% or more, and generally in elections something bigger than that is considered a big win, maybe a landslide. In the vast majority of American geographies it was not close. People tended to lean very heavily in one direction or another. It is a fair criticism, and in fact there is a Supreme Court case right now about the issue of gerrymandering and whether lines are drawn fairly or whether they are drawn to lock in one party or the other. As it happens, the historical Supreme Court position has been that it is a matter—it may be bad—but it is a matter for the political branches that they ought not meddle in. I have no idea what they will do in this one.

Even if it's a good idea for the court somehow to step in against gerrymandering, it may be a little late. In the geographic concentrations I just talked about, you could draw the fairest, squarest, most geographically compact lines around the so-called common communities of interest, just the way the law contemplates, and you would still get a one-sided outcome, because our population has concentrated in this novel way. You would almost need to reverse-gerrymander. You would almost have to draw salamander-like districts in order to throw, let's say, Democrats and Republicans together in some even mix.

At our school, this is a good thing in some ways, but not necessarily for the poor schmo at my job. Whoever holds the job gives the commencement speeches. It's my biggest homework assignment of the year. And in each of the last three (and I'll probably do it again, because I'm so fixed on this idea), I have said in one way or another to our graduates something like the following:

> You have never thought of yourselves as an aristocrat, but starting today you are one. It's not the aristocracies we've known throughout time. It's not based on your family's name, or inherited land, or a title. It's not based on great wealth. It's not based on your father's membership in the totalitarian party that rules the country. It will be based on this [pointing to head].
>
> You are about to leave here with one of the great emblems of achievement available anywhere—a degree from Purdue University. You are highly likely in the natural course of things, without intending to, to end up working with people like you, living near people like you, marrying somebody much like you. You will have kids who are much like you. Please don't let that happen. It will take an extra effort that previous generations never had to think about. I don't know what the right answer is. Join a softball league, attend a church on the other side of town. Do something so you don't lose touch with people who aren't favored with the cognitive advantages that you have just earned for yourself here.

It's a fact of life that we have and are likely to continue separating along these lines.

Some other causes I think emerge from our modern communication media. What was at its outset called narrowcasting, the division of the electronic media into more and more channels, hundreds of them now, has made it possible for people to naturally gravitate to the information sources that they agree with. Or, as they say, "confirm their biases." That's a very natural human tendency. And now we know that the large majority of Americans tend to listen to, watch, or read those sources that do reinforce their current views.

There is some research on this now that is very convincing. People in a closed or somewhat closed system—where the information they receive, the arguments they hear, and the facts provided to them furnish what is called "confirmation bias"—wind up with more extreme views, more rigid views. It's only common sense, only natural, but we know this empirically now, and I think we see it all around us.

Finally, there is another sort of media which has erupted over the last historical blink: so-called social media. Maybe we should start calling it antisocial media. I don't partake of it much, but everybody knows what is there and sees pieces of it. In many ways, I think you'll agree, it encourages the worst tendencies. People will say things they would never say face-to-face with someone else and sometimes wind up in cycles of vituperation, one to the next, back and forth, back and forth. Lincoln might have worried about the worst angels of our nature if he had seen today's social media.

Some of this is probably inherent in the economy we have, in the society we have, in the media, the tools, in the technologies that we develop. Maybe some of it was just absolutely built in from the start. But I think some of the causes are more self-inflicted.

Very few of the students emerging from our high schools today have what I would consider even a basic grounding in the facts of American history or American government. You've seen all the surveys too—they would be funny, if they weren't so worrisome—about how little our young people, and now not so young people, know about our system and about the proud history that produced it.

In some corners of the K–12 system I think it's worse than that. In some places it's not only a matter of leaving children ignorant and uninspired about the country and about its past, but there has been a relentless assault on our unifying myths. By myths I don't mean things that are fictional, I mean those stories that any society or any culture passes down which remind us of the things that should make us proud, that remind us of things that should unify us, and that we could all feel good about. The pilgrims, Valley Forge, Lewis and Clark, Gettysburg. The great tinkerers and inventors Whitney and Bell and Edison. Normandy, Hiroshima.

Many of the young people, including some that I encounter on our campus, have been taught a twisted, I think distorted version of our history, which focuses only on the obvious flaws and imperfections and misses the overriding reality, the fundamental truth: that this nation, at each stage of its history, has been pushing out the boundaries of freedom, expanding the opportunities of humans to be men and women in liberty; that the direction and the march has always been upward toward what Churchill called "the sunlit uplands."

Another fallacy, perhaps the most ignorant fallacy that is extant today, has now been given the label "presentism." This is the notion that we in this historical moment are uniquely wise, uniquely knowledgeable, uniquely moral, and that those who went before were deeply flawed individuals, whose memories are not worth preserving, maybe should be disintegrated, defaced, torn down.

As I've pointed out to some of our students—they may be there to see it in a hundred years, given the advance of the life sciences—I'll make a very confident prediction. In a hundred years, if the species *Homo sapiens* is still in charge, if our machines haven't either turned us into domestic pets or worse, I promise you, they will look at you as an intellectual and moral midget. I don't know on what basis, but before you get really smug about those who went before, recognize that they lived among different challenges, they lived with more hardships, they lived with a range of choices and understandings. It's your job to put yourselves in their minds, not to imagine that you can transpose your way of thinking on them. That's a reality that we have drifted into.

Rolling all of this together, too many of our fellow citizens on both sides of this tribal divide have come to the tragic conclusion that if you and I disagree, you're not just wrong, you're evil, you're "other," and there is no talking to you, let alone compromising with you. The undisguised disdain of one tribe for the one that more generally prevails in, let's say, Fort Wayne, Indiana, was to me the decisive factor in the shocking events of the 2016 election. Yes, economic frustration was a part of it. Yes, there is a natural rhythm in our politics—one side is in for a while, the other side has a better chance of prevailing the next time.

But I think the absolutely decisive factor was the sense among many people that they were being read out of the American family, that they were not worthy, that views and values that seemed eternal until very recently were now not only changing, but those who held them were some subspecies that could be looked down on. I told a number of friends who were deeply disappointed by the outcome of the last election that if you look down your nose at people long enough, one day they will punch you in it. And making no case on either side for where we are as a country, I think this is what happened. The outcome of that election, many of the people who prevailed, were not a cause of our current divide. They were very much a symptom of all these factors that I've just outlined and probably others I'm not savvy enough to see through.

In any event, we awaken to find ourselves in this place where mere disagreements have been elevated to fatal character flaws. Where really awful words—hate, racism, bigotry—are not to be reserved for the worst tendencies among us but are thrown around so loosely and so often. I think some of them are being stretched and cheapened by overuse. Someone recently wrote that maybe the worst bigotry of all is political bigotry, the kind that I've been talking about.

Did you read the serious suggestion by one national writer who was writing, in this case, to her fellow women? If one's husband was so hopeless that he somehow favored the current president, she should divorce him. Now think about that. These days, Andrew Sullivan's culture of compromise is viewed on both sides of this divide as not only not the essential ingredient of progress and freedom and our society, but as a dirty word and as perhaps the original sin.

I would love to say that having painted this rather distressing picture I have some prescription to recommend to you for our national affliction. I'm not smart enough yet to see one. I do suggest maybe this: Is there a chance that Indiana could be different? That we could strike a different direction, a different tone, perhaps with different results that at least separate us from what I believe is a dangerous new direction in the country? Who knows? Maybe we could induce others at some point to think about heading in that direction themselves.

We have been different, in other ways, in the not-too-distant past. We have neighboring states who are headed for bankruptcy, if that's an option open to them. We are an island of solvency. We have a business climate that has led to full employment. I just looked at a map earlier today that graphically shows how widespread full-time employment is in Indiana compared to other places. We have built infrastructure in ways that other states have only dreamt of and talked about. We've worked on health care in a way that the nation may, for all I know, now use as a model for broader reforms. We conserved more land than at any other time in the state's history and perhaps, relative to our size, in any state's history.

How did these things happen? The results were almost always marked by and almost always enabled by civility and at least, even during the strongest disagreements, a positive presumption about those with whom one was in dispute. I said in the book I mentioned that if we would expect the best from our fellow citizens, we must assume the best about them. I think in Indiana, it's fair to say, with very few exceptions, we tend to assume the best about each other and keep our arguments from becoming personal, and bitter, and tribal.

Some of the things I found most gratifying about and experienced in my last job were only achieved with people from both parties pitching in, because we had a divided legislature much of that time. Full-day kindergarten, telecommunication reform, property tax reduction and reform, and maybe the best example: in 2008, this state voted for Barack Obama for president, while the Republican candidate for governor set a record number of votes that still stands.

I remember in that campaign I would frequently mention to audiences that one thing I felt very good about was knowing it was going to be my last tour in elected politics. It was the only job I was ever interested in. That I had run three campaigns, a primary and two general elections, and never ran a television ad that attacked anyone's character, motives, or background. It was the biggest applause line of any speech in which I thought to mention it. Hoosiers thought that was a really good thing, and I just don't believe we have somehow had a massive change of heart in just eight years.

I look around today and think it is fair to say, as others have said, that we have a governor who is open and friendly and constructive, and hoping to work with people who are willing to work with him. I think we have two senators, one of each party, who meet that description and are frequently mentioned as somewhat rarities in that body now, because they might not be fully predictable, not totally dug in on one side or another. And I think our General Assembly seems to conduct itself with a degree of decorum and civility. This has positive effects that ought not be overlooked or underestimated.

I thought one of the most and gratifying things that happened in the late stages of my last assignment was when a fifty-state survey showed Indiana had the second highest percentage in the country, 77%, when people were asked, "Do you believe your state government does a competent job?" South Dakota was first.

Why did I think that was a big deal? Because we want our fellow citizens to have confidence in their government. We need government to do important things. We can argue about what they are. We can argue about how much of them they should do, but we need it, and we will not be an effective nor a successful society if we break down into tribes who can't even agree on the goodwill and motives of those who see the world a little differently. So maybe our contribution here in Indiana, our way of "resisting," is to avoid the vilification, the tribalism, that for now at least seems to be strengthening in the country. Is to keep on keeping on in the way we have. Maybe we can be a sanctuary for civility in a nation that seems to have very few.

We don't yet need another Lincoln. Although it's quite possible that if things don't change, we will have to pray for one. We could sure use some more Ians right now. As rare and unique as he was, I don't think that's too much to hope for.

His example is so recent for us all. Ian Rolland, as I remember him, was a voice of calm in stormy arguments. He was a good listener when others were shouting. We could use him, but in his absence we must make do with his example, and maybe we can emulate it and set the example ourselves, each of us in our own small way. Maybe collectively the broader community of the state might over time catch the attention of others and influence them to step back and think about doing something similar. One way or another, we have to bring our nation back from the brink of tribalism to become again the free and cooperative society the United States was always meant to be.

Thank you very much.

2018 Philip Merrill Award for Outstanding Contributions to Liberal Arts Education
American Council of Trustees and Alumni
Washington, D.C.
Re-liberalizing the liberal arts
October 2018

Surely I'm not the only person here thinking about Bob Meusel. For the few to whom the obvious comparison has not occurred, I'll remind you that Bob Meusel was the New York Yankee third baseman who, though a creditable player in his own right, followed Babe Ruth and Lou Gehrig in the Yankee batting order, and is therefore largely forgotten. Following Dr. Robert Zimmer and the Ferguson–Ali tandem to this podium leaves me in a similar position.

Given the Hall of Fame–level impacts of their intellects and sheer courage, anything I've contributed to the cause we honor this evening is minor league. That fact leaves me all the more appreciative for your selection.

I may be almost as miscast tonight as Andrew Jackson was when honored at Harvard. Challenged by a mischievous dean to respond in Latin, President Jackson declaimed, "E pluribus unum, my friends. Sine qua non!" And sat down. I regret to inform this audience that you won't be quite that fortunate.

I was already deeply indebted to each of those gracious souls who risked their credibility by seconding the choice. There is no one from whom I have learned more, or whom I have quoted more frequently, than Charles Murray. That a person so wise, caring, and intellectually honest should ever have been abused in places of alleged "higher" education is a travesty of the first order.

Erskine Bowles ranks among the great citizens of our time. To cite just one of his contributions, Erskine did more for his university in five years than I could hope to do for mine if I stayed for twenty. He has introduced me to more fascinating people and learning opportunities than anyone I can name.

Nadine Strossen is an icon of single purpose in an age of double standards, of fidelity to principle in an environment awash in hypocrisy. I value our friendship, especially because it coexists so amicably with our many disagreements.

During my last job, I chose Jeb Bush as my role model in all matters, but particularly education. I often consulted my imaginary "WWJD" bracelet when a difficult call presented itself. My deepest thanks go to each of these wonderful individuals, and my apologies at having imposed on their time and goodwill.

Relative merit aside, the brevity of my time in academic life makes me a highly unlikely choice for tonight's recognition, or for any involving higher education. I have served only one institution, and that for less than six years, hardly enough time to make a serious dent in affairs. Moreover, I work not at a university known primarily for the liberal arts the award celebrates, but at one from the other end of the spectrum.

At Purdue, by our land-grant heritage and by our current conscious strategy, the so-called STEM disciplines predominate. More than 60% of our undergraduates, and an even higher share of our graduate students, pursue engineering, chemistry, physics, agricultural and biological science, and the like. We are by that measure the third most STEM-centric school in the country. Not where "outstanding contributions to liberal arts education" seem likely to come from, unless one recalls that the medieval quadrivium was the STEM curriculum of its time. Whatever the logic of your choice, I am deeply grateful for it and will work hard to live up to it in the remainder of my working days.

But reflecting ahead to this evening, and to the critical objective of redeeming, restoring, reviving, recovering, rejuvenating—pick your favorite "re" word—the liberal arts as we know them today, I began to think that it is a struggle for which newcomers and outsiders are not so poorly suited. Said differently, if we wait for reform from within the ranks of today's liberal arts fields, we may wait forever, or at least a fatally long time. The concerns most often voiced about the current university scene—conformity of thought, intolerance of dissent, and sometimes an authoritarian tendency to quash it, a rejection of the finest of the Western and Enlightenment traditions in favor of unscholarly revisionism and pseudo-disciplines—these and other problems are not unique to the liberal arts departments, but a host of surveys document that they are most common and most pronounced there.

A monotonously one-sided view of the world deprives students of the chance to hear and consider alternatives, and to weigh them for themselves in the process we call critical thinking. But, as this audience knows so well, something even larger is at stake. The entire enterprise of knowledge advancement depends on the clash of competing ideas.

It's encouraging to see John Stuart Mill enjoying a modest revival. It was Mill who taught, "Both teachers and learners go to sleep at their posts as soon as there is no enemy in the field." Former Stanford provost John Etchemendy has written, "Intellectual homogeneity weakens the academy." He labeled the ad hominem attacks that today's homogenous tribes often direct at dissenters "the death knell of inquiry." Perhaps Princeton's Keith Whittington has stated the point most concisely: "Ignorance flourishes where free inquiry is impeded."

Incidentally, the widely criticized policy of lifelong tenure was created to protect diverse viewpoints from discrimination. Where is its rationale in schools where everyone thinks exactly alike?

Still, one hears the suggestion that it's not really a problem in an ever more technological world. If some of our English departments and sociologists want to render themselves irrelevant, let them. So be it.

I couldn't feel more differently. The worn out joke about the stakes being so low in higher ed debates does not apply to this one. In the struggle to define what a genuine liberal education should be, the stakes could hardly be greater. Because it can be argued that we have never needed effective teaching in the liberal tradition more than today. Even the most gifted young people often emerge from today's K–12 systems appallingly ignorant of either the history or the workings of their own nation's free institutions. Authoritarians of both left and right are eager to take advantage of their ignorance. There was a reason that the last sultans of the Ottoman Empire banned the teaching of literature and history throughout their realms.

The most vexing issues generated by the social media and biotechnology revolutions already have shifted from the technical to the philosophical, psychological, economic, and political. Next month at Purdue's fifth annual Dawn or Doom conference, scholars will examine the societal implications of these innovations, with philosophers and anthropologists and psychologists in leading roles.

The conference is part of our 150th anniversary, which we are celebrating with a year-long, homecoming-to-homecoming ideas festival. As we discuss what a world of 9 or 10 billion people, migration of our species beyond our planet, or an end to human mortality might mean, the scientific questions are mere prelude. For the big matters, we'll be calling in the humanists, from the disciplines that gave humanism its name.

The long drift—perhaps slide is a more accurate description—from the finest that has been thought and said to the denigration of obvious greatness and the celebration of mediocrity has led to some natural confusion.

Few words I can think of generate more such confusion these days than the word "liberal." Its use in politics morphed over the years, from describing policies aimed at liberating individuals into a complex of ideas designed to herd them into groups and limit their personal freedom. The dissonance became so apparent that its advocates have recently abandoned the term altogether for the label "progressive." Fans of irony can savor the fact that self-styled campus progressives tend to be the most reactionary voices whenever something novel is proposed, pedagogically or administratively.

In the university context, the liberal arts have in many places become centers of the most illiberal viewpoints. Speech codes, forbidden words, compulsory "thoughtcrime" reeducation, and other repressive policies have replaced the lively clash of ideas.

Conformity of thought, enforced by heavy-handed peer pressure and reinforced by generations of self-perpetuating personnel practices, has by now achieved comi-tragic proportions. At one prestigious eastern university, a friend recounts that, when he asked the history department chairman if he had any Republicans in his faculty, the answer was, "Have any? We don't *know* any."

Evidence of shoddy scholarship is another dilemma. Hopelessly abstruse, jargon-laden papers from so-called studies programs read like self-parodies. The recent findings that fewer than half the published studies across the social sciences can be replicated threaten to impugn entire disciplines.

Worst of all, too many practitioners have achieved the difficult feat of making the liberal arts boring. History has been rewritten without the heroes, the drama, the glory, the human elements. When the most captivating and thrilling literature the past has given us is not being deconstructed by inferior talents, it is being displaced by trendy treacle by eminently forgettable authors.

The groupthink and deep ideological loyalties that now prevail so monolithically across the liberal arts probably make widespread reform from within impossible. But, to twist a phrase, despair is not a strategy. There are some reasons for optimism.

Appreciation for the best of the liberal tradition is growing in other quarters, specifically in the categories of study sometimes disparaged as pedestrian or vocational. Businesses constantly tell us that, while technological understanding is essential in today's workplaces, so too are the soft skills of communication and empathy. Here and there, one sees evidence that supply is rising to meet this demand.

At Purdue, our College of Liberal Arts has responded to this interest by crafting a two-year bundle of courses specifically chosen to equip a STEM graduate with the essentials of a liberal education. Enrollees in the Cornerstone Program will read Locke, Hobbes, and Jefferson, as well as other works in the Great Books tradition. Our Engineering College is strongly encouraging its students to sign up, and our Polytechnic Institute has made it mandatory.

I want to pause for a moment to introduce two pals who came with me tonight. One is the dean of that College of Liberal Arts, David Reingold; the other is the chairman of our Board of Trustees, Mike Berghoff. I'll just observe that the day that a majority of American colleges and universities have boards like ours, chairs like Mike, and deans of liberal arts like David, ACTA [American Council of Trustees and Alumni] can close up shop and declare victory.

Our liberal arts colleagues were also the first to respond to our appeal for the creation of three-year degrees. By devising academic maps, through which a student adds a course in certain semesters and takes others during the summer, often online, the college now enables participants to complete the same number of credits in the three years that are conventional in many other countries, launching their careers a year sooner and saving substantial money in the process. Due perhaps in part to this new option, we were delighted to see enrollment in the College of Liberal Arts grow this fall for the first time in years.

I am happy to report that many of our liberal arts faculty have been active in shaping and promoting a free speech environment at our school. I am even happier to note that both our undergraduate and graduate student governments petitioned us to promulgate strong free speech policies, which, with Bob Zimmer's permission, our board did by adopting verbatim the statement I always refer to as the Chicago Principles. Entering freshmen are walked through that policy and then view a series of talks and skits illustrating the value of free inquiry, and the appropriate reaction to speech one finds wrong or, in the current vernacular, offensive. With the memorable chancellor of the California system Clark Kerr, we believe that a proper university "is not engaged in making ideas safe for students. It is engaged in making students safe for ideas."

We have not been without our arguments on these topics. Like many campuses, we experienced a small-scale replica of the eruptions at the University of
Missouri. On a campus of some 42,000 students, maybe 1% or 2% took advantage of our "anytime, anywhere" protest protection policy and expressed their dis-
content. I invited about a dozen of the event's chosen leaders into my office and
listened to a list of their demands.

Although I'd been instructed by one young woman, obviously well-rehearsed
by one of our faculty members, not to interrupt with questions, at one point I
did so in order to point out an example of the common ground I had told them
I knew we shared. When she announced, "This demand is nonnegotiable," I did
interject: "Yes, you see there's something we agree on. Because there aren't going to be any negotiations." We believe it is the duty of university leadership to
show great respect, but not deference, for the opinions of the young people who,
after all, are paying us a lot of money because there is so much they *don't* know.

The first line of adult supervision must be occupied by people in roles like
mine, and many have failed that assignment. But of the various actors who have
weakened the performance and reputation of American universities, I'm sad to
say none has more to answer for than the trustees who over the years have abdi-
cated their legal and fiduciary responsibilities. ACTA's central mission of recall-
ing these officers to their duty is ideally chosen, and absolutely essential.

I am frequently in front of audiences packed with business, civic, and political figures. No topic more interests such people today than higher education. I
always implore them to use the influence they undoubtedly have at one or more
institutions to press for the kind of reforms ACTA advocates with such clarity and tenacity.

I relate to them my observation that some of the toughest-minded business-
persons and professionals I know become strangely compliant when they get near
Dear Old Alma Mater. I suggest they use their positions to ask questions like,
What is our free speech policy? If we haven't adopted the Chicago Principles or
something closely akin, why not? I know about our commitment to racial and
social diversity. How diverse are we intellectually? What is our ratio of administrative to teaching positions? Why are we charging students so much and what
are we doing to hold those costs down? And, Can you prove to me that they're
learning anything for all that money?

ACTA has courageously been posing these and other important questions
now for better than two decades. There must have been times when the dominance of the reactionaries has left you discouraged. Please press on. Signs of better days are visible.

Incidents of disinvitations and speaker abuse were down last year. Maybe shame still has its effect. As faculty have learned that the student harassment that seemed so amusing when aimed at conservative speakers can next haul them in front of campus tribunals for saying something "offensive" in class, an obvious shift away from coddling such behavior has begun.

So do press on. Your work is important far beyond the academies you seek to redeem. A nation at risk of losing sight of its true greatness, and its unfinished mission to the world, needs you. A world in search of answers to the new challenges presented by our scientific genius needs you. Young minds, in danger of missing what Alan Bloom called "civilization's last chance to get hold of a person," need you most of all. In so many ways, yours is the essential cause, and organization. In so many ways, I am profoundly honored to be your guest, and your ally. Thank you and good evening.

Reason Foundation's fiftieth anniversary keynote address
Los Angeles, California
November 2018

Somehow this wound up a big year for anniversaries. Our university's 150th; our alumnus Neil Armstrong's moon landing's 50th; my wife and I hit number 40; and now this great mile marker for my favorite think tank. Please know I'm not just being ingratiating; nothing else I can think of would get me to leave hearth and home for Los Angeles on a Saturday night. Unless it was a Dodgers game.

When your kind invitation arrived, I had that familiar reaction: Who canceled? Surely there are a number of people to whom this genuine honor might more fittingly have been extended.

Perhaps it's because I have been not just an avid student, but an occasional practitioner of the policy prescriptions Reason has innovated over the years. Of all the accolades that my home state garnered during the years of my public service, none was more gratifying to me than Indiana's rating as the third freest state. Largely through aggressive employment of Reason's privatization proposals, Indiana now has the fewest state employees per capita in the country.

Our ranking, by CNBC among others, as having the nation's best infrastructure traces directly to this organization's decades of excellence in imaginative transportation policy. We built P3 toll bridges, entirely private bridges, and by leasing an existing toll road, harvested nearly $4 billion for reinvestments that resurfaced half the state's highway miles, rebuilt a third of its bridges, and constructed over 200 new projects, many of which had been languishing in the netherworld of unkept government promises for decades. They haven't named any of them for Bob Poole yet, but one day someone should, because that's where we got the ideas.

And, in 2011, on one of the happiest days of all, we passed sweeping education reforms that included the nation's first universal, statewide voucher program. Here, too, we called on Reason Foundation experts and their scholarship. How I wish Milton Friedman, who dedicated his own personal foundation to this specific purpose, had been there to see it. In one of life's most important decisions, the education of one's children, all Hoosier families are now truly "free to choose."

Whatever and whoever was behind this opportunity, I'm deeply grateful. It's uplifting to be among friends who place primacy on individual dignity and autonomy. Some days it feels as though staunch friends of freedom are getting harder to find.

It's a night for remembrance and celebration, not warnings and discouragement, but this wonderful organization has always looked forward, not back, and followed facts and reality where they appeared to lead. To me, today's realities suggest that liberty may be more, not less, jeopardized than in years past, and thus that Reason and its allies will be more, not less, essential in the next half century.

I now inhabit that sector of our society where once sacred freedoms are suddenly at risk. Where some speech is forbidden, other speech is sometimes compelled. Where due process and the presumption of innocence are often discarded, with gross injustice a frequent consequence. Where tomorrow's Americans leave their formal education abysmally ignorant or misled about our history, the rationale for our free institutions, or the superior morality they embody.

Boone Pickens says, "The first billion is the hardest." I'm tempted to speculate that, in the modern-day defense of freedom, the first fifty years are the easiest. That would have seemed absurd in the depths of the Cold War, when two totalitarian governments between them enslaved hundreds of millions and pledged themselves to bury the West and its effete institutions.

It would have seemed even further-fetched just a couple of decades ago when, with one of those regimes on history's ash heap and the other discovering the wonders of capitalism, we all learned that history had come to its end, with the full and final triumph of liberal democracy and free market economics.

Oops.

It's not as though bossiness ever went entirely out of fashion. We've always had those among us who, as someone once said, don't care what you do as long as it's compulsory. But lately one gets nostalgic for the good old days when the worst threats to liberty came from our "benevolent betters," those loving paternalists who dedicate themselves to protecting us against choosing the wrong light bulbs, the wrong insurance policies, those dangerous soft drinks and even more deadly plastic straws, or unregulated lemonade stands.

In the two brief decades since freedom declared victory, new threats have emerged which are arguably more, not less, menacing than those against which Reason has contended its first half century. Looking back, the Cold War did of course present the danger of nuclear holocaust, but there was no chance that a sclerotic twentieth century totalitarianism would ever overtake, let alone bury, nations where human ambition and innovation were free to flourish. It was communism, not capitalism, that contained within it the seeds of its own destruction.

I'm not sure that can be said of a hybridized system that takes advantage of freedom's economic power while tightening the bonds of statist control on the political and social lives of its subjects. If Stalin, in one historian's memorable phrase, was "Genghis Khan with a telephone," then we must hope President Xi or a successor does not turn out to be "Mao with an algorithm."

Further away, but if anything more frightening, lies the specter of a world so automated that our inventions render millions of us superfluous, idle, docile, and ripe for supervision by the masters of that new universe, or even by the inventions themselves.

But maybe the most ominous, and certainly the most clear and present danger, lies in a poisonous domestic politics that incites authoritarian impulses not just on the left, where they come naturally, but also reactively on what has historically been the pro-freedom right.

Not only on college campuses but across society at large, tolerance for intolerance has spread like a computer virus. The brilliant comedian George Carlin got a lot of laughs, but also broke a lot of barriers years ago, when he cataloged "the seven words you can't say on television." Today, you can hear those words and much worse all over television, but there is a new verboten vocabulary of others, a single utterance of which will end a career, even years after the event, at the hands of linguistic lynch mobs.

In my hometown recently, a longtime radio personality met his professional end for repeating a joke with today's most forbidden word in it. Fair enough; that has come to be expected. Then, after he identified the person from whom he thinks he had heard the joke years before, that person also was exiled to PC purgatory. But the mob's lust was not sated. The second party's son, a professional race car driver, who had never even heard let alone told the joke, became a collateral casualty when a cowardly corporation pulled its sponsorship of his car rather than risk social media sliming.

A contest between "live and let live" and "do it my way or else" is what we call asymmetrical combat. Those devoted to the liberal tradition defend the free expression of even their most radical opponents and seek to contest arguments on the basis of—what else? Reason.

By contrast, people who see their adversaries not as errant in their thinking but as evil in their souls will not hesitate to employ the power of government, if they can seize it, to enforce their version of cultural virtue on the sinners around them. And since that authoritarian temptation most often coexists with a statist view of economics, limits on permissible speech and thought will inevitably be accompanied by new infringements of the right of free exchange. Liberty looks to need a heavy dose of eternal vigilance these next few years.

When a couple of his aides got a little too hotheaded, Ronald Reagan admonished us, "No. We have no enemies, only opponents." Today, it seems most of our public officials, and many private citizens, have inverted that formulation.

A few years back, I wrote a book in which, while expressing deep concern about our national fiscal future, I was obstinately optimistic about the capacity of Americans to govern ourselves—in particular, to grasp and rally around changes that halt the current plunder of the next generation, the economic decline if not ruin of the country, and the loss of sovereignty and autonomy that hopeless indebtedness brings with it. To opt for policies premised on individual human dignity and responsibility, not condescension and the cultivation of dependency.

I ventured the thought that the great untested theme in our politics is "These folks don't think you can cut it, but we do." As a banner for this set of ideas, I suggested bending a then prominent slogan into "Change that believes in *you*" to appeal to our fellow citizens as completely equal adults, fully capable of making all the important decisions about their own lives and about the nation's future. This was not a fantasy case for abandoning all programs of mutual assistance. Reasonable income transfer programs are almost universally supported and here to stay, but they need not bring with them patronizing, demeaning supervision.

I've not met many people who would welcome the idea that they are ignorant, gullible incompetents who need their benevolent betters to supervise and shepherd them through life. Nor many who would knowingly exploit their own children and other younger Americans by borrowing enormous, unrepayable amounts of money and spending it not on future investment but on their own current consumption.

I've been forced to ask myself lately if I'd write the same book today. While clinging to an obstinate optimism about the innate character of the American people, I confess that for now that conviction is more faith than factual. I cannot cite a single public opinion survey that supports the policies of ordered liberty, or that reveals a will to the self-control and mature self-governance that true liberty requires to endure. If there is an actor on today's public stage who speaks in this fashion, I haven't caught his or her act. But America has always produced such leaders, and I have to believe in time she will again.

When they do arrive, ultimately, their wisest, probably Reason Foundation–inspired policy prescriptions will be secondary to a more fundamental societal decision through which they must guide us.

Above all others, or maybe I should say comprising all others, the question Americans must answer in the next few years is, What kind of people will we be? Resolute advocates of liberty, or acquiescent helots submissive to the orders of others? Respecters of each other's values, privacy, and personhood, or mini-dictators determined to enforce our worldview on the subhumans around us? Creatures of dignity, or objects of therapy?

Nations bound by ethnicity, or tribalism, or a common religion have no trouble defining their identity. Typically, it has been defined for them, by history or by whatever tyrant holds sway at the time. Our unique nation, bound solely by the historically novel/unprecedented ideal of individual liberty and the self-government of civic equals, cannot, as the man said, "long endure" without a common definition of its citizens' roles and personhood.

The lyricist stated the principle in nine words: "Confirm thy soul in self-control; thy liberty in law." When the founders spoke of "ordered liberty," they knew that a people that would preserve order for themselves must first resolve to live free, self-disciplined lives, then insist on a rule of law and not of men, subject to the tyrant's temptation.

At Purdue's commencement ceremonies, over which the poor person with my job presides, the climax is the conferral of the degrees which, at our university at least, students have worked very hard to earn. The boilerplate language includes the phrase "with all the rights, privileges, duties, and responsibilities of that degree." I always enunciate the last two nouns of the series more clearly and loudly.

In more than one commencement address, I have drawn the audience's attention directly to those words in advance. "We live in an age," I have observed, "when people are quick to demand what they claim are their rights and privileges, but far less often recognize any attendant duties or responsibilities." I have followed that observation with a call to protect our freedoms through lives that are active civically and responsible personally.

Joseph Sobran once mused, "How is it that every time someone asserts a new right, the rest of us wind up less free?" We await new leadership and new generations that, by both action and individual example, revive and fortify the premises on which authentic freedom depends.

Except that this great organization has never waited. You have with nearly unique persistence and unique fidelity to principle upheld our liberties, constantly innovating and advocating measures to guard and extend them. Unless my worries are misplaced, your vigilance, grasp of technology, and intellectual courage will be needed more than ever in the free nation I dream of my grandchildren inheriting.

On perhaps the most memorable single evening of my working life, as I thanked the people of Indiana for giving us the chance to bring major change to our state, I finished by saying, "When the music stops and the last confetti falls, get a good rest. Get your courage up and your game face on because the real work starts tomorrow."

I know no such counsel is needed here. Reason Foundation has always looked to tomorrow, and with you on freedom's ramparts America's tomorrows will always dawn brightly.

 Indianapolis Economic Club luncheon
Indianapolis, Indiana
February 2020

Remarks, followed by an interview with Allison Melangton, senior vice president of the Economic Club of Indiana

As I looked ahead to this particular occasion, it occurred to me that today I get to give more or less the speech that I always hoped I could give here or somewhere, and this is the perfect place and audience to do it. I had always hoped over the last couple of decades that there'd come a time in a gathering like this when we'd be able to celebrate a state as we often used to say "of genuine promise and prosperity." Although we've got too many holes in the Swiss cheese and much, much work left to do, there's just so much to celebrate about the Indiana of today, and this is the place to do it because you are the people who have done it.

The epicenter of our growth is Metro Indianapolis, and it's the enterprises who are here and the enterprising men and women who created them and lead them that have made so much opportunity for so many others. We are a place of essentially zero unemployment—more jobs than people to fill them, as we read so often. We're a place where the population now is growing, not as fast as we'd like, but faster than any place between Iowa and Maine, a place so much more diverse in its economy with thriving life sciences and IT communities that were only dimly visible twenty and even ten years ago. Year after year now the state is ranked as having the number one infrastructure in the country, a state that's rated very high for its business climate, and a state that has taken care of the tax-payers' dollars and remains one of the few triple-A credit ratings in this country, a state with a credit rating better than the federal government.

We said over and over in my last job that government does not create jobs and never did. Governors, presidents, they don't run economies. It grates on me whenever you read a news story that uses that terminology. No, government at its best creates the conditions whereby men and women of enterprise create jobs and opportunity and wealth for each other. At its worst, it drives those things away or makes them difficult or impossible to do. But you and the organizations that you represent have a whole lot to feel good about, and on behalf of your fellow citizens, I just want to thank you for it.

I thought that perhaps the way to approach our reflections together today was to talk very briefly about how we got here, how we stay here, what we do next, what we guard against, and what's on the worry list.

The answer to the first question, how we got here, is not overnight, and it wasn't accidental. Permit me just the briefest of walks down memory lane. In the first act of the first day of the first term of my previous job, I signed an executive order creating the Indiana Economic Development Corporation, a nonprofit corporation that everyone could participate in, so we could have some first-class staff, some people who knew business, and knew how to attract it. Later it was codified in the first bill passed in what some historians believe was the most active legislative session certainly in memory, and possibly in the history of our state. That was number one because it was always job one. We established that the governor, whoever she or he was, would be the chair of the corporation to remind that person what comes first.

I made it a practice that at every cabinet meeting the secretary of commerce[10] sat directly at my right hand, and economic development was always the first agenda topic. The question was, What's going on that might bring more investment and jobs to this state? If the secretary needed the Transportation Department, or the secretary of health and services, or the environmental officer to do something to make the next investment more likely, we wanted to hear about that first. Many thanks to my successors. They have maintained their discipline and their focus on this fundamental assignment. It's so simple, but so overlooked in other states. I see constantly, particularly for those who are on life's first rung or a lower rung, that when more opportunity and growth comes, all of the other work of government becomes easier, and all of the other problems that we worry about together are alleviated.

In that same year we began our march out of bankruptcy. Later, we built reserves which are still there and have been protected by my successors. We cut taxes and later capped property taxes at some of the lowest levels in America—another great sales tool for the businesses we hope will continue to come here and join this club.

Imagine that as recently as fifteen years ago, we used to waive the tax on tools of manufacturing, but not on the tools of the information economy, which was already so obviously becoming dominant. If you bought a new drill press, you didn't pay sales tax. If you bought a spectrometer or a new computer, you did. We left that era behind. Until then, Indiana levied tax based on three factors: if you built things here, if you had property here, and if you hired people here, we taxed you. Now, we want you to sell in the world "and that's all we will tax you on."

We found out that state government was spending well over half of all its procurement dollars on goods and services from outside the state. We reversed that and ultimately increased in-state purchasing to 90%.

We made other changes, including the Right to Work law,[11] always looking for that next step forward to make Indiana a welcoming place, a hospitable place, and a place of encouragement to those who wanted to grow a business, or start and build one.

So, what's next? Even by the time I changed jobs, now seven years ago, it was very obvious that the next challenge, that "the unchecked box," I often used to say, was human resources—people skills, workforce, and so forth. The box we couldn't check was the quantity and quality of labor, particularly for the evolving economy. And that remains a big challenge. Our governors, legislators, and our business community have been very focused on this now for years, and it's exactly what they should be doing.

This unfortunately is the hardest needle to move, so much more difficult than the other challenges that we have addressed as a state. What should we do about it? Well, the effort must never end to improve our K–12 education system, but that is not going to fix this problem. It is too slow, too stubborn, too resistant to change—in some cases too reactionary. Although there have been improvements, we will be left behind if we wait on the long process of today's youngest people becoming adults educated to a level necessary to support the enterprises of the country.

What else do we do besides that? We educate adults. We brought Western Governors University (WGU) to Indiana,[12] and at our university we have now entered the online education world through Purdue Global.[13] There are three-quarters of a million people in this state who started college and didn't finish. I'm not talking about people who dropped out of high school, or people who stopped at a high school diploma. These are people who attempted college, and something got in the way. It's an enormous opportunity. It's a much smaller step to help a person, particularly someone who has now built experience in the workforce, complete a credential which will enable them to earn substantially more money. That is what WGU does; that is what Purdue Global does. It's an enormous opportunity, and I'm glad that our state is seizing it in a way that not every place is. I urge you to take the opportunity to be supportive of that mission.

Indiana's research universities are another great asset and resource for us, and I don't say that just because I happen to be employed at one right now. In the knowledge economy and technologically driven economy in which we live, research-intensive universities are not just sources of great new talent, leadership, and occasionally innovations, but also can be economic engines. In Indiana we have three of them, not to mention their outposts like Indiana University–Purdue University Indianapolis. They employ people directly, they spin off all sorts of additional enterprises and secondary investments, and they originate new businesses. At Purdue, we are certainly trying to be aggressive at business creation—we were third in the country again last year in new startup businesses, behind MIT and Stanford, and well ahead of number four, which was an obscure university in Cambridge, Massachusetts.

There's a project in regional development which another of Indiana's crown jewel assets, the Lilly Endowment, conceived and launched around our university. Last year, Tippecanoe County[14] was number one in America in the growth of wage gains. Bloomington is another great source. South Bend can be a greater one than it is now. It has been so important that the endowment and others have seen the value of these resources and are trying to encourage more indigenous activity and more collaboration between them.

The project in the area around Tippecanoe County is a ten-county endeavor. When Saab, Schweitzer Engineering Laboratories, Rolls Royce, and other employers locate on the boundaries of our campus, they can hire people from all ten counties. In the world we're in, these regional consortia are great assets that not every state has to the extent that we do.

A third thing we can do is change our mentality and become aggressive about gaining brains. When I first ran for office and encountered people who asked, "What are you doing this for?" I was a no-name first-time candidate and I used to reply, "I'm tired of seeing our best young people leave and go somewhere else, not because they don't love this state, but because they fear that they won't find the economic opportunity here that fits their hopes and dreams." We've come a long way. We've had a net ingress of college graduates, if you take that as a rough proxy, over the last two or three years. There need to be more, but the flow has reversed.

Meanwhile, we need to get on offense in a way that we haven't been before. There's an endeavor going on now which Purdue is certainly supporting, and other schools are taking part in, that has identified a million people out in the world who have a nexus to Indiana. They either grew up here, went to school here, or both. These are people who also have shown some propensity to mobility. They may have moved recently, changed jobs recently, and there is some reason to think they might be interested in coming back. The last time I checked, more than 200,000 of them have been contacted, 5,000 were involved in active conversations, and there are now multiple success stories of people who have actually been matched with an employer and come home, or come back.

If we're aggressive about it, I look to this to be a great possibility. And let's not overlook the 60,000 prospects who are here now. I'm talking about the students from other places who are on the Purdue campus, the IU campus, and all the other schools that we're so blessed with in Indiana. Those students are sitting right here, and they will get an exposure to the advantages of this state, if we are clever enough and industrious enough to bring it to their attention.

I confess I was too slow to think about this, but starting two or three years ago, the first thing our incoming freshmen see on the first day of their orientation period is a video that says, "Welcome to Indiana." Of course it talks about Purdue, but it shows the rest of Indiana. It shows our businesses, it shows our parks, it shows our recreation facilities, and our cultural offerings. It is an introduction to the place that they're going to spend the next three or four years, and we hope much longer.

And we ought not overlook another fantastic asset we have in this respect, and that is Illinois. There's a Facebook site called Leaving Illinois. We have a ton of Illinois students on our campus. Whenever I meet one, I say, "Oh, a ref-ugee. Welcome." I say, "We have a very generous asylum policy here in Indiana."

I shouldn't digress, but I just have to tell you that I've got a million stories about this. But my favorite is, I was asked to give a speech on the topic of eco-nomic development in Chicago a few years ago. One of the people who preceded me that morning was a strong supporter of business, and he got up and almost gave a commercial about Indiana. He said, "Oh my gosh, their taxes are fair, their regulation is fair, their infrastructure is great." He basically gave our speech. He said, "We've been talking to folks over there. They all talk like businesspeople and they want to help us solve our problems. They looked at it from our side." And on and on. He said, "Not only that, the next day the governor of the state called me, and he talked like a businessperson. Before we hung up, he gave me his personal email and cell number." He says, "Now that's the way you do business." When they started the Q&A period, the first person said, "I have a question, but before I get to it, I need to tell you something. Here in Illinois when they give you the governor's cell number, it means something different." I did not make that up.

We've come a long way, and we think we know what works. There are some things we can be doing, all of us together. What to worry about? In business if you don't have a worry list, you're not looking close enough. There are two or three on mine.

Complacency would be one. The competition does not stand still. States like Ohio, Michigan for sure, and Wisconsin were great to compete with ten and fif-teen years ago. They have changed in many ways and improved. For a long time, Indiana was the only non-Sunbelt state in the top tier of any business rankings, but here and there you'll now find some of our neighbors. That's a great thing about the federal system: people copy what works, and observe the mistakes of others, and avoid them.

Let me finish with just a couple of words of reminder about the importance of continued innovation, continued improvement, and certainly of speed. As we say so often in this world, whether you're a state or a business enterprise, if you slow down, someone will pass you. If you tread water, you will sink. I say to our public officials, "Congratulations, but take us further. Don't worry too much about the slings and arrows that any suggestion of change always, always brings."

I used to tell colleagues wherever I was at the time, "Don't worry about the mud balls and the criticisms. Results are trump." I sometimes repeat what one Hoosier said to me at a low moment when we were receiving a lot of criti-cism. She said, "Oh, Mitch. Don't fret too much about that. Just remember, dogs don't bark at parked cars." And she was right. So, wherever you are, whatever organization you're a part of leading, I would encourage you, never park the car. If you keep it moving, sooner or later you leave the dogs behind. Thank you very much for having me back.

MS. MELANGTON: As governor, you had a lot of stubborn problems to address. Of all the things you accomplished in those eight years, what was the most stubborn problem that you weren't sure you'd get accomplished, but you did by the time you got out the door?

MITCH: I always felt that the number one challenge we had was to try to spread a mentality of excellence and an insistence on breaking out of the pack, which has not been associated with our state historically, but can be. I was hoping that the accumulation of things that we might do, targets we might aim at, would persuade a critical mass of people to never settle for middle of the pack and to be a leadership state. I see evidence of that happening, certainly in our business community, and nothing would make me happier than to have that become the profile of our state.

MS. MELANGTON: As the parent of a recent Purdue grad, thank you for all you have done to keep tuition costs flat. What advice would you give other universities to follow your lead?

MITCH: I've always been really shy about prescribing anything we've done at Purdue to any other school. Every school is different. Every school has to make its own choices. At Purdue, we should prize accessibility—we're a land-grant school. Even in Indiana, a lot of people overlook this. But we should never lose sight of the goal of being accessible to any student who can meet our standards. So yes, of course, I believe that it should be part of the responsibility of anybody in this day and age, when higher education has become so expensive, to do anything they can to keep the cost of tuition down. People worry about student debt, and there are hundreds of ideas about what you ought to do about it, but I keep saying, "Well okay, fine. But the first thing you could do is not charge so darn much in the first place."

MS. MELANGTON: We knew this one was going to come, and I have several of them. Can we talk you into putting your name in the hat for 2024?

MITCH: What hat? No, people now and then will say something like that. When they say it up around our campus, I always tell people, "At this point in life, I am not taking the demotion."

MS. MELANGTON: Would you personally like to see a viable third party in the United States?

MITCH: The two-party system should not be lightly abandoned. It has served this country very well. Just go look at the multiparty democracies. You wouldn't want to be Italy or most of the European countries—it can lead to paralysis. And if you think we have some division now, just start carving us up into even smaller slices.

The system is not performing well at the moment, but it has been resilient, and I hope this will return. Its resilience has usually come when the party not doing well figures it out. And maybe we ought to be more inclusive. Perhaps we ought to reach out and try to find the center so we can win again. I guess I'm still hoping that that will occur, so I'm not rooting for a third party, although as scholars have noted, there certainly is a so-called exhausted middle that is uncomfortable with what it perceives as the somewhat extreme views of the parties as they are led today.

MS. MELANGTON: Your thoughts on the current national deficit and how to start digging out?

MITCH: To me, it might be the single biggest indictment of the two parties that neither one of them is talking about this at all. It is really not just a fiscal issue, it's not just an economic menace, although it is certainly both those things. To me, it's a test of our democracy. We are borrowing unbelievable amounts of money that we are not investing in the future. We're spending it on current consumption, writing checks to ourselves. That is an incredible disservice to the young people of this country and a problem that we're going to deposit on them. And everyone in this audience, with the exception of the very youngest, should feel a little bit guilty about this. Until two or three years ago, we could say that if we just got going, we could manage the problem. It's getting harder to say that—just look at the arithmetic.

What should be done about it? Pretty simple. Nothing makes any difference if you don't deal with the safety net programs. We have to save the safety net. Anyone who opposes reforms in Medicare, Social Security, and Medicaid doesn't care about low-income people and has it absolutely backward. If you care, you want to make those changes now because we're not going to be able to take care of them on the current track.

Social Security is the easiest one to talk about. We should raise the retirement age further because we're all living longer. We should concentrate the money on those who need it most. We should means-test it. There's a long story about why we don't, but most of us in this audience could do with either a little or less, or very little income support from the federal government.

And we over index it for inflation right now. It's absolutely fine to keep up with the cost of living, but that's not what we do. Those are three things that would protect those we care about and those for whom the programs are most intended, while protecting those taxpayers of tomorrow who are otherwise going to be dealt an impossible hand.

MS. MELANGTON: A couple of questions on township government. Will Indiana ever eliminate township government?

MITCH: Yes, I think one day eventually. We have work on the shelf, by the way. This is one we don't have to start over, we don't have to commission any new studies, we don't need any additional commissions. A great bipartisan group led by my predecessor, Joe Kernan, and Randy Shepard, our then chief justice, led a group which produced twenty-seven suggestions to modernize our antique system of local government. Seven of them became law, but some of the biggest ones, including township government, did not. We did not get rid of township trustees.

In this state, supposedly a small government, conservative state, we still elect more people to political offices than any state in the country. So yes, I still think at some point someone will pull out the work they did—it will probably still be evergreen fresh—and pursue those reforms. But good government reforms of that kind are not the kind of things political careers are made of. Nobody leads torchlight parades for cleaning up the machinery of government. But once in a while it needs to be done, and I think it does have some bipartisan possibilities, so maybe someone will summon the energy to go after it again.

MS. MELANGTON: How can we make progress on breaking down the economic and racial barriers that exist in our state to get a more equitable system?

MITCH: The starting point is "lift all boats." In this national economy, and I have no reason to think it looks any different here, incomes at the bottom are rising faster than incomes at the top. And we need a long, sustained period of that. That's a starting point. I have to be honest and say that although there are barriers, and there are injustices, and unfairnesses, I don't think that is at all a total explanation for the continuing inequities that we have. There are certainly educational differences. Purdue has started two high schools in this town because we can't wait for the current system to turn up enough students. We're desperate to educate to a Purdue standard more low-income students, first-generation students, and minority students. So, we're going to create our pipeline, and I hope we're well embarked on doing that.

It's going to take efforts like that in education, and I would certainly go back to something I talked about earlier. Go look at who goes to WGU. Go look at who goes to Purdue Global. A majority of our students are adults who didn't complete college the first time. The majority of our Purdue Global students are minorities, and a majority are women. There are things you can do without waiting for the miracle or the millennium at the K–12 level.

MS. MELANGTON: You're an avid reader. What's the book that everybody here should be reading?

MITCH: I'll betray both a friendship and a preference—George Will's *The Conservative Sensibility* is a remarkable book even if you don't agree with his conclusions. I encourage our students to read history and biography—history if they want to understand that very few things are happening for the very first time, and biography if they are interested in leadership. I've never found a how-to book that I thought was very valuable. But if you hope to have positions of responsibility in any of our three sectors, to me the best reads are about people who have led successfully, what they did well, and where they fell short. And so I've devoured a lot of those.

MS. MELANGTON: Well, thank you. What a great afternoon with Mitch!

Remarks upon the inaugural conferral of the Daniels Prize
Indianapolis, Indiana
October 24, 2013

The Mitch Daniels Leadership Foundation was created in honor and affirmation of the service of Mitch Daniels as Indiana's forty-ninth governor. The purpose of the foundation is to encourage leadership that refuses to accept the status quo as good enough, constantly aims higher, and executes courageously, lifting the arc of progress in Indiana. The foundation established two awards, the Daniels Prize and the Mitch Daniels Leadership Grant, and the inaugural recipients were:

Tim Solso, retired CEO of Cummins, Inc., a Fortune 250 company that designs, produces, and sells diesel engines, power generation equipment, and related components worldwide

Earl Phalen, CEO and founder of the nationally renowned
Summer Advantage USA and Reach Out and Read organizations and the founder of the Phalen Academy charter school
in Indianapolis

I want to thank Tim and Earl for the lives they have led, the service that led to
their selection for their gracing this occasion, and agreeing to be part of what we
hope will be an enduring movement in our state.

Tim, who turned around a great company, created untold opportunities for
others—the essence really of a free economy and a free society—who then took
that company global in a new way and used the benefits of success to help others
in a myriad of ways. Just a perfect example of corporate citizenship at its finest.

And, Earl, who I'm coming to know now, I just have boundless hopes for you,
what you've already done and what I know you are going to do for the children
in Indiana who need it most. There is no greater cause and there is no place in
our public life where a person needs more courage, more gumption, more persistence than in trying to change our educational system.

When I think back over the last eight years, I tend to think of those things
that we tried to do and didn't get to the finish line, but I appreciate reminders of
those things we did do. It was never about the specifics; it was more about two
overriding goals that we took into public office and tried never to lose sight of.

First, we were out to rebuild confidence in our public institutions. We live in
a time of understandable cynicism and a corrosive distrust of government and
the people in it. We said in Indiana we are going to do everything we know how
to deliver—lean and clean government, government that can shoot straight, that
can do things well for people and can do big and bold things to make life better for everyone.

I hope we did advance that ball. Hoosiers certainly said so a year or so ago. At
a rate unmatched in America, they said they had confidence in their state institutions. A free people should feel good that the people and the structures to whom
they have entrusted public leadership have their interest at heart, are reasonably
competent, and are trying hard every day to live up to the public trust. There is
a group of people in this room who are a part of the finest administration the
State of Indiana ever saw and may ever see. And from my experience quite possibly the finest such collection of public servants of any state in America based
on their results and on their record.

Our second goal, maybe our transcendent goal, was to try to transform a state known for its inferiority complex, known for settling for the status quo, a culture of complacency, into a culture of excellence, action, and high aspiration. This we worked on every day and worried about every day.

Robert Kennedy said that progress depends on change and change always has its enemies. And there are two sets of opponents to almost any change one advances in public life. One set with whom we can feel some real empathy are those who are just reluctant and fearful of what the unknown might bring.

I came across an interesting line in a book of history I was reading. It turns out that in the nation of Spain which, of course, went from a leading world power to a sadly unimportant country, there was a common phrase that lasted well into the late nineteenth century: "Que no haya novedad." Let nothing new happen. It could have almost been a Hoosier phrase.

We watched some segments from past State of the State speeches, and in 2006 I read into the record a fragment of a letter that a gentleman in Lafayette, Indiana, wrote to his newspaper about one of the reforms we had advanced. He said, "I'm an old-timer, and old-timers don't like change. I know that's just the way I am, but I don't need a reason for anything." I expressed sympathy with that gentleman and replied, "I'll give you a million reasons. That's the million children in schools in our state, all of whom deserve a better future, all of whom deserve to live in a great state—a state that is renowned and distinctive, and known for doing things first, better, and bolder than others."

That same night we proposed a bill which we walked on coals finally to pass—it seems odd now. I talked that night about the dreams all over this state for major new public infrastructure. Roads—fictional roads at that time—like U.S. 31 continuous to South Bend, Interstate 69, new bridges over the Ohio River, and a road called the Hoosier Heartland Corridor, which opened two days ago. It was a great celebration for towns from Lafayette, to Delphi, to Logansport, to Peru, to Wabash. And of course it eventually extends, through investments that that bill made possible, all the way to the Port of Toledo. New hope to some of the proudest towns in Indiana history.

These were the dreams we had, and in so many cases made real and made happen. It never, never, never happens without discord, and criticism, and concern. It was a Hoosier farmwife who first taught me the saying, as she tried to comfort me, "Oh, Mitch. Don't fret too much about that. Just remember, dogs don't bark at parked cars." We were determined that we were never going to park Indiana's car while we were assigned to drive it. We were always going to try to move forward.

In a Civil War history, I read about the Confederate General Beauregard, whose best battle was his first battle, First Manassas, and after that he became known for his caution and care. The historian wrote something that I shared with a lot of our team: "A soldier is on the wane from the moment he begins to think more of reputation than of opportunity." We tried to discipline ourselves to not worry about reputation—it will take care of itself; to seize the opportunity . . . what's the next goal, the next step forward, the next step upward.

There is a second group of people who can be counted on to obstruct or try to impede change—and these folks are a slightly less lovable group—whose vested interests are threatened by potential improvements or reforms. Earl and Tim, God bless you for your willingness to take on the toughest of those interests as you attempt to bring change and new methods, options, and choices to students in this state who deserve it. You will be a great voice for positive change. I know you will be busy, but I hope you can make as many of those appearances as this award contemplates, to share with the people of this state your own sense of ambition for children and refusal to accept less than the best for them. You'll inspire them as you inspire us all tonight.

Finally, I would just say to everyone present, don't leave it up to Earl and Tim. They will be great voices, but what this state needs, and the reason I agreed to collaborate on this prize, is a constituency—a growing and permanent constituency for positive change and a restlessness with anything less than the best for the citizens of our state. We need people to defend the change agents when the complacent or the self-interested attack them. We need each of you not merely to say, "Isn't it too bad that somebody took a shot at Earl's new school." We need you to step forward and say, "No, this is right, this is good," and there is a proud purpose to be served in defending it.

I hope everyone here will be an infectious agent of optimism, courage, and encouragement of others to think big, and to think about that next improvement, that next point of differentiation for our state, which has now begun to assume a position of distinction among the states of this country.

I hang out with a lot of brilliant people now; and in the language of quantum mechanics, if you add energy to an atom, an electron can jump to a new orbit. That's what we tried to do in Indiana—add enough energy that the whole place jumped to a new orbit, a new position among its peers.

The last fifty years have been very tough on Indiana and states like ours. The transition from a manufacturing economy, with hundreds of thousands of solid middle-class jobs, into an information economy, where there are fewer, has wreaked some very serious damage on states like ours. But unless our entire nation collapses and loses its momentum and the positive economic growth that it has always been characterized by, the next fifty years are going to be very promising for this state and for states like ours if they have their act together.

We'll have so many advantages of location. We will have water and apparently lots of affordable energy—the kind that powers an economy like ours. We'll have a low-cost environment that we've always enjoyed. We are solvent because we take care of the people's business and don't make the mistakes that now threaten so many of our brothers and sisters on the various coasts.

The door to great opportunity and true greatness is open to us, but the next few years will tell whether we seize it or not and whether the last eight years were really, as we hoped, a bold new departure, or an interruption. Whether they were a dawn or a meteor, the spring of which we sometimes metaphorically spoke, or just a misleading week or two of Indian Summer. I just hope that in your busy lives you will take time to support Tim and Earl, as well as the people who conceived and brought together this evening, in establishing and constantly nurturing a permanent constituency for greatness in a state that we now know is fully capable of achieving it. Thank you.

MESSAGES TO THE PURDUE COMMUNITY

Statement upon selection as Purdue University's twelfth president June 21, 2012

No institution of any kind means more to Indiana today or tomorrow as Purdue University. It educates at the highest level the engineers, scientists, agricultural experts, and information technologists on whom our state and national success disproportionately depend.

Its research gives rise to the innovative new goods, services, and companies on which American and Hoosier prosperity must be built. I can conceive of no other assignment in which a person has the chance to contribute more to building the kind of Indiana of which we dream.

My old friend and former colleague Art Hansen, Purdue's eighth president, once said that, at any university, no one learns as much as the president. That will most literally and necessarily be true of me.

I have not made a life in the academy, but I have spent my life reading, admiring, and attempting to learn from those who do. I am not a scholar in the sciences, but I am as avid a student of their advances as a lay person can be, and have taken every step I could think of to elevate the scientific disciplines in the eyes of our citizens and in the educational paths of our young people.

I will have to earn the honor of this appointment through strenuous work to build the understanding, alliances, and personal relationships, especially with faculty, required for a successful presidency. I likewise look forward to as much direct engagement with Purdue students as they are willing to have with me.

Off campus, I hope to become an audible and credible voice for the critical role of higher education in the nation's future, and an effective advocate of Purdue to those who might support its growth in quality and reputation.

I am troubled but persuaded by the many who assert that American higher education is now challenged to modernize its traditional practices and to reconfirm its value to students and society. Perhaps Purdue, a premier community of problem-solvers, can lead in this transition and the innovations that will shape it.

The balance of this calendar year, I will use the time not consumed by my current duties to begin this process of earning by learning. Effective immediately, I will recuse myself from any partisan political activities or commentary.

I will come to this assignment filled with appreciation for the Purdue we know and excitement for the still greater Purdue that can be. Helping this great institution achieve even higher levels of research and intellectual excellence, by recruiting the finest minds and students anywhere in the world, and delivering to those students an exceptional, affordable education, is the highest calling to which anyone who loves this state as I do could aspire.

Remarks at the memorial service for Purdue student Tyler Trent
Purdue University
January 9, 2019

In a community as big as ours, it's inevitable that tragedy will now and then descend on us. On April 15, as we do every year, we will hold the Golden Taps ceremony, at which we honor and mourn those students taken from us during the year. We will remember Jessica Lin Marrs, Matt Klenosky, Erin Davis, and Tyler Stephan. Every student life is precious to us. With every loss, the poet's bell tolls for us all.

But it's right that we gather tonight to pay tribute in this special memorial to our most recently departed son and brother. Through no intention or effort of his own—he just camped out outside a ticket office—Tyler Trent became a symbol and an inspiration to everyone in the Purdue family, and to millions elsewhere.

We have asked Savannah Bratcher, president of Purdue Dance Marathon, and football co-captain Elijah Sindelar to speak about two of the ways in which Tyler left lasting footprints during his too-brief days with us.

A word one hears a lot here and around higher ed these days is "grit." It's slang for that combination of qualities like diligence, persistence, and the resilience to face life's inevitable adversity with fortitude. We look for it in potential Boilermakers because it's a proven indicator of academic success. We want to encourage every student that comes here to develop these traits, to help them through Purdue and all through life.

Tyler Trent was grit personified. Dealt a hand worse than anyone here is facing, or God willing ever will, he never stopped working, or fighting, or moving ahead. He never showed a trace of self-pity. If you tried to mumble through some awkward expression of sympathy, he'd shrug it off and change the subject to his coursework, or Purdue football, or the money he was raising for Riley Children's Hospital.

Life brings trouble, and fear, and sadness to us all. But it's not supposed to come in this form, at this age. The death of any bright young life always hits us harder. We think of the lost potential, all that might have been, and just how darned unfair it seems.

A century ago, millions of men Tyler's age went to their deaths in what a naive world called "the war to end all wars." In France, one in every four men between 18 and 34 was killed. Then, twenty years later, it happened again. It's hard for us today to imagine the horror and heartbreak of such events.

But at least when a young soldier dies, those left behind can tell themselves that there was a reason. A cause served. A nation protected. A value in exchange for their terrible loss. An answer to the haunting question, Why?

When death comes as it did to our friend Tyler, an answer sometimes doesn't present itself. We're just left wondering, and frustrated, and empty in our grief.

But we're not in that position tonight. Tyler Trent answered the why question for us, over and over. His courage, and faith, and even cheerfulness amid such bad luck set an example none of us could miss, and all of us will be better for witnessing firsthand.

Next time you confront a big challenge, Tyler will be there to help you meet it. If you don't think he had something to do with 49–20 [margin of victory at the Purdue v. Ohio State football game in the fall of 2018], ask one of our players.

Will anyone here not remember Tyler, next time a tough moment comes? That scary exam, insensitive friend, or disappointing interview ought to seem a little more bearable with Tyler's example in front of you.

Just like the Ohio State win that he and he alone predicted, he will never be forgotten. He's now in the pantheon of Purdue heroes. Years from now, we'll all be telling people, "I was at Purdue with Tyler Trent."

Adios, Tyler. Literally, "To God." We know there's an extra ration of grit in heaven tonight.

**Message to the Purdue Community announcing plans
to reopen campus for the fall 2020 semester
April 21, 2020**

To the people of Purdue:

The global pandemic which has altered every previous reality of daily life has, of course, inflicted great harm on the nation's colleges and universities. American higher education, often criticized for its antiquated ways and its slowness to change them, has improvised and responded with admirable, even amazing alacrity to enable students to finish this semester with the progress they anticipated.

The central question now, assuming governmental authorities permit reopening of our schools by the customary August start dates, is should schools do so, and with what new rules and practices. Purdue University, for its part, intends to accept students on campus in typical numbers this fall, sober about the certain problems that the COVID-19 virus represents, but determined not to surrender helplessly to those difficulties but to tackle and manage them aggressively and creatively.

Institutions committed to the on-campus educational experience face special difficulties in returning our operations to anything like their previous arrangements. At Purdue, we have pursued a conscious policy that promotes density of our population. Our campus master plan aims at bringing people more closely together. Our housing policies, with significant success, have been designed to encourage on-campus living. And there are far more of us; we have grown our entering classes, both undergraduate and graduate, by some 25%, while investing heavily in programs like learning communities that foster higher retention and graduation.

There were sound reasons for these steps. Serving more students is our most worthy social mission. Making the campus more convenient and walkable likewise has obvious merits. Most important, all the evidence reveals that students who live and spend more of their time on campus succeed academically at higher rates. The learning experience is enhanced not only by being closer to faculty, labs, and classrooms, but also by being closer to other students, especially those from different backgrounds.

Now, sadly and ironically, the very density we have consciously fostered is, at least for the moment, our enemy. Distance between people—that is, less density—is now the overriding societal imperative. It could be argued that a college campus will be among the most difficult places to reopen for previously regular activities.

But in other respects, a place like Purdue may be in a better position to resume its mission. Our campus community, a "city" of 50,000-plus people, is highly unusual in its makeup. At least 80% of our population is made up of young people, say, 35 and under. All data to date tell us that the COVID-19 virus, while it transmits rapidly in this age group, poses close to zero lethal threat to them.

Meanwhile, the virus has proven to be a serious danger to other, older demographic groups, especially those with underlying health problems. The roughly 20% of our Purdue community who are over 35 years old contains a significant number of people with diabetes, asthma, hypertension, and other ailments, which together comprise a very high percentage of the fatal and most severe COVID-19 cases.

We will consider new policies and practices that keep these groups separate, or minimize contact between them. Literally, our students pose a far greater danger to others than the virus poses to them. We all have a role, and a responsibility, in ensuring the health of the Purdue community.

The approaches below are preliminary, meant to be illustrative of the objectives we will pursue. View them as examples, likely to be replaced by better ideas as we identify and validate them.

They could include spreading out classes across days and times to reduce their size, more use of online instruction for on-campus students, virtualizing laboratory work, and similar steps.

We will look to protect the more vulnerable members of our community by allowing (or requiring, if necessary) them to work remotely. Like the rest of society, we are learning a lot right now about which jobs are most amenable to remote work, and about new and better ways to do such work.

We intend to know as much as possible about the viral health status of our community. This could include pretesting of students and staff before arrival in August, for both infection and postinfection immunity through antibodies. It will include a robust testing system during the school year, using Purdue's own BSL-2 level laboratory for fast results. Anyone showing symptoms will be tested promptly, and quarantined if positive, in space we will set aside for that purpose.

We expect to be able to trace proximate and/or frequent contacts of those who test positive. Contacts in the vulnerable categories will be asked to self-quarantine for the recommended period, currently fourteen days. Those in the young, least vulnerable group will be tested, quarantined if positive, or checked regularly for symptoms if negative for both antibodies and the virus.

Again, these concepts are preliminary, intended mainly to illustrate an overall data-driven and research-based strategy, and to invite suggestions for their modification or exclusion in favor of better actions. They will be augmented by a host of other changes, such as an indefinite prohibition on gatherings above a specified size, continued limitations on visitors to and travel away from campus, required use of face coverings and other protective equipment, frequent if not daily deep cleaning of facilities, and so forth.

Whatever its eventual components, a return-to-operations strategy is undergirded by a fundamental conviction that even a phenomenon as menacing as COVID-19 is one of the inevitable risks of life. Like most sudden and alarming developments, its dangers are graphic, expressed in tragic individual cases, and immediate; the costs of addressing it are less visible, more diffuse, and longer-term. It is a huge and daunting problem, but the Purdue way has always been to tackle problems, not hide from them.

Closing down our entire society, including our university, was a correct and necessary step. It has had invaluable results. But like any action so drastic, it has come at extraordinary costs, as much human as economic, and at some point, clearly before next fall, those will begin to vastly outweigh the benefits of its continuance. Interrupting and postponing the education of tomorrow's leaders for another entire semester, or year, is one of many such costs. So is permanently damaging the careers and lives of those who have made teaching and research their life's work, and those who support them in that endeavor.

The COVID-19 virus will remain a fact of life this autumn. Natural immunity, which has been slowed by the shutdown, will not yet have fully developed. No vaccine can be counted on until 2021 at the soonest. It is unclear what course other schools will choose, but Purdue will employ every measure we can adopt or devise to manage this challenge with maximum safety for every member of the Boilermaker family, while proceeding with the noble and essential mission for which our institution stands.

Sincerely,
Mitchell E. Daniels, Jr.

Twenty-fifth anniversary of the Purdue Bell Tower
Message included in the time capsule
installed in the Tower's foundation
October 14, 2020

Dear members of the Purdue community,

I write to you as we mark the twenty-fifth birthday of the Purdue Bell Tower, a campus icon and a symbol of our great institution's persistent pursuit of the next giant leap—of our dedication to remembering our past while striving to achieve even more by going "one brick higher" as we work to build a better world.

Ordinarily, a twenty-fifth birthday might not call for a letter to the future from the university president and its students, or a new time capsule to be opened by those who we expect will celebrate this tower's hundredth birthday in 2095. This birthday, however, coincides with the most unique year in our 151-year history. You will no doubt have read in your history lessons about the worldwide COVID-19 pandemic of 2020, about the loss of hundreds of thousands of lives and the disruption to the lives and livelihoods of millions more. I hope you also will have read or heard stories of the year 2020 at Purdue University, and about the dedicated faculty, staff, and students who collectively and collaboratively found innovative solutions to ensure the continuity and even expansion of our learning, discovery, and engagement missions.

Within the time capsule you are opening, you will see some of the material artifacts of our efforts: a COVID-19 test kit, which was provided to all students before their arrival on campus for fall semester; a wellness kit, including Purdue-branded face masks, a thermometer, and hand wipes; a copy of our full Protect Purdue Plan and Protect Purdue Pledge, which we believe enabled us to prepare and adapt to the changing circumstances and to understand each of our roles in protecting ourselves, each other, and our campus. We have great hope that advances in medical science will long since have eliminated the need for any such items. We place them here so you might know more about what your predecessors experienced in the year 2020.

Before the disruption of the pandemic, there were already many questions being asked about the future of higher education: What is its true value? Is there a need for residential campuses? How can we provide an affordable, accessible, world-class education for learners no matter where they are and throughout their lives?

Our university is answering those questions better than most. At Purdue now twenty years into the twenty-first century, we've identified affordability and accessibility, transformative education, world-changing research, and leadership in the science, technology, engineering, and math disciplines as our focus. Our students and our faculty are among the most innovative in the world (in fact, we've just been named the fifth most innovative university in the U.S.).

We've held tuition and fees to the same levels for eight and soon to be nine years, helped our students reduce their debt loads, and provided opportunities for them to shorten their time to degree through initiatives designed by our outstanding faculty and staff. Our research enterprise has grown to record levels, and those discoveries are the basis for new businesses, boosting the economy and impacting citizens around the world. In addition, we've expanded our land-grant mission beyond the residential campus in West Lafayette to online degrees and curriculum via Purdue Global and Purdue Online, where learners from around the world can have access to our high-quality faculty and programs.

Those of us who are stewards of Purdue in 2020 believe that with continued focus on innovative solutions and the right reforms, higher education will remain valuable, and that this capsule will be opened by young people pursuing learning and personal growth at a place called Purdue.

Whoever you are, thank you for taking the time to read this missive from the past. I wish you all the best, and on behalf of the Purdue community of 2020, I wish a happy one hundredth birthday to our Purdue Bell Tower.

Message to the Purdue community regarding
the harassment of a Chinese student
December 15, 2021

Dear Purdue students, staff, and faculty,

Purdue learned from a national news account last week that one of our students, after speaking out on behalf of freedom and others martyred for advocating it, was harassed and threatened by other students from his own home country. Worse still, his family back home, in this case China, was visited and threatened by agents of that nation's secret police.

We regret that we were unaware at the time of these events and had to learn of them from national sources. That reflects the atmosphere of intimidation that we have discovered surrounds this specific sort of speech.

Any such intimidation is unacceptable and unwelcome on our campus. Purdue has punished less personal, direct, and threatening conduct. Anyone taking exception to the speech in question had their own right to express their disagreement, but not to engage in the actions of harassment which occurred here. If those students who issued the threats can be identified, they will be subject to appropriate disciplinary action. Likewise, any student found to have reported another student to any foreign entity for exercising their freedom of speech or belief will be subject to significant sanction.

International students are nothing new at Purdue University, which welcomed its first Asian admittees well over a century ago. We are proud that several hundred international students, nearly 200 of them Chinese, enrolled again this fall.

But joining the Purdue community requires acceptance of its rules and values, and no value is more central to our institution or to higher education generally than the freedom of inquiry and expression. Those seeking to deny those rights to others, let alone to collude with foreign governments in repressing them, will need to pursue their education elsewhere.

Sincerely,
Mitch

PART II

The Columns

O NE SET OF OPPORTUNITIES TO ELEVATE PURDUE'S NATIONAL RECOGNITION BE-came larger than I had ever anticipated. I was well trained as a writer—thank you, Mrs. Heckle, Mr. Jenkins, and all those terrific teachers I had at the outstanding public schools I attended—and have done a lot of it over the years. Besides three books, I had authored dozens of newspaper columns in national magazines and periodicals. I had hopes that journals like the *New York Times*, the *Wall Street Journal*, and others which had found merit in my submissions in the past would occasionally be interested if I submitted something from my new perch at Purdue.

That happened from time to time during my early years in the job. But then came an unexpected invitation. At a conference at the Aspen Institute—another of those influential audiences I wound up in front of due to past relationships—the opinion editor of the *Washington Post* asked me to become a regular on his pages.[15] The late Fred Hiatt, a wonderful person and a journalist of the highest integrity, said that he had found my occasional *Post* columns useful, and that I should become a contributing columnist.

Over the next few months, I probably irritated Fred as much as I had irritated the Purdue search committee and trustees during my period of rumination in 2012. As gratifying as the *Post*'s offer was, I was very dubious about accepting.

First, I was uncertain that I could generate enough ideas to supply something worth anyone reading on a regular basis. I was even more doubtful because I knew I would be staying away from all the political subject matter that dominates most op-ed pages. And I weighed the upside, putting Purdue's name in front of the *Post*'s large and prestigious readership, against the chance that some opinion I expressed would redound negatively somehow against our university.

Fred was persistent, and patient, and finally I talked myself into accepting. Five years and some sixty columns later, I am satisfied it was the right call. I have enjoyed the challenge of producing thought pieces that fit between the seams of things the *Post*'s other columnists are writing about all the time. I think I sometimes was able to bring a viewpoint in a different voice, from far outside the proverbial Beltway bubble to which most *Post* readers restrict themselves. And, month after month, a byline reminds thousands of powerful individuals that there is a place of higher education out in Indiana from which an occasional new and provocative idea emerges.

I miss Fred Hiatt. I'll always be grateful that he stayed after me until I awakened to the great opportunity he was offering me, and Purdue.

COMMON SENSE

This book has a vital message, and method, for our times.
January 3, 2023

I recently noticed the reissuance of a book from whose original version I had learned a lot, so I obtained and devoured the update. Nicholas Eberstadt, perhaps our finest modern demographer, first published *Men Without Work: America's Invisible Crisis* in 2016, and just recently its post-pandemic edition. The book is valuable first for its substance, but its mode and method might have just as much to teach.

Eberstadt depicts in deeply documented fashion the "invisible crisis" that is the "decimation" of the adult male workforce in America. By his calculation, some 10 million American men of prime working age are neither working nor looking for work. This "continuing calamity" is first of all a national economic albatross. He states flatly, "The United States cannot prosper unless its prime age males do."

The social damage might be even worse. What someone has termed the "New Misery" comprises a set of pathologies ranging from drug abuse to gambling addiction to the simple moral squalor of chronic idleness. AWOL working-age men watch almost six hours of television per day. They are far less likely to read newspapers, participate in volunteer activities, or attend religious services than their female or working male counterparts. Eberstadt sums up their condition as "infantilization."

Working in higher education, one knows that the situation is not improving. The decades-long retreat of men from higher ed has, like the adult nonworker phenomenon, been largely ignored until lately. But as the college-going percentage has dropped to 63%, and the share of men in the nation's universities dipped close to 40%, alarm bells have belatedly rung in both professional and general audience publications.

So the issue Eberstadt analyzes is critical, and the book is a significant contribution. But what might deserve equal attention is the form in which the author has chosen to present his findings and arguments. The new edition commits the last 10% or so of its pages to "Dissenting Points of View." Two other eminent scholars are given the floor to critique Eberstadt's analysis and conclusions, which they do powerfully but graciously.

Henry Olsen, a *Post* columnist, asserts that Eberstadt assigns too much weight to the lure of entitlement programs and too little to deindustrialization and other structural changes in the economy. He also notes the neglect of other possible causative factors, such as the shrinkage of military service where young men previously learned skills and discipline conducive to productive adult life.

Jared Bernstein challenges the book's claim that the decline in male workforce participation is linear, finding a more cyclical pattern. While concurring that the disability insurance program now suffers from rampant abuse, he concludes that Eberstadt exaggerates its role in creating the crisis.

The book wraps up with a few words of rebuttal from the author, presented as thoughtfully and politely as the dissenters expressed their criticisms. The reader, or at least this one, learned more from the give and take than he would have in its absence. He might have thought of these counterarguments on his own, but the odds are against it.

The contrast with most of today's public debates is instructive. First, the author decided to reexamine his original position to see whether the pandemic had produced evidence of refutation or altered circumstances. As a comment attributed to economist John Maynard Keynes is sometimes quoted, "When the facts change, I change my mind. What do you do?"

The invitation to others to challenge the work is a welcome departure from today's more common approach, even in scientific debates, of vitriolic certainty. In purely political clashes, that posture is merely repellent. But in the pursuit of knowledge, it is dangerous and unacceptable.

Depressing examples abound, but the vilification of the thousands of scientists who suggested in 2020 that pandemic lockdown policies might prove to be net negative is as clear as any. They were right; their assailants were wrong. But even if the Great Barrington Declaration signers had turned out to be in error, the condemnation they incurred was profoundly anti-intellectual and anti-scientific.

Knowledge advances through the clash of ideas; the contrarian is often the herald of a new insight; labels such as "settled" and "consensus" are the cudgels of fundamentalists.

One man who never declined to work, Albert Einstein, wrote letters to scientific peers urging them to conduct experiments that might disprove his theories. He saw the imperative need for the critical input of others. When he sensed that his *Entwurf* equations were errant, he said, "I do not believe I am able to find the mistake myself, for in this matter my mind is too set in a deep rut." When other physicists denounced his general theory, he didn't dismiss them by saying, "I represent science." Instead he replied, "I enjoy controversies."

We need not enjoy controversies to understand how essential they are to finding truth and expanding human understanding. Nicholas Eberstadt's book and its dissenting guests have furnished a model worthy of wide emulation. And not just in works of scholarship.

It's good to run into an optimist these days.
A roomful is even better.
October 3, 2022

It had been quite a while. For a decade such stops were a regular calendar item, but a recent speech at a small-town service club was the first such appearance I'd made in a similar number of years. I'd forgotten what I was missing, and, although they were tasty, it wasn't the eggs or the biscuits and gravy.

I agreed to speak to the Warsaw Breakfast Optimist Club in Warsaw, Indiana, as a favor to an old friend. My view now is that he did me the favor. First, in providing me reassurance that essential virtues, values, and voluntarism still thrive, at least in some places. Second, by fortifying my resolve to keep looking and hoping for the best in a nation beset with division and self-inflicted problems.

The Optimist Club national organization was founded in 1911 before going international a few years later. They now have more than 2,500 local clubs—there's more than one in Warsaw—and can teach us a little about maintaining a bright outlook through dark times.

The meeting's preliminaries included lightning-round reports on recent youth service activities, the charity golf tournament, and, in a tone of regret, the first dues increase in many years. Such was the civility and community of this crowd that even the last report received a round of (tepid) applause.

To me, the highlight of the meeting came immediately after the invocation and Pledge of Allegiance when, without prompting, the 150 men and women present stood and recited from memory the 158-word Optimist Creed. A couple of passages can be read as inner-directed ("Forget the mistakes of the past and press on to the greater achievements of the future." "Be so strong that nothing can disturb your peace of mind"). But most point the person taking the pledge toward others: "Make all your friends feel that there is something in them." "Be just as enthusiastic about the success of others as you are about your own." "Give so much time to the improvement of yourself that you have no time to criticize others." And, of special salience in this age of self-pity and freely spewed malice,

"Be too large for worry, too noble for anger." Peaceful people, with good will toward all. How countercultural.

Values like those produce practical results. Warsaw, population less than 16,000, through the ingenuity and work ethic of its people, became the orthopedic capital of the world. Globally renowned companies such as Zimmer, Biomet, and DePuy grew up in Warsaw, and some 50% of all the world's artificial joints come from there. If you or a loved one has benefited from the miracles of hip, knee, or other joint replacement, odds are heavy that your new body part came from this modest-sized town.

Entrepreneurs such as Dane Miller, in the grand tradition of American tinkerers, invented and steadily improved these products. Miller, co-founder of Biomet, was an engineer who began his operations in a barn. To persuade skeptical surgeons of his insight that titanium would be a safe and superior material for orthopedic products, he had a rod implanted in his own arm and proved his theory correct. Forty years later, the company he founded employs about 20,000 people and, now merged with Zimmer, continues to improve lives all over the world.

Current unemployment in Warsaw is 2.5%. The mayor dropped by the meeting and told me his biggest problem is attracting sufficient housing for the workers the town needs. An independent contractor named Charlie said his challenge is finding enough workers to keep up with the work.

An hour with the Optimists served as a partial antidote to the grim mood I've been warding off while reading Victor Davis Hanson's *The Dying Citizen: How Progressive Elites, Tribalism, and Globalization Are Destroying the Idea of America.* Hanson's diagnosis of our current social condition hits like a visit to an oncologist with a bad bedside manner. But, as always with his work, the scholarship is formidable and the documentation inarguable. One can reject his views of the previous presidency, but his alarming longer-run conclusions are hard to dismiss.

The falsification of U.S. history, the poisonous divisiveness of identity politics, the conflation of residence with citizenship, and the usurpation of democracy by unelected bureaucrats have plainly altered the conception of Americans' responsibilities to the nation and to each other.

There are those who find these changes acceptable or even preferable. Hanson argues powerfully that they are destructive and potentially fatal to our country's prosperity, but more important to our precious, historically unique experiment in self-government. Even an obstinate optimist comes away from the work in need of cheering up.

A trip to the Optimist Club helped. Warsaw is exactly the kind of place, filled with exactly the kind of citizens, whose disappearance Hanson foresees and laments. Here's hoping that, despite his sharp insight and erudition, he's wrong this time.

It happens that I have a major vocational change coming up, and no plans yet for what's next. I'm thinking maybe I should start by looking for a nearby Optimist Club.

In a nasty era, insisting on basic politeness is a revolutionary idea.
July 19, 2022

"Be Kind or Leave." The newspaper article, and the restaurant sign that inspired it, caught my eye. The owner of an Erie, Pennsylvania, eatery posted the notice after tiring of obnoxious, belligerent customers berating his employees and sometimes each other.

It seems the escalating—make that descending—level of boorish behavior in our society has many in customer-facing enterprises rethinking their traditional "all are welcome" policies. As a Rhode Island hotel manager put it, "The customer was always right. Well, they're not." One consumer research consultant said he now advocates drawing of clear and firm rules: "If you don't meet our expectations of decorum, leave."

These folks should have met my friend Jan Williams. The owner of one of hundreds of Indiana diners, taverns, and other small establishments I visited during a decade of constant travel through our state, Jan ran her Bainbridge Tap with, shall we say, high standards. On the first of many drop-ins at the place, I was intrigued by a cardboard sign taped to the kitchen door. It listed ten or twelve names under the arresting heading Barred for Life.

Even though I had just met Jan, I had to ask, "Really? For life?" (Answer: "It means what it says.") "Okay," I said, "what gets a person barred for life?"

The range of transgressions included fighting; breaking a beer bottle over another guy's head (that he was dancing too close to the perp's girlfriend was not deemed exculpatory); breaking a beer bottle over your husband's head (Jan's rules were gender-neutral); bringing a minor into the bar, or being the minor brought in; trying to run over Jan in the parking lot; or, most memorably, throwing a dead possum in the back of Jan's pickup truck. Jan gave no second chances and brooked no appeals of her convictions. In the Tap, rules were rules.

Encouragingly, signs that Americans are fed up with the trampling of what once were called manners have spread beyond diners and smaller communities such as Erie and Bainbridge. The profanity, vitriol, and sheer personal nastiness swirling across social media platforms have led companies such as Google and Twitter to devise filters that try to reduce overly hostile expression, as opposed to trying to regulate content. Google's Perspective artificial intelligence product is now in use not just at Reddit and other sites but also, to their credit, at a number of news originators, including the *Post*.

One wishes these new politeness police every success and wide emulation. But if not, life will go on, just less pleasantly.

In the real world, beyond the reach of any machine learning, antisocial behavior is increasingly common where America can least afford it: in public school systems. There, disruptive, sometimes barbarous conduct is blighting the futures of innocent children and inflicting lasting damage on our society.

One doesn't have to be elderly to recall times when even minor misbehavior was grounds for removal from the classroom and maybe from the school itself. The schools didn't carry the whole burden of keeping order. In proposing a bill, as Indiana's governor in 2008, to protect discipline-enforcing teachers from lawsuits, I observed, "If I had ever gotten in any big trouble at school, my dad would have come right down there. But he wouldn't have been looking for the principal." And that was when a mere disrespectful remark justified banishment from class.

Today, when an astonishing 10% of public school teachers report not just misbehavior but threatened or actual physical violence directed at them, the damage to the young lives exposed to this conduct is irrefutable and tragic. In one of many such studies, the National Bureau of Economic Research found that classroom exposure to just one disruptive boy in a class of twenty-five reduced test scores, the likelihood of receiving any degree, and lifetime earnings—all by significant margins.

Anyone who has talked with inner-city parents on charter school waiting lists or, where they are available, rushing to utilize vouchers or choice scholarships knows that for many, if not most, the first goal is not academic quality but a setting free of chaos.

Impeding any school, but especially those serving low-income and minority students, from maintaining order in the classroom is worse than mindless; it's inhumane.

It has been a few years since my last visit to the Bainbridge Tap, and when I called there recently, I learned that Jan sold the place a few years back. Christie, an employee of twenty years, told me that the Barred for Life sign is gone but that the uncompromising standards—for both conduct and the Tap's signature frog legs—still apply.

Jan Williams was a great small-business person, but I sometimes wish she'd have chosen to become a school principal instead. She'd probably have posted a sign: "If you don't meet our expectations of decorum, leave."

I never thought I'd miss the Gridiron Club dinner, but I think now maybe I do.
June 8, 2021

In a sometimes-public life, there are certain speaking invitations that are equally irresistible and intimidating. One of these, which came my way some years ago, is the annual Gridiron Club dinner bringing together the Washington press corps and political class. It's one of those "can't say no, but better be good" occasions. Preparing and delivering ten minutes of topical jokes sounds like great fun until you try it, in front of one of the tougher crowds a stand-up act can face.

A tough crowd with long memories. That was brought home to me at an intermission after my little show, when someone said, "Do you remember how bad ___ was?" Amid the guffaws and eye rolls, I asked, "Oh, was he here last year?" and was told, "Oh, no, it was five years ago."

I never thought I'd catch myself missing the Gridiron, but I think now maybe I do.

To be honest, I always viewed attending this event, nearly mandatory when one holds a certain kind of job in Washington, as more of a chore than a treat during the two tours I served in the federal government. The stand-up monologues were only occasionally funny, the skits amateurish and often lame, the dress code stiffly formal, the evening wearingly long. All told, not the ideal Saturday night. And just as well that it isn't recorded or televised.

Looking back, I think a big reason I escaped the fate of the unnamed presenter above was that I spread the jokes around. By my count, the script some friends and I wrote took nine jabs at President Barack Obama (who was sitting nearby) or other Democrats, three at the media, seven at other Republicans, and seven at myself.

At a distance, at least, one can't tell that people in Washington laugh at themselves anymore, or at much else. To some extent that just reflects an entire nation that seems to have lost its sense of humor. Entertainers such as Jerry Seinfeld and Chris Rock have lamented the hazards of their profession in an era when every audience is guaranteed to have at least a few members yearning to be "offended" and play Twitter Gotcha while the show is still on. Try getting a comedian to come to a college campus these days.

And yet . . . in these times I'm tempted to think we need this seeming anachronism to make a comeback. The Gridiron dinner, traditionally held in March, was canceled in 2020 by the coronavirus and wasn't even scheduled this spring, owing to uncertainty that one suspects was only partly medical, and partly hesitation about the institution's viability in the Washington of today.

The idea of members of both parties taking a night off to socialize, forget about their differences, and share a few laughs together is hard to picture right now. A media that has, with few exceptions, cast aside any pretense of objectivity or nonpartisanship is awkwardly suited to host a program of evenhanded good humor.

The Gridiron's motto has always been "Singe, not burn." In a town where people reach for the blowtorch on a daily basis, it may prove challenging to gather a jovial, bipartisan crowd and to confine the evening's scripts to singe level. But it wouldn't hurt to try.

As bad luck would have it, the nation lost longtime *Post* reporter David Broder a few days before my Gridiron appearance. Deeply serious about his craft, scrupulously fair-minded, critical but never contemptuous of the imperfect humans he covered, Broder was, for good reason, probably the most respected journalist of his generation.

Broder loved the Gridiron. I doubt he ever missed a year, and many dinners would find him putting himself out there as a bit player in some silly skit.

In my post-jokes wrap-up, I paid tribute to that great man, and suggested that the club consider opening his favorite evening to live coverage. I said, in part, "To me, 'Singe, not burn' means to tease but not ridicule those who must find answers that serve the interests of us all. It's the humor I encounter all the time among the regulars in Indiana coffee shops: The humor of common struggles, common purpose, and genuine, if carefully concealed, affection. The humor of the needle, not the dagger."

I finished by suggesting, "It is not for a visitor to say, but maybe this event should be shared more openly with our fellow Americans. Because it would be a fine thing for us all if the spirit of the Gridiron spread widely across this great but troubled land."

Bring back the Gridiron Club dinner. But before its spirit can be spread, first the city, and its press corps, need to recapture some of that spirit themselves.

Why the Midwest is seeing a resurgence.
March 9, 2020

The cheery woman grabbed me on my way to the stage. She couldn't wait to tell me that, after a long career in the Washington area, she was moving to the Midwest. About the great house she found at half the price and a fraction of the property tax. The quick, easy trips to work, stores, and everywhere else. The proximity of parks and bike trails and open, rural spaces. Packed and ready to go, she was the happiest person I met all month.

It's an increasingly familiar story. The event I was attending was a CNBC-sponsored program titled Growth in the Heartland, a contradiction in terms for most of the past half century, but now a real phenomenon and a possible long-term trend. Studies now detail the resurgence of a host of Midwestern cities such as Kansas City, Missouri, and Minneapolis, including some in what has been called the Rust Belt, such as Columbus, Ohio, and Madison, Wisconsin. In recent years, gross domestic product in the Great Lakes states has been outgrowing that of the East Coast.

To an extent, the shift reflects natural economic adjustment. Decades of slippage have meant that wage rates, housing prices, and overall costs of living are far lower than those prevailing on the coasts. The median home can be purchased in the Midwest for 60% of what it would cost in the Northeast, and barely half what it costs on the West Coast. The computer engineer who commands $108,000 in California can be hired for $79,000 in Michigan.

Another price of past coastal success is paid in the currency of time. Half of the nation's shortest metro-area commutes are in the Midwest. One needn't tell Washingtonians where the longest are, clocking in at more than twice the drive time one faces in Wisconsin or Iowa.

Small wonder, then, that even in a society where mobility has slowed, the hemorrhage of people out of the Northeast and California is now unmistakable, and it's less and less masked by international immigration. Net domestic migration from the Northeast now runs more than 350,000 per year; California is losing population, and likely a congressional district, for the first time in its history.

These changes are more than just a pendulum swinging. Some of the turnaround is the product of conscious, thoughtful public policy. Places such as Wisconsin, Michigan, Ohio, and my home state of Indiana have built some of the country's most business-friendly climates. Many have reformed and strengthened public education and seen positive results. Five of CNBC's top 10 states for infrastructure are Midwestern, led by Indiana at No. 1.

(Of course, there are exceptions. Illinois, where local wags claim the state slogan is "Come for the corruption, stay for the high taxes," is ours. But Chicago is losing 200 residents a day, and last year Illinois sent 30,000 people to Indiana, twice those going in the other direction.)

But let's give credit where it's due; we would not be getting by without a little help from our friends. If the Midwest impulse is to do whatever we can to lower the burden of investing and hiring, our friends elsewhere seem to think that if they let you build something and employ someone, they are doing you a favor.

One friend totaled the regulatory cost of building a home in California at eighteen months and $100,000, and that was before construction could start. The state's new law penalizing independent contracting will hit screenwriters, freelance journalists, owner-operator truckers, and the entire California-born gig economy in an ironic act of economic infanticide.

Overall tax burdens are lower in the middle of the country, but especially so at higher income levels. California is notorious for collecting half of all its revenue from less than 1% of its citizens, but the practice is common elsewhere. In Connecticut, which trailed only New Jersey and Illinois in last year's survey of outbound moving vans, more than half the fleeing refugees came from upper income brackets (greater than $150,000 a year). This is what is known as a death spiral.

Blackouts, anyone? Whatever problems middle America still faces, keeping the power on, as California and New York now struggle to do, isn't one of them.

And then there are the quality-of-life choices. Public authorities tolerating discarded needles, aggressive vagrants, and you-know-what on the sidewalk are hard for us provincials to understand. But when Oracle moves its annual tech conference out of San Francisco because of "poor street conditions"—at a loss of $64 million for the city—we sure get that.

No one is claiming a Midwest miracle or a full reversal of a decline that has gone on for decades. But no one fifty years back saw how far Detroit, Cleveland, and other once-strong cities would eventually fall. One has to resist succumbing to that four-syllable German word I always struggle to pronounce. And we can stifle any urge to say, "Last one to leave, turn out the lights." They'll probably just go out by themselves.

Set political disagreements aside for the holidays.
December 20, 2019

When one golfing buddy of mine hits an especially bad shot—it's not that uncommon—he sometimes slams his club to the ground in frustration and shouts, "If it weren't so damned important!" We're in between golf seasons where I live, but I think of him and that funny line often these days, when what should be the season of peace is now, we are told, frequently marred by arguments among family and friends over . . . politics.

Holiday news coverage once tended to take a break from the grim and gloomy, dealing with topics like how to dodge the worst highway traffic, experiment with a new libation, or prepare the perfect cranberry relish. In the past couple of years, the articles have seemed more likely to advise readers on how to navigate political minefields during the holidays.

Thanksgiving now brings helpful guidance not on how to enjoy your turkey but rather how to deal with the one at the end of the table, when he starts spouting whatever dogma his group adheres to at the moment. Tips like "Don't make it an issue if you don't have to"—why in the world would you have to?—and verbal coaching ("I feel like I'm not being heard") are offered up to keep relatives from hurling dinner rolls at each other. Also provided: cautions about the headache or stomachache that might come from the stress of political discord. Gee, couldn't it just possibly have been the oyster dressing?

Elsewhere, we read depressing surveys about friendships ending over Medicare for all or impeachment or maybe plastic straws.

It seems that many of us have outgrown the old "I wouldn't want my child to marry one" bias in its religious or racial forms, only to substitute ideological marriage tests. Pew Research Center found in 2014 that 45% of Americans who are "consistently" or "mostly" conservative would be unhappy if a family member married a Democrat, and 31% of "consistently" or "mostly" liberal Americans would be unhappy if a family member married a Republican. The hostility has almost certainly worsened since then. Don't get me started on the vile practice of assaulting heretics from one's own views in restaurants or even at their homes.

How we arrived at such a sad pass is hard to say with certainty, but some root causes are evident. The intrusion of a sprawling, nosy federal government into seemingly every corner of American life has made its actions and workings relevant in ways they once were not. The nationalization of news, and the corresponding collapse of state and local coverage, has pushed whatever Washington thinks is important to the top of everyone's information feeds. The atomization of life, the retreat of too many into their smartphones and laptops, has reduced the number and variety of human interactions that actually do make for interesting dinner conversation. And, of course, the politicization of cultural issues and culturalization of public debate have helped force politics onto the table with the gravy and mashed potatoes.

Seriously, folks. Can we all blow into the paper bag for a minute? This nation has been through the Vietnam War, Watergate, stagflation, 9/11, and a genuine Great Recession just within the lifetimes of today's 50-year-olds. Momentous as those events were, one doesn't recall arguments over them spoiling millions of holiday gatherings.

Samuel Johnson wrote that to be happy at home is the ultimate aim of all human endeavor. Years from now, the joys or the difficulties of marriage, children, personal health, career—not to mention the soccer league, church choir, or United Way—will have more to do with our happiness at home than whether the Democrats hold on to Virginia's 7th District or the exact amount of the minimum wage.

It is possible to care deeply about politics without losing all perspective on things of truly permanent consequence, and on things that bind us together whatever our views on temporal matters. Remember that old line about ending life not wishing one had spent more time at the office? It also applies to not wishing one had tried harder to persuade Uncle George that a border wall was a good idea.

A personal wish for this and all your future holidays is that, with full appreciation for the civic value of passion about our public life, you give yourself even the briefest of respites from all that. Set aside the political harangues (and while you're at it, how about your cell phone, too?) and remember what, and who, matters most.

Like that 7-iron I pulled into the trap on 18. Now that was important.

Sadly, political cartooning is becoming a lost art.
July 31, 2019

The digital age, for all its beneficial wonders, has left some regrettable casualties in its wake. No loss has been more troublesome for many of us than the decline of print journalism as our principal medium of information. For all their flaws and variability, newspapers bring a depth of information, a degree of editorial quality control, and a capacity for self-correction of errors that are difficult to find in what now passes for "news" journalism.

With that development, we're losing something I have always appreciated almost as much. The political cartoonist, an influential voice in public debates for centuries, is among our most endangered species. According to *Drawn & Quartered*, a history of American political cartoons by Stephen Hess and Sandy Northrop, 2,000 editorial cartoonists were employed a century ago; estimates of the number of staff cartoonists working today range from about 2 dozen to maybe 40.

The famous 1,000-to-1 words-to-picture ratio may be understated when it comes to the political cartoon. A case can be made that public opinion has, over time, been more often shaped by these artists than by the words of their polemicist colleagues on the nation's editorial pages. A salient political point made with humor can pack more punch than the same idea draped in invective. Many citizens who would not take time for a lengthy essay have learned of an issue or taken a cue from a well-drawn sketch and a clever caption.

I confess that, during my younger days spent in Washington, I read an occasional op-ed—but I never skipped a Herblock cartoon in the *Post*. If and when the political cartoonist's genre goes extinct, we'll have lost more than an occasional chuckle.

The cartoonist I'll miss most laid down his pen for the *Indianapolis Star* earlier this year. For a quarter century, including the eight years I spent in elective office, Gary Varvel delighted and illuminated the fortunate readers of the *Indianapolis Star* with his craftsmanship and his insight in equal measure. To someone who can't draw a circle with a compass, Varvel's seemingly effortless ability to capture the essence of his subjects was inexplicable. To someone who was working daily in public life, his grasp of events and clarity of thinking brought, not infrequently, second thoughts or even a change of viewpoint.

Even before newspapers began to homogenize and wither, Varvel was an unusual and especially valuable figure in Indiana life. He carried on the tradition of cartoonists who, at their best, have served a particularly American service by satirizing the pretensions of the political class.

Our greatest cartoonists have reminded us of the foibles, frauds, and failures of those imperfect people to whom we entrust power over us. They have helped to maintain the healthy skepticism that protects liberty against its enemies, whether would-be dictators or those who simply consider themselves our benevolent betters.

During the current president's recent trip to Britain, the interest group Led by Donkeys lampooned him with sarcastic images projected onto buildings and billboards. The group's leader explained, "By laughing at them, you can reduce their power." It's a vital role. A Varvel cartoon almost always poked its fun at those who would infringe upon rather than protect our freedoms.

Though it is a common misconception that the word "nasty" derives from the work of Thomas Nast, who is considered the father of American political cartooning, the myth did ring true. In recent years, public discourse has coarsened unmistakably and drearily, but much political cartooning was already there. For all his great wit and artistic skill, Varvel was always playful but never cruel.

A Varvel caricature stopped short of ridicule; its caption aimed to make the reader laugh, not smirk. And many times—see his post-9/11 drawing of a weeping Uncle Sam holding a fallen firefighter in his arms, or his "Bush Reunion" piece after former president George H. W. Bush joined his wife, Barbara, in death, portraying the couple embracing on a cloud—he made us shed a tear.

The best cartoonists can be appreciated for the smiles, the artisanship, or the principled philosophy that usually underlie their oeuvre. One needn't agree with their opinions to appreciate the skill of those who see public debates and participants through more imaginative eyes than our own. That is especially so when their work is drawn in a spirit of genuine humor and goodwill. Like the tough copy editors and corrections columns of yesteryear, they'll be hard to replace.

In farm children, I see virtues that one sees too rarely these days.
June 11, 2019

Along with the rise of women and the expansion of civil rights, the most important social transformation of America's first quarter millennium has been the triumph of modern agriculture over famine and the ceaseless, backbreaking effort simply to feed oneself that had been the dominant fact of human life through-out history. Most of those who preceded us lived their entire lives on the farm. A little more than a century ago, a third of all Americans were farmers.

Successive revolutions in mechanization, horticulture, and biotechnology have been an enormous blessing, enabling a tiny percentage of Americans—to-day fewer than 2%—to feed the rest of us and much of the world. Incalculable human talent has been liberated to invent all the other miracles we enjoy. We spend less of our income on food than any society ever.

But this blessing, like most, is not an unmixed one. Other valuable talents, and much precious social capital, have diminished with the share of Americans liv-ing and working on the land.

During a decade in elected office in Indiana, I made it my practice while trav-eling the state to stay overnight in Hoosier homes rather than hotels. Because of geography and, candidly, personal choice, probably a third of those 125 over-nights were with farm families. There I witnessed virtues that one sees too rarely these days—hard work, practical manual skill, a communitarian ethic—woven tightly into the fabric of everyday life.

I saw teenagers and even younger siblings rising at 5 a.m. to feed animals or do other chores before cleaning up and heading to school. It was fun to return home and tell those stories to four suburban daughters whose idea of a tough as-signment was clearing the table and washing the dishes.

At county fairs, I would always ask that the 4-H officers be the ones to take me around. Every one of those young people had raised animals for competition, and they showed me projects—artistic, scientific, or community service—with the special pride that comes from creative, arduous individual effort.

After shooting the breeze with some FFA members in their northwest Indi-ana town, I was musing to a local friend about what fine characters and purpose-ful attitudes farm kids seem to have. "Absolutely," she said. "Our circuit judge has been on the bench here for twenty-plus years. Once I asked him, in all that time, how many FFA or 4-H members have come before you? He said, 'Uh, none I can remember.'"

At the Gerber family's farmhouse near Boston, Indiana (population 130), I learned about the year that Doug, the father, was hit and nearly killed by a train while trying to clear storm debris off a railroad crossing. He said that when he returned home after weeks in a coma, the first thing he saw was his neighbors sowing his crops and feeding his livestock so that his family would have income that year. "They wouldn't even let me pay for the diesel fuel," he recalled.

At the Indiana State Fair, held on grounds now surrounded by inner-city Indianapolis neighborhoods, urban kids can witness, in person, the birth of pigs and calves. Once I asked a boy who had arrived at the fair on a school bus from across town, "Do you know where milk comes from?" He said, "Sure. The grocery store." A couple of hours later, he knew better and just maybe had a little sense of awe and gratitude for the work and skill it takes to fill that grocery store.

Thomas Jefferson believed that democracy could work only in a society of agrarian yeomen, living in small political units, who would be invested in their society and resolute in defending their liberty against the encroachments of government. We'd better hope he was wrong or, to the extent that he was on to something, that we can recognize and preserve the characteristics that make yeomen (and women) such good citizens.

The cultural fiber that an agricultural upbringing once brought to society will of course not return through numbers. But there are ways other than state fairs to expose modern young people to its value and its virtues. One-third of today's 4-H members now live in urban areas. Summer jobs detasseling corn or baling hay are still occasionally available as an alternative to *Fortnite* practice or soccer camp. In their constant quest for diversity, universities should not overlook the benefits that rural students can bring to their big-city and suburban classmates.

The distance that has opened between the producers of our food and the beneficiaries of their hard work, and between rural and urban Americans in general, has been sadly apparent in our politics and popular culture. More than tolerance is in order. Some true appreciation, and even some emulation, would be helpful right now. There's a lot to learn down on the farm.

Want to study abroad? Check out America.
March 11, 2019

A growing staple on the menu of most colleges and universities is the opportunity to study abroad, through which a student earns credits by traveling to a foreign land for coursework or a special project assignment. It's a fine idea. The lives and careers of today's young people will be inextricably bound up with global events. Simply to be a knowledgeable, effective citizen will require a grasp of previously unfamiliar places and some practice mixing and empathizing with the people who inhabit them. At Purdue University, we have boosted the number of graduates with at least one international experience by 70% in five years, to al-most a third of the latest class.

Yale University, with the goal of producing graduates who have immersed themselves in the ways and the thinking of an exotic culture that is utterly alien to their own, offers undergraduates a fascinating option: the chance to under-take a "study abroad" experience in . . . America.

Students in the school's Grand Strategy program, having read such classic authors as Thucydides, Clausewitz, and Machiavelli, as well as modern masters such as Henry Kissinger, can earn credit for a summer odyssey in the form of a road trip across their own country—or anywhere else in the world, provided the odyssey isn't dangerous. Yale helps finance the trip, and a written account of the journey becomes a part of the final grade.

John Gaddis, who along with fellow historian Paul Kennedy and former dip-lomat Charles Hill founded the Grand Strategy seminar in 2000 (they still teach in the program), told C-SPAN in May that their conception represented "our small effort to try to break down some of the isolation that somehow the elite universities have locked themselves into, the bubbles into which they have placed themselves." It was a great idea, and now is timelier than ever.

At each Purdue commencement, I find myself imploring our graduates not to accept the invitation from America's knowledge economy to cluster together professionally, residentially, and socially with other academically successful con-temporaries. More than their personal growth is at stake; the country's drift into mutually distrustful, even hostile, cultural camps is near the top of almost every-one's national worry list.

By equipping some with the skills and credentials for success, while cocoon-ing them in what are often highly homogenous intellectual environments, the United States' higher education institutions contribute to the growth of this cul-tural crevasse.

There may be no better example of that cocooning than Yale, home of Hallo-ween Hysteria (when a faculty member was savaged for suggesting that students were mature enough to pick their own costumes) and the official censorship of political signs, cartoons, and T-shirts that include the word "sissies" (quoting F. Scott Fitzgerald on Harvard men).

After seeing Gaddis's interview, I called him to talk about the Grand Strategy program. I wanted to know more about summer odysseys across America, and he supplied me with a paper by one of his students, a Massachusetts native who set out on a 7,200-mile trip that took him through 22 states and included multi-week stays in a town in South Texas, an Indian reservation in South Dakota, and an inner-city Cleveland neighborhood. His 90,000-word account of the journey is a catalog of revelations, a genuine voyage of discovery.

In Cotulla, Texas, he became friends with a 45-year-old ranch manager and part-time musician. When the student asks about the revolver on the floor of his pickup truck, the ranch manager casually says, "If it comes to me or them, it's gonna be them." "Them" turns out to mean drug runners who don't merely trespass on private property: "If they see ya," he says, "they shoot ya." Our wide-eyed Yalie thinks to himself later, "Where I come from, black ice was the greatest threat to our safety."

Elsewhere, he attended, and was moved by, a small Sunday church service, apparently the first he could remember taking part in. As a stranger welcomed into the service, he noted the way it provided a "moral foundation" that promoted "kindness, humility, and generosity," helping to keep families and the community together.

At each stop, our young Odysseus met other Americans his own age, none of whom had a chance of going to Yale or, in too many cases, to any higher education institution. Regardless of setting—urban, rural, small town—he discovered the overwhelming impact of family and culture on the life prospects of children. Coming from an intact, scholarly family, he at first is stunned by the notion of homes where values are not taught and education is not encouraged. Soon he grasps that it is among our society's true root problems.

"Study abroad" remains a valuable concept. Yale's wonderful innovation merely reminds us that in our sadly balkanized age, we must work to build cultural competence across the abroads right here on shore.

I've met people of all stripes. I have my motorcycle to thank.
October 5, 2018

Late fall lowers my spirits for a lot of reasons, but one of the saddest comes on that dreaded day when it's time to winterize the motorcycle and put it away until spring. It's almost a half century since I bought my first bike, and now the season's end comes with a little extra wistfulness, as I contemplate that my riding career is about over.

That was supposed to happen this year. An increasingly aggressive lobbying campaign by the five Daniels women ("Really, Dad, don't you think it's about time?") had persuaded me to call it quits. I sold one of my two Harleys and made plans to donate the other, which is too much of a custom keepsake for eBay, to a friend's collection. But—guy story trigger warning—at the last minute, standing in front of the waiting trailer, I just couldn't bring myself to do it. Down went the garage door, and I sneaked back into the house, reinstated the registration and insurance, and started working on my spousal and fatherly alibi.

Aside from the fun I'll miss in riding retirement, I find the prospect rueful for a second reason. Motorcycling has always been a hobby through which riders can encounter a wonderfully wide spectrum of fellow enthusiasts. More than any other pursuit that comes to mind, it has long attracted people of all types. Even as America became a nation of flyover air travel and interstate highway travel, motorcycle riding remained a pastime that took you on old roads and into small towns, where you were apt to meet people from geographically distant parts and socially distant backgrounds.

Outside one Indiana diner, I encountered a group of riders in matching leather jackets whose colors said Boozefighters. That was the name of the gang that inspired Marlon Brando's *The Wild One* back in 1953. I asked one of them about it. "That's right," he said. "We're drinkers with a motorcycle problem."

In the 1950s and '60s, as the sport sought to expand, it adopted a more genteel face. A Japanese company with eventual designs on the American auto market unveiled its initial two-wheel offerings with the slogan "You meet the nicest people on a Honda." The Beach Boys sang, "It's not a big motorcycle, just a groovy little motorbike."

According to the Motorcycle Industry Council, the number of motorcycle registrations exploded from 2.8 million in 1970 to 8.6 million in 2015. With that growth has come a wide diversification in participants. A surge in female ridership—from 8% in 1998 to 14% in 2014, the council says—is one of the more recent positive trends.

With most riders often wearing similar clothing and sharing a deep interest in equipment, accessories, and tales of the road, one can never assume anything about the new acquaintances a ride often brings.

In one typical encounter, at a huge charity ride—motorcyclists of all income levels tend to be inordinately generous and are constantly organizing events for good causes—I was bantering with members of another motorcycle club, the

Outlaws, getting a kick out of the fact that every one of them had a nickname: Blackjack, Deadeye, Papa Smurf, and the like.

When a bearlike, long-haired fellow sauntered up, dressed in studded leather like the others, I asked him if he had a nickname. "Everybody calls me Doc," he replied. "Okay, Doc," I said. "Are you a member of the Outlaws?" "No, I'm an anesthesiologist over here at Methodist Hospital." You just never know.

In this social clustering, self-segregating era, that aspect of biking is especially enjoyable, and meaningful. There are fewer and fewer organizations, activities, or recreational pursuits through which Americans of very different stations meet one another on equal terms, with entirely common interests. That fact of modern times is not, some of us believe, a trivial factor in the cultural estrangement now afflicting our social and political life.

In my previous job as a politician, I tried whenever possible to stay overnight in citizens' homes, from inner cities to small towns to the most remote farms, with people of every income level. The practice was invaluable, bringing new friends, new insights, great anecdotes, and examples for the next speech. But mainly it was a lesson in our commonality, the values and concerns that we share instead of dividing over. One might say, stereotypes die in the light of personal interaction.

So if you don't have a cross-cultural hobby, think of trying mine. It's a ton of fun, it may be the last place where you can't possibly text or expose yourself to antisocial media, and you'll get to know some good folks whom life won't otherwise bring your way. Take it from me (but don't take my Harley just yet), you'll meet the nicest people.

Is anyone ever wrong anymore?
December 6, 2017

A recent whim prompted me to reread Stephen Ambrose's *To America*, a collection of reflections on the historian's craft and many of the topics and individuals Ambrose wrote about during his prolific career. The book might have been titled *Second Thoughts*, because virtually every chapter describes some significant issue on which the author changed his mind over the years: his estimation of presidents such as U. S. Grant, Theodore Roosevelt, and Richard Nixon; Harry Truman's decision to use the atomic bomb; the "robber barons" who built the transcontinental railroad; the reality of Soviet tyranny; and several more.

In many cases Ambrose relates how he came to dispute conclusions that his university professors and advisors peddled to him in his younger years. Elsewhere, he takes issue with his own previous views. But in each instance, he explains the evolution of his thinking, and the grounds for it, without defensiveness or embarrassment.

When the book appeared, early in this century, one would not have found such admissions especially noteworthy. In 2017, they take on a more striking cast, because ours is an era when it seems no one ever confesses to being wrong. Moreover, everyone is so emphatically right that those who disagree are not merely in error but irredeemably so, candidates not for persuasion but for castigation and ostracism.

Social historians will need some time and perspective to determine exactly what led to the new closed-mindedness, but some of the causes seem plain. One is the effect of narrowcasting, in which people find the sources of information (or the sources' algorithms find them) that fortify their existing viewpoints and prejudices. Confirmation bias has mutated from a hazard of academic research to a menacing political and social phenomenon.

Meanwhile, those institutions of higher learning—the adjective now almost needs quotation marks—that should cultivate and model openness to debate and refutation too often have become bastions of conformity and thought control.

John Maynard Keynes is frequently credited with the aphorism "When I find I'm wrong, I change my mind. What do you do?" Today, the problem may less be an attitude of stubbornness than that fewer people than ever recognize their mistakes in the first place.

In a well-documented fashion, steady doses of viewpoint reinforcement lead not only to a resistance to alternative positions but also to a more entrenched and passionate way in which thoughts are held and expressed. When those expressions are launched in the impersonal or even anonymous channels of today's social—or is it antisocial?—media, vitriol often becomes the currency of discourse and second thoughts a form of tribal desertion or defeat. Things people would not say face-to-face are all too easy to post in bouts of blogger or tweeter one-upmanship.

So honest admissions of error are more eye-catching these days. In recent years, the *Post*'s Bob Woodward has recounted how, a quarter century later, he had come to a very different interpretation of Gerald Ford's pardon of Richard Nixon. And how he wasn't the only one; Senator Ted Kennedy, who excoriated Ford at the time of his decision, joined Woodward in that assessment, and conferred an award for political courage for the act they had once deemed a corrupt bargain.

A few months back, the world lost Jay Keyworth, nuclear scientist and presidential science advisor to Ronald Reagan. Keyworth had assembled the evidence to advocate an antiballistic missile (ABM) system, which establishment opinion of the time relentlessly derided as "Star Wars"—a fanciful and impractical notion, and one in conflict with the then sacred doctrine of mutual assured destruction.

Now, with one rogue nation perfecting both weapons and rocketry capable of annihilating U.S. targets, and another perhaps only years from joining it, the conversation is all about the effectiveness of our ABM system and why the heck the government hasn't made our national safety more certain. We're still waiting for that conversation to include "Thanks, Jay. You were right, and we weren't."

Ambrose wrote his book near the end of his life. In fact, it is dedicated to his cancer doctor and nurses. Maybe such honest introspection comes more readily under the imminence of the great event. But our everyday exchanges, and indeed the life of our republic, would be greatly improved by the more common utterance of those three magical little words: "I was wrong."

EDUCATIONAL CHALLENGES

Student loan forgiveness and the national debt:
Purdue students learn to be responsible while their
peers get bailouts. There will be a reckoning.
Wall Street Journal
September 1, 2022

The colorful Ohio governor Jim Rhodes once likened George Romney's run for the presidency to "a duck trying to [make love to] a football." I wish he had been around to put a label on the federal student loan program. In the sad catalog of its failures, the federal government has set a new standard. President Biden's debt cancellation announcement represents the final confession of failure for a venture flawed in concept, botched in execution, and draped with duplicity.

The scheme's flaws have been well chronicled. It's regressive, rewarding the well-to-do at the expense of the less fortunate. It's grossly unfair to those who repaid what they borrowed or never went to college. It's grotesquely expensive, adding hundreds of billions to a federal debt that already threatens our safety net programs and national security. Like so much of what government does, it's iatrogenic, inflating college costs as schools continue to pocket the subsidies Uncle Sam showers on them. And it's profanely contemptuous of the Constitution, which authorizes only Congress to spend money.

When the federal government took over the loan program in 2010, President Obama claimed it would turn a profit of $68 billion and that "we are finally undertaking meaningful reform in our higher education system." Credit where due: a dead loss of hundreds of billions of dollars and tuition costs that continued to soar can fairly be described as meaningful.

There are, and long have been, better ways. Colleges should always have been at some risk for any non-repayments by graduates. One can view such defaults as a breach of warranty, as degrees could be thought to imply that their bearers were prepared to be productive citizens, with the market value and personal character to live up to their freely chosen obligations.

Even a modest percentage of shared liability for non-repayments would have significantly affected schools' behavior. The financial exposure and potential embarrassment would have driven material changes in the rigor of teaching and the amounts they charged and encouraged students to borrow. Such a system would have amounted to a fair request that institutions stand behind their product.

Of course, much of this unpaid debt would never have been accrued if colleges hadn't raised their prices at the highest rates of any category in the economy. Thanks to the subsidy gusher, that was easy to do. But it wasn't right or necessary.

I have been asked countless times about Purdue's record of holding tuition and fees flat since 2012 while lowering room, board, and book costs. It is less expensive to attend our university, in nominal dollars and for all students, in-state or out, than it was a decade ago.

I'd like to claim that this was a triumph of managerial brilliance, but I can't. We simply asked ourselves each year, "Can we solve the equation for zero?"—meaning what would it take to avoid a fee increase? Placing top priority on containing student costs has driven lower ratios of administrators to faculty, less goldplating on new buildings, modernized and consumer-driven health plans, and other simple changes. Meanwhile, not coincidentally, enrollment and revenues have surged.

Ten years on, more than 60% of our students graduate debt-free. Debt per student has been cut in half, to just over $3,000. Had Purdue raised tuition at the national average, students' families would have sent us more than $1 billion more than they have.

Along with marketable knowledge and skills, Purdue aspires to foster character in its students. Watching each year as more than 99% of our graduates honor their student debt obligations, we take pride in them. But I'm uncertain what to say to them as they see their less-responsible contemporaries bailed out—with, adding insult to injury, a portion of the tab handed to them as taxpayers.

When, not if, our national debt forces a traumatic reckoning, asset sales will likely be part of the emergency plan to preserve safety net payments and some vestige of discretionary government. Along with surplus federal land and structures, it will make sense to sell whatever remains of the student loan portfolio. That will be a fitting end to a bankrupt lending system born of bankrupt policy choices.

It looks like pay-for-play in college sports is here to stay. Too bad.
May 26, 2022

The two archrivals had met during the regular season, Notre Dame coming away with a 2-point overtime victory over Purdue. They collided again in the tournament's final game, this time the Irish winding up on the short end of a 53–48 barnburner, and a new national basketball champion was crowned. The crowd of about thirty diehard fans erupted, their cheers echoing around the not-so-famed Highmark Center in Erie, Pennsylvania.

You didn't see it on *SportsCenter* or anywhere else. It was the championship in late April of the National Club Basketball Association, an organization promoting a newly novel concept: college athletes, genuine student-athletes, playing a sport for the pure love of the game and the camaraderie of a team.

Unlike those "exploited" varsity players at Division I schools such as theirs, these players enjoy no free tuition, no special food or housing, no lavish practice facilities, and no personal trainers, nutritionists or psychologists. Any tutoring or academic coaching comes to their aid only if they take the initiative to seek it out.

They coach themselves, drive themselves to all away games, raise their own funds to hire officials, and cover any other expenses.

But they can play ball. Every one was a high school starter; every one could play collegiately at some level, if basketball were their top priority. Among the club championship players, two plan to go to medical school. Another will be an engineer. One who's headed to an IT job in Houston told me, "I ultimately passed up the chance to play small-school basketball because education was the most important thing to me."

Meeting these young men, and celebrating their success this spring, struck me as especially meaningful, given that it occurred at a time when college athletics are plunging down the bobsled run into full-blown professionalism.

In the past year, the agents, lawyers, politicians, sportswriters, and would-be union organizers rooting for free-for-all player compensation have largely won the battle. They made a convincing case that athletes should be able to earn income from the fame their talents bring them, while elsewhere a court struck down prohibitions on direct payments to players by schools.

All agreed solemnly that it's just about "fairness" and, mercy no, we can't and won't let this become a vehicle for recruiting, poaching or run-wild booster involvement.

Right. Before a single recruiting season has passed, big-money payments are everywhere, they are boastfully open, and apparently we are all to suddenly understand that this is just the way it is going to be.

There is a precedent for the world that many university athletic programs are now hurtling into. From 1947 to 1961, the National Basketball Association had a highly competitive rival league. The National Industrial Basketball League (NIBL) comprised teams sponsored by companies as a way to promote their names and reputations, an earlier version of the stadium and event sponsorships of today.

Teams such as the Peoria Caterpillar Diesels and Akron Goodyear Wingfoots contended with Milwaukee Allen-Bradley, the Denver Central Bankers, and some two dozen others over the fourteen years before the league succumbed to the competition of a rising NBA.

My friend Bobby Plump, whose last-second, real-world jump shot in 1954 for Milan High School made the movie *Hoosiers* possible, compared an opportunity with the NBA's Minneapolis Lakers with one from the Phillips 66ers of the NIBL and chose the latter. He led them to a league title and a lot of publicity for the company. Bobby and his teammates might have made an occasional public appearance on behalf of their firm, but their job was to play ball.

That may become the model for our brave new pay-to-play world; a top tier of young athletes will be handsomely compensated to boost the recognition of their sponsoring universities. Period. "Let's welcome the Crimson Tide, sponsored by the University of Alabama!"

Schools comfortable spending huge donations on recruiting the best players—funds that might have been used to strengthen their academic missions—will be free to do so. When that happens, they should drop any pretense that these are students and any requirement that anyone attend classes or pursue a degree. Offer education, as more and more employers now do, as an optional fringe benefit of the job.

Only a couple dozen sports factories will be able to compete successfully in the pay-to-play echelon. The rest will be left with a Hobson's choice between permanent also-ran status and dropping down into a further segmentation of today's system, hoping that they can still fill stadiums and negotiate TV contracts to watch actual students play. Meanwhile, they will be deciding which nonrevenue sports to cut so athletic department budgets come close to balancing. Maybe they can expand club sports.

My guess—okay, hope—is that such an arrangement can work. Meanwhile, I'm sure the new league of sponsored professionals will be highly entertaining and a huge financial success. Just please don't call it "college" sports.

Hail to mothers, even those who can't let go of their college-age kids.
May 6, 2022

Can I get something on the record? I love moms. I really love moms. They're the most important people we have, as individuals and as a society. A caring mom provides the best chance, sometimes the only chance, a young person has of turning into a responsible, self-reliant, high-character adult. No mission is nobler.

However, ahem, even moms are subject to that fundamental caveat of life—up to a point. Working daily with and on behalf of tens of thousands of other people's children, one encounters moms who, let's just say, carry things a little far.

Like the lady who insisted, without ever providing any documentation, that her child was allergic to all nonorganic food. She ordered food multiple times a week, accompanied by specially selected spices, and had it delivered to our dining courts with a demand that the staff cook it separately for him, to her specs. (They did, for a year, until the demands, or maybe the allergies, ceased.)

Or the woman who wrote and called eight times to complain about her daughter's accommodations. She was sure there was mold (the test she ordered came back negative), and that the water was tainted (she sent it out for tests, negative again). The oven handle was loose. (Has your daughter tried a screwdriver?)

We often receive helpful advice about adding streetlights or other measures to enhance physical security, on a campus found every year one of the statistically safest in the nation. After the university acceded to one mother's demands and moved her daughter to different housing, she continued to complain on behalf of other people's children who apparently hadn't realized the extent of their own jeopardy.

Of course many of the grievances are justified, and we try to act on them promptly. But after years on the receiving end of such entreaties, the term "helicopter parent" no longer seems adequate to capture the closeness of the hovering. "Mom mowers" might be more descriptive.

This is not to exonerate the fathers. Although paternal complaints make up a much smaller fraction of the campus mailbag, they can be just as difficult. One father was the source of thirteen emails and three phone calls about how miserably lonely his son was, insisting he be moved to a different residence. When visited, the student reported having lots of friends, several extracurricular involvements, and zero interest in being moved.

Such parent–student disconnects are not uncommon. One mother was persistent and belligerent because her son's bed was too short for his six-foot-three frame. When visited to see if the university could make a different accommodation for him, he picked up his cell phone, called home, and bluntly asked Mom to butt out.

As extreme as such examples are, it is impossible not to empathize with a parent who, rationally or not, worries about the physical safety or comfort of their child. More dubious are parental attempts to shield their offspring from failure, or the academic challenges that higher education, if it's doing its job, presents to its young clients.

Like the mother who insisted that we gather all her son's homework assignments daily and fax them to her so that he and she could work on them together every evening. Or the one who requested an "advance interview" for herself the day before her daughter's own interview so that she could "explain her daughter's qualifications" for the award in question.

Or, a personal favorite, the mom who impersonated her son—yes, son—at his teaching assistant's virtual office hours, to present his homework solution and push for a 100% grade. Even with the Zoom camera off, the TA detected the subterfuge.

When my wife and I dropped off the oldest of our four daughters at college, the day's program ended abruptly in midafternoon. Parents and kids had attended separate orientation sessions at lunchtime, and when we saw our daughter again it was for only five minutes, before the adults were politely excused.

The message was clear: a new era has begun for your child, and that means for you, too.

In a country where the number one cause of our various social sadnesses is irresponsible parenting, one cannot fault those who love their children to the point of overprotection. But protection from challenge, and from the occasional failure, which is often the best teacher, can be endangerment of a different kind.

So bless all the moms, and dads, including those who go a little over the edge. We'll do our best to be responsive. But remember; when your kid graduated from high school, maybe it was time for you to graduate, too.

Happy Mother's Day to all.

Imagine if a lemon law penalized schools for rotten educations. February 14, 2022

I think it's fair to say that we Americans, whatever our other different predilections, are pretty demanding shoppers. We expect good value in the goods and services we buy and exert ourselves to obtain it. We pass lemon laws and have well-developed doctrines of implied warranty that require sellers to stand behind their claims.

A growing chorus comprising voices from left and right argues that it is past time to bring a similar accountability to one of our most vital services, the education delivered by U.S. colleges and universities. Whether by fining them a fraction of their graduates' student debt defaults, charging them an insurance premium against such failures to repay, or some similar mechanism, the concept of schools sharing the risk of inadequate performance with the taxpayers has wide and growing support.

That's a sound principle as applied to higher education, but why stop there? A parallel approach might inject a degree of accountability into the K–12 area, where the performance record is, if anything, worse, and the consequences even more destructive at both the individual and societal levels.

Year after dreary year, hundreds of thousands of high school diplomas are awarded to young people who, it turns out, are not nearly literate or numerate enough to identify the main idea of a reading passage or to perform basic computations. We're not talking about readiness for MIT. Even at the nation's community colleges, 40% or more of students require remediation, which amounts to factory recall repair work for a defective original job. The beleaguered taxpayer pays twice for the same service, which far too often fails a second time.

Federal and state governments have rightly focused on high school graduation rates as a paramount goal. The diploma has long been recognized as the first essential step toward productive adult life. My home state of Indiana, in one typical initiative, prohibits dropping out of high school without a personal conference attended by the student and parents, where the likely negative consequences are reviewed in detail. Graduation rates are widely publicized, and schools scramble to look as good as possible.

But the opportunity to grant exceptions on graduation requirements—justifiably intended for those for whom English is a second language or who have special needs—can turn into a gaping loophole, exploited to "waive through" students who fall far short of any adequate preparation for either work or citizenship. In pre-pandemic 2019, an encouraging 87% statewide graduation rate was tainted by a record 12.4% of diplomas granted through waivers.

Through one of the educational reforms for which I advocated as governor, Indiana prohibits the so-called social promotion of children from third to fourth grade until they pass a reading test. It's well-established that up to that point, children must learn to read, so that beyond it they can read to learn. Yet far too many schools choose to shuffle along kids who are not reading-ready, in most cases dooming them to struggle and failure later on.

The reform worked, in a uniquely rapid and emphatic fashion. In the first post-reform cycle of national assessments, Indiana fourth graders jumped from twenty-seventh to fourteenth. Two years later, the state ranked ninth. The extra costs for summer tutoring, or the reputational bruise from too many youngsters having to repeat third grade, clearly got the system's attention.

So a little accountability can go a long way. But whenever the K–12 system can devise ways to disguise its shortcomings, it will. Last year, Oregon made a cryingstock of itself by ending proficiency exams for its high school graduates. Obviously too few students, including too few in specific demographic categories, were learning what they were supposed to. A lot of losing football coaches in Oregon wish they, too, could just stop keeping score, but, of course, football is too important for such nonsense.

Turns out the idea of an education warranty flickered briefly, a couple of decades ago. A few isolated high schools around the country, and even the Los Angeles Unified School District, touted guarantees of proficiency in reading, writing, and problem-solving, with free retraining for graduates not meeting that standard. But all sank without a trace.

After a decade in higher education, I'm sure that even a modicum of risk to an institution would produce behavior change. If there's anything that motivates college administrators as much as money, it's reputation, and getting a bill for a share of graduates' debt defaults would deliver a hit to both. The reaction in the K–12 world would be similar.

When a coffee pot, a lawn mower, or a smartwatch fails to deliver as advertised, we don't hesitate to ask for a remedy, and we don't expect to be charged a second time. When, aside from public safety, the most important service we purchase from government breaches its warranty, why do we settle for so much less?

How higher education can counter the dangerous weakening of American self-governance.
December 13, 2021

Add to the long list of Johns Hopkins University's services to the nation the book its president, Ronald J. Daniels (as much as I wish I could claim a familial connection, there is none), recently published. It makes an important contribution to not one but two urgent and topical subjects: the weakening of American self-governance and the overall role of higher education in countering that dangerous trend.

That contribution begins with the book's title: *What Universities Owe Democracy.* The occupational sector in which I have now worked for almost a decade is not, shall we say, much given to self-criticism. I have sat through innumerable speeches and panels about what a benighted, unappreciative society owes us—credit, respect, and always, always more money—but few, if any, that started with a question about reciprocal obligations and whether our institutions collectively might be failing to fulfill them.

Daniels devotes relatively little space to documenting the problem. He doesn't need to. Americans' ignorance about the workings, the theory, and the fundamental values inherent in their country's system of self-government have been painfully plain to see for decades now. The book's essence is a series of thoughtful and constructive suggestions for addressing the problem, to the extent that higher education can do so.

Those proposals start with an end to legacy preferences in admissions, to expand opportunities for first-generation and minority students. Daniels advocates reforms to make scientific research more open, transparent, and verifiable, to begin repairing credibility damaged by conflicts of interest, foreign influence, and too many overhyped, unreproducible, and spurious research studies.

Closer to the core of the problem, he calls for "purposeful pluralism," a cluster of actions to "deliberately design campuses with an eye to engagement and dialogue." These include randomization of first-year roommate assignments, curricular changes that require broader exposure outside chosen major subjects, and other steps to move students outside their "enclaves of familiarity."

He notes that universities are among those increasingly rare places where Americans of different backgrounds are sure to encounter one another, quoting John Stuart Mill: "It is hardly possible to overstate the value ... of placing human beings in contact with other persons dissimilar to themselves, and with modes of thought and action unlike those with which they are familiar." To those who have "adopted a hands-off approach toward campus interaction" or, worse yet, enabled or encouraged self-segregation, Daniels says, "Universities were not built to referee; they were built to educate." Novel concept.

Between the goals of "engagement" and "dialogue," achieving the latter is probably the harder slog. As with civic illiteracy, the monotonous groupthink on the nation's campuses, and its frequent enforcement against dissidents, were long ago documented beyond debate. Daniels calls for adoption of the Chicago Principles of free expression, diversification of monolithically left-wing faculties and, interestingly, a revival of the debating societies, sometimes called "little republics," that he nostalgically reminds the reader were once at the center of university life. He hopes schools will "infuse debate into campus programming."

One of his boldest proposals is that universities adopt a "democracy requirement" for graduation. Daniels believes that propounding, and living, the values of tolerance and individual dignity, while cultivating competencies such as basic historical knowledge and the skills of peaceful reasoning and persuasion, are now a central obligation of his school and all its counterparts.

The heart of his case is that our universities, as much as any institution in society, should be exemplars of democratic behavior and values, "at the forefront of modeling a healthy, multiethnic democracy." Brave as the book is, the author is too gentle about the degree to which today's colleges fall short of this ideal.

He says they have been "passive" about promoting diversity of thought and open dialogue among differing opinions. But in countless cases, they have been not passive but complicit, allowing, or even colluding in, the squelching of departures from dogmatic fads of the day. Many have been not models of healthy democracy but of its opposite. A first step back in paying what those universities "owe" would be Hippocratic, to stop making the problem worse.

Anyone with my job can benefit from Daniels's wisdom, and high standards. Our university has no legacy preference, but we still have curricular silos and we do permit entering students to choose their roommates. We have implemented a civic literacy requirement, but not one as extensive as Daniels appears to have in mind. We enacted the Chicago Principles, but cannot claim to have truly "infused debate" into daily campus life. He has given us a lot to contemplate.

One hopes that Ronald Daniels's sterling academic reputation, and that of his institution, leads to a wide readership among those in the sector to whom he addresses himself. But for those higher ed leaders who do not get around to it, let's hope they at least notice the title.

Kids can't write. Parents, this is your chance to help.
April 8, 2020

Looking for another useful shut-in activity? How about one that helps your child while addressing a serious national shortcoming, the sorry ineptness of young Americans at writing the English language? Try being an amateur Mrs. Heckle.

She was that teacher you never forget. Tough, uncompromising, as intimidating as a grizzly, though she barely weighed a hundred pounds. Nina Heckle taught us ninth-grade English the way I imagine Vince Lombardi taught football. We were convinced the principal had dialed Hollywood: "Hi, Central Casting, can you send me the classic severe English teacher? You know . . . bun hairdo, half glasses, perpetual frown?" Wherever Mrs. Heckle (an obvious Hollywood stage name, we thought) came from, we were lucky to be assigned to her class.

There was reading, lots of it, and nothing fluffy or trendy on the list. There were grammar drills, and sentence diagramming, and vocabulary quizzes. But most of all, there was writing. Book reports, essays, short stories, our juvenile attempts at poetry.

When she returned our homework submissions, there were corrections all over them. Even the best efforts, the rare As, would come back with constructive suggestions for clearer syntax or a brighter metaphor. And woe to the author of an incomplete sentence, a mistake in punctuation, or, terror of terrors, a misspelled word.

As memorable as Mrs. Heckle was, my classmates and I would have turned out to be passable writers even if we'd missed her. At our fine, late-1960s public high school, we encountered writing assignments, and their rigorous correction, in virtually every class that wasn't math.

Watching my four daughters move through high school, I knew things had changed. But that still didn't prepare me for firsthand exposure to the truly sad state of the English language in the hands of today's students—even postsecondary students, and even the most otherwise talented of those.

Finding myself employed in higher education in late career, I undertook to teach a course, one that I have subsequently offered for several years. As I expected, I learned more than my students probably did, especially about how much effort it takes to construct a useful curriculum, convey essential content, and try to excite young minds to pursue that content further.

But by far the lesson that hit me hardest was that the kids can't write. Even in a course fully subscribed by students from our Honors College, a class full of future doctors, business executives, computer engineers, and the like, the quality of written expression was almost uniformly—sorry to choose this word—pathetic.

In higher ed circles, this is now a very old topic. Now and then, one can find an "it's not really so bad" analysis, but the vast weight of the literature comes to the same conclusion I did when grading papers and final exams: even our best and brightest all too often don't write like it.

Some will claim that a digital, electronic world has obsoleted written communication. They're not talking to the world's employers, who are expressing a renewed appreciation for the value of the humanities, and more and more concern about the inability of new hires to communicate well, either orally or especially in writing. In a 2018 national survey by the National Association of Colleges and Employers, written communication skills were at the top of the list of qualities prized by today's businesses.

As in other respects, we must keep trying to do better at the K–12 level, but we can't count on that system to fix the problem. As the American Psychological Association reported on a study of adolescents' media use from 1976 to 2016, students are reading less and less, of less and less rigorous material. It's pretty hard to write excellently if you haven't read any excellent writing.

And the amount of writing assigned in today's high schools has dwindled dramatically. Most recently, colleges of education, including the one at the university

I lead, are reporting that tomorrow's teachers will struggle to teach good writing because their own writing skills are so weak.

The thought occurs that, unlike much else about a modern youngster's education, home remedies might be possible—especially when the coronavirus has corralled so many students at home. Mom or Dad might not be able to solve that differential equation or explain the second law of thermodynamics, but they could give writing assignments of their own. A journal of the family vacation, a report on a book the family read together, an actual letter (on actual paper!) written to Grandma or Uncle Russ might produce more composition practice than all of next semester.

Because all the evidence says that we just don't have many Nina Heckles anymore.

Mrs. Heckle, I feel you watching, and I know "obsoleted," above, was a somewhat clumsy usage. But it is a legitimate transitive verb. I looked it up.

Here is a powerful alternative to student loans.
November 28, 2019

Robert F. Kennedy used to observe that all progress depends on change, and change always has its enemies. Occasionally, a new idea can be menaced not just by its foes but also by its friends. So it is with the income share agreement, or ISA, a partial response to the bleak outlook regarding student loan debt.

In an ISA, a student borrows nothing but rather has his or her education supported by an investor, in return for a contract to pay a specified percentage of income for a fixed number of years after graduation. Rates and time vary with the discipline of the degree achieved and the amount of tuition assistance the student obtained.

An ISA is dramatically more student-friendly than a loan. All the risk shifts from the student to the investing entity; if a career starts slowly, or not at all, the student's obligation drops or goes to zero. Think of an ISA as equity instead of debt, or as working one's way through college—after college.

By contrast, student debt sits there and compounds, whether a borrower does well or poorly in the working world. Every day we read of young people—and some not so young anymore—who got behind on their loans and may never catch up.

Not surprisingly, the ISA concept has attracted plenty of interest. At Purdue, the university I lead, hundreds of students have such contracts in place, and other colleges large and small are joining the ISA movement. Beyond traditional higher education, coding academies and other skill-specific schools are making the same offer: study for free, and pay us back after you get the good job we are confident you'll land.

Although the very nature of ISAs protects the participant, early adopters such as Purdue have built in safeguards. A user-friendly computer simulator provides quick, transparent comparisons with various public and private loan options. No investee pays anything for the first six months after graduation or until annual income exceeds $20,000. For those graduates who get off to fast career starts, a ceiling of 250% of the dollars that purchased their education limits total repayment. One of the rare issues drawing broad bipartisan support these days, ISAs are the subject of pending legislation in Congress that would enact similar boundaries.

We never recommend an ISA in lieu of taxpayer-subsidized federal loans—you can't beat their artificially low rates—but compared with higher-interest private loans or federal "parent-plus" loans, they are often far preferable. And they always carry the advantage of shifting the risk and fixing the payment obligation at an affordable share of income.

ISAs have emerged principally in response to the wreckage of the federal student debt system, but they also represent an opportunity for higher education to address another legitimate criticism: that it accepts no accountability for its results. As the lead investor of the two funds Purdue has raised to date, our university is expressing confidence that its graduates are ready for the world of work.

One of many ironies in the higher ed world is that so many people who style themselves as modern or progressive are reflexively reactionary at the first scent of a new idea or a change in business as usual. Objections to ISAs span the spectrum from sophistry to silliness.

Facts or logic being unavailable, critics of ISAs often resort to name-calling. A favorite is "indentured servitude," an enjoyably ironic brickbat because servitude is a good description of federal student loans, which keep growing regardless of life circumstances and are difficult to escape even in bankruptcy. My personal favorite attack came from a former Obama administration education advisor, who, stumped for anything rational to tell the *Wall Street Journal* about ISAs a few years ago, fell back on "It feels icky to me." Got me there, pal.

It's no surprise when lifers in any sector leap to quash a new idea that challenges either their credentials or profits. But the ISA could also fall victim to the well-intentioned embrace of its new fans. The Education Department, noting ISAs' many advantages, has talked about offering its own version of the agreements. Advocates of the programs appreciate the affirmation, but we worry about becoming friendly fire casualties if the federal government decides to become a competitor. Uncle Sam nationalized student lending a decade ago, and we've all seen how well that worked out.

The best test of an innovation is its acceptance and performance in the marketplace. Whether strangled or hugged to death, a young innovation trying to grow is always at risk of asphyxiation. Here's hoping that both enemies and frenemies will stay their busy hands and allow income share agreements, and perhaps even better ideas, a chance to try to improve the financing of higher education.

For college admissions, let's value grit over GPAs.
November 28, 2018

Resuming a debate that has arisen occasionally in the past, some U.S. colleges have announced that they will no longer require applicants to provide standardized test scores, but instead will look to high school grade point averages and subjective information.

The institution I lead, Purdue University, will not be joining that group. A review of all the data tells us that no admissions criteria that ignores either the SAT or ACT exams can predict with equivalent accuracy a student's college performance, or his or her best placement level in critical freshman courses such as mathematics. Accepting a high school A at face value and enrolling a student in a calculus course beyond his or her capabilities does the student a serious disservice by risking an avoidable failure.

Still, assigning greater weight to high school grade point averages has its merits. In many cases, the GPA proves to be a reliable indicator of discipline, persistence, and resilience—characteristics necessary to succeed at the college level (to say nothing of in adult life). In the current vernacular, these traits are often collectively called grit. Enrollment experts agree on its significance. The problem is in knowing when a high GPA reflects it and when it doesn't.

The challenge for today's college admissions officer is like the one faced by corporate recruiters: In an era of rampant grade inflation, which grades can you believe? Businesses began learning years ago not to put much stock in diplomas from schools where the average graduate's GPA is 3.5 or higher and may not be at all indicative of real learning or readiness for the modern workplace.

Last year, researchers reported that nearly half of high school seniors in 2016—47%—graduated with an A average. That's up from 38.9% in 1998. As ordinary students increasingly "earn" higher marks, teachers help top students stand out by granting them extra credit of various kinds. The result: It is now not unusual for colleges to see high school GPAs above a "perfect" 4.0. Soon, it will be time to get real and reset the scale with its top at either 5.0 or 6.0. This GPA inflation occurred while national ACT and SAT scores were going down.

It is increasingly clear that, though a strong high school GPA may indicate grit, it can also just be a sign of lax grading—producing not resilience but its opposite.

The emotional fragility of many young people today is, by now, a well-documented phenomenon. College students' psychological problems and mental illness are very real; every school I know of approaches the matter with utter seriousness and responsibility. Running a college necessitates ever-growing numbers of counselors and therapists, but keeping up can be difficult. Requests for appointments start almost as soon as a new class arrives. This fall at our school, at least one freshman sought a counseling session before setting foot on campus.

The trend has spawned a host of explanatory theories. Many have pointed to parental overprotectiveness as the primary cause, and, no doubt, that is a real factor. In the new book *The Coddling of the American Mind*, co-authors Jonathan Haidt and Greg Lukianoff write that many young people, having too rarely handled problems or adversity on their own, now instinctively run looking for an adult at the first whiff of difficulty.

On campuses, one sees plenty of support for the authors' contention. Calls and emails from worried parents—not only to the student but also directly to university offices—are a daily fact of life. The phrase "helicopter parent" is no longer adequate; now you hear about "lawnmower parents."

Many problems brought to our counselors are of social origin—loneliness, cyberbullying, just plain homesickness—but many others stem from academic anxiety, and small wonder. Freshmen who rarely saw a B during their K–12 years can be severely jolted when handed back a paper marked C. Too many participation trophies when growing up is lousy preparation for life at a reasonably rigorous university, let alone in the real world beyond.

Of course, one easy solution for colleges is just to go with the grade inflation flow, and obviously many institutions of higher education have chosen that route. Places determined instead to stretch and challenge students, aiming to help them achieve their full potential, will have to take on the trickier task of identifying and fostering true grit, providing quality counseling everywhere it's needed without worsening what is already an overly therapeutic culture.

Meanwhile, let's hope the College Board comes up with a new GPA—Grit Potential Assessment. I guarantee you, our university will be the first customer.

Health care isn't our only ludicrously expensive industry.
February 6, 2018

Just for fun, let's design an economic sector guaranteed to cost too much. Then you guess what it is. For openers, we will sell a product deemed a necessity, with little or no option for the customer to avoid us altogether. Next, we will arrange to get paid for inputs, not outputs—how much we do, not how well we do it. We will make certain that actual results are difficult or impossible to measure with confidence. And we'll layer on a pile of complex federal regulations to run up administrative costs.

Then, and here's the clincher, we will persuade the marketplace to flood our economic Eden with payments not from the user but from some third party. This will assure that the customer, insulated from true costs, will behave irrationally, often overconsuming and abandoning the consumerist judgment he practices at the grocery store or while Internet shopping.

Presto! Guaranteed excessive spending, much of it staying in the pockets of the lucky producers.

You say, "Oh, sure, this is American health care." As soon as we took the fatal misstep of untaxed health insurance—compounding the error of World War II–era wage and price controls with a greater mistake—we were doomed to a future of overly expensive medical care.

Your answer is correct but incomplete. It worked so well in health care, we decided to repeat the formula with higher education. Some sort of postsecondary education is, in fact, necessary for a fully productive life in this economy, but by evading accountability for quality, regulating it heavily, and opening a hydrant of public subsidies in the form of government grants and loans, we have constructed another system of guaranteed overruns. It is the opposite of an accident that the only three pricing categories that have outpaced health care over recent decades are college tuition, room and board, and books.

Health care has been crab-walking its way toward a modicum of consumerism through higher co-payments, deductibles, and health savings accounts. Foolishly, the federal government has generally thrown obstacles in the path of these adjustments, but it has tried in its own clumsy way to effect some cost reduction by putting providers at some risk for poor performance and results.

In much the same manner, a promising movement is advancing in education to put some of the risk of lousy results—students who do not graduate or who graduate without having learned enough to earn their way in the world—on the institutions that educated them. It is about time. This game has been skinless far too long.

Various approaches are being examined as Congress advances a long-overdue rewrite of the Higher Education Act. As a condition of participating in the federal student aid programs, universities could be required to either guarantee a percentage of the dollars loaned to their students, or be penalized a specified amount based on default rates. Or be charged a yearly premium for an insurance fund that would, at least partially, protect taxpayers against what has turned into the latest massive driver of national debt. With more than $1.4 trillion in student debt, and nonpayment rates climbing past 45%, the multibillion-dollar write-offs we have seen already are just the leading edge of what is coming.

All these approaches have merit, and any of them would be a huge improvement over the built-for-excess model under which we've been operating. Just as health care spending can be adjusted for the health status of a given population, schools' exposure or premiums could vary with the characteristics of their student bodies.

My guess is that even a small degree of risk-sharing in higher education would cause significant behavior change. While the hydrant gushes unimpeded, schools have been free to duck hard choices—or even modest priority-setting. Most practice "incremental budgeting," an unintentionally self-indicting term that indicates that each year's budget spreads additional funds around evenly, with no serious thought given to ending obsolete or useless programs, and no meaningful prioritization among existing activities. Even a small charge, plus the embarrassment of its public announcement, would probably jar many schools from their complacent ruts.

Better counseling of students and their families, more attention to reducing the time it takes to earn a degree, and, most straightforward of all, controlling how much is charged in the first place would all likely become more common. Progress is not impossible; at Purdue University, these actions in combination have reduced total student debt by 37% over the past five years.

Some of my higher ed colleagues have recently described themselves as "blindsided" by growing criticisms of our sector. In the case of student debt, everyone should have seen the issue coming. An important secondary feature of the at-risk reforms is that they have attracted a unique level of support across our fractured political spectrum. Members of Congress and think tank scholars from both sides are actively advocating these changes in one form or another. These days, when a proposal leads people to lay down their partisan cudgels and cooperate, it must be an exceptionally good idea.

Dear Condoleezza Rice: Good luck fixing the NCAA. February 1, 2018

Dear Condi,

That invitation to speak on our campus still stands, but I see that you'll be a little too busy this spring, now that you've accepted yet another service opportunity as chair of the new commission tasked by the NCAA to help it reform college basketball. You've always been a sucker for a good cause; and if ever a cause qualified, this one does.

When the FBI revealed its findings about the corrupt connections among shoe companies, agents, a few big-time college programs and coaches, and the Amateur Athletic Union, or AAU (the first *A* increasingly looks like a misnomer), no one near the sport was shocked. The existence of this part of the cesspool has been in plain view for years. Those in a position to stop the scandals spawned by the one-and-done era—in which many top-tier players were required to enroll in college for one year before bolting for the NBA—have been either powerless to do so or actively interested in perpetuating the status quo.

When it was discovered that, at what we've always considered an academically admirable school, championships had been won by teams loaded with players who took completely phony classes, most of us were sincerely shocked. We were stunned again when, after years of cogitation, the NCAA delivered a penalty of . . . nothing. It was a final confession of futility, confirming the necessity of this special commission if any meaningful change is going to happen from the collegiate end.

If the NCAA is impotent to stop the abuses, the NBA is all but an unindicted co-conspirator. The current arrangement works out beautifully for the league: it gets a free minor league player development system, a massively televised show-case for its next round of stars, and one less argument with a players union that prefers to limit, through its ineligible-until-age-19 rule, the number of competitors for the few hundred NBA roster spots. The league has every incentive to keep dragging its feet, so the most promising avenue for reform is to make the college game inhospitable to NBA exploitation and the rotten collusion that the one-and-done world fosters.

As for solutions, one can start by observing that almost no change could make things worse. I don't pretend to know the single best answer, but it's not hard to list a number of possibilities.

We could require a year of readiness, meaning that freshmen could practice but not play while they became acclimated to college life. This was the NCAA rule for many decades, and it makes great sense unless a "student" really has no intention of pursuing a real education.

Or the NCAA could simply use the rule already in effect for baseball, which gives young aspirants a choice between going professional straight from high school or entering college and staying a minimum of three years. Either of these approaches separates those seriously interested in higher education from those forced by the current system to pretend they are.

Another idea would be to allow players to depart early for the NBA, but the scholarships they received would be required to remain vacant for the balance of their four-year terms. Coaches who want to chase that next championship with full-time players masquerading as students could do so, but the following few seasons might be tough with rosters filled with walk-ons.

I'm convinced the college game would be more, not less, popular if a handful of would-be pretend students, whose names fans barely get a chance to know, instead went straight from high school to some sort of professional league. Doing so would certainly bring more parity and fairness to the college game. The play would still be amazingly athletic—most of us fans would not be able to tell the difference—and schools with genuine academic and conduct standards would no longer be at such a competitive disadvantage.

It's startling how concentrated the phenomenon is. In the past five years, 45% of all five-star recruits, and 58% of all one-and-dones, have gone to just five schools. Our entire fourteen-member Big Ten conference, by contrast, has had

9.2% of the first category and 6.4% of the latter, collectively. One could tell conferences like ours that if we don't like today's situation, we can just establish our own rules, but unilateral disarmament never seems like a good idea.

It troubles me to give up on my friends and neighbors at the NCAA, but when the FBI beats you to a monstrously obvious problem in your own backyard, you're clearly never going to fix it on your own.

So thanks for serving, Condi, and best of luck. If you thought Iranian sanctions or North Korean nukes were hard problems, wait until you try this one. And take your time about that invitation. Go save us from ourselves.

How student debt harms the economy: In 2010–13,
the percentage of younger people owning part of
a new business dropped to 3.6% from 6.1%.
Wall Street Journal
January 27, 2015

To the growing catalog of damage caused by the decades-long run-up in the cost of higher education, we may have to add another casualty. On top of the harm high tuition and other charges are inflicting on young people, and the way their struggles are holding back today's economy, we must add the worry that tomorrow's economy will suffer, too.

Ever-escalating tuitions, especially in the past dozen years, have produced an explosion of associated debt, as students and their families resorted to borrowing to cover college prices that are the only major expense item in the economy that is growing faster than health care. According to the Federal Reserve, educational debt has shot past every other category—credit cards, auto loans, refinancings—except home mortgages, reaching some $1.3 trillion this year. Analyses in the *Wall Street Journal* and by Experian in 2014 show that 40 million people, roughly 70% of recent graduates, are now borrowers. In the class of 2014, the average borrower left with an average load of $33,000.

Even though the debt balloon is a fairly young phenomenon, several damaging results are already evident. Research from the Pew Research Center and Rutgers shows that today's 20- and 30-year-olds are delaying marriage and delaying childbearing, both unhelpful trends from an economic and social standpoint. Between 25% and 40% of borrowers report postponing homes, cars, and other major purchases. Half say that their student loans are increasing their risk of defaulting on other bills. Strikingly, 45% of graduates aged 24 and under are living back at home or with a family member of some kind.

Now comes evidence that it's not just consumer spending that these debts are denting, but also economic dynamism. A variety of indicators suggest that the debt burden is weighing on the engine that has always characterized American economic leadership—and the factor that many have assumed will overcome many structural and self-imposed challenges: our propensity to innovate and to invent new vehicles of wealth creation.

For instance, the U.S., despite its proud protestations about how creative and risk-taking it is, has fallen in multiple worldwide measures of entrepreneurship. A drop in such activity by the young is playing a part. From 2010 to 2013, the *Journal* reported on January 2, the percentage of younger people who reported owning a part of a new business dropped to 3.6% from 6.1%. Over the past ten years, the percentage of businesses started by someone under 34 fell to 22.7% from 26.4%. Common sense says that the seven in ten graduates who enter the working world owing money may be part of this shift.

New data strengthens this hypothesis. Working with the Gallup Research organization, Purdue scholars devised last year's Gallup-Purdue Index, the largest survey ever of U.S. college graduates. Among its findings: 26% of those who left school debt-free have started at least one business. Among those with debt of $40,000 or more, only 16% had done so.

Controlling the cost of higher education, and expanding access to its undeniable benefits, is first of all a social and moral obligation of those in a position to affect it. Purdue is midway through what is so far a three-year tuition freeze. Coupled with reductions in the costs of room and board and textbooks, these actions have brought down our total cost of attendance for each of the last two years, for the first time on record.

Aggressive counseling of students about the dangers of too much borrowing and the alternatives available to them has also helped, as total Purdue student borrowings have dropped by 18% since 2012. That represents some $40 million these superbly talented young engineers, computer scientists, and other new workers will have to spend, or perhaps invest in their own dreams of enterprise. At Purdue, where we give students the ownership of any intellectual property they create and support their attempts to give birth to new products and companies, a significant number of such dreams are likely to become real.

Today's young Americans have a very legitimate beef with previous generations. A pathetically weak recovery has left millions of them unemployed, underemployed, and with falling incomes, not the rising ones their predecessors could expect. And, never forget, they are already saddled with a lifetime per capita debt of some $700,000 (to date) to pay not for debts they incurred, but for those run up in entitlement programs such as Social Security, Social Security Disability, and Medicare, explicitly designed to tax the young to subsidize their elders.

For future generations to enjoy the higher living standards America has always promised, nothing matters more than that the U.S. remains a land where miracles of innovation and entrepreneurship happen consistently. As a matter of generational fairness, and as an essential element of national economic success, the burden of high tuitions and student debt must be alleviated, and soon.

KEEPING OUR DEMOCRACY (GOOD POLICY AND PRACTICE)

Sincerity in policy debates? Of course.
Seriousness? That's another matter.
August 22, 2022

Countless times during the Daniels girls' adolescence, usually around music preferences or sartorial choices, I got the sardonic question, "Dad, seriously?" Often these days one has that same reaction, listening to a number of national debates over topics that stir strong passions but weak prescriptions. It leads one to worry that the vaunted American practicality—the do-what-it-takes instinct that has served the nation so well—is being superseded by an impulse that values winning an argument more than actually improving the world or solving a problem.

It isn't necessary to dispute the sincerity of an opponent's viewpoint to be exasperated by its indifference to plain facts, or to any credible ideas about how to improve the outcome at issue. It's distressingly easy to find examples of the syndrome on both sides of our partisan and cultural crevasse.

Consider the essential goal of feeding a growing world population a far better diet than has been within its reach historically, and doing so in ways that protect the planet and its resources. Modern bioscience and agricultural technologies can enable huge improvements in pesticide reduction, insecticide reduction, and water conservation, all while producing more and better food on less land, food with more nutritional value and even therapeutic benefit. Yet, many of those proclaiming their commitment to feeding the world take every opportunity to deprecate and obstruct the use of these proven safe technologies. Let's postulate their sincerity; the problem is they aren't serious.

Or the unwillingness of those who, with full justification, call for reasserting control of our borders but have no realistic suggestion about the millions of immigrants already here illegally, many now with firm roots in this country.

Or those who lament an obsolete, decaying national infrastructure but insist on the wage laws and absurd permitting requirements that make rebuilding impossibly slow and expensive.

Or those bemoaning the massive, truly dangerous state of the federal debt but are unwilling to advocate the far-reaching entitlement reforms without which no combination of policies can make much difference. Sincere, but not serious.

But enough griping. On at least one front, we are seeing some green shoots of practicality.

After decades of blocking the development of nuclear power, some of those most dedicated to the goal of reducing net carbon dioxide emissions to zero have begun to recognize that the goal is a fantasy without nuclear power as a major factor. The *New Yorker* has covered the phenomenon in an article headlined "The Activists Who Embrace Nuclear Power." In June, the *Economist* editorialized, "Politicians need to tell voters that their desire for an energy transition that eschews both fossil fuels and nuclear power is a dangerous illusion."

This growing awareness is fortified by a host of positive technological developments. New modular designs incorporate passive safety systems obviating the risks of human error or mechanical failure that remain possible in earlier generation plants. Smaller than the plants of today, assembled by experienced workers in dedicated facilities, and transported to the site of operation, these small modular reactors, or SMRs, should be far less expensive to build.

The environmental benefits go far beyond the primary goal of carbon dioxide reduction. Eliminating fossil fuels without deploying more nuclear energy would entail massive degradation: huge new mines to extract minerals like copper, aluminum, and lithium, vast land areas to host the wind and solar capacity of which some advocates dream, toxic disposal challenges of batteries and worn-out windmills and solar panels on a scale that makes handling nuclear waste seem trivial.

The ever-escalating demand for more electricity is a global phenomenon, but few places experience it more directly than a growing, research-intensive university. Our institution has launched an exploration, led by scientists, engineers, and other experts, to examine whether an SMR might be the best long-term way to achieve net-zero carbon while meeting the tests of affordability and reliability. Sincerity requires that we give it a serious look.

The savvy political analyst William Schneider once wrote that an ideologue is someone who believes that if something is wrong, it can't work, whereas a pragmatist believes that if something works, it must be right. He went on to say that most Americans are pragmatists.

Or we were. Schneider offered that formulation in the 1980s.

Maybe if someone isn't prepared to be serious about the means of solving a problem, they weren't really all that sincere after all.

Let in every last Ukrainian who wants to come here.
April 6, 2022

He was already well up in years when I first met him. A distinguished professor of economics at a nearby university, he had offered his advisory services to a young Senate candidate, Richard G. Lugar, who would become one of the nation's great statesmen over nearly four decades. In a delightful Eastern European accent that I wasn't cosmopolitan enough to identify exactly, János Horváth would dissect and explain plainly inflation, oil crises, stagflation, and other dreary, complex phenomena, somehow always with a twinkle and a smile.

The accent turned out to be of his native Hungary. When I later learned his life story, not from him but from his colleagues, I wondered how he came by the relentless good cheer, because his story was not an easy one.

As a promising young academic after World War II, Janos had become active in pro-democracy politics and had earned a place in the short-lived Hungarian national government of 1956 as the president of the National Reconstruction Council. A grainy photo from that fateful November shows a youthful Horvath on the floor of the Hungarian parliament.

Then the tanks rolled, and the Soviet dictators did what such people always do after quashing freedom. They went after those most likely to cause trouble again: the political leaders, the journalists, the non-quisling academics. Like thousands of his countrymen, the cream of Hungarian society, Horvath was forced to flee for his life. And where better than the land that best embodied the freedoms he had hoped to bring to his own country?

The rest of his story is extraordinary only in its ordinariness. He was forced to redo his doctorate from scratch. Legend has it he worked his way through Columbia University as a janitor. Like millions of immigrants, but especially those who came to the United States not only for economic betterment but to find political freedom, he loved this country and its traditions more than so many of those pampered and spoiled by the good fortune of having been born here. It's commonly observed that immigrants make great Americans. I dissent slightly; those I've known make the best Americans.

A catalog of the immense human talent that has fallen into the lap of this country, thanks to the bestiality of statists abroad, can and has filled volumes. Half of the Americans who won the Nobel Prize in physics from 1943 to 1969 were European refugees. Other examples: from Hungary, Intel pioneer Andrew Grove; from Germany, Henry Kissinger; from Cuba, Coca-Cola chief executive Roberto Goizueta.

And from Czechoslovakia, the wonderful Madeleine K. Albright, who died last month. It was Albright, as secretary of state, who in 1998 labeled the United States "the indispensable nation." Some native-born Americans obviously disagree, but few of her fellow "Americans by choice" do.

Immigrant populations are the product of highly promising self-selection. By definition, they are adventuresome risk-takers. The millions who have come here seeking economic betterment make great workers. At least in places where they cannot become instant wards of the state, they are prepared to work hard and provide for themselves.

The most valuable of all are those fleeing political repression. They, too, become great workers and citizens. As mentioned, they are likely to bring unusual talents with them, the kind that might get them jailed or shot at home but can flower powerfully when turned loose in a free economy and polity.

So here we are again. Millions of Ukrainians already have fled the dictator's tanks. And although the Horvaths of their nation are mainly still at home fighting, there is every chance that again many will have to rebuild their lives in the American refuge. It won't be merely compassionate and humane for the United States to take in every one who seeks to come; it will be smart.

The university I serve has committed resources to support Ukrainian scholars who feel forced to flee their homeland, and we are in touch with several already. Our hope is to provide them a haven to continue their scholarship until they can return to a safe and free Ukraine. But if, as in Hungary, Czechoslovakia, and elsewhere, the dictator's tanks prevent that for a long time, the United States will experience yet another windfall, of both talent and appreciation for the "blessings of liberty."

Janos Horvath waited more than three decades. But after the breakthrough of freedom in 1989, he offered his wisdom—as he had offered it to Richard Lugar and countless American young people—to his native land. Another, highly moving photo shows a 70-something Horvath (he died in 2019 at 98) in the same chamber, being sworn in as a member of the new, post-Soviet Hungarian parliament.

We hope for a Ukrainian victory and the survival of freedom in that brutalized country. But until that survival is ensured, we should take them in, not just some arbitrary number, but every one who wants to come. It's as much in our interest as theirs.

Rebating tax dollars doesn't "cost" a state anything. It's your money!
March 21, 2022

A newspaper account early this year reported on pending legislation that would "slash billions of dollars' worth of taxes" in my home state of Indiana. The article was more interesting for its word choices than for its content. Twice, it stated that the proposal would "cost the state" money. Twice, it warned that the state would "lose out" on large sums. And the article capped its evident alarm by labeling the bill a "potential hit" against both state and local governments.

This is not to pick on the writer. As yet another young reporter in the parched landscape of what was once local journalism, she couldn't bring a firsthand, historically informed philosophical understanding to the assignment. The article simply showed the implicit biases now thoroughly ingrained across what these days is referred to as the corporate press. The negative slant about the tax policy in question, a legitimately debatable matter, is less important than the mentality it reflects about whose money we're discussing.

I can't and don't pretend to objectivity about the policy, which provides that, when state reserves exceed a specified percentage of the annual budget at the end of a two-year fiscal period, they are automatically returned per capita to the taxpayers, the same amount for every return. I proposed the concept while seeking reelection as governor in 2008, and it was enacted in 2011.

In a TV ad suggesting the idea, I said of surpluses: better the money stays in your pocket than burns a hole in the pocket of government. That seemed to make sense to the citizens who employed me, and ultimately to a large majority of their elected representatives.

The refund was first triggered in 2012, with millions of Hoosiers receiving $111 each, or $222 on joint returns. For 2021, when the surplus reached 23% of the budget, more than 4 million taxpayers will receive—or, better said, retain—a slightly larger per capita amount. If current revenue forecasts are even remotely accurate, a third and still larger refund would occur in 2023.

The refunds are the same for all taxpayers for two reasons. It is administratively simple, so that the public can readily understand it, and a large bureaucracy can execute it without errors. Secondly, it is progressive, more valuable to people of moderate means than to their wealthier neighbors.

The original bill has been tinkered with a couple of times since its author left public life. Now half of the "surplus surplus" goes to further strengthen already solid pension funds. And this year, an almost unanimous, bipartisan General Assembly extended the refunds to people not paying income taxes, on the sensible basis that these citizens do pay sales and excise taxes to the state.

Readers in a city where mere billions of dollars are rounding errors, and which is surrounded by some of the nation's richest counties, cannot be expected to be impressed with sums like these, although I can attest that for many Indiana households they are not immaterial. But the amounts refunded, or even the fiscal brake of getting excess dollars out of the government's hands before someone invents a way to spend them, were never the central point.

The real point, one hopes a didactic one, was that property in a free society belongs not to the state but to its people, and it should be expropriated by the state only for truly necessary purposes, in truly necessary amounts.

It's more than just a matter of money, because every act of taxation imposes a diminution of freedom.

During many visits to high school classrooms, I often engaged in a little stunt in which I would ask if anyone was carrying a $5 bill. When some unsuspecting student produced one, I would walk over, grab the bill, saying, "Many thanks," as I pocketed the money, and keep walking. When the tittering subsided, I would feign surprise, but before returning the cash, I would make the point that their classmate was now slightly less free than a moment ago, no longer in possession of the five bucks or the option of deciding what to do with it. As I said in that original TV ad, "After all, it's your money."

Next month, Indiana taxpayers will receive checks restoring to them some $125 apiece of income they earned. While by then it might buy only a couple of gasoline fill-ups or family meals, it will convey an important message: "After all, it's your money."

An old saying in our state holds that "when a feller says, 'It ain't the money, it's the principle of the thing'... it's the money." Good line, and generally true. But sometimes, it actually is the principle.

Let's have more than two candidates in the general election presidential debates.
November 11, 2019

The candidates and issues in presidential campaigns vary wildly from cycle to cycle, but one constant for decades has been the general election televised debates. Ever since the two major parties asserted control over the process in 1987 by creating the Commission on Presidential Debates, the number, timing, and format of these events have been almost unchanged.

One other feature hasn't changed, but maybe it should. That's the cast of participants, restricted with only one exception to the Republican and Democratic nominees. Only in 1992, when the two parties' campaigns suggested H. Ross Perot's inclusion—a masterstroke by one side and a fatal miscalculation by the other—was the stage widened to permit a third player.

The 2020 general election campaign should be the next time. A commission that has stiff-armed pleas to admit a third candidate and fought off lawsuits challenging its refusals ought to take the idea seriously this time around. Circumstances have changed; the two-only policy should reflect that and change with them.

I was a member of the Commission on Presidential Debates during the 2016 cycle. Critics' suspicions that the CPD is motivated solely by bipartisan protectionism were not supported by my experience. I observed only civic-minded people trying to serve the public interest as they understood it.

The core of the commission's commitment to its major-party restriction is the conviction that the debates should be limited to those with a chance to win. That view was convincing, or at least arguable, for the presidential elections of the commission's first three decades, but it is ripe for reevaluation today.

Since its emergence in the republic's earliest years, the two-party system has served the nation well. A look at the travails of Italy, Israel, or even Britain today should be enough to deter those tempted by a fragmented, multiparty alternative.

The principal contribution of two-party domination has been the incentive each has felt to reach for the center. In their policies, their selection of candidates, and in those candidates' presentations in broad forums such as the presidential debates, success generally depended on persuading—or at least not driving away—voters in a wide middle. But, as we all know, that was then.

In 1988, the first CPD election, nearly one-third of Congress voted at least 20% of the time with the other party. Now, the degree of overlap is in the single digits. A nomination process that no one designed, or would have, tends to produce nominees who cater to the fringes. Researchers find an "exhausted majority" leery of the extremism and weary of the harshness of the two parties as they exist today. An unprecedented four in ten voters decline to identify with one of the two parties.

For years, another civic-spirited American has been appealing for greater access to the commission stage. Peter Ackerman has invested millions of his own funds appealing to and ultimately suing the commission, without success. As far as one can tell, his cause is as selfless as one sees in public life: He seeks no office, supports no candidate or third party, is currying no access or favor from anyone. He simply believes that the national dialogue needs improvement.

The commission employs a complex qualification test utilizing selected public opinion polls, which so far no third candidate has passed, and Perot would not have met if it had been in effect in 1992. Ackerman's prescription, involving a national petition process, is awkward; quite possibly a better means could be devised. This time around, the CPD should attempt one.

However valid in the past, the "only someone who can win" argument is less than ideal in a time of radical polarization, with the pandering to extremes and the cheapened discourse it brings. A third voice on the stage, even one with no realistic chance of capturing 270 electoral votes, could in this troubled era raise issues the Big Two are ducking (the pending collapse of the social safety net, the national debt tsunami, etc.). He or she might model a bit of the civility and respect for the nation's highest office that earlier aspirants, whatever their differences, once took for granted.

In his quest, Ackerman attacks the catch-22 nature of the commission's position: only a potential winner will be allowed to debate, but only a debate participant has a chance to win. A candidate who made it to the debate stage and performed very well could, especially in today's instant-communications world, vault to genuine contender status. Stranger things have happened. Recently.

In virtually every economic and social realm, we are a world away from 1987. That's obviously true of national politics, too. While there is plenty of time to fashion a better way, it would behoove the good people of the commission to reexamine their rigid attitude that three's a crowd.

Good government gets plenty of lip service but no respect.
October 8, 2019

Former governor Jim Edgar, a Republican, left Illinois in reasonable shape twenty years ago. When asked last year to comment on the state's current wretched condition, he replied, "Good government is boring." Sadly, that's true. Yet the effects of incompetent government are anything but boring, in the damage done to the quality of life in the short term and to public confidence over the long haul.

The sheer incompetence of government at all levels ought to be a generator not of sarcasm but of bipartisan consensus and cooperation. If there's anything America's fractured polity should agree on, it's that, whatever the size and scope, public activity ought to achieve its stated goals and produce maximum value for the dollars it consumes.

Instead, good government is an orphan issue. Executive branch leaders who could make effective service a priority usually pay it little attention. Legislators empowered to oversee executive performance are more likely to reward failure by protecting the funding of plainly unsuccessful programs than to demand an increase in the programs' effectiveness.

In the abstract, one would expect the opposite. Proponents of larger, more expansive government might be expected to be the most insistent voices for competent delivery of the services they were so eager to provide. Advocates of more limited government would scrutinize each dollar spent and criticize each shortcoming aggressively. Both camps would place the burden of proof on the activity in question.

Of course, that's not what happens. Democrats pretend that even the most obvious fiascoes are fine, just fine, and any exposure of their shortcomings equals a heartless lack of "care" for their intended purpose. Republicans celebrate the failures in "I told you so" mode but rarely expend effort trying to find better ways to attain worthy public objectives.

Why is government so generally hapless, and why is there so little interest in fixing it?

Most people come to elected office with little or no experience—and too often no particular interest—in actually managing anything for real-world results. They are likely to surround themselves with people similarly unprepared: lawyers, PR experts, campaign operatives.

When the politician is in office, or pursuing it, the incentives are, if anything, negative. Candidates are rewarded electorally for rolling out shiny new models, not cogent ideas about how to operate the old clunkers already in the garage. No one organizes marches on Washington to demand faster permitting times or job-training programs that actually place people in lasting jobs. More money for the flops we have now, sure, but not better performance or accountability for those in charge of them.

In 2001, a naive crew of which I was a part inaugurated a systematic evaluation, by the Office of Management and Budget, of every discrete program in the federal government. Over five years, each of more than a thousand activities was rated based on objective measurements, with the findings duly reflected in President George W. Bush's budgets and in reports to Congress.

Many of the programs—the National Weather Service and the Special Supplemental Nutrition Program for Women, Infants, and Children come to mind—showed clear goals and excellent effectiveness in meeting them. Many, many others merited a failing grade. The aspiration was that Congress would reinforce those programs with proven results and reform, reduce, or terminate those without them.

We should have saved our time and the government's money. If even a single change was imposed on the scores of failures, I must have missed it.

The saddest consequence of inept, indifferent government isn't even the dollars it wastes, it's the cynicism it fosters. Viable self-governance depends on at least a modicum of public confidence in institutions. Chronically lousy service undermines such confidence.

In another job I had, as governor of Indiana, I set out with colleagues in state government to instill genuine effectiveness in public administration in agencies large and small. The techniques were simple but not easy to implement: rigorously measuring outcomes, liberating managers from paralyzing labor agreements and archaic civil service laws, and recognizing and rewarding the success of individual workers and units. Eight years later, taxpayers received refunds in days, not months; citizens were in and out of Bureau of Motor Vehicles branches in ten minutes; and polls showed public confidence in the efficiency of state government at 77%.

Some believe that the United States is past the point where any incremental government reforms can matter. One of the most insightful thinkers on these topics, Philip K. Howard, argues persuasively in *Try Common Sense*, published this year, that nothing will suffice short of replacing today's entire rules-based, hyper-prescriptive, compliance-obsessed edifice with a radically simplified system based on individual judgment under strong oversight. I wish him well. But I'm doubtful that such ideas will find vigorous sponsorship. After all (like, I'm afraid, this column), the whole subject of good government is just so ... boring.

America needs a Democratic Richard Nixon.
August 21, 2019

Sorry to be so obvious, but isn't it clear that what the United States needs is a Democratic Richard M. Nixon?

No, not that one. We've had plenty of truth-bending, political dirty tricks, and abuse of authority from both political parties over recent years.

I'm thinking of the "other" Nixon, the one who longed for a place in history and whose shrewd instinct for the political center produced the Environmental Protection Agency; arms talks with the same Soviet Union he had built a career on denouncing; wage and price controls that violated every canon of his party's philosophy; and, of course, the opening of relations with "Red" China.

That sort of Nixon, with a Democratic pedigree, is the figure our republic could use sometime soon.

The breakthrough needed now doesn't involve China (though relations there certainly could be improved), it's about national solvency. After radically swelling an already dangerous national debt under the most recent presidency, the nation is on track for a similar run-up during the next few years.

There is no need to restate all the ruin that unpayable debt does to nations that indulge in it. Debt such as what we are now piling up will end badly. With entitlements and interest payments devouring available funds, the result will be some combination of economic catastrophe, the collapse of basic services, or a disastrous weakening of national defense. For anyone still in denial, the Flat Earth Society is accepting applications.

No Republican can even put a dent in this problem. The party's Scrooge stereotype, however unfair in many cases, is too burned into the public and media consciousness to permit the necessary ideas to be advanced from that quarter. The ludicrous but effective slandering of then representative Paul D. Ryan (R-Wisconsin) in 2012 for his interest in Medicare reform—a TV ad portrayed the then Republican vice presidential candidate as literally pushing an elderly woman in a wheelchair over a cliff—is all the evidence one needs. And anyway, under present management, the GOP shows zero interest in even raising the issue of the national debt.

Hope must come from the other direction. Just as Nixon, one of his era's most vigorous anti-communists, used the credibility of his personal record and party label to undertake his startling initiatives, a Democrat—and only a Democrat, protected by the party's tribune-of-the-poor reputation—can lead the country fiscally where it desperately needs to go.

Arguments fully consistent with the Democratic image and catechism are already available, and if they are politically premature today, they will become more apparent and viable with each passing year of procrastination. Modernizing the public safety net is not about trashing it, as our puerile public debate now asserts, but about saving it. Absent significant change, Social Security, Medicare, and Medicaid will go bust, and no one will be harmed more than those most dependent on the programs.

Continued entitlement drift is choking the discretionary government most dear to Democrats—a squeeze that will grow inexorably tighter. Saving public housing, mass transit, federal education funding, and (fill in your favorite social program here) will become ever-stronger rationales for what must be done. Attempting to enact even the tiniest portion of the latest Democratic policy fads will require creating some fiscal space on the spending side.

For the moment at least, the Democratic brand is strong among younger voters. These of course are the Americans about to be plundered and gouged by the wanton borrowing in which we, their elders, are engaging: borrowing not for appropriate investment in their future but for our current consumption.

Today's young may not know much about the nation's history or civic institutions, but they will not remain forever oblivious to this giant, unconscionable threat to their economic futures. Here, too, a Democrat has a far greater entree to share the stark facts and make the case for change.

Nixon was a practitioner of the maxim "If your base isn't a little mad at you, you're doing something wrong." A considerable portion of the Democratic core will remain obdurate on entitlements, determined never to be confused by the facts. But it may be possible to lead a large and growing segment to see their self-interest being positively affected by reforms such as means-testing and moderating the increases in autopilot transfer payments.

It's fair to observe that China, as a political "third rail," was never as high-voltage as Social Security or Medicare. But that's where the legacy opportunity comes in. Assuming that our republic summons the maturity and discipline to steer away from a fiscal Niagara Falls, the leader at the helm of that achievement will be rewarded with what every president must yearn for: a place of historical honor. More likely than not, that person will be a Democrat.

As a politician, I vowed not to attack my opponents. Where's that ethos now?
November 9, 2018

If America has any better writers than Cormac McCarthy, I haven't found them.

McCarthy hasn't written a political novel—goodness knows we don't need any more—but indirectly, almost allegorically, maybe he has.

In his dark masterpiece *No Country for Old Men*, the protagonist is a long-time county sheriff in south Texas who watches what has always been a rough-and-tumble environment descend rather suddenly into levels of violence and brutality that even that weathered veteran cannot cope with, or even comprehend. Even though "bein' sheriff was one of the best jobs you could have and bein' a ex-sheriff was one of the worst," by the book's end, sheriff Ed Tom Bell is ready to quit.

Many of today's politicians must feel similarly. Viewing the savagery of the current public arena, others may decide to not even attempt a political career.

Just a decade ago, but in what now seems a parallel universe, one could run for public office without vilifying one's adversary. In fact, you could even make a virtue of it.

Running in a primary as a first-time candidate, I wrote and recorded an ad nominally directed at my fellow party members, but really aimed at the larger electorate I hoped to be addressing in a general election. In the ad I said, "I've never run for public office before, and before you vote, you should know there are a few things I won't do to win one, like compromise a fundamental principle, or attack anyone's personal background, character, or motives."

For years after, I found a surefire applause line in a public appearance was to mention that, through three contested campaigns including that primary, we had never run a negative ad breaching that pledge. In the most irritating moments, I tried to bear in mind President Ronald Reagan's admonition: "We have no enemies, only opponents." How far away such a world seems today.

In the past few months we have just endured, candidates left and right heaped new levels of personal scorn on their opponents. Epithets such as "liar" and "thief," which not long ago would have backfired on the person employing them, have become boringly common. Attachment of disparaging adjectives to the other person's first name has migrated from middle school yearbooks to the heart of our self-governance process.

Third-party interest groups and hired mercenaries, with no responsibility and probably little interest in the actual work of government between elections, are, if anything, even more vicious in their language and tactics. In case words aren't adequate weapons, sticks and stones have entered the repertoire in the form of physical confrontation and intimidation in public spaces or doxing, the release across the Internet of personal addresses and information.

Oh, I know. "Politics isn't beanbag," and never has been. But, like Sheriff Bell's Terrell County, it has never been like this.

The sheer obnoxiousness of scorched-earth campaigning is actually only its second worst problem; worse is its high opportunity cost. A would-be elected official on the campaign trail will have no better chance, not even if gaining office, to communicate directly with the citizens he or she seeks to serve. To describe a better future and steps we could take to achieve it. To secure understanding and, given sufficient success, a "mandate" to pursue those steps. In other words, to campaign to govern, not merely to win.

Of course, that presumes you had some such purpose for running in the first place.

A former political practitioner gets frequent requests for advice from aspiring candidates. I've often suggested that the younger ones build some private sector experience and credibility first, but have always encouraged ambition in men and women who have the new talent that a healthy democracy needs to refresh itself.

I'm more hesitant with that advice these days. When people of the finest character and best motives are nearly certain to be slimed and slandered, if not assaulted, for the sin of disagreement, it's with mixed feelings that one cheers them on into the Coliseum.

Looking out on his own transformed arena, Sheriff Bell says, "I can't say that it's even what you are willin' to do ... I think it is more like what you are willin' to become. And I think a man would have to put his soul at hazard. And I won't do that. I think now that maybe I never would."

Unless and until a national revulsion with character-assassination politics requires some degree of civility and constructiveness in electoral competition, this will be no country for old men, or women. And not much of one for young ones, either.

Get Washington out of Washington. Put it in Omaha.
November 6, 2018

Agriculture secretary Sonny Perdue announced in August that he wanted to move the Economic Research Service and the National Institute of Food and Agriculture out of Washington, to places where the type of scholarship they rely on is centered. Now the department is considering proposals submitted by interested parties (including my university) to host the headquarters for those subagencies.

You might assume that such a move would be regarded as a commonsense exercise in sound administrative and academic practice. But you would be wrong—at least in the eyes of the client organizations that seek funding from these mini-bureaucracies. Their protests came promptly and loudly after Perdue's announcement.

The Housing Assistance Council complained that moving the Economic Research Service away from Washington "is yet another way rural voices will be out of earshot." The National Sustainable Agriculture Coalition wrote that the plan meant "America would experience a disastrous reduction in its agricultural research capacity." You'd have thought someone had suggested moving the Washington Monument.

But what exactly is so unthinkable, especially these days, about dispersing more of the federal government's sprawling assets somewhere into the 99.998% of America's land mass that isn't the District of Columbia? The Economic Research Service and the National Institute of Food and Agriculture together comprise less than 1% of total Agriculture Department employees, a large majority of whom already work elsewhere in the country. The Centers for Disease Control and Prevention, one of the more respected and effective federal agencies, is headquartered in Atlanta.

The idea of getting Washington out of Washington has come up periodically for decades. In 2002, I was part of a small group in the George W. Bush administration assigned to study whether the government's various units with a relationship to what came to be called Homeland Security should be gathered together in a new cabinet-level department. Ultimately, President Bush decided that taking this step would be wise, and he commissioned a draft of the necessary legislation.

I proposed locating the new agency anywhere but D.C., for what seemed to me some highly logical reasons.

First, given that the Department of Homeland Security would make an attractive terrorist target, prudence would dictate not placing it immediately adjacent to Washington's many existing targets.

Second, technology has rendered distance and physical place less important than ever. Enterprises of all kinds now operate perfectly well across multiple locations as data moves instantly, and teleconferencing has advanced to a "same room" feel.

Third, locating DHS somewhere other than Washington would have made much better economic sense. Under the government's statutory geographic compensation formula, the savings in salary and benefits alone would have been significant, to say nothing of other operating expenses. A GS-13 Step 2 employee who is paid $100,203 in Washington would cost less than $91,000 in Kansas City or Indianapolis.

You can guess how far the idea got. The chemical weight of lead is insufficient to describe that particular balloon. The idea might have seemed far-fetched back then, but it should be less so today.

Washington is becoming unlivable. Its cost of living index has exploded: Housing prices have doubled since 1988 and are up a third just since the end of the recession. A meal at a midrange restaurant costs almost half again above the national average.

Commutes have stretched to Seattle or Silicon Valley dimensions. Traffic gridlock, with its attendant pollution and lost productivity, ranks with the nation's three worst areas. Average commutes exceed an hour a day. Waldorf, Maryland, has the nation's longest average, at forty-three minutes each way.

Leaving aside all the security and administrative advantages, relocating bureaucracies can offer important intangible pluses. Parts of the nation now estranged from the federal government—and cynical about it—might feel more invested and sympathetic if more of its officials were seen as neighbors and not as faraway, arrogant paper pushers.

And federal workers themselves might benefit, not only from quality of life improvements but also from a perspective on their work enriched by closer exposure to its real-world consequences. Might there not be at least a little logic in having, say, the Interior Department located somewhere in the country's … interior? The USDA's Economic Research Service near some actual farmers?

Then again, the idea of relocating federal bureaucracies could be one of those sensible choices that Washington finds simply unthinkable, such as reforming Social Security before it implodes.

Maybe it's just as well. A friend recalls a lighthearted moment in the Senate chamber in the 1980s during an especially pompous and boring oration when someone in the back suggested moving the capital to Omaha. Senator Robert Dole, always ready with a quip, replied, "What have you got against Omaha?"

President George H. W. Bush is an extraordinary example for our times.
June 11, 2018

They come less and less frequently now, because fewer and fewer of their subjects remain. With the youngest now in their 90s, obituaries of the World War II generation strike some of us with a special poignancy. They evoke thoughts of those who gave their lives back then, and what they might have been and done. They remind us how relatively safe, prosperous, and sheltered those of us who came after them have been.

One of the very biggest has, happily, not yet come. Though we sadly have recently lost his beloved Barbara, a fortunate nation is still blessed with the presence of George Herbert Walker Bush, at once an extraordinary figure in our history, but still so emblematic of the times and the generation from which he came. Hoping that it remains years away, I think often of the memories to be revisited when we do ultimately lose him.

Virtually every quality the first President Bush personifies has faded from our national life. He was astonishingly forgiving of those who wronged or defeated him. Today, it's more common for leaders to practice the rugby coach's instruction to "get your retaliation in first."

In contrast to today's showboat, look-at-me, dance-in-the-end-zone world, George H. W. Bush was resolutely undemonstrative, drilled from childhood to avoid bragging, self-satisfaction, or, worst of all, self-aggrandizement. His upbringing instilled in him an instinct to always give the credit to others.

Highly educated, successful in business, friend to innumerable influential people of all kinds, he was a member of the "elite" by multiple definitions. We have watched as that former synonym for excellence has become a term of derision and disparagement.

Slandered by some detractors as aloof or out of touch, this was a man who twice walked away from offers of an easy Wall Street life to forge his own path in the high-risk world of wildcat oil. Who swept floors and lived with his family in an apartment so small they had to share a bathroom with prostitutes. Who volunteered for the armed services of his country, where he fought side by side with men from every part of the country and generally from backgrounds radically poorer than his own had been. Who endured perhaps the cruelest loss possible, the death of a young daughter. Run through the roster of today's leading politicians in search of a person more in touch or empathetic with the lives and concerns of ordinary people. But, sometimes to his detriment, he never wore it as a pose or affectation; he left those life experiences understated, or simply unstated.

He served in an unmatched series of public capacities. He not only held more high positions than any previous president, he is the only person ever to have been CIA director, ambassador to China, UN ambassador, and national party chairman before assuming our highest office. These days, it is outsider status that is prized; a life of public leadership like the one that 41 lived can seem a virtual disqualification.

When reports came early in 2016 that Bush was experiencing a dangerous illness, I caught myself wondering whether, should we lose him then, the certain outpouring of affection and appreciation might force a little national introspection, maybe even jolt that depressingly negative and cynical election onto a different course. Mercifully, he remains with us, and so we'll never know.

Looking ahead, one thinks about the near truism of our politics, that the electorate looks for qualities in a next president that were lacking in the last one. It's a perplexing thought experiment to ask whether, if Bush 41 showed up as a candidate in 2020, he'd be welcomed as just what the doctor ordered or run out of the field before the first caucus or primary.

We were so lucky to have him at all. What if that parachute hadn't opened in 1944? Or the life raft had not inflated? Or his fellow pilots not spotted him and strafed away the Japanese boats as they attempted to machine gun the downed American flyboy? Or if, instead of paddling furiously away from it to his discovery and rescue by a submarine, he had drifted to the nearby island, to almost certain capture and execution? Our nation would have been deprived of argu-ably its finest single life of patriotic service.

Is it too much to hope that the final contribution of this giant life might be to cast before the country an example of virtues that have eroded and nearly disap-peared? The very virtues that have sustained the American Experiment through its hardest trials?

It was discreetly and respectfully suggested to me that I prepare a short essay in advance of 41's passing, to be available when the inevitable occurs. By leave of the editors, I submit it now, as we celebrate his 94th birthday Tuesday, in the faint hope that the qualities George H. W. Bush embodies might stage a come-back, rather than pass forever from the national scene.[16]

Someone is watching you.
March 27, 2018

Isn't technology wonderful? At Purdue University, the same IT infrastructure that enables us to manage student assignments and grades, operate residential and dining facilities, and support a leading community of scientific researchers produces as a byproduct a massive amount of fascinating information. We know where each student is anytime—which is virtually all the time. Their mobile de-vices are connected to our Wi-Fi network. When they enter their dorm, or din-ing court, or recreational facility, they swipe in, and a machine captures the time and place. Whether they're in class or in their rooms, a machine knows when they're online and where they're going while there. Forget that old ominous line "We know where you live." These days, it's "We know where you are."

University people are curious by nature, and much of today's big data era was born at our school. So it's only natural that we would want to delve into this trea-sure trove of information in search of illuminating patterns—especially those that might prove helpful to those same students, whose academic success is the heart of our mission.

Does the data say that too many days away from campus, or too many absences from class, or too much in-class browsing of websites unrelated to the course, or too few visits to the gym, correlates with lower grades? Does eating meals with the same people day after day appear to help scholastic performance? If so, shouldn't we bring this to the students' attention, for their own good?

For the past two years, virtually every entering Purdue freshman (there is an opt-out option that few exercise) has been given a mobile application through which the university sends them personalized information about ways to improve their chances of academic success.

So far, the information employed and the ways we're using it have not seemed at all problematic. "Is that combination of courses you chose a historically tough one? Here's where you can find a tutor." "Did you know that students who wait as long as you did to sign up for courses are more likely to struggle? The registrar's office opens at 8 a.m. tomorrow."

But that's today. With the best of motives, schools like ours will feel the urge to use more and more personal data, through more and more insistent tactics, all in the "best interest of the students."

Much has been written in recent years about the possibilities for "nudging" people to do things they otherwise might not choose to do. In particular, would-be social engineers who have run into trouble, and often political backlash, when trying to order people to change their behavior have looked longingly on more subtle means of influence.

So when does "nudge" come to "shove"? We don't have to theorize about the far end of that spectrum. The future is now, in the form of China's new "social credit" system, already in effect for volunteers and becoming mandatory in 2020. Citizens conforming to governmentally approved behaviors will earn a high numerical rating; nonconformists can expect unhappy consequences. Those with high scores will enjoy a multitude of preferences, ranging from VIP hotel rooms and air travel to better schools for their children. Paying your bills, or spending money on work clothes instead of video games, will be worth points. But to protect your high rating, be sure to say nice things, and never, never skeptical things, about the government, in your digital life, or be linked to others who do. This all is designed to deliver, in author Rachel Botsman's apt coinage, "gamified obedience."

This subject needs a highly public examination sooner not later. The data is here, it is in fact "Big," and it calls out to the sincerely curious to be analyzed and utilized for good, in all the institutions suddenly knowledgeable about the previously most private aspects of our daily lives.

Somewhere between connecting a struggling student with a tutor and penalizing for life a person insufficiently enthusiastic of a reigning regime, judgment calls will be required and lines of self-restraint drawn. People serene in their assurance that they know what is best for others will have to stop and ask themselves, or be asked by the rest of us, on what authority they became the Nudgers and the Great Approvers. Many of us will have to stop and ask whether our good intentions are carrying us past boundaries where privacy and individual autonomy should still prevail.

COVID AND OUR AFTER LIFE

Let's talk about the grim realities of the
coronavirus at the dinner table.
March 19, 2020

After days of worrying over and grappling with the coronavirus pandemic, can a person be forgiven for a moment of groping for a bright side? Granted, facing almost certainly the worst societal threat of this century, even Ronald Reagan's apocryphal young optimist would have to shovel awfully deep to find his pony. But can we permit ourselves to try, just briefly?

Might the family meal make a slight resurgence? A YouGov survey in October found that 44% of Americans eat together fewer than four times a week, and 10% only on special occasions. Maybe a little extra togetherness could ensue. Social distancing doesn't mean eating in separate rooms.

Across the economy, private and nonprofit enterprises are going to discover what work they do, and which expenditures are really essential. Much of the travel canceled this year will prove in retrospect to have caused no damage by not happening. In higher education, the sector I inhabit, it's the season for academic conferences. One sarcastic friend labeled them "the leisure of the theory class." Many are clearly vital, but reading over some of the agendas, it's clear he has a point.

I have never seen a business that has eliminated all nonproductive spending, but higher education needs housecleaning more than most. The role of bloated administration in pushing up tuitions and student indebtedness has been documented for years, but too many schools have yet to act on the problem.

The next few months will expose many functions that make little or no contribution to the core mission of thousands of the nation's businesses. In higher education, that mission is teaching and research. Maybe some of the frills will come out and not be replaced in the aftermath of the pandemic. Meanwhile, businesses of all kinds, ours included, will come out of this knowing a lot more about telecommuting and telemedicine than we do now.

COVID AND OUR AFTER LIFE

The forced shift to remote delivery of education should provide some long-term benefit. Very little of the coursework on the scale now required will be of the quality that is feasible online; think PowerPoints and audio-only lectures, not streaming video and an almost-classroom experience. Most schools have procrastinated in creating such offerings and will only just now be developing them. COVID-19 should accelerate a future of more flexible, affordable offerings to students, and more rapid progress to degrees, when normalcy returns.

I'll wager that the next flu season, or whenever we return to epidemiological normalcy, will be measurably moderated. Each year I roll up my sleeve for the annual "Everybody get your flu shot" publicity photo knowing that only about half my Purdue co-workers will take me up on it. Next year, I'm sure we will see a much higher compliance rate, not to mention a far greater level of handwashing, elbow-bumping, and cough-covering.

Among the most prescient books of recent decades one must include John M. Barry's 2005 book *The Great Influenza*, a history of the misnamed Spanish flu a century ago. Warning that "the clock is ticking, we just don't know what time it is," the author recommended a variety of preparatory measures that could have been taken over the past two decades in recognition that an event like this was likely. We will take those measures now.

And the book reminds us poignantly of a reason to feel slightly better about today's nightmare, which has reserved its greatest lethality for us elderly types. In a phenomenon not understood to this day, the 1918 epidemic visited some of its worst effects on young people. Worldwide, tens of millions of young lives, with incalculable future promise, were snuffed out. One needn't traffic in the bloodless arithmetic of QALYs (quality-adjusted life years) to be a bit grateful that the danger this time seems to be the reverse of that tragedy.

For those of us troubled by today's tribalism, it's been common to imagine that a good old-fashioned crisis, something of external origin affecting us all, might bring the nation together. One wouldn't know it from the hair-trigger partisanship of our Washington leaders, but elsewhere there are signs of unity and voluntarism and communitarian caring.

That about does it in the desperate search for good-news scraps. No, wait. I forgot a big one. Someone finally found a way to shorten the interminable, almost meaningless NBA regular season. (Of course, I'm not sure why suspension was necessary; most teams play social-distance defense until the playoffs start, anyhow.)

Enough scrounging for upsides. As comedian George Carlin reminded us, "Outside every silver lining, there's a dark cloud." Time to refocus on the grim realities, and the tasks at hand. Maybe we can talk about it at the dinner table.

**When this pandemic is over, let's avoid the partisan blame game.
May 5, 2020**

What follows is not a prediction. More of a precaution, based on a premonition. While I'm wearing out the prefix, let's call it a preventive prescription.

I'm worried about preventing a sickness, one we've been through before—much more recently than the last pandemic flu. It's our tribal eagerness to employ 20/20 rearview vision and castigate the Other Side for its mistakes, even those made in all sincerity, even those the second-guessers failed to dispute, or even endorsed, at the outset. Since everything these days seems to call for a snappy abbreviation, let's use HRD, for Hindsight Recrimination Disorder.

In the first years of this century, the consensus conclusion of multiple national intelligence agencies was that Iraqi leader Saddam Hussein had or was close to acquiring weapons of mass destruction. Based on that "expert" information, the United States organized a large number of nations in a massive campaign to eliminate the threat, which proved unjustifiably expensive in both human and economic terms.

Because the intelligence was wrong. The WMDs weren't real; they proved to be a dictator's bluff. A reasonable postmortem would have been to review the performance of those who misread the information and try to learn lessons that might help us avoid repeating the error. Decision-makers of the time could have been criticized for not seeing through faulty data they had been given, without being trashed as liars or scoundrels pursuing personal agendas.

Of course, that's not what happened. People who had examined the information and come to their own conclusion favoring military action developed a contortionist amnesia in order to denounce the exact viewpoint they had once held, or even voted for. Conspiracy theorists were permitted, even encouraged, to foment the slander that someone fabricated the inaccurate intelligence. Today's poisonous, partisan atmosphere carries some of the toxins from the ugly Iraq War aftermath.

It's easy to imagine the coronavirus producing the same potentially deadly symptom. None of us knows how this is going to turn out. It could be that the maximalist measures we've taken, with all their brutal consequences in lost jobs, dashed dreams, interrupted educations, second-order deaths—from forgone care, postponed surgeries, addiction relapses and suicides, you name it—will all prove warranted.

I, for one, hope so. I earnestly hope that our public officials, who are acting on the best (they believe) intelligence available to them, have chosen wisely. Because I think we pay a frightful societal price when we fail to establish social distance from HRD.

The conspiracists will have a lot of raw material to exploit. Even more than in the Iraq experience, it will be simple to identify special interest motives and claim they drove a campaign that deceived the rest of us into an overreaction. The public health community, underappreciated in normal times, has been handed a fabulous limelight opportunity. They're not only on TV daily; they're also calling the public policy shots.

Heretofore obscure politicians have also been handed plenty of airtime to pronounce on the pandemic. At least in the short term, they are "saving lives"; hard to be unpopular doing that. Of course, trading near-term benefits they collect for long-term costs someone else can deal with is what politicians do (#nationaldebt).

Most industries are taking a terrible beating, but the news media are suddenly on a roll, at least in audience. All those eyeballs stuck at home, and desperate for news about the virus that is the reason. There has been a lot of smart and responsible reporting but also a ton of the other kind: anecdotal, sensationalist, alarmist. The old print maxim "If it bleeds, it leads" now has its modern-day update: "If it's sick, it clicks."

Again, my hope is that what we've been doing will be fully vindicated. I want us to discover that this was the wisest course, that the ghastly price we're paying was all worth it. But it's the long term that matters. I can already hear the outcry claiming, "They lied to us."

Sweden (hey, wasn't it just yesterday we were being lectured to admire and emulate its health care system?) has been criticized for a high per capita coronavirus death rate after declining to shut down its entire society. But what if after a year or two Sweden's rate is far below ours, due to the herd immunity we are postponing? What if people as thoughtful as *New York Times* columnist Thomas Friedman have been right about protecting the most vulnerable without ruining the futures of millions?

Let's not reprise Iraq. How about we self-vaccinate against HRD and all agree that, whatever comes, people right now are doing their best with the information they have. If their judgments turn out to be mistaken, let's avoid another orgy of tribal recrimination and agree that we won't repeat the errors. Here's a type of HRD immunity we can achieve without becoming ill ourselves.

Why failing to reopen Purdue University this fall would be an unacceptable breach of duty.
May 25, 2020

On February 1, watching the outbreak of a new virus in China, our university suspended travel to that country. On February 26, we extended that ban to visiting other countries reporting the infection. On March 10, we decided to close the Purdue University campus for the spring semester and move to remote instruction. On March 17, we canceled our traditional commencement.

At the point when the campus was shut down, if we had needed to decide on our plans for the fall, we would have felt compelled to resume with remote instruction and keep the campus closed. For all we knew, COVID-19 posed a danger across all lines of age and health status, and a place as densely populated as our campus would be defenseless against it—operations couldn't be responsibly restarted.

We have all learned a lot since then. What would have been a reckless and scientifically unjustified decision in late March is now plainly the best option from both a scientific and a stewardship standpoint, at least for our particular institution. The *Post* asked me to explain here what has gone into our thinking. (We're not alone: two-thirds of the more than 700 colleges surveyed by the *Chronicle of Higher Education* have now come to the same conclusion and will reopen with in person instruction in the fall.)

The most salient discovery the world has made during these terrible two months is that COVID-19 is a very dangerous disease, specifically for the elderly and the infirm, particularly those with diabetes, hypertension, other cardiovascular illnesses, or the obesity that so frequently leads to these disorders.

The companion discovery is that this bug, so risky in one segment of the population, poses a near-zero risk to young people. Among COVID-19 deaths, 99.9% have occurred outside the 15-to-24 age group; the survival rate in the 20-to-29 age bracket is 99.99%. Even assuming the United States eventually reaches 150,000 total fatalities, COVID-19 as a risk to the young will rank way below accidents, cancer, heart disease, and suicide. In fact, it won't even make the top ten.

This is fundamental information for institutions with radically skewed demographic compositions. If you're running a nursing home, it means one thing. New York unintentionally ended hundreds of lives prematurely by ordering COVID-19 patients into such homes, the worst possible places for them.

But if you're running a university, the science is telling you something diametrically different. Our campus, including its surrounding community, has a median age of 20.5. More than 80% of the total campus population is 35 and under. We may have the population density of New York City, but we have the age distribution of Uganda. The challenge for Purdue is to devise maximum protection for the unusually small minority who could be at genuinely serious risk in order to serve the young people who are our reason for existing at all.

Here's something else we've learned. Our students (and, one suspects, their trapped-at-home parents) overwhelmingly are eager to continue their educations, in person and on campus. We know it is not the case everywhere, but at Purdue, tuition deposits by incoming freshmen have shattered last year's record, and re-enrollments of upper-class students are at normal levels.

Forty-five thousand young people—the biggest student population we've ever had—are telling us they want to be here this fall. To tell them, "Sorry, we are too incompetent or too fearful to figure out how to protect your elders, so you have to disrupt your education," would be a gross disservice to them and a default of our responsibility.

Instead, we have spent every waking minute of the past eight weeks planning changes to almost everything we do—how we house and feed students and preserve the value of the tutelage and mentoring by faculty and advisors, while maintaining a safe physical distance between the two groups. A panel of scientists and clinicians is guiding our choices.

We will make our campus less dense in multiple ways. At least one-third of our staff will be required to work remotely. Our technologists have applied what they've learned about social distancing to redesign 700 classrooms and labs and 9,500 dormitory rooms, all of which will be reconfigured with lower occupancy limits. All large-enrollment courses will be offered online as well as in person to accommodate those who cannot or choose not to come to campus and to further reduce in-class numbers.

We will test systematically and trace contacts of anyone testing positive for the coronavirus. We will forgo the concerts, convocations, and social occasions that ordinarily enliven campus life. It will be a quieter fall without fraternity parties, but first things first.

Perhaps most important will be the cultural change on which we have to insist because, in another lesson of the coronavirus spring, nothing makes a more positive difference than personal behavior and responsibility. Wearing masks indoors and in any close-quarters space reduces viral transmission dramatically all by itself. Combined with rigorous hygiene and prudent social distancing, facial protection can probably provide more protection than all the extra disinfecting, plexiglass barrier installation, HVAC improvements, and other measures we take.

On arrival in August, each Boilermaker will receive a kit including face masks and a thermometer for daily temperature-taking as well as the Protect Purdue Pledge asking for a commitment to at least a semester of inconvenience, not primarily for the student's own protection but for the safety of those who teach and otherwise serve them. I will urge students to demonstrate their altruism by complying, but also challenge them to refute the cynics who say that today's young people are too selfish or self-indulgent to help us make this work.

A final thought: We recognize that not every school can or should view the decision to reopen as we do. Unlike Purdue, many colleges were already struggling with low enrollment and precarious finances when the pandemic hit. But given what we have learned, with 45,000 students waiting and the financial wherewithal to do what's necessary, failure to take on the job of reopening would be not only anti-scientific but also an unacceptable breach of duty.

Even amid a pandemic, the kids are "alright."
December 16, 2020

A few years ago—no, it was almost eight months, but like everything else about 2020 it feels longer—we decided to reopen our university this fall. Like almost all hard calls, the choice had to be made with a less-than-ideal amount of information in hand. Experience warned us against procrastination; the operational difficulties of the task ahead clearly were going to require every possible day of planning and preparation.

We did reopen Purdue University in late August, and with great relief just completed a semester with more than 40,000 students taking courses on campus. More than two-thirds of their classes were either partially or totally in person. Their organizations sponsored more than 17,000 events and meetings, two-thirds of those in person. Our residence halls were 86% occupied and, while dining shifted to mainly outdoor and carryout modes, we provided tens of thousands of meals each day.

It was far from the typical resident experience, but our students' educational progress continued uninterrupted.

I can only hope that they learned as much as the stewards of their university did in wrestling with the pandemic. It turned out that two-thirds of our faculty and staff preferred to work remotely, reducing their exposure to the possibility of infection. Like many enterprises today, we expect remote work to be a permanent feature for many employees even after the pandemic is over.

A particularly welcome finding was how thoroughly we were able to guard against viral spread in labs and classrooms. Through masking, distancing, daily disinfection, plexiglass shielding, and other measures, not a single infection was traced to any encounter in one of our 784 classrooms. "Safe spaces" took on a different meaning at our school.

By far the most crucial learning involved a central factor in our original decision: that this particular virus, while very dangerous to the elderly and those with certain existing conditions, presents a threat to the young as close to zero as one sees in this life. Strongly suggested by the worldwide evidence available in the spring, eight months' more data now makes this phenomenon decisively clear. People our students' age represent 0.2% of COVID-related deaths; their chance of dying from the disease even after infection is 1 In 20,000.

An American between ages 15 and 24 is 1.5 times as likely to die from heart disease, 2.5 times more likely from cancer, 11 times more likely from suicide, and 21 times more likely to die from an accident than from COVID-19. Had the science not seemed persuasive on this in the spring, we would not have risked reopening. As it accumulated and strengthened globally, mercifully we saw it borne out in our community.

Of the 2,770 positive coronavirus test results for students during the semester, 82% were either asymptomatic or had only one minor symptom. Less than 1% rose above even the fourth level of a six-level severity index.

But the most gratifying lesson, and the one most essential to our navigating the semester safely, involved our students. Their compliance with the burdensome restrictions and impositions in what we called the Protect Purdue Pledge confounded predictions that student behavior would doom any reopening college to catastrophe.

Throughout the fall, students submitted to testing, tracing, and quarantining as necessary. When found positive, they moved from in person to online instruction and back again. They constantly reminded and encouraged one another to stick to the pledge. They observed and, if anything, over-complied with masking and distancing requests. One curious senior parked himself along a major campus corridor and tallied 94% of his schoolmates wearing masks outside on a breezy, sunny day.

The students adhered to the pledge so strictly for the best of reasons: to help and protect others. They knew full well how tiny the risks were to themselves. Their sacrifices were made for their vulnerable elders and their fellow students, enabling the school to remain open.

I have stifled the temptation to write back to those who sent gracious messages labeling our reopening decision "crazy," "stupid," or "delusional" (those are the more polite ones). But I might make an exception for those who directed their cynicism at our students. The critics deserve to know, as I knew from years of direct interaction with today's young people, that an ability to act responsibly, along with a spirit of altruism, runs deep among them. I'm not imagining that we're raising a generation of angels, but neither do I believe our Boilermakers are wholly atypical.

Next semester looks even tougher, with high infection rates in Purdue's surrounding communities and new risks that, like many hospitals today, we might face shortages of essential staff. But one problem we won't worry about is the behavior of our students. With a nod to the Who, the kids really are "alright."

Lockdowns needed a warning label, too.
December 31, 2020

The arrival of effective vaccines against the COVID-19 virus is a miraculous achievement that needs to be universally welcomed and embraced. Like other licensed drugs, they will come with a package insert describing downside risks, however small, that are inevitable with any active pharmaceutical. Anyone too sensible to pore over the inserts' fine print will be familiar with their gist from the ubiquitous television commercials for today's prescription medicines.

The founder of the drug company for which I once worked was remembered for the aphorism "Show me a drug with no side effects, and I'll show you a drug with no effects." But we develop these products because the harm they prevent is vastly greater than the costs they impose. We should use them, but carefully, not indiscriminately, or in cases where the risks of not using them are too great.

Maybe we need package inserts for nonmedical prescriptions, too. Had the most common, and often vitally necessary, societal treatment for the pandemic we are enduring come with a Food and Drug Administration label, it would have read something like this:

Lockdown® is approved for the temporary relief of overcrowded hospital emergency rooms. Common side effects include postponement of annual physicals, screenings, and other important preventive care; delayed treatment of diseases such as heart disease, asthma, and diabetes; severe stress; increased risk of depression and suicide; and overuse of alcohol, opioids, and other dangerous substances.

Do not take Lockdown® if you are troubled by income inequality, educational inequality, or unequal treatment of like individuals under law. Other complications reported are severe learning loss in children, increased domestic violence, the extinction of small businesses, and the obliteration of life savings.

An FDA reviewer would have required much, much more, but you get the picture. The vaccines now becoming available are miracles not only in the speed with which they arrived—please, let's adopt permanently the streamlined, anti-bureaucratic waivers that enabled such speed—but also in their apparent efficacy, with some reported protective rates above 90%. We need an equally efficacious program to deliver them swiftly to entire populations, and to persuade everyone to take advantage of them.

We will do so in the certain knowledge that, very rarely, vaccinated individuals will suffer serious, possibly fatal, injury. The measles vaccine has led to anaphylaxis in a tiny percentage of children. The swine flu vaccine induced Guillain-Barré syndrome in 1 of every 100,000 individuals, leading to fifty-three deaths. Very small numbers of fatalities have been caused by vaccines for yellow fever, smallpox, and rotavirus.

The nation has been well served in 2020 by its scientists and epidemiologists. Their expertise and, therefore, their advice have been focused on the minimization of viral spread; no one asked them for guidance about damage to educational attainment, economic prosperity, or even other health consequences. Factoring in those questions was someone else's job: governors, mayors, school boards.

Harry S. Truman, among others, felt that experts should be "on tap, not on top." Positions of broad responsibility are at their very core about the duty to weigh and balance competing interests, to make and not duck often-excruciating trade-offs. Abdicating that duty in the pandemic, or delegating it to advocates for the most important—but not the only—criterion in a complex decision, may well have ultimately caused more harm than good. A "Lockdown" label would have included a black box warning about the dangers of overdose, along with a reminder, "Use only as directed."

"If it saves a single life . . ." That oft-heard statement is at once so natural, so human, so admirably empathetic . . . and so vacuous. If applied to the wondrous new vaccines, it could be taken to mean we should not inoculate anyone, because inevitably someone, somewhere, will be harmed or even perish from them.

We must excuse members of the lay public whose compassionate impulses led them to such careless thinking. But people steeped in the realm of medical science, statistics, and assessments of relative risk should not have been blind or indifferent to the enormous side effects of the lockdown policies. Or, if they were, then those with ultimate authority should have taken those effects fully into account, and many did not.

In the pandemic's early months, a maximalist approach was understandable, and excusable. As time went on and the costs, future as well as present, became more and more clear, caution became dereliction.

God willing, we will soon have vaccinated an entire population against the infection that has brought so much heartache and ruin to the world. As we do so, we will be making a reasoned, wise judgment with an open acceptance of the risks involved. If only we thought that way all the time.

An economist predicted work from home in 1979.
Here's what he expected.
April 1, 2021

My beloved late pastor used to say that a Presbyterian was someone who fell down a flight of stairs and says, "Well, I'm glad I got that over with!" One needn't be a Calvinist, or one of their theological descendants, a scientific determinist, to appreciate a good coincidence.

A delightful one happened to me just the other day. Seeking to double-check a dubious assertion in a book about World War II, I pulled down John Keegan's authoritative history of the conflict, undisturbed on my library shelf for who knows how many years.

When I opened the book, a yellowed section of a newspaper—they used to come on paper, you may recall—fell out. It was the Outlook section of the *Post* from September 2, 1979, as long ago now as the war was when it was published. Headed "The War That Changed the World," the section marked the fortieth anniversary of that ghastly conflict's start.

Most of Outlook's eight pages were devoted to the war, its origins and consequences. But my eye fell on an unrelated feature on the first page: "Working at Home Can Save Gasoline" by one Frank W. Schiff, then the chief economist of the Committee for Economic Development. He was reflecting on a completely different crisis than the current pandemic—namely, the "energy crisis" of his day. But the prescience he displayed was stunning, and fun to read.

After listing societal problems such as "gasoline consumption, traffic congestion and air pollution" and "mental and physical stress," Schiff marveled at "the contribution which could be made by working at home one or two days a week." He noted that "the share of service industries has risen ... to over 60 percent," that a majority of jobs "are now centered in information-related activities." He imagined "engineers, computer programmers ... medical researchers, lawyers, accountants" among many others, moving their daily work back home.

Along with economic transformation, he saw even bigger changes in the "machinery" of work. Among new advances he cited were "today's hand-held 'programmable' scientific calculators"; "computer terminals ... in portable form"; the encoding of "large files and entire libraries" on microfiches, which could be "carried home" and displayed "on portable viewing machines."

And Schiff thought that this was only the beginning, that in the next few years "the sophistication of machines available at home is likely to increase tremendously ... machines that combine the functions of television sets, videophones, computer terminals, electronic files and word and data processing systems and that can be directly connected with offices and other homes."

About all he missed was the 3D printer. Beyond the obvious savings in personal time and expense, Schiff went on to predict gains in productivity and quality of life, as "couples could spend more time together and with their children."

Student of business operations that he was, Schiff (who died in 2006 at age 85) anticipated the criticisms that working from home would draw: "How can one tell how well they are doing or whether they are working at all?" Employees would be "cut off ... from needed contacts with their co-workers and others." There would be "too many distractions and the lack of a quiet place in which to work." His rebuttals of these concerns mirror almost exactly the answers that real-world, large-scale experience began providing in 2020.

What would it take to bring about this back-to-the-future transition? Only here did Schiff's clairvoyance fail him. "No single dramatic step is likely to provide the solution," he wrote, only a concerted campaign of persuasive public advocacy. Too bad such a campaign didn't get here before COVID-19 did.

As Yogi Berra never said, predictions about the future are especially tricky. But when so many in retrospect turn out to be bunk, it's a treat to trip over one as wisely farsighted as Frank Schiff's.

PS: It wasn't until I finished carving quotes from the Schiff essay that I spotted yet another coincidence. Right next to his piece was an article with the grabber headline "The Mad Gasser of Mattoon, Ill." It recounted a "mass hysteria" from thirty-five years before, which the article demonstrated the "stunning" potency of the American media.

In Mattoon, Illinois, an elderly woman reported that she believed someone had pumped gas into her bedroom, sickening and paralyzing her. The "mad anesthetist" made for juicy headlines, and soon, newspapers around the country and even *Time* magazine were reporting breathlessly about dozens of Mattoon residents suffering similar symptoms.

The symptoms were real, even though the Mad Gasser did not exist; it was just someone's diagnosable case of hysteria. Citing a University of Illinois psychologist who investigated the episode, the article said it was "testament to the power of a newspaper to influence not just public opinion, but even public health." Good thing I'm out of space. That could have generated another column.

The post-pandemic era needs a return to risk-taking creativity, not lingering fear.
May 5, 2021

The editors of the *Economist* are always worth our attention, so they got mine recently when they wrote that the 1918 flu pandemic ushered in "a ferment of forward-looking, risk-taking social, industrial and artistic novelty," and speculated that the current pandemic might do likewise.

Let us hope so. But the past year, and those preceding it, have offered ample reasons to fear the opposite outcome.

Even before the virus arrived, there were signs of a diminution in the willingness of Americans to take the risks that have characterized our national rise to greatness—and from which all human progress springs. Rates of physical mobility, new business formation, and that boldest of bets on the future, child-bearing, were all declining and now give signs of falling further.

The irony is powerful. We live in the safest time, by far, in human history. Na-ture, starvation, violence, war, and disease are all dramatically less likely to harm us than ever before.

Of course, we don't see it that way. As great psychologists such as Daniel Kahneman demonstrated years ago, we fall victim to the "availability heuris-tic," through which, because tragic events are so memorable, we drastically over-estimate their probability. The fact that we so rarely experience them person-ally—compounded by a click-conscious media that ensures we all hear about them instantaneously and graphically—heightens the fear factor.

Barbara A. Bichelmeyer, the University of Kansas provost and executive vice chancellor, wrote wisely to her campus community last summer, "In times of such high anxiety, it is human nature to crave certainty for the sense of safety it pro-vides. The problem with craving certainty is that it is a false hope; it is a craving that can never fully be met."

Our collective reaction to the COVID threat has reflected that impulse—and its consequences. Draconian lockdown policies that fallaciously promised max-imum safety remained in place, and retained strong public support, even as they failed to stem the spread and as the collateral damage they inflicted mounted massively. A central question for the years ahead is what lesson we take away from this experience.

As early as April of last year, economists Julian Kozlowski, Laura Veldkamp, and Venky Venkateswaran documented in a National Bureau of Economic Re-search paper the "belief-scarring effects" of the pandemic. They predicted "a per-sistent change in beliefs about the probability of an extreme, negative shock" and "long-lived responses of beliefs to transitory events, especially extreme, unlikely ones." Through indecipherable equations and delightful terms such as "kernel density" and "martingale" properties, they made a simple point: we scare easily, and we stay scared a long time.

Manifested in economic behavior, these scholars project, such scarring would seriously damage long-term growth prospects. Carried over into other realms of life, it could produce a widespread risk aversion that is the very last thing the nation can afford now.

With luck, we will draw just the opposite conclusion from the recent trauma—namely, that boldness and well-calculated risks are superior to the futile quest for perfect safety. The near-miraculous speed with which effective vaccines have arrived furnishes one example, because it is hard to identify a riskier venture than vaccine research.

Many of the largest research-based companies in the world have exited the field due to scientific failure, regulatory obstacles, huge economic losses, and often severe criticism for the sin of trying. As *STAT* reported in 2018, the French pharmaceutical company Sanofi Pasteur abandoned its effort to produce a Zika vaccine after losing millions of dollars while enduring "horrible PR" for its trouble.

The COVID vaccine program at Merck, long one of the finest research organizations of any kind anywhere, ended in failure earlier this year. They are in good company: scores of firms attempted to solve the COVID puzzle, losing untold millions along the way. Novavax, a small Maryland firm, appears to have produced an approvable COVID vaccine. If so, it will be the firm's first success after being in business for thirty-four years.

But, as always, the risk-takers that succeeded have delivered enormous societal benefits, including the possibility that this pandemic will be conquered—or at least made manageable by the new vaccines they discovered.

Mark Twain wrote that a cat that steps on a hot stove will never do it again, but it will never step on a cold one, either. Here's hoping we draw the right lessons from our current trip across a very hot stove.

OUR CULTURAL CREVASSE

California's ham-fisted war on pork offers some useful lessons.
January 14, 2022

An intriguing feature of recent political life has been the sudden discovery by much of the American left of the virtues of federalism. Oh, there has been no conversion to the principle of subsidiarity, that decisions ought to be made at the levels closest to daily life. The leftists' credo still calls for overruling the choices of their benighted fellow citizens regarding labor laws, voting procedures—virtually anything where outcomes can be dictated centrally.

But, at least in cases where it has proved difficult to impose their will nationally, those of the statist persuasion have decided to move ahead in places under their control, and that has some indirect value to us all.

Consider the current case study of California's Proposition 12, which includes a provision whereby the state's voters were persuaded to ban the sale of pork from feeding operations unless they meet standards virtually nonexistent in the industry today.

The proposition, approved in 2018 and effective as of January 1, imposes criminal and civil penalties on anyone selling pork from a facility where sows live in less than twenty-four square feet or might touch an enclosure when turning around. A trace percentage of the nation's livestock farms meet this test, and those that do serve almost entirely niche local markets.

The Supreme Court is now weighing whether to take a case from the agriculture industry challenging the proposition. (The U.S. Court of Appeals for the Ninth Circuit allowed it to stand.)

Here is not the place, and the author is not the person, to argue either the scientific merits of California's radical new requirements, or the legal prospects for a rule that would have impacts so large and so far beyond the state's borders.

Suffice to say that both are dubious. The proposition was cooked up not by anyone with expertise in agriculture or food safety, but by people whose sole concern is animal rights. As the agriculture community's Supreme Court brief says, "The law is based on a human health rationale so patently false that California has declined to defend it."

The extraterritorial reach and burden of the California rule might well lead to its being struck down. The state imports about 99% of its pork, so the entire burden of the new requirements will fall on producers elsewhere, especially small farmers, either to fork over an estimated total of $300 million to $350 million for building entirely new facilities, or to forgo selling in California, about 13% of the U.S. pork market.

One extraordinary provision of Prop 12 declares that agents of the California Department of Food and Agriculture are free to come on the property of producers to inspect for compliance. Visualizing a ponytailed, clipboard-toting coastal type marching onto a hog farm in Iowa or North Carolina suggests a new entry for one of those "world's most dangerous jobs" lists.

A state action more plainly burdensome to interstate commerce would be hard to imagine, and the Ninth Circuit has over the years had the highest reversal rate of any federal appeals court.

And yet, the nation could benefit from the ensuing spectacle should the law be allowed to stand. The first to feel the effects will be Californians themselves. Whatever the industry response to the new regime, they will quickly be paying much more for pork, when they can find it at all. As you sow, so shall you reap. Sorry.

The famous phrase "laboratories of democracy" is still the most apt description of our federal system and, along with its protection of local liberties, its greatest advantage. For instance, the legalization of marijuana in many states is furnishing real-world evidence for others to study in making their own decisions.

An activist governor or mayor is constantly watching for successful innovations elsewhere to copy and adopt. But the negative lessons are just as valuable. Most lab experiments fail, and science learns as much from those as from those that finally succeed.

The accelerating out-migration from high-tax states (California prominent among them) is an instructive caution to governments elsewhere. The more extreme anti-law-enforcement policies have already demonstrated their absurdity, sadly at a tragic cost in human life.

Occasionally, actions work out so unfortunately that the jurisdiction reverses field itself. Kansas chose to undo tax reductions that went too far, and a number of cities are now refunding the same police they so recently defunded. But even where some poor citizens remain stuck with the consequences, folly in one place serves as a valuable caution to all the rest.

So, if California's ham-handed approach to pig production takes effect, there will be a lot learned. One doubts the results will affirm its wisdom. This latest novelty from the once-Golden State almost certainly will fit in the "for heaven's sake, don't" category. But such mistakes, and the system that permits them and the teaching moments they provide, serve us all very well.

This must be what it felt like to be a loyalist in 1770.
September 7, 2021

This must be what it felt like to be a loyalist in 1770 or so. He knows that he is a citizen of the Greatest Nation, and is grateful, but he lives among many who feel increasingly mistreated, disrespected, even held in contempt by the Crown and by the courtiers who surround the throne of power in a distant capital.

Many direct their ire at the king's ministers, or at a parliament in which they feel they have no voice, but the sense of estrangement grows steadily. The loyalist remains devoted to his nation and its institutions, but wishes that his rulers were more attuned to the extent of the restiveness in what they seem to regard as their empire, and more sensitive to the legitimacy of many of those concerns.

Out here in what I'll call the colonies—the lands beyond the centers of power—rules that must seem wise and just to the national lawmakers often come across as clueless, contemptuous edicts. Our voting laws, land use policies, labor laws, fiscal freedom to lower taxation, all are to be overridden.

A tiny parliamentary majority seeks to pad its paper-thin margin, enhancing its ability to continue such trespasses, by creating what is known as a "rotten borough"—with few voters but a seat at the legislative table nonetheless.

People here, where government lives within its means, watch in wonderment as those in authority run up unimaginable mountains of debt, accumulated not for investment in the long-term future but for current consumption. Doomed to face the inescapable burden of servicing and repaying those debts, our children will experience true taxation without representation.

Escalating migration to the provinces demonstrates that dissatisfaction with current government is shared even in the power centers, but when the new arrivals reach their refuges, they may find that the impositions they were fleeing have followed them. There are even rumors that the taxing authorities they thought they were escaping will try to tax their income in their new homes.

One can try to rationalize that these actions, as the imperialists of old told themselves, are motivated by a sincere missionary spirit, a desire to evangelize and convert the heathens, by force if necessary, "for their own good."

But my neighbors who still cherish traditional ways of life must be forgiven if they do not surrender meekly and instantly to what they interpret as an unprovoked and unwarranted assault on sincere and legitimate customs and beliefs. Blanket denunciations of entire regions or categories of people only serve to strengthen the credibility of the most strident and radical anti-establishment voices.

Observing the growing discord, a loyalist hopes for ways to defuse this ill will and accommodate understandable resentments before they become even more virulent.

Perhaps the best idea for a better way forward is to devolve or, better said, restore more decisions to lower levels of government. The idea has been suggested by numerous commentators, but it is especially well defined and defended by Brian Riedl in his recent paper for the Manhattan Institute. Riedl argues that returning more authority to states and localities would foster more competent, flexible, creative government, arrived at by less hostile, more bipartisan means.

He names health care, education, welfare, and infrastructure as logical realms in which states would be likely to deliver services more competently, flexibly, imaginatively, and with far greater accountability than the federal government ever does. He notes that Europe is full of countries smaller than most American states, who manage to operate effectively in these areas. To the challenge that some states might not handle these tasks well, he replies, dispositively, "Compared with what?"

The most important benefit of a Riedl-like plan might not be its superior competence but an alleviation of alienation. To those ideologues among us who are "so convinced of the superiority of their policies that nothing less than their implementation from sea to shining sea is acceptable," who believe that "the other party's approach is so destructive that no American should live with its consequences, even if local voters unwisely choose to vote for it," Riedl recommends a dose of "humility, modesty, gradualism, and acceptance."

That's an appealing list, although he missed a chance by not also playing today's ace and king of trump, "diversity" and "inclusion."

My disaffected colonial neighbors aren't seeking to universalize their ways and values, only to be afforded the tolerance to live by them without harassment or disdain. Humility and modesty seem quaintly out of fashion, and central authorities almost never turn loose of power once they have seized it, but even small gestures of "acceptance" and understanding would go a long way.

The Chinese Communist Party's 100th birthday vs. America's 250th.
August 9, 2021

Two anniversaries, one just concluded and one approaching, should prompt some thinking about the nature and purpose of such occasions, and specifically those of national scale.

This summer, the Chinese Communist Party commemorated its centennial in the style at which dictatorships specialize. Everyone from the smallest children to the highest officialdom was "invited" to applaud the successes of the past hundred years—the latest 2% of Chinese history. The events were uniformly grandiose and uplifting. Never was heard a discouraging word.

This nationwide gala coincided with a surge of nationalistic fervor, much state-sponsored but much apparently spontaneous, among many Chinese citizens and, it is reported, especially the young. Enthusiasm for Confucianism, with its emphasis on obedience and respect for authority, is growing in concert with calls for *wenhua zixin*, or cultural self-confidence.

President Xi Jinping's speeches and party propaganda during the centennial pounded the theme of China's coming dominance over an economically fading and culturally decadent United States. The picture presented to the nation and the world was of a China about to resume its rightful place as the center of the world after a brief interruption by effete Western values.

Meanwhile, July Fourth celebrations reminded many Americans of the imminence of our own next big anniversary, the 250th, semiquincentennial (yikes, can we find maybe a four- or five-syllable term for it?) of the Declaration of Independence in 2026.

It will be an unusually telling occasion. The way we choose to commemorate that event will define not only who we are as a society today but also who we will be—a successful, world-leading society or, as Xi sees us, one en route to self-imposed decline.

Predictably, and sadly, the first calls are being heard for using the 250th as yet another occasion to dwell on America's shortcomings. One interest group looks forward to a "new" patriotism based on "radical honesty" about the nation's systemic betrayal of its ideals and vital principles.

Well, that would be one way. Boy, I'm sure glad I'm not on the invite list when these folks celebrate family landmarks. They must be a real blast: "Happy anniversary, dear. Here's a list of all the things you've done to disappoint, anger, and betray me over the past year." Or "Happy birthday, son. Let's go over all your failures and unacceptable actions during your life so far." But that's the use to which some believe we should put our 250th.

Imagine what even a tiny gesture of non-radical honesty would have led to during the Chinese Communist Party's centennial. We can be sure there were no apologies for Mao Zedong's murdered millions, no wreath-layings at Tiananmen Square, or protests at the gates of Uyghur concentration camps, no teach-ins about the dehumanization of omnipresent state surveillance and "social credit" systems. Anyone murmuring about any of these systemic wrongs would risk finding himself on the receiving end of the holiday fireworks.

No one is calling for ignoring any of America's inequities, past or present. Americans' capacity for self-criticism is a laudable, essential part of our democratic tradition, and a major reason for the improvements we continue to make in extending freedom. The question raised here is whether a historic anniversary is the time for even more of it, or whether there is not value in pausing now and then to appreciate and recognize the good in a person, or a nation.

July 4, 1776, marked a huge step forward out of a world of monarchy into a new world of freedom, opportunity, and self-government. It was very far from the last step, or a complete step, but undeniably it was a forward one. The autocrats of the time understood that and trembled. The oppressed of the world understood that and drew heart from it. It was a watershed event in human history.

We have all year, every year, to examine—I almost said "wallow in"—our shortcomings. There should still be moments when, welcoming differing views, as always, we accentuate the positive, celebrate the goodness of our people and the good that the nation has done in its first quarter millennium.

We should welcome the new attention to Juneteenth as a new day of celebration, for the most positive of reasons. It marks not the largest blot on our history but its eradication, the stamping out of slavery, by a white-dominated nation resolved to take its next step forward. That victory was accomplished through the sacrificial death of hundreds of thousands of its men. That is cause not for self-recrimination but for pride, as July 2026 should be.

A successful society for all requires constant self-examination but also a strong degree of confidence and morale. A nation with our history, whose main adversaries today are a seventh-century theocracy, an oligarchic kleptocracy, and a totalitarian autocracy, has every reason, at least on a landmark birthday, to observe author Alex Haley's maxim: "Find the good and praise it."

**Tossing around "Nazi" and "fascist" as insults
is reckless and historically illiterate.
July 11, 2021**

Words matter. They're not weapons or violence, in the fatuous formulation one still occasionally hears these days. But some words are freighted with so much historical or emotional heft that their casual or imprecise use comes with a cost.

For instance, it has been suggested that commentators avoid applying the term "genocide" to China's persecution of its Uyghur population. Even given the anti-Uyghur campaign's massive scale, involving millions of victims, and the genuine horrors it entails, the argument holds that the Chinese practices stop short of true genocide, which means the mass slaughter of an entire people. Accusations of genocide, as opposed to, say, "crimes against humanity," risk "diminishing the unique stigma of the term," the *Economist* wrote earlier this year.

Agree or disagree, the call for caution before applying the most damning labels is a worthy one. Allow me to nominate two more such words to be reserved more carefully for their proper place and time.

Inapt use of "Nazi" is not new but has proliferated in recent years, hurled by hands both left and right. It was thrown at presidents George W. Bush and Barack Obama. The term has been used to criticize immigration enforcement by one side and pandemic lockdowns by the other. Even in the early Internet days, in 1990, writer Mike Godwin formulated the theorem that "as an online discussion continues, the probability of a reference or comparison to Hitler or Nazis approaches 1."

Such reckless verbiage is, of course, not just grossly disproportionate and non-analogous to the real thing, it's historically illiterate. The Anti-Defamation League has frequently had to issue reproaches such as, "Glib comparisons to Nazi Germany are offensive and a trivialization of the Holocaust."

The term "fascist" is, if anything, even more absurdly misused, also by both of today's tribes. From one side, fascist has been applied to proponents of gun control, mask mandates, and speech codes. From the other side, to almost anyone who deviates from their various orthodoxies: people dubious about cutting police budgets during a crime and homicide surge, committed feminists who balk at today's more extreme demands on gender issues, college presidents supportive of free expression, and so on. A Christmas Day article on Salon attacked Hallmark movies as "fascist propaganda." I'm not making that up.

Here, too, ignorance reigns. The inventor of fascism a century ago, Benito Mussolini, also defined it: "Everything in the state, nothing against the state, nothing outside the state." That sounds closer to one side of today's arguments than the other, but let's stipulate that neither really is advocating the complete eradication of voluntary, intermediating institutions or of all forms of personal freedom. At least not yet.

The loosening of discipline around the terrible insults that "Nazi" and "fascist" represent has crept beyond the fevered denizens of Internet chat rooms and fringe "activists." Thinkers I admire deeply, such as Michael Gerson and Jonah Goldberg, have launched the Other F-bomb—Gerson at the supporters of the previous president, Goldberg in his 2008 book *Liberal Fascism*. The *New York Times* columnist Michelle Goldberg spat it at a U.S. senator for suggesting the use of federal troops in a public safety emergency. Good idea or not, it hardly merited the fascist slur, any more than it did in Little Rock 1958, Detroit 1967, or D.C. 2021.

This is not an argument for either side of any of these issues. It isn't a plea for "safe spaces" because of the hurtful character of such invective. They are, after all, only words. It's just a suggestion that words packed with this much meaning not be thrown around so loosely, and ignorantly.

Somebody once said—maybe it was George Carlin; gee I miss him—"What's another good word for synonym?" Instead of "Nazi" or "fascist," how about "tyrannical," "autocratic," "coercive," "despotic," or "dictatorial," just for starters?

Because, God forbid, we may one day need to use those other words accurately again, and if so, it would be important that we not have cheapened them and erased their actual meaning from memory. There are real concentration camps in this world, but they're not in El Paso or Portland, Oregon. Innocent people are executed for their ethnic background or religious beliefs, but not in Seattle or Tuscaloosa, Alabama. As a people, we are nowhere near the kind of polity that produces such atrocities, and we ought not talk to each other as though we are.

Free speech's worst enemies aren't who you'd expect.
August 29, 2018

Within weeks of each other, two prominent speakers visited the university where I work and made strikingly similar observations. Nadine Strossen, former longtime president of the American Civil Liberties Union, and Geoffrey R. Stone, a renowned constitutional scholar at the University of Chicago, each noted with bemusement that the people whose freedom of speech they had most often labored to protect are now too often its worst enemies. Their careers had begun by defending leftist causes against autocratic rules and institutions, they said, but now involve arguing against the intolerance of those who had typically been allies.

Thank goodness we still have thinkers such as these, ones who are willing to stay engaged with the free-speech debate. The resolute advocacy of people such as Strossen and Stone—invaluable in its credibility and admirable in their courage to express it—is the nation's best hope to veer away from the new authoritarianism now threatening our democratic system.

No one has stronger credentials. Stone may be America's most honored First Amendment authority, the producer of a host of award-winning books and the editor of the Oxford University Press's Inalienable Rights series of works on the topic by other respected authors. Strossen, the youngest person and first woman to head the ACLU when she began her seventeen-year tenure as president in

1991, has led for decades across virtually the entire spectrum of liberal causes, including abortion rights, affirmative action, and marijuana legalization, always from a staunch civil-liberties perspective.

Both grew up defending, as they saw it, the rights of minority groups, anti-Vietnam War protesters, and others involved in causes commonly characterized as left-wing. Now, in maintaining their lifelong defense of free expression, these two liberal lions find themselves often aligned with more-conservative camps that might have once represented the opposition. And they are arguing with, occasionally being maligned by, those who fancy themselves today's leading leftists.

But they are undeterred. A few years ago, Stone led the drafting of a clear and forthright statement in defense of free expression at his university that is so well done that others of us in higher education have labeled it the Chicago Principles and adopted it verbatim at our schools. Strossen travels and lectures and recently published a book for the Oxford series Hate: Why We Should Resist It with Free Speech, Not Censorship, challenging the growing orthodoxy about so-called hate speech.

In a factual and dispassionate way, Strossen's book demolishes the case for government censorship of hate speech. Laws that attempt to block it are unavoidably overbroad and vague from a constitutional standpoint. Such speech causes little or no real harm, let alone that "serious, imminent" injury that justifies government limitation. There is no justification for having one rule for some identity groups and a different rule for everyone else. Such censorship may imagine that it acts on behalf of minorities, but invariably it endangers minority rights and sooner or later is likely to be used against them.

The principled consistency shown by Stone and Strossen is depressingly rare these days. On both sides of the current political tribal warfare, people have shown themselves quick to abandon supposedly core convictions in rationalizing the actions of their tribe.

It's hard to name anyone more credible to make the case for free speech than these two, with their unimpeachably liberal records. The same assertions made by people of a different philosophical profile, or by those on the receiving end of today's repression, are easily dismissed or ignored by the perpetrators and, too often, by the news media.

It's even harder to think of a more courageous stance on free speech than Strossen and Stone's. Taking on the dogma of one's political brethren is tremendously harder than chiming in against traditional adversaries. It's a familiar truth that the most brutal fights tend to be between close allies; ask pro-life Democrats or "McConnell Republicans."

The gross excesses of today's would-be authoritarians, on campus and elsewhere, have started generating an encouraging back pressure from the only kind of voices that are likely to prevail against them. Here and there, academics terrorized in their own classrooms and journalists attacked for unwelcome coverage have begun to speak up.

But all along, a few brave stalwarts such as Geoffrey Stone and Nadine Strossen were standing in the breach, defending the most basic right of a free people. Let's hope many others will take wisdom from their advocacy and courage from their example.

We won't know how foolish we look until a long time from now. April 20, 2018

At the first meeting of a class I teach about the causes and consequences of World War I, each student is assigned a seat at a table with the flag of one of the combatant countries in the center. I explain that during the semester they will be asked to speak about and defend the actions of "their country" from the perspective of a citizen of that time and place. Hindsight is not permitted; they are to put themselves as much as they can into the position and the mindset of the French, British, Germans, Austrians, Russians, or Turks of a century ago.

We spend a part of the first class discussing the fallacy of "presentism," through which the values, mores, and conventions of the present day are used to judge, almost always harshly and sanctimoniously, our predecessors. Will Durant wrote of the tendency for humankind, at each point of the modern era, to imagine that history is a straight line upward, leading to the "us" of the current day. We seem especially vulnerable to this conceit these days.

The European peoples of a century ago fell hard for the errors of presentism. They were riding the tide of a century of stunning economic improvement and technological advances, every bit as transformational as those of the past few decades. Between 1815 and 1914, Britain's per capita gross domestic product grew nearly three times as fast as it had in the preceding century. The steam engine, the sewing machine, the railroad, electricity, the telegraph, the telephone, the airplane, and so many more breakthroughs convinced the people of 1914 that a golden age had arrived, in which a benevolent science was on its way to conquering distance, want, and the tedium of daily work.

Moreover, humanity was not only wealthier but so very much wiser. The barbarity of war was surely a thing of the past, left behind by the more mature, enlightened, and sophisticated people of the time. A runaway best seller, absorbed by elites across the continent, was Norman Angell's *The Great Illusion*, which asserted that the "interdependent" industrialized nations would see and avoid the stupidity of fighting, or that if a war did start, the obvious economic damage would lead them to put a quick stop to it. A few years later, 20 million were dead, most at the hands of machine guns, aerial bombs, and other recent products of scientific progress, and perhaps 50 million more by a war-spawned influenza their "modern" medicine proved powerless to stop.

Even worse, the collapse of their golden age ushered in a new dark age over much of the globe, in which totalitarians such as Hitler, Stalin, Mao, and Pol Pot murdered tens of millions and enslaved the survivors within their reach. It is presentism's smug folly to assume that we in the present day are superior intellectually and morally and that the past has nothing to teach us.

Presentism's principal tributaries are a lack of knowledge and a deficient capacity for empathy. One of today's premier historians has written that "historical illiteracy is the new normal." How dismally true that is. The list of basic facts today's Americans don't know is too embarrassing and discouraging to repeat. The fundamental civic concepts of which majorities of both young and old are ignorant is equally appalling.

The quality of empathy, the ability to discern and understand the feelings of others, was denoted by Adam Smith as the most distinctive of human traits. Evidence of its erosion is everywhere these days in the burgeoning cultural estrangement we now aptly call tribalism.

It finds further expression in the sneering denigration of America's history and, it seems, almost all those who made it. A better reading is that the storyline of America, with all its imperfections past and continuing, is about the steady expansion of human freedom and unprecedented, widespread material prosperity.

That ongoing journey took its longest step forward in the lives and work of the so-called founding generation. Their work was incomplete, but essential, and all that their times made possible. They made—gasp—compromises. They declined to let the ideological perfect be the assassin of the achievable good. And so a world of freedom, justice, and equality was brought much nearer by their heroic efforts.

Those who indulge in the arrogance of presentism can be assured that, a century from now, we will be looked on by our descendants (or whatever genetically enhanced or computerized species has displaced us) as hopelessly ignorant and morally backward, in ways we cannot foresee. More time spent trying to understand and empathize with those who struggled with harder problems than ours might enable us to learn from their accomplishments as well as their mistakes, and look a little less absurd to our successors when their "present" comes.

BAD POLICY AND ITS TRAPPINGS

Modern monetary theory, debunked everywhere
except among government big spenders.
November 8, 2022

The Piltdown Man hoax, about finding the "missing link" between humans and apes, escaped exposure for forty-one years. Phrenology had a similar run of credibility; even some widely respected scientists thought the contours of a person's cranium could be "read" for what it said about intelligence and character. Lysenkoism was around long enough that, to his eternal disgrace, the proponent of the bizarre theory of plant heritability got his name attached to it.

Blatant bogosity—to employ a college roommate's useful coinage—is no guarantee that a preposterous idea will die quickly.

These days, transparent nonsense can be shielded by tribalism or the groupthink of "elite" opinion. If a notion is convenient enough in justifying a preferred outcome, it can survive despite mountains of evidentiary, or just commonsense, refutation. Think of imaginary stolen elections or defunding police in an era of exploding crime.

One recent bit of hogwash appeared to have expired quickly. A concept dubbed modern monetary theory (MMT), after percolating for years on the fringes of economics, enjoyed a brief run of massive publicity a few years ago when an academic trying to popularize it was, for a time, taken seriously in suggesting the modern equivalent of alchemy. The suggestion was that a government could borrow unlimited amounts of money in its own currency and repay it without risk simply by printing more of that currency.

There was nothing modern about a government spending wildly beyond its means and searching for an easy way out. In 1455, Henry VI granted patents to those pursuing alchemy for the purpose of "enabling of the king to pay all the debts of the crown in real gold and silver." "Medieval monetary theory" would have been a more apt label for the recent version of Henry's fantasy.

And yet for those whose zeal for bigger government was not sated by the trillions already on or headed for the government's books, MMT offered a fig leaf of validity. It came under George Orwell's familiar heading of an idea so absurd that only an intellectual could believe it, and the theory probably only attracted any attention at all because the academic in question was associated with a presidential campaign.

MMT died a quicker death in the public square than its predecessors in quackery, or so it seemed. First, a host of intellectuals, of all persuasions, did not buy it and said so. A survey of economists by the University of Chicago's Booth School of Business found zero in agreement and nearly three-fourths strongly disagreed with the theory's basic assertion.

Many of the earliest and most emphatic critics were especially credible because their policy preferences are not hostile to more expensive, more interventionist government. Prominent economists, including left-leaners such as Larry H. Summers and Paul Krugman, were quick to dismantle and dismiss the MMT notion.

Summers, likening MMT to the more extreme version of supply-side economics, labeled it a "fallacious" product of "fringe economists" that would lead directly to inflation or even hyperinflation. Krugman, attacking MMT more than once, has called it "indefensible" and "the cryptocurrency of macroeconomics."

The same points made by limited-government advocates or debt-fretters such as my colleagues at the Committee for a Responsible Federal Budget might have been ignored as familiar and predictable, but when even the likes of the Progressive Policy Institute chimed in, the last rites for MMT had been performed. Or at least they had in intellectual terms. But it's hard to tell from the federal government's continuing behavior.

MMT's academic cover might have been blown, but that has not slowed the unprecedented torrent of spending—of borrowed dollars—gushing out of Washington. Each recent administration has outdone its predecessor for profligacy, but records are made to be broken and the current regime seems determined to break them. Collectively, Washington's actions over the past couple of years have taken the nation's debt well beyond $30 trillion and driven inflation to multidecade highs.

The Federal Reserve Bank of San Francisco calculated that the "stimulus" bills during the pandemic added about three percentage points to the current price rise, just as Summers predicted. Unfazed, the federal government belched forth yet another twelve-digit spending bill earlier this year, this time with the chutzpah to label it "inflation reduction." The MMT theory might be dead, but its zombie lives on.

Ronald Reagan used to say that an economist is someone who sees something work in practice and wonders if it works in theory. When something fails in both theory and practice, one would think that would pretty well settle the matter. Apparently not.

We stopped measuring the shape of people's skulls a long time ago. These days it's our national leaders who, as my mother used to say, "need their heads examined."

The Biden administration's "workarounds" damage the machinery of democracy.
November 8, 2021

In a job that keeps a person in regular contact with brilliant and ingenious engineers, one develops a deep admiration for people who run toward hard problems and devise inventive ways to solve them. When one of SpaceX's recent private astronaut flights developed a sensor problem in a waste management system, flight managers quickly took the sensor offline and found workarounds for the hazard. And we all remember the glorious nerds who saved Apollo 13.

But what's commendable or even lifesaving in operating complex machinery is problematic or even dangerous when applied to the machinery of democracy. Such attempts are hardly new, and no workaround was ever more flagrant than the persistent attempt to undo a presidential election result. But the pace and deviousness of these machinations have, if anything, increased under the new regime.

At summer's end, the Biden administration directed the Labor Department's Occupational Safety and Health Administration to promulgate an "emergency temporary standard" ordering all private employers of one hundred employees or more to require coronavirus vaccination or face punitive fines. No seeking statutory authority, no rulemaking and comment process, just a sudden ukase from on high.

Faced with likely unanswerable challenges to the constitutionality of such a diktat, the White House staff chirped (meaning: issued a cheerfully triumphal tweet) that the OSHA maneuver was a "workaround."

This end run of all prescribed procedures joined a growing parade of such maneuvers. A new majority at the Federal Trade Commission in September peremptorily jettisoned a formal rule on vertical acquisitions that had been widely lauded for bringing clarity to merger decision-making. More than a year of internal deliberations and public comments were cast aside in days.

In fact, this particular move constituted a rare double workaround. Now, with no guidance as to which mergers are likely to receive FTC approval, many companies will opt for caution and never attempt them, sparing an agency overtly hostile to such transactions the work of actually studying proposals and building a case against them. Maybe "preemptive workaround" is a better phrase for this especially clever move.

On the legislative front, the ruling party has many advocates for chucking long-standing procedures, most notably the Senate filibuster. But as that's proving difficult, maybe they can just intimidate the parliamentarian into calling immigration or pro-union labor law changes "budgetary" matters, and therefore legal for incorporation into a reconciliation bill. Call it the "involuntary surrogate workaround."

The pandemic, which furnished abundant case studies in public sector incompetence, also offered countless workaround opportunities, and excuses for them. A White House approval of "booster shots for all" not only short-circuited the Food and Drug Administration's "gold standard" approval process, it ignored a contradictory agency recommendation. Two scientists resigned in protest but, hey, what's the fuss? It was just a simple workaround.

Ideas for redesigning the machinery of self-governance are always in order, and sometimes badly needed. But discarding or violating rules while they are still in effect is corrosive of the trust on which all depends. It furthers the already pervasive notion that, rules be damned, the fix is in.

In a recent campus appearance, Russian chess champion and human rights advocate Garry Kasparov surprised his audience with two answers, one to a question about threats to democracy, and another about how to lower the level of polarization afflicting American society.

Kasparov, who unlike today's pseudo-socialists has the advantage of actually having lived in Utopia, replied to both questions not by espousing specific policies or issues but by defending process. He confessed error in his early support of Boris Yeltsin, whom he said was correct in opposing a return to communism but wrong in resorting to force to do so. Kasparov linked that action to the nation's subsequent collapse back into tyranny:

What we didn't understand is that democracy is a process, not a result. The moment you go against the process, the moment you accept that your guy, who has the best intentions in this world, can violate the rules, can rig the result with a little bit of a tweak—it starts with little tweaks here and there—then that's it.

And a little later:

As I said, it's about protecting the process . . . I'm really worried that you see on one side people say, "Oh, since we lost, the election was rigged." On the other side you say, "Oh, we won, so we have to rig the system to make sure we will win next time."

Eschewing "working around" and returning to "working within" would be a step back toward the comity, community, and public confidence we now see so little of.

That entitlements can is getting heavier, and we're running out of road.
June 6, 2018

So another congressional session is half over and, we're told, is likely to go by without a mention of the moose on the American table, our preposterously out-of-control federal debt. It's not as though the stakes are high: just our standard of living, national security, all the discretionary activities of government, and literally our future as an autonomous, self-governing people. Every honest observer knows what will cause the coming crunch, so aptly termed by Erskine Bowles as "the most predictable crisis in history": the runaway autopilot programs we call "entitlements." Without changes there, no combination of other measures can come close to preventing the reckoning.

We all understand the silence. Our political class was long ago scared witless by the career-killing cheap shots aimed at anyone daring to commit candor about the topic.

So far, no one has fashioned a vocabulary that an elected official can use to level with voters about Social Security and Medicare and live to tell about it politically. Everyone believes, and polls confirm, the fabled third rail is as electrified as ever.

A well-functioning democracy would, by now, have had a mature national discussion marked by a recognition of the need to set priorities among finite resources, as well as the intergenerational unfairness of the status quo, the ethical wrongness of borrowing for current consumption instead of investing in the future, the feasibility of alternative remedies if only we would start now, and so on. Regrettably, but realistically, our republic at this point doesn't seem capable of discussions like that. Meanwhile, action really can't wait much longer; the can is getting heavier, and we're running out of road.

Maybe we should try rolling with the zeitgeist. Since we, for now, inhabit a polity dominated by cynicism, distrust, and the belief that "they" are misleading everyone else, maybe a pitch aligned with those dispositions—and embracing the attachment Americans plainly have to programs that are bankrupting our government—would work better. Something like:

Good evening, folks, and thanks for coming. Our topic tonight is the way those Washington elites are destroying the crucial set of government programs we call the "safety net," especially Social Security, Medicare, and Medicaid. It makes me furious when I think of how our politicians, from both parties, have put the safety net in terrible danger and tried to cover it up. And we have to take some action to save it from them. Let's start with Social Security.

They're not telling you this, but the money is running out, fast. They told us it was being held for our retirements, but instead they've been blowing it for years on all sorts of less important things.

That's not all. They've lied to you about how the system actually works. During your working years, your taxes pay the benefits for those already retired. The deal has always been that, when it's your turn, those still working will pay for yours. If you didn't know that—if you thought you were just getting your own money back—it's not your fault. The politicians didn't want you to know what was really going on. But starting soon, there won't be nearly enough workers, and nowhere near enough money, to keep the promises they've made to us. Shame on the whole lot of them.

Here's the good news: There is still time to do some simple, common-sense things to save the safety net. Just for one example: Why do we send retirement checks to Warren Buffett? When the system is running out of money, shouldn't we let the millionaires and billionaires provide for themselves, and conserve the money for those who really need it? There are plenty of other steps we could take that won't hurt anyone now or soon to be in the system, or anyone ever who really needs the protection. But the big shots don't want you to know about them, because then they'd have to admit to the mess they've made of our great Social Security system.

Our political class has botched a lot of things these past few years, and the way they've undermined our safety net is one of the worst. Let's pull together to save it while there's still time. Our parents left us peace of mind, and security. Let's fire the politicians we've got and elect some who will do the same for our kids, and theirs.

They're wrecking Medicare, too, by the way. But let's get into that at next week's town hall.

Nah, never mind. Even on this topic, where such rabble-rousing is actually pretty accurate and fair, one cannot really countenance it. Another crying need of our times is to stop tearing at and start rebuilding confidence in our institutions and those leading them. But the debt danger is, as they say these days, existential. Facts and fastidiousness have gotten us nowhere. If not a little demagoguery, what do you suggest?

We were right to worry about the nation's fiscal future.
But I know when to fold 'em.
January 27, 2021

Like most people, I really hate to admit defeat. Okay, some take it a little further than others, but it's among the most common of human traits. On a matter in which I've invested no small amount of time and worries, I'm throwing in the towel. Regarding our national fiscal future, as the man said, you've got to know when to fold 'em.

In a variety of public employments and from various posts in private life, I've been among those urging that we take greater care with our public finances to ward off serious, permanent damage to the economy and, just as important, to the safety net on which so many vulnerable Americans rely.

Until recently, I've held on tightly to two beliefs essential to long-term fiscal survival.

The first, grounded in actuarial reality, was that, if we began acting now, we could keep the promises of Social Security, Medicare, and the other so-called entitlement programs.

The second, always as much a matter of faith as of proven fact, was that the American people could engage in an adult conversation about the subject and support the needed changes, before it was too late. Surely someone eventually would appeal successfully to our reason and to our concern for our children, grandchildren, and the country's future.

I conclude, reluctantly and dejectedly, that it's time to face the unpleasant facts. The past decade demonstrates amply that our political process is not capable of the kind of decisions that are necessary. The temptation to savage anyone proposing safety net reform (the sine qua non of any serious fiscal rescue, really the only issue that matters) remains electorally irresistible and invariably effective.

From very different directions, either of the past two presidents could have led the nation to a safer place, but neither had any interest in doing so. Instead, both perpetuated the "noble lies"—"You're just getting your own money back," "We owe it to ourselves," etc.—by which the public has been misled through the years.

Even the modest, painless actions we could have started with, such as means-testing, or small, distant future increases in the age of eligibility, or correction of the system's over-adjustment for inflation, have never had a ghost of a chance.

Meanwhile, the inexorable arithmetic of dollars times demography has taken us past the point of no return. It's no longer possible to say that, by starting now, we can avert massive, and massively unfair, changes in the promises we have made, or that current beneficiaries have nothing to worry about. That line was crossed even before the emergency budget blowout of 2020 added trillions to the debt tab we will dump on younger generations.

There are parallels with other long-term, nation-threatening challenges of our time. We should have seen the pandemic coming and prepared for it. If the climate change computer models prove accurate, it is already too late to prevent the world's thermometer from rising to levels deemed unacceptable. While calling on us to take what preventive measures we can, the more serious leaders on these topics are hard at work on the goals of mitigation and adaptation.

However likely the climate problem or next pandemic is, the unraveling of the safety net is far more so. No computer models are needed to see that there is zero chance of delivering on the promises already in place, let alone the fresh, astonishing proposals in Washington to make these commitments even larger.

A start on mitigation would be for the Social Security Administration to begin including in beneficiary bulletins a disclosure that, starting soon, the system cannot fulfill all of its commitments. The disclosure could then provide sample calculations of the amount of savings a given recipient will need to replace those expected payments under alternative scenarios. Something similar could be done for doctors and medical students, projecting the deep cuts in reimbursement rates to which Medicare will resort.

Allowing the fiction of full payment for all to persist will only add the rage of betrayal to the hardships imposed by the now inevitable sudden cuts in benefits and huge tax increases. If you think confidence in the federal government is shaky now, wait until it starts reneging on these "sacred" promises. Better to come clean, and help people plan, starting now.

I recall watching with sad admiration decades ago the dauntless activism of what was once known as the captive nations lobby, those brave refugees and descendants from the Baltic states then subjugated by Soviet communism. One had to feel sorry for people pouring their energy into such a just but hopeless cause. I'm beginning to see those of us still pleading for safety net reform in much the same way.

Of course, for the captive nations activists, a miracle happened. A cataclysm only Ronald Reagan and a few other visionaries foresaw brought the liberation that their lobbying and demonstrations never could have achieved. It's too late for any such rescue of America's safety net. Might as well face it, and shift our efforts to the task of getting ready.

Senate Republicans could restore a bit of civility by confirming Neera Tanden.
December 22, 2020

On a wall somewhere, I have a historical artifact. It's only two decades old, but it might as well be on papyrus in Aramaic. It's the Senate tally sheet from January 23, 2001, recording my unanimous confirmation as director of the Office of Management and Budget. Along with Colin Powell's as secretary of state and Donald Rumsfeld's as defense secretary, my confirmation was moved through a Senate controlled by the opposition party on its first meeting day of the new year.

The pattern of permitting new presidents to form cabinets of their own choosing, and enabling them to get started promptly, began to erode after the inauguration of the administration I served. President Barack Obama saw four of his fifteen nominees delayed beyond his first weeks in office. Then President Trump was blocked on all but three. Now we read that an opposition Senate—if that is what results from the coming runoff elections in Georgia—may challenge a large number of president-elect Joe Biden's nominees.

News reports indicate that one nominee to be so targeted is Neera Tanden, proposed for the office in which I once served. Let's hope a different view prevails regarding Biden's choices, starting with that appointment. It may sound

Life in academia has a rhythm all its own, welcoming a crew of freshmen every August and watching their predecessors graduate every May. At Purdue, our new student orientation, Boiler Gold Rush, is a week of activities designed to set freshmen off on solid footing. Among my favorite events was the chance to see their expectant faces arrayed in Ross-Ade Stadium, knowing that tomorrow's great astronauts and accountants, engineers and entrepreneurs were in the crowd. (August 2021)

The other end of the academic year, commencement, is a deeply gratifying time at any university, and nowhere more so than at Purdue. After all, it is the reason institutions like ours exist in the first place and is a time of great traditions, both solemn and boisterous. At Purdue, one long-standing custom among aeronautical and astronautical engineering grads is to launch paper airplanes at the stage, with a hearty competition to see whose plane goes the farthest. In my office I always kept a collection of the winning models and invited the designers to stop by to autograph their creations. (May 2014)

Between freshman orientation and graduation, I tried to spend as much time as my schedule allowed with students. If you ever feel the least bit down about our nation's future, spend some time with Purdue students. Energetic, hardworking, and intellectually engaged, they never failed to impress me with their thirst for learning and eagerness to take on any challenge before them. (January 2013)

My personal photo album is filled with images of the terrific students I met during my ten years at Purdue. I had students join me for dinner at my on-campus home as often as possible. This beautiful late spring evening was spent with just a handful of our many student leaders. (May 2022)

In my own classroom or as an invited guest instructor, I always found teaching to be a deeply rewarding experience. Purdue is home to more than 3,300 immensely talented full-time faculty at its flagship campus in West Lafayette. We made hiring a priority, growing the full-time faculty by over 20% and ensuring that the faculty-to-student ratio remained among the highest of any land-grant university in the country. (November 2018)

Even on a campus of 50,000 top students, one comes along now and then who claims our hearts like none other. One such student was Tyler Trent, a superb young man whose life was cut tragically short at age 20 by osteosarcoma. Tyler had suffered bouts of the disease prior to joining the freshman class of 2017, but that didn't stop him from becoming a superfan of Boilermaker football, energizing the campus with his sheer determination, and captivating the empathy and support of Americans far and wide. Tyler's legacy lives on at the university he impacted so deeply, with the "T2" gate at Ross-Ade Stadium, a Courage and Resilience Award in his honor, and a research endowment at Purdue's Cancer Research Institute. (December 2017)

A principal goal I established early on was to elevate the reputation of Purdue University and to ensure that it attracted the national and international visibility it deserved but had never seemed to attain fully. One way was to augment our students' classroom learning and enrich the general intellectual environment of the university by bringing to campus some of our nation's most influential and impressive minds. This photo of renowned historian Walter Isaacson brings back great memories of the fascinating evening he treated the audience to. I hope you will take the time to read the excerpts of some of the Presidential Lecture Series events in part III of this book and to watch the full recordings. (September 2019)

In September 2017, we celebrated the installation of an authorized exact replica of Emanuel Leutze's *Washington Crossing the Delaware*. Thanks to the family of Ann Hawkes Hutton and the Washington Crossing Foundation, the awe-inspiring painting is on long-term loan to Purdue. National Book Award and Pulitzer Prize–winning historian Joseph Ellis joined us for the installation and gave an erudite and riveting lecture on George Washington's bold leadership in the Battle of Trenton, which was so pivotal to our nation's founding. Here, the curtains swing open, revealing the painting in its new home, the Great Library of the Wilmeth Active Learning Center, where I hope generations of Purdue students will be inspired by Washington and will be reminded of the blessings of liberty to which his courage and character gave birth.

Purdue is justifiably known as the "cradle of astronauts," with twenty-seven Boiler-makers having undertaken at least one mission into space, including Neil Armstrong, the first man to walk on the moon, and Gene Cernan, the most recent. In fact, nearly a third of U.S. spaceflights have included a Purdue graduate. In 2014, seven of our astronaut alumni returned to campus for a weekend reunion. A packed hall of more than 6,000 students, faculty, and community members were riveted by an on-stage conversation with Mark Brown, Gene Cernan, Drew Feustel, Gary Payton, Loren Shriver, Scott Tingle, and Charles Walker. It was a genuine thrill to share a stage with those remarkable, courageous men. (April 2014)

Some might rightly say we at Purdue will stop at nothing to tout the remarkable contributions our astronaut alumni have made to America's space program. So, when our
faculty and trustees voted to award an honorary doctorate to our very own Drew Feustel,
who at the time was orbiting Earth in the International Space Station, I thought it only
logical to confer the degree via satellite uplink. Thanks to our friends at NASA, some

technical wizardry, and Drew's good cheer, we managed to honor him live, with
some help in the hooding process by fellow Boilermaker-astronaut Scott Tingle.
After the conferral, Drew and Scott thrilled the assembled graduates by floating
up and out of the picture. (May 2018)

As a prelude to our April 2019 Presidential Lecture Series, we arranged for a special homecoming for the rare Lafayette meteorite, which had been blasted off the surface of Mars by an asteroid strike millions of years ago. Nearly a century after the meteorite was found in a drawer on campus and sent for identification to the Field Museum in Chicago, the fine folks at the museum generously agreed to return it to campus. West Lafayette mayor John Dennis (*above, center*) joined in the homecoming. On occasion new presidents at peer institutions call for advice, and I always tell them, "Be fortunate enough to have a terrific mayor for a partner." Through the enormous economic growth we triggered on and proximate to campus, and a nearly one-third increase in our student and population, the university and city never suffered the town–gown conflict so prevalent at other places. Purdue and I are eternally grateful for Mayor Dennis's leadership, collaborative spirit, and true friendship.

Another big part of our work to heighten Purdue's reputation was to attract major new investment on campus, within our research park, and in areas adjacent to campus. The opportunity to partner in innovative research with the university's outstanding faculty, as well as our focus on commercialization of research and business-friendly climate, gave Purdue a leg up when it came to some of the most recognizable companies. Here, on a beautiful July day in 2014, General Electric Aviation broke ground on a $100 million LEAP jet engine plant.

Over the years, we hosted dignitaries of every stripe, from corporate CEOs and presidents, to ambassadors and foreign elected officials, to U.S. cabinet members, undersecretaries, and assistant secretaries from three presidential administrations. No occasion was more special than the chance to host U.S. Secretary of Commerce Gina Raimondo

and Secretary of State Antony Blinken. The visit, at their request, was to discuss restoring our nation's semiconductor industry and included a tour of Purdue's advanced technology labs and conversations with the faculty who lead them. Joining the group was Indiana's own U.S. Senator Todd Young (*foreground, right*) and Governor Eric Holcomb (*background, right*). The visit concluded with an enlightening on-stage conversation. (September 2022)

Heightening Purdue's reputation also included broadening its land-grant mission. It didn't take long to realize that our state's urban public schools were never going to produce an acceptable number of low-income and minority students ready to succeed at Purdue. So we designed our own pathway to a Purdue education and, in 2016, opened the first Purdue Polytechnic High School in Indianapolis. We have started two more since then and are well down the road to opening a fourth. The first graduation ceremony, captured in the photo above and at the QR link, was a remarkable day, followed a few short weeks later by the arrival at West Lafayette of the first PPHS alumni to become Boilermaker freshmen. (June 2021)

Our land-grant mission didn't stop at our physical campuses and high schools. We knew we had to serve the population of adult learners for whom life interrupted their first attempt at a college degree. It became clear that building our own online platform and standing up an entire catalog of academic programs would take too long and cost far too much. So when presented with the chance to purchase for $1.00 the long-standing Kaplan University, we seized the opportunity. Since then, the newly branded Purdue Global has graduated tens of thousands of adult students who otherwise may never have returned to higher education.

Purdue's growth, especially in STEM disciplines, necessitated major investment in academic facilities. We built more than two dozen new facilities, adding more than 2 million gross square feet of classrooms and research space to campus. The Active Learning Center, whose dedication we celebrated with great fanfare in August 2017, houses twenty-seven classrooms designed to promote project-based, interactive learning.

Spring 2020

Fall 2020

Fall 2021

COVID dramatically changed the way we all did business, interacted, and lived our lives. Like every institution in the U.S., Purdue was forced to go online for the second half of the spring 2020 semester. But we were determined to use every bit of our ingenuity, flexibility, and talent to reopen campus for residential education in the fall 2020 academic term. Communication, to the entire community, was a priority. So we created dozens of videos and websites, isolation and quarantine housing, a mammoth testing facility, and ultimately a vaccine center. In this photo, two of our Protect Purdue ambassadors help me deliver a video message to the campus community. (August 2020)

The Protect Purdue Plan became the set of guiding principles for keeping our students, faculty, staff, and community as safe as possible during the pandemic. A key feature was a pledge we asked every member of the Purdue family to sign. Among other safety protocols, it committed every person on campus to wear masks in all public places on campus, and as you can see in this photo, it extended to the Purdue Polytechnic High Schools as well. Our students were absolute models in taking the Protect Purdue Pledge seriously, and I consistently credited them with Purdue's success in remaining fully open and providing the education every Boilermaker deserved. (September 2021)

Since its founding, Purdue has held steadfastly to its tradition of calling each graduate forward to receive a personalized diploma at commencement. Reportedly, we're the last university of any size to do so, and it means holding seven ceremonies. But in May 2020, when COVID forced us to move to a virtual ceremony, we were committed to holding the best remote commencement we could. I donned my cap and gown and delivered the commencement address to a lone videographer in an otherwise empty auditorium. (April 2020)

Yes, that's a motorized couch and a very fine way to arrive at commencement. Thanks to two enterprising and innovative Boilermakers, the couch cart was seen zooming all over campus during the spring 2021 semester. When COVID meant holding commencement in Ross Ade Stadium, I figured showing up on the couch cart would bring some levity to our typically solemn occasion. Our marketing team took it one step further with a fun video. (May 2021)

Well before the couch cart, I seem to have developed a reputation among students as a guy who would do just about anything they asked . . . within reason. I suppose it started with my daily workouts among the students at Purdue's recreation facility and gained momentum from there. Here, I was enlisted to "jump the tracks," elbows linked with a group of freshmen. Some tracks preserved from an old rail line nearby were later installed on campus in trib-

ute to our "Boilermakers" nickname. A new tradition of jumping the tracks emerged as part of Boiler Gold Rush, symbolizing students' official entry to Boilermaker status. (August 2013)

And speaking of doing just about anything for our students . . . Here I am surrounded by some Tark Sharks. The students of Tarkington Hall, one of Purdue's oldest residence halls, have established a relatively new tradition of wearing shark onesies to home games and cheering on their Boilermakers with great gusto. I was proud to don a shark suit for a segment of "Where's Mitch?"—a fun addition to Purdue football games in which I ensconced myself in the student section, giving that week's group a special appearance on the stadium's video screens. As for the onesie, it was beautifully monogrammed for me by one of the Tark Sharks. (November 2021)

And then there were the football games when a groups of students asked me to pose for a photo alongside images of . . . well, myself . . . including a giant poster of my head and a mock *Vogue* cover. It was always great fun, and spending time with students during the games was a real highlight of our home games.

Somehow, I let Purdue's All-American Marching Band convince me to ride my Harley onto the field during the halftime show at one of our football games. The band was established in 1886 and is a true icon at Purdue—especially impressive since our university does not offer a music major. Whenever I have the chance to brag about it, I note that the band's 380-plus members represent nearly every academic discipline, from engineering to pharmacy. (September 2013)

Purdue is home to some of the finest science, technology, and engineering students found anywhere in the world. And when it comes to go-cart racing, in Purdue's own Grand Prix or in international races, they are fiercely competitive. When some of our students asked me to suit up and hit the track for ten laps at top speed in the electric racer they built, it was a quick "Yes." (October 2018)

Purdue wouldn't be the top STEM university it is if it didn't go all out to observe the first total solar eclipse to be visible in the U.S. in a century. It was a great chance to join a couple of thousand students who turned out, equipped with free viewing glasses and all sorts of do-it-yourself viewing paraphernalia. (August 2017)

Some events come around . . . well . . . every 200 years. When in 2016 Indiana's bicentennial celebration included a relay through every county, I was thrilled to put on my running shoes and carry the torch past the resting place of John Purdue, our university's founder. And you've got it—that torch was designed and produced by students in Purdue's College of Engineering. (October 2016)

Being Purdue's president came with one or two perks that I was unashamed to take advantage of. When some Harley Davidson execs came to campus to promote the company's new Livewire electric motorcycle, they didn't have to ask twice when offering me the chance to take a test-drive. The company consistently recruits Boilermaker interns and graduates, with more than forty company employees holding Purdue degrees. (September 2016)

One birthday I was given a personalized T-shirt cannon proudly bearing the Purdue *P*. It was a lot of fun to take to home games, both basketball and football, and let loose into an enthusiastic crowd. My technique definitely improved over time. (January 2020)

At any university, raising funds is among the president's core responsibilities. At Purdue, it was never a hard sell to get help from loyal Boilermakers, but creativity never hurt. For our second annual Purdue Day of Giving, our development team had the clever idea to offer zip line rides across the football field in exchange for donations, and I was the first to "volunteer." Armed with a selfie stick and assurances that the operators knew what they were doing, I took my own Giant Leap. In every successive year, the Purdue Day of Giving raised a new record in donations, going, as I said, "from an intriguing experiment to proven success." (April 2015)

old-fashioned, but to me there is no good reason to depart from a presumption of deference in this instance.

Republicans have legitimate grievances after a record-shattering, well over 300 cloture votes obstructing Trump nominees. And some senators, we're told, have individual reasons to oppose Tanden. Apparently indulging in another collapsed standard of our times, she in the past tweeted or otherwise emitted a number of unkind, personal nastygrams aimed at some of those who now will consider her nomination.

Shame on her. But, in the recent toxic wasteland of national affairs, if we disqualify everyone who ever unleashed a smarmy or juvenile cheap shot, we'd have very few people left in Washington. Don't tempt me.

Another reason for Republicans to stay their hand is, frankly, the Office of Management and Budget isn't that important, or at least it's not likely to be for the next few years. OMB can be an enormously effective instrument, but it depends entirely on the philosophy and governing approach of whoever is president. As a general rule, administrations favoring big spending, hyperactive regulation, and unfettered departments and agencies don't have as much use for OMB. Odds are that the next administration will prefer higher levels of spending and rulemaking, and OMB will have correspondingly less influence over events.

Deferring to Biden's OMB choice, as well as most if not all others in this initial round, would be not an endorsement of any individual but just a small display of the respect once shown to the other side's presidents and to the office they hold. One day, when Republicans return to the executive branch, they might be glad they did.

Confirmation of Tanden in particular would demonstrate a willingness, not seen often in recent days, to overlook the personal and the petty, to honor the biblical injunction and "return no one evil for evil." I'm presuming here that senators are, as they frequently claim to be, troubled by the harshness and crudity of our current political discourse. So here's a chance to demonstrate it, along with a degree of magnanimity. (You remember what that is.)

Conversely, a confirmation hearing dominated by histrionic recitations of previous little insults and so's-your-old-man rejoinders will just make a dreary situation worse. The issue isn't whether payback is deserved. The very fact that it arguably is would make refraining that much more magnanimous.

Acquiescing in this appointment would not preclude for a moment confrontations over policy as vigorous and even rancorous as senators think warranted. Goodness knows, I had them. All these years later, people still occasionally bring

up to me C-SPAN duke-outs I had with such senators such as Robert Byrd and
Fritz Hollings, who had been among the one hundred ayes on that OMB confirmation tally sheet.

My own previous encounters with Tanden were invariably adversarial. When
I was governor of Indiana, her interest group attacked our state reforms of health
care, infrastructure, and education, always harshly (and, as the subsequent evidence showed, unjustifiably). I was once disinvited from a forum her organization
was hosting for the sin of disagreeing about yet another issue. But, were I voting
in the Senate, I would save my criticisms, and negative ballots, for the substantive arguments to come, regardless of who is at OMB.

Sadly, from public profanity to violence on TV to the collapse of objective
journalism, we have seen that it is rare if not impossible to revive standards once
they have decayed and ratcheted downward. The tradition of granting deference
to a new president's picks may not yet be beyond resuscitation, but one more cycle like the last one and it probably will be. Confirming Neera Tanden would be
a small and cost-free step toward reviving the comity and civility we have lost.

Lotteries manifest all the elements of bad taxation.
April 9, 2019

A decade and a half ago, as a new governor confronting a chronically unbalanced
budget and a massive debt owed to schools, universities, and localities, I sought
to lighten a fiscal brainstorming session by saying, "Hey, I know a great new revenue source. We'll put the state in the cigarette business. We'll call 'em 'Hoosier
Smokes.' The margins will be terrific and the take enormous."

My teammates looked properly shocked, but then I confirmed that, of course,
I was kidding, but wanted to make a different point: The state already operates a
lucrative, high-margin business that promotes addictive, often self-destructive
behavior and preys primarily on poor people. It's called the lottery.

We found more appropriate ways to balance the books and pay off the debts.
But the spread and growth of state lotteries as a public finance tool has never
stopped troubling me. I recognize that my view is an isolated one. Among
the many ways that governments extract money from the public, lotteries are
uniquely popular across income, social, geographic, and political spectrums.

I once proposed a plan not to end the Hoosier Lottery but merely to cap its
revenue at current levels and devote the monetized value of their future growth to
making community college free to young people of moderate means. Republicans

were unenthused, and Democrats were actively opposed. The bill went nowhere. As far as I can tell, the result would have been the same in most other states.

One would expect second thoughts to be more common. Lotteries manifest all the elements of bad taxation. Although the payer/player knows he is handing the government his money, it's unlikely he realizes how much of his dollar the state is planning to keep. And the double taxation—by the lottery itself and by the taxes on any winnings—means that the "benefit" even for the occasional winner further obscures the amount of the rake-off.

But the biggest and most obvious offense is these systems' severe regressivity. While somewhat higher percentages of upper-income citizens report participating in lotteries, their play is much more casual. A 2002 study at the University at Buffalo's Research Institute on Addictions, echoed by a Bankrate.com report earlier this year, found that top-quintile players spend well under half as much as bottom-quintile players. As a percentage of income, the money spent by low-income people is ten times that of wealthier residents who play the lottery.

If the nature of lottery taxation is a bit deceptive, the way it has been marketed is an outright con job. In state after state, lotteries were sold as benefiting education. It has seldom happened. Repeated studies find no correlation, or even a negative correlation, between lottery revenue and K–12 or higher-education spending. Give credit for candor to the National Association of State and Provincial Lotteries, whose formal position is "The lottery is simply a form of entertainment that happens to benefit your state." Maybe we should view state lotteries as a modern twist on the bread and circuses public entertainments of antiquity, only in this version the government supplies only the circus, and the people fork over the bread.

Since this regressive, addictive, partially hidden tax is here to stay, might a little improvement still be conceivable? Beyond their other unsavory features, state lotteries far and away offer the lousiest odds in an expanding American gambling universe. As a national average, only about 60% of dollars gambled on lotteries are paid out to winners. In many places, one's chances are even worse: Delaware pays out 27%, Oregon 25%, South Dakota only 20%.

If my Syrian-immigrant grandfather had offered odds that crummy in the numbers game he ran out of his pool hall, he'd have been chased out of Monessen, Pennsylvania. I used to point out to fans of the lottery system, "The Atlantic City mob let you keep 92%." Here's a modest suggestion: States should consider reducing their skim of the wagers; at 73%, even Massachusetts's leading payout seems unfairly skimpy. No state would go broke sharing a little more of the take; in only nine states do lotto revenues amount to even 3% of total state receipts.

My sources tell me that the long-standing enterprise called "pea shake," a traditional form of numbers gambling prevalent for decades in my Indiana hometown's inner-city neighborhoods, is down to two operators and likely to close up shop soon. Local law enforcement has played a part, but competition from the Hoosier Lottery is cited as the biggest reason.

By all accounts, a pea shake player had a shot at 80% to 90% of the pot. Wouldn't it seem that our public servants could give their suckers at least that fair a shake?

The State of the Union is a tasteless, classless spectacle. It must go.
January 25, 2019

One needn't be a hidebound traditionalist to appreciate the value of our national civic ceremonies, those uplifting occasions when Americans pause even briefly to be reminded of our shared citizenship and our fortune to live in a government subject to the people's consent. The wreath-laying at the Tomb of the Unknowns on Memorial Day; public naturalization proceedings, when we welcome new Americans into the national family; state funerals such as those last year for Senator John McCain and former president George H. W. Bush; the peaceful transition of authority at a presidential inauguration, which not even the occasional subpar speech can fatally depreciate.

A fractured country needs, if anything, more such moments for reflection on common bonds and mutual obligations. Events that dignify, unify, and signify our membership in this special polity, and all the reasons we should be grateful for it, faults and all. Mark me down as a big fan of them.

But one such event has long since passed its sell-by date. It no longer fulfills the civic purpose that might once have justified its existence. On the contrary, it diminishes rather than elevates respect for the United States and its institutions. I refer to the tasteless, classless spectacle of the modern State of the Union speech. Or SOTU, in White House parlance. The political mud wrestling over the State of the Union address in recent weeks only underscores the reasons for my belief that it's time for this affair to be retired.

President Woodrow Wilson has a lot to answer for in U.S. history: his disdain for constitutional limits and prescriptions, his introduction of rule by unelected "experts," his refusal to disclose an incapacitating illness. But among Wilson's

most regrettable legacies, at least these days, is the delivery of the constitution-
ally required annual message to Congress through an in person speech.

Although George Washington and John Adams had read their messages
to Congress, Thomas Jefferson, to prevent its becoming, as Wilson biographer
A. Scott Berg put it, a "throne speech," sent his messages in writing. The precedent lasted 112 years. Then Wilson, prompted by a journalist's suggestion (another, ominous precedent: the publicity-minded getting involved), requested that
Congress convene to receive his report in 1913, and away we went. A brief return
to reticence by Calvin Coolidge and Herbert Hoover, who briefly restored written submissions, failed to take.

Franklin D. Roosevelt, the first modern media president, knew a PR opportunity when he saw one. Why just report when you can propagandize? As the
official House website relates, "Designed to reach the largest possible radio audience . . . the address touted the accomplishments of the Roosevelt administration and the New Deal."

Even discounting for the horn tooting, the occasion retained its dignity. Done
with what was once customary ritual and decorum, State of the Union addresses
served the communitarian civic purpose very well. Members of both parties, representatives of the judiciary and the military all listening respectfully, applaud-
ing sincerely and appropriately, made for one of those rare and valuable national
convenings.

That was then. The throne speech temptation proved irresistible to skilled
stage managers in the TV era. It was the Reagan White House, predictably, given
its Hollywood roots, that took the speech even further from the printed word and
the mere "information of the State of the Union" stipulated by the Constitution.
The positioning in the balcony of Lenny Skutnik, an authentic hero of the 1982
Air Florida crash into the Fourteenth Street bridge in Washington, set a trend
that reached its ad absurdum status when President Barack Obama mentioned
by name four of his more than twenty guests during his 2015 address.

After President Ronald Reagan's innovation, it dawned on everyone involved
that the supporting cast need not be confined to the balconies. Members of
Congress got in the act, on both sides of the aisle. Effusive, cued applause, camera-
conscious backslapping, stony-faced growls of disapproval, and eventually even
catcalls from America's lawmakers have drained what little was left of a serious tutorial about national challenges and priorities. What remains: a tired, far-
cical theatrical experience more likely to promote cynicism than citizenship in
its viewers.

Give Wilson and Roosevelt credit on one score: They addressed their audiences on a higher plane than their successors. On the Flesch-Kincaid readability index, their first State of the Union addresses measured at post–high school reading levels. Ever since, the vocabulary of presidential first-timers has plummeted, save for an uptick in 1982 with Reagan's debut. The most recent State of the Union required a ninth grade reading level.

Although Wilson inflicted this now-debauched custom on the nation, he got one thing right: his first State of the Union address lasted all of nine minutes. After Reagan (who presumably knew the attention span of TV viewers), the speeches have averaged forty-five minutes or more, gusting beyond an hour in the cases of presidents Bill Clinton, Obama, and Trump.

Herewith, an anguished appeal to future presidential candidates to forswear in advance the worn-out, counterproductive State of the Union spectacle, and return to the dignity and sobriety of a written report. Something different is worth a trial period; I'm thinking 112 years might be good.

Government "transparency" has gone too far.
August 13, 2018

Dave Eggers's 2013 novel *The Circle* depicts a world where demands for "openness" annihilate privacy and personal autonomy, creating a dystopian nightmare. Public officials in the tale try to outdo each other in going "clear" by wearing body cameras and microphones every waking moment. For most readers, the book is far-fetched science fiction, but for those active in public life, Eggers's conception doesn't seem all that implausible.

It's hard to determine when too much of a good thing becomes truly too much. And the more laudable the goal, the harder it generally is to reel in the excess, because any suggested retrenchment is viewed as an abandonment of the goal itself. At the risk of being misconstrued, I venture the heretical thought that we have overshot in the pursuit of governmental "openness" and "transparency."

There's no question that American government at all levels is better off for the open door and open record reforms of the past half century. Knowing that the public is watching, public officials generally behave more responsibly in the conduct of their duties.

I'm a true believer. As the director of the Office of Management and Budget in the early 2000s, I worked in perhaps surprising collaboration with Ralph Nader to open the federal government's contracting process to broader public inspection.

During my service in Indiana as governor from 2005 to 2013, we made similar changes as a part of wider ethics reforms.

But even water has a fatal dosage level. Too much exercise can be unhealthy. Attempts to eliminate almost all forms of confidential interaction in government come with downsides.

We've seen the unintended consequences of overzealous reform before. Badly needed civil service and procurement reforms initially worked, but they expanded over time until they paralyzed the federal government to a comical degree. Federal employees are in greater danger from a lightning strike than termination for lousy performance, and the procedures for buying, say, a new computer are so byzantine that the machines are outdated by the time they arrive.

The current obsession with transparency is starting to take a similar toll. In a host of ways, government has been rendered less nimble, less talented, and less effective.

Honest people are now compelled to become scofflaws in the good faith pursuit of their duties. Under open meeting requirements forbidding members of governing bodies to confer privately, the result is furtive hallway conversations or executive committee meetings where the discussion might not technically fall into the category of exemptions that permit such meetings.

Open records laws have had the same effect. Government took a serious wrong turn at the dawn of the email era when somebody decided that these online exchanges are documents. Every emailer knows that, perhaps apart from attachments, they are conversations.

I'm rarely on a conference call with other public university presidents that doesn't include someone reminding the group: "No emails!" Even the most deliberative of discussions is vulnerable to later being spread across a newspaper front page.

In sarcastic moments, I sometimes point out the gaping loophole in our public records laws: Public officials are talking on the phone, and we don't know what they're saying! Clearly, we need a wiretap on every government line and, while we're at it, their home and cell phones. And we'll need surveillance cameras because, next thing you know, they'll switch to speaking in person!

Overall capability in government suffers, too. The excessive background checks and disclosure demands of today's federal employment discourage countless talented people from serving. I watched the number and quality of aspirants to Indiana state judgeships decline over the years. Like many other states, Indiana requires the immediate public identification of interested judicial candidates, and far too many outstanding lawyers, worried about angering their law firms, clients, or employers, stay on the sidelines.

Maybe the worst net negative effect of the openness obsession is on the spirit of compromise—a spirit that is prized, ironically, by many transparency advocates. There is a reason the Constitutional Convention of 1787 was held privately and no official minutes were kept. Men who argued fiercely against certain provisions preserved their ability to accept second-best outcomes, and to go home and advocate ratification of the overall agreement.

None of this is to suggest a major rollback; we are better off for the sunshine. But for the best of reasons, transparency has risen to sacred status, and even moderate change will be difficult. A news media accustomed to rummaging through email records and visitor logs may be especially unsympathetic. Still, it's time for us all to consider broadening the definitions of what communications should remain confidential and to grant more leeway for the kinds of meetings that are often essential to producing workable compromises.

I hope I've made myself . . . clear.

Connecticut is drowning in debt.
Should the rest of us have to pay?
July 23, 2018

In 1787, when the Constitutional Convention and an infant republic hung by a thread, two imaginative New Englanders solved the problem and saved the day. Roger Sherman and Oliver Ellsworth, both representing Connecticut, proposed a bicameral legislature made up of one house representing population and the other giving each state an equal voice. The Connecticut Compromise—designed as a safeguard against the domination of smaller states by the more populous neighbors—entered history as perhaps the most crucial of all the bargains that enabled a new nation to be welded together out of the ramshackle Articles of Confederation.

But Connecticut, which today, along with a number of other states, faces a seemingly insurmountable budgetary crisis, may end up regretting the statesmanship of its illustrious forebears. Sherman and Ellsworth's two-members-per-state system stands as a bulwark to prevent reckless states—Connecticut included—from raiding their more responsible brethren. Let's thank them for their innovation.

Over the past few years, several of today's fifty states have descended into unmanageable public indebtedness. In Illinois, vendors wait months to be paid by a state government that is $30 billion in debt and one notch above junk bond status.

And in terms of per capita state debt, Connecticut ranks among the worst in the nation, with unfunded liabilities amounting to $22,700 per citizen.

Each profligate state is facing its own budgetary perdition for different reasons, but most share common factors. The explosion of Medicaid spending, even before Obamacare, has devoured state funds just as it and its entitlement cousins, Medicare and Social Security, have done at the federal level. This has crowded out other vital public activities, as striking teachers in most states experiencing such hardships know.

In parallel, public pensions of sometimes grotesque levels guarantee that the fiscal strangulation will soon get much worse. In California, some retired lifeguards are receiving more than $90,000 per year. A retired university president in Oregon received $76,000 per month—and no, that's not a typo. These are the modern-day welfare queens, and they are the reason for some of the nation's worst budget crises. California's pension shortfall, $250 billion under the rosiest of assumptions, is more likely close to $1 trillion.

With things this far gone, even an aroused public or a sudden eruption of statesmanship is unlikely to prevent a crash. In some states, government unions have barricaded their benefit levels behind a Maginot Line of legal and even constitutional protections.

More and more desperate tax increases haven't cured the problem; it's possible that they are making it worse. When a state pursues boneheaded policies long enough, people and businesses get up and leave, taking tax dollars with them. We see this often in the headlines: GE leaves Connecticut, General Mills exits Illinois, Chevron and Waste Management flee California. But also watch the U-Haul rental data: Illinois and California are first and second, respectively, in net rentals leaving vs. coming into the state.

So where is a destitute governor to turn? Sooner or later, we can anticipate pleas for nationalization of these impossible obligations. Get ready for the siren sounds of sophistry, in arguments for subsidy of the poor by the prudent.

In fact, this balloon was already floated once, during the crunch of the recent recession. In 2009, California politicians called for a "dynamic partnership" with the federal government. Money from other states, they said, would be an "investment" and certainly not a bailout. They didn't succeed directly, although they walked away with $8 billion of federally borrowed "stimulus" money. Such a heist will be harder to justify in the absence of a national economic emergency.

In the blizzard of euphemisms, one can expect a clever argument might appear, likening the bailout to another important compromise of the founding period:

the assumption of state debts by the new federal government. But that won't wash. Those were debts incurred in a battle for survival and independence common to all thirteen colonies, not an attempt to socialize away the consequences of individual states' multi-decade spending sprees.

Sometime in the next few years, we are likely to go through our own version of the recent eurozone drama with, let's say, Connecticut in the role of Greece and maybe a larger, "too big to fail" partner such as Illinois as Italy. Adding up the number of federal legislators from the fifteen or twenty fiscally weakest states, one can count something close to half the votes in the House.

The Senate—thanks to Ellsworth and Sherman—will be our theft insurance. These statesmen could never have imagined governments as sprawling and expensive as those even today's more cautious states operate. But had they somehow foreseen that their own beloved state would be among the worst offenders, one of those most likely to try to fob off its self-inflicted problems on its counterparts, I think they would only have felt better about their handiwork.

A guide for luring Amazon to your city—and what not to do.
November 20, 2017

The Amazon "HQ2" headquarters auction is in full swing, so prepare to witness some reckless behavior out of the reported 238 bidder states and localities. Like groupies in a 1960s rockumentary, public officials will be throwing themselves at the stage trying to catch the star's attention.

Nothing in public life is more dangerous to the public interest than politicians chasing jobs with the people's checkbook. They can buy their way into the ribbon-cutting photos knowing that, if they grossly overbid, they won't be around when the bills come due. Chances are the Amazon winner will fall into this category.

Abuse of this practice is robustly bipartisan. As many Republican as Democratic officeholders have lost their fiscal virtue when a big score seemed in prospect.

The best defense against this all-too-human behavior is to establish some rules in advance and make them transparent to citizens and potential business investors alike. In Indiana, from the 2005 inception of a reconstituted public–private state economic agency, its board (which is chaired by the governor, to underscore his accountability) established boundary conditions to govern negotiations with firms seeking investment incentives. Examples of these include

No upfront cash. Any assistance must be strictly conditional, receivable only as promised new jobs materialize.

Only new, incremental jobs are eligible; no incentives for merely staying put. A state creating such a precedent almost ensures a run on the bank. Shortly after Illinois paid Navistar $65 million not to depart for another state, it found itself giving Motorola $100 million and the Chicago Mercantile Exchange $100 million more, without the requirement of a single additional job.

An explicit clawback mechanism. Things change in business and will over the span of a multi-year agreement to support a company's expansion. Competitive pressures or economy-wide slowdowns alter the most careful of plans, so a subsidy agreement should contain a provision for the repayment of any incentives tied to jobs that later were eliminated, as well as a mechanism for regularly auditing and certifying those that are still active.

Governments should measure and report to the public the efficiency of their economic recruitment efforts. Incentive dollars per new job and per dollar of new capital investment are two good places to start, with the obvious objective of driving those ratios down as far as possible. In Indiana, the new agency brought the first number down from $36,000 to $9,000 per job within a year. Tracking those figures over time can help establish another critical boundary: a walkaway level beyond which negotiators are instructed not to go in a given transaction.

I concede that Amazon may be the exception that justifies some bending of these rules. The new headquarters' enormous size, and the highly paid, high-tech nature of its workforce, may make it appropriate for bidders to assume a multiplier effect on the surrounding economy and to assign some premium to intangible, "transformative" benefits. But even if so, such premiums should be rigorously calculated and debated, not the product of wild guesses or heat-of-the-moment attempts to outbid the state next door.

Remember that this is a multi-decade decision a company is making. The most important criteria in its thinking will be long term: What taxes are we likely to pay? How high is the cost of living and what will our wage scale have to be? (There are enormous differences here. A computer hardware engineer who costs $137,000 in California would cost only $91,000 in Tennessee or $82,000 in Nebraska, with equal purchasing power). How burdensome or collaborative are state and local governments? Are permits and regulatory approvals quick and reasonable or ponderous and hostile? If—make that when—we are sued, are the local courts fair or do they operate in cahoots with predatory litigators?

Front-end goodies are not unimportant, but they are almost certain to be outweighed by the twenty- or thirty-year effect of these factors. If you are the people's negotiator, it's your job to understand and remember that. Indiana has routinely captured new business when other aspirants were offering much higher incentives. Too many officeholders enter these discussions without business experience, and their taxpayers pick up the tab.

So let the auction begin. Amazon is dangling a big prize, and aggressiveness is perfectly appropriate. But establish your limits, and keep your head. Anyone in business learns that often the smartest deal of all is the one you didn't make. The people's business should be no different.

Washington's wake-up call: Sky-high debt and dismal
growth are testing Americans' faith in democracy.
Wall Street Journal
September 13, 2016

When I testified on Capitol Hill last week on the subject of the national debt, I found myself in the odd position of hoping our elected representatives would find my testimony of little value because it would strike them as so obvious.

As I told them, they know, or should know, that our federal deficits have been running at historically unprecedented levels, so much so that another half trillion dollars this year was met with a yawn.

They know, or should know, that our national debt has reached a peacetime record and is heading for territory where other nations have spiraled into default, or into the loss of sovereignty as creditors use their leverage to dictate terms.

They know, or should know, that public debt this large weighs heavily on economic growth, crowding out private investment and discouraging it through uncertainty. And that much faster growth than today's is the sine qua non of the greater revenues necessary to meet federal obligations, let alone reduce our debt burdens.

They know, or should know, that the unchecked explosion of so-called entitlement spending, coupled with debt service, is squeezing every other federal activity—from the FBI to basic scientific research to our national parks to the defense on which the physical survival of the country depends.

They know, or should know, that the problem is getting worse, and fast. Even if reform began today, past overpromising and demographic realities mean that the entitlement monster is going to devour accelerating amounts of additional dollars, all of which are scheduled to be borrowed rather than funded honestly.

They know, or should know, that official projections of growing indebtedness—even the appalling estimates I just referred to—are built on a foundation of wishful thinking: productivity assumptions are too high, interest rate assumptions too low; growth too high, spending too low. As each of these is proven unduly rosy, more zeros will be added to the bill we hand to the young people of this country.

So let me offer an appeal on behalf of those young people and the new Americans not yet with us. The appeal is for a shift in national policy to the growth of the private, productive economy as our all-out, primary priority. And for decisive action soon that begins the gradual moderation of unkeepable promises and unpayable debts that will otherwise be dumped on coming generations.

A national government that, year after year, borrows enormous sums and spends them not on genuine investment in the future but on current consumption, passing the bill down to others, pretending that the problem is smaller than it really is, lacks not only good judgment but integrity. It is not hyperbole to label such behavior immoral. For a long time, people have gone to Congress decrying the intergenerational injustice of this policy, yet things keep getting worse.

A near-decade of anemic growth and the weakest postrecession recovery on record has eroded Americans' economic optimism. A 2015 Rasmussen survey found that nearly half (48%) of likely voters "think America's best days are in the past." As this new pessimism has deepened, it has turned into an ugliness, a meanness, a new cynicism in our national life, with a search for scapegoats on the left and the right.

For nearly two and a half centuries, Americans have shared a resilient determination to be self-governing, to guard against tyranny at home, and, on occasion, to resist by force its spread elsewhere. But lately there are alarming signals of a different outlook.

According to the World Values Survey, as reported by Roberto Stefan Foa and Yascha Mounk in the July edition of the *Journal of Democracy*, in 2011 a record one in four American citizens said that democracy is a "bad way" to run the country, and an even larger number would prefer an authoritarian leader who didn't have to deal with the nuisance of elections.

When today's young Americans learn the extent of the debt burden we have left them, they will legitimately question the premises of self-government. When tomorrow's older Americans finally understand how they have been misled about the nature and the reliability of our fundamental social welfare programs, it may be the last straw breaking the public confidence on which democracy itself depends.

In fairness, a few members in each political party have tried to address the coming crisis. To them, all thanks and credit. To those still in denial, or even advocating steps that would make our debts even higher, please reconsider. Your careers may end happily before the reckoning. Your re-elections may not be threatened by your inaction. But your consciences—and what Lincoln called "government of the people, by the people, for the people"—will be.

LESSONS FROM SCIENCE

This climate change contrarian gives us an
important reminder about science in general.
October 12, 2021

Clichés, however shopworn, can retain their usefulness provided they continue to describe their object with some accuracy. One cliché that has lost almost all value is "speaking truth to power." These days, it almost invariably is attached not to an act of genuine courage but to its opposite, the spouting of some politically favored bromide. The speaker runs no risk of negative consequences from any power, individual or institutional; on the contrary, lavish praise and short-term celebrity are assured.

Steven E. Koonin is a genuine example of someone daring to challenge a prevailing orthodoxy. Impeccably credentialed both scientifically (New York University physics professor; National Academy of Sciences member; chief scientist for BP, focusing on alternative energy) and politically (undersecretary for science in the Obama Energy Department), Koonin has written probably the year's most important book.

Not because of its conclusions about climate, about which his contrarian views might be completely wrong. Rather, because *Unsettled* is surfacing the anti-intellectual, burn-the-heretic attitude that has infected too much of the academic and policy worlds.

The ad hominem epithets began flying from the moment the book was pub-lished last spring. He is a "crank" and a "denier" who thinks climate change is a "hoax," according to a dozen scientists writing in *Scientific American*.

That is false. Koonin stipulates firmly that Earth's climate is changing and be-coming warmer, and that human influence is playing a role. He is eager to iden-tify and advocate actions that will address these changes effectively. But he is deeply troubled—"appalled" is one of his terms—by the misuse of science, his life's work, to persuade rather than inform, and by the near-hysterical pressure to stifle and vilify any deviation from the dogma of the day.

As detailed in the *Post* earlier this year, the book uses government and aca-demic reports' own data to challenge the scientific "consensus"—about rising sea levels, droughts, extreme weather—now repeated endlessly and uncritically.

Doesn't the world face economic catastrophe, absent wrenching, unimagin-ably expensive actions to reduce greenhouse emissions? Not according to Koonin, who cites the United Nations' own report stating plainly that any such effect would be minor at most and decades away.

Koonin also points out how wildly climate computer models disagree with each other. Having written one of the first textbooks on such modeling, he is especially harsh on the "fine-tuning" of models to adjust for unwelcome find-ings. He says that such manipulation often crosses the line into "cooking the books."

We have never expected much truthfulness or integrity from our politicians, whose self-interest in publicity and campaign dollars too often outweighs any scruples about scientific precision. Nonprofit public interest groups raise fortunes on forecasts of doom, often on the flimsiest evidence. The modern news media, chasing the dollars that titillating, click-catching headlines bring, have been, if anything, worse than the political class in discussing climate change. Koonin serves up multiple examples, with descriptions such as "deliberately misleading" and "blatantly misrepresenting."

The truth's last line of defense should be the scientific community, but here Koonin indicts those of his fellows who have discarded a commitment to the truth—the whole truth, and nothing but—in favor of their own view of wise policy. "Distorting science to further a cause is inexcusable," he says, a violation of scientists' "overriding ethical obligation."

Even if such people ultimately prove right, and Koonin wrong, about climate, he is correct to label their willful distortions "dangerous" and "pernicious."

Scientific research has already suffered serious self-inflicted wounds over recent decades. The discovery that as many as half of all published papers cannot pass the basic test of replication has yet to be meaningfully addressed. Researchers' deep financial ties to foreign funding sources raise the specter of compromised security and integrity of results.

An ethical and responsible scientific community, including those who strongly disagree with Koonin's findings or conclusions, would welcome his book as the latest contribution to an important debate. As vital as identifying the best climate strategy is, a broader issue involves the willingness of scientists, and the citizens who seek their advice, to tolerate—and maybe even welcome—the dissident who has the courage to speak the truth as he sees it to the powers of his age.

The calumny and name-calling that greeted Koonin's book has helped to make his point. One must hope that his courage and sense of scientific morality, if not his specific viewpoint on climatology, will prevail. Knowledge advances only through the collision of hypotheses and the facts that ultimately prove one theory superior. Galileo, not the high priest inquisitors who condemned and ostracized him for his heresies, is the person we remember.

The U.S. put a man on the moon. But it might be harder to do the same on Mars.
February 25, 2021

The thrilling success of NASA's Perseverance mission to Mars has captured well-deserved national attention. As occurs intermittently, the air is filled with bold predictions of a revived U.S. human spaceflight program, with Mars as its goal and the moon as its staging area.

I hope it happens. A national commission I co-chaired a few years ago concluded that, for reasons tangible (scientific discovery, economic spinoffs, national security) and intangible (inspiring of young talent to scientific pursuits, national morale and prestige, the elevation of human aspiration and imagination), a resumption of our attempts to reach beyond low Earth orbit was justified.

If and when humankind reaches that next frontier, though, there are reasons to doubt that it will be a U.S. government space project that leads us there. Ironically, the society that put a man on the moon may be just the wrong one to succeed in this next great endeavor, at least through a grand national project like Apollo.

In launching what became Apollo, President John F. Kennedy said we should attempt it not because it was easy, but because it was hard. As dazzling as the Perseverance achievement is, it involves radiation-proof robots, not fragile humans, and a seven-foot, one-metric-ton craft, not the forty-metric-ton, two-story system that a human landing, life support, and ascent vehicle would require.

It will be exponentially harder for humans to fly safely to Mars, establish a sustained presence, and survive to return to Earth. To do so, our commission concluded, would require making the goal a central, single-minded priority of the U.S. space program; a relentless, unswerving multi-decade commitment to a preagreed path to reach the goal; and constant investments in amounts well above the rate of inflation. American democracy is not very good at any of those things.

Our system affords us, thank goodness, a chance to change national direction every two years, and presidential leadership quadrennially. That competitiveness and responsiveness enables the quick correction of mistakes and the flexibility to navigate changed circumstances. What it doesn't excel at is sustaining long-term projects of distant or indirect benefit to the voting public.

Each new national administration brings its own agenda. Presidents are always more interested in starting initiatives than in extending those they inherit. Fiscal, economic, and other national policies can be altered frequently, and often should be. Yet this pattern has also applied to space policy, jerking NASA through a series of major strategic shifts, from Apollo to the space shuttle to the International Space Station to asteroid capture and, finally, to thinking about reaching Mars with a manned mission via the moon.

"Finally," I should say, for now. The new Biden administration's overall agenda is bigger and more expensive than any before it, yet it appears to leave little or no space for space.

With a micromanaging Congress resetting budgets on an annual basis, picking out a priority for NASA and sticking to it for twenty years or more is likely not in the cards; we've proved very poor at "perseverance." Plus, our legislators regularly carve out NASA dollars for favored non-exploratory causes such as environmental monitoring, and fiercely protect multiple space centers and resulting costly redundancies.

Even if a consensus plan were reached, and some magical mechanism invented for maintaining it over changing administrations, the money wouldn't be there.

The nation's elected representatives continue spending vastly beyond revenue and legislating promises that cannot conceivably be paid for. The odds are that a crisis in the safety net—forcing some combination of massive tax increases, benefit reductions, and further asphyxiation of discretionary programs such as NASA (which has never registered more than tepid public support)—will arrive here before we arrive on Mars.

So if our system is ill-suited to the task, what kind of nation would be most likely to reach this next frontier? Oh, in theory, one with a patient, farsighted culture, accustomed by history to taking the very long view. A country with an authoritarian regime, capable of commandeering the massive resources necessary without making concessions to public opinion. Perhaps one with a "leader for life" intent on establishing his realm as dominant in both reputation and technological power. Just speaking hypothetically.

Will Americans spend the next half century watching Chinese astronauts or robots "boldly go where no man has gone before"? My hopes that I'm wrong rest with the same freedoms that operate politically to make a U.S. government Mars mission so difficult.

The superiority of free enterprise has given birth to nimble private companies, unencumbered by political realities, backed by private fortunes imbued with the explorer spirit and, in some cases, a dream of profits. Either on their own or through increasingly harmonious partnerships with NASA, they give us the best chance that, despite our mismatched system of government, the first human on Mars, as on the moon, will be a free citizen of a free country.

A fishy campaign against salmon.
February 12, 2020

What should one make of the following set of facts? A federal government, urged on by self-designated advocates for the public interest, blocks for a quarter of a century the availability of an irrefutably safe product that would improve Americans' health, lower consumer costs, and deliver a host of environmental benefits. Sound fishy? You're right.

For about three decades, science has known how to genetically modify salmon so the fish can be safely and economically raised anywhere, not just in the seaside pens that have long been the only alternative to the continuing depletion of the world's ocean stocks. Scientists worldwide have attested for over a decade,

without credible opposition, to the safety of these fish and their essential indis-
tinguishability from other salmon. But only in March last year was this long-
stalled technology released from regulatory purgatory by the Food and Drug
Administration and cleared for operation in the United States.

Consider the advantages we have been forgoing. Salmon is a healthy food,
strongly recommended by the American Heart Association, the Mayo Clinic,
and, ironically, the federal government's own nutritional guidelines for at least
the past twenty years. Consumers aware of its heart-friendly qualities increasingly seek out salmon—consumption is rising rapidly, leading to overfishing
of wild populations, and the knock-on overfishing of other species taken for
the up to five pounds of fish meal necessary to grow one non–genetically engi-
neered salmon in today's coastal farms. (Some scientists believe the world's natural supply has hit "peak fish," with more than 90% of stocks having no capacity for more production.)

Because they grow to market weight in sixteen to eighteen months rather than
the thirty-two to thirty-six months for conventional varieties, genetically engi-
neered (GE) salmon use 25% less feed, alleviating the overfishing problem while
reducing production costs and therefore consumer costs by 20%. GE salmon
are efficient sources of protein, needing only one pound of feed to produce one
pound of weight. This compares with tilapia and chicken at about two-to-one,
pigs at three-to-one, and cattle at eight-to-one.

Another benefit to the environment: reducing the reliance on oceanfront pens,
which generate polluting organic and inorganic waste material. These pens are
prone to parasitic infestations that can spread to wild salmon; at inland facilities,
the infestations could be quarantined and managed.

If those inland facilities were built near population centers, the salmon steak
being trucked from just down the road would entail far lower carbon dioxide
emissions than if it were shipped, as much salmon is, from Norway or Chile.

Unlike today's coastal fish farms, GE salmon will come from almost entirely
self-contained production processes. The emissions involved are primarily recy-
cled water well suited to vegetable or greenhouse growing, and small amounts
of filtered solids usable as fertilizer. Because the salmon are by design infertile
and raised only in secure, inland, indoor facilities, there is zero chance of cross-
breeding with native species.

So, you say, what's been the problem? As usual when a seemingly clear public interest is being anomalously violated, one can look for the involvement of a
special interest. In this case, it's commercial fishing interests, most notably from

Alaska, which have been eager to squelch such a cost-competitive competitor. At least we can understand their motives.

But the years of opposition by the self-styled green lobby is less logical. Given the positives for the environment from GE salmon, the greens' obstruction has to be added to the list of bizarre cognitive dissonances to which this community has proved so vulnerable. We have seen the reflexive attacks on carbon-free nuclear power, and on fracking, even though the natural gas it produces has done more to reduce U.S. carbon dioxide emissions than every other factor combined. Then there is the anti-scientific blockade of GE crops that could dramatically improve the lives of those in some of the world's most impoverished countries.

The green campaign against beta-carotene-rich golden rice—which could save hundreds of thousands of poor and undernourished children from blindness and death caused by vitamin A deficiency—prompted more than one hundred Nobel Prize winners to write to Greenpeace in 2016 challenging its baseless attacks. At some point, those who would ask us to trust them on environmental issues should try to align their heads with their hearts on issues such as these.

Ultimately, the worst damage of anti-science lies in its opportunity costs. Because they are not yet apparent to ordinary citizens, such costs do not generate an outcry commensurate with the harms they impose. No congressman or bureaucrat has ever been put out of work because of the innovation that was blocked, its benefits never realized. Salmon shoppers had no idea that they were being shafted on every purchase by a combination of fishing interests, self-appointed advocates, and compliant regulators. At least in the case of the latter two groups, let's just say they had better fish to fry.

A genuine Big Idea that could fix the border problem.
May 3, 2019

So here we are in another presidential campaign season (when aren't we?), and the air is thick with greenhouse gas of the political variety. When candidates take a break from talking about themselves, they generally turn to "bold" policy pronouncements that they hope will prove eye-catching enough to separate them from the thundering herd of wannabe Washingtons and Roosevelts.

Thanks to the modern primary-dominated process—designed with the goal of returning nominations to "the people" but, instead, captive to the parties' political fringes—these policy ideas tend to fall in two unfortunate classes. The first consists of those crafted to massage the erogenous zones of extremists. The second is those policies chosen for their divisiveness quotient, the extent to which they underscore the stark difference between Us and Them, and the proponent's passionate commitment to Us.

Almost all share the common denominator of absurd impracticality. They have given us a new definition of the admirable adjective "aspirational," now taken to mean "I know it's preposterous, so don't hold me to it."

But now, thanks to some wildly imaginative researchers at a group of universities—including Texas A&M, Arizona State, Cal Tech, and Purdue University, where I work—candidates have available for inspection a genuine Big Idea that just might transcend these dreary categories. As reported in *Scientific American* and elsewhere, this consortium of more than two dozen scientists and engineers proposes an "energy-water corridor" along the nearly 2,000 miles of the U.S.–Mexico border. It is that rarest of modern phenomena: an ecumenical concept with unifying potential; an idea that even sworn enemies can love.

The scientists envision a chain of green-energy installations, powering seawater desalination that could make the desert bloom Israel-style, ease water shortage concerns in several southwestern states, and trigger enormous economic possibilities in both the United States and Mexico. And, oh yes, provide through its necessary, concomitant protective features a major new physical barrier to illegal immigration.

Any idea this big faces daunting feasibility questions, but the proponents have spent a fair amount of time thinking through and costing out their plan. They seem on unchallengeable ground that the border regions of California, Arizona, New Mexico, and Texas are as conducive to solar and wind power as virtually any place on Earth. Nearby, potentially enormous natural-gas deposits could complement the renewable energy and provide power day and night. The attractiveness and opportunities for private capital could be immense.

A solar park with a width of just five one-meter panels—about sixteen feet—running like a ribbon along the corridor's entire length would produce some sixteen gigawatt-hours of electricity per day, on the same order of magnitude as all the hydropower along the U.S.–Canada border, or at a full-scale nuclear power plant. The estimated cost is $4.5 billion installed, with the investment recouped in less than ten years.

The 8 million panels needed, according to the scientists' report, would be within the present capacity of the U.S. solar industry, and would provide a strong economic jolt for those American businesses in their competition with Chinese and other manufacturers. A major shortcoming of solar energy is its inconsistent energy production; a corridor reaching from the West Coast to the Gulf Coast would address that problem by enabling load-shifting from west to east and east to west depending on time of day.

Alongside the solar farm, the consortium imagines a network of wind turbines, taking advantage of some of Earth's windiest geography. The turbines' annual 1.2 gigawatts of energy, powering two reverse osmosis desalination facilities, could provide more than 2 million acre-feet of water per year, covering, for example, the annual commercial and agricultural consumption of Texas.

The proposal doesn't stop there. There are suggestions of a "super-pipe" system to move the water to where it's most needed within a free-trade zone, one hundred kilometers wide (about sixty-two miles), on both sides of the border. As the authors somewhat slyly put it, the fencing or barriers attendant to all this solar and wind infrastructure would constitute a "border security" system with "instant feedback and surveillance capability throughout the entire region."

Sure, there are implementation issues galore. We haven't been shown cost projections or rates of return for several big features of the plan. Unless the United States adopts some of the breakthrough regulatory reforms championed by thinkers such as lawyer and author Philip K. Howard, the country's insanely cumbersome antidevelopment laws would likely strangle this greenest of initiatives in its infancy. In fact, the smartest modification for the plan might be to build the whole thing on the Mexican side of the border.

But based on the work to date, the energy-water corridor looks vastly more practical than some presidential candidates' proposals for trillion-dollar-plus loan forgiveness and "free" (the quotation marks should be journalistically mandatory) everything.

Perhaps the United States and Mexico, two nations that have been squabbling, will find a reason to work on it together. The two nations into which America itself has split might even do the same.

Things really aren't that bad. But we like to think they are.
December 26, 2018

Human nature being as it is, every decade or two someone has to write a book to set us straight and cheer us up. People all too readily overlook astonishing improvements as they rapidly become parts of daily life, and swallow uncritically assertions that disaster waits right around the corner. The books are the works of scholarship, sometimes dry and sometimes sly, that debunk the doomsayers and remind us how fortunate we are to be alive in these times.

During the 1970s, it was futurist Herman Kahn and his merry band at the Hudson Institute who demolished the "limits to growth" forecasts of the Club of Rome cognoscenti—think Davos before it was invented—that the world was about to run out of darn near everything. In *The Next 200 Years* and *The Resourceful Earth*, Kahn and his collaborators piled fact upon fact to argue the opposite, that an era of unprecedented growth and abundance was about to open.

The debate was memorably settled in 1980 when Hudson's Julian L. Simon proposed a wager to leading doomsayer Paul R. Ehrlich. The wager: Ehrlich would pick any five commodities he liked and bet $10,000 that during the next decade they would rise in price rather than fall, indicating increasing scarcity. Simon won easily—Ehrlich was 0 for 5. But he could afford it, as the author of the best-selling and equally wrongheaded *The Population Bomb* (1968) and the recipient of a $345,000 "genius" grant from the MacArthur Foundation in 1990—the same year he lost the bet. (MacArthur should have asked for a refund.)

But lamentations of impending economic, social, and environmental catastrophe grow back like pests on an organic farm, and the record of progress periodically needs to be reestablished. Demographer and author Ben J. Wattenberg took his turn in 1984 with the whimsical but fact-laden *The Good News Is the Bad News Is Wrong*. Among his many bracing observations: the increased incidence of cancer wasn't a sign of an epidemic; it showed that people were living longer and not dying of other causes.

In our day, the task of rebutting the pessimists has fallen to Harvard cognitive psychologist Steven Pinker, whose contribution is the best one yet. In *Enlightenment Now*, Pinker catalogs the irrefutable evidence that "life has gotten longer, healthier, richer, safer, happier, freer, smarter, deeper, and more interesting" through the application of reason, science, and humanism. It is only the abandonment of those Enlightenment ideals, he says, that can threaten humankind's continued upward trajectory.

One by one, the author exposes alleged crises as overhyped, misrepresented, or, in many cases, just plain wrong. Deaths from war and genocide have plummeted; genuine poverty and hunger are in steep decline, and famine has virtually disappeared; economic inequality is vastly overstated in the United States and is shrinking dramatically worldwide. Life expectancy in the poorest country on Earth is now nine years greater than it was in the richest country two centuries ago.

Pick your favorite worry and it's likely to be getting better, not worse. Deaths from car and plane crashes, drownings, and workplace injuries are all way down.

If a 453-page book, dense with facts and averaging one chart or graph every 6 pages, can be a delightful read, this one is it. Pinker enlivens it with aphorisms from the past ("The Stone Age didn't end because the world ran out of stones") and of his own devising: "Despair springs eternal," and "Intellectuals hate progress. Those who call themselves progressives really hate progress."

In touting the epistemological superiority of science, the book is harshly dismissive of religion. Pinker strikes out at "right-wing politicians" and their disrespect for empirical facts. But he is equally direct in criticizing "politicized repression of science ... from the left" on matters such as overpopulation and genetically modified organisms.

Where Pinker goes beyond his doom-dispelling predecessors is in explaining why so many people so readily accept pessimistic predictions or wild conspiracy theories. He walks the reader through such phenomena as the availability heuristic (we overestimate the frequency or probability of things that are shocking or otherwise memorable), negativity bias (we dread losses more than we enjoy gains, dwell on setbacks more than we savor good fortune), and identity-protective cognition. We are awash in this last syndrome today, on both left and right, as "certain beliefs become symbols of cultural allegiance," however unfounded those beliefs may be.

Given the way we humans take progress for granted, "enlightenment now" will not be the last corrective required. Somewhere out there a farsighted doctoral student should start collecting data for the next era when, despite all the evidence, people are disinclined to believe that life is getting better.

Avoiding GMOs isn't just anti-science. It's immoral.
December 27, 2017

Of the several claims of "anti-science" that clutter our national debates these days, none can be more flagrantly clear than the campaign against modern agricultural technology, most specifically the use of molecular techniques to create genetically modified organisms (GMOs). Here, there are no credibly conflicting studies, no arguments about the validity of computer models, no disruption of an ecosystem nor any adverse human health or even digestive problems, after 5 billion acres have been cultivated cumulatively and trillions of meals consumed.

And yet a concerted, deep-pockets campaign, as relentless as it is baseless, has persuaded a high percentage of Americans and Europeans to avoid GMO products, and to pay premium prices for "non-GMO" or "organic" foods that may in some cases be less safe and less nutritious. Thank goodness the toothpaste makers of the past weren't cowed so easily; the tubes would have said "No fluoride inside!" and we'd all have many more cavities.

This is the kind of foolishness that rich societies can afford to indulge. But when they attempt to inflict their superstitions on the poor and hungry peoples of the planet, the cost shifts from affordable to dangerous and the debate from scientific to moral.

From campus to Congress, it's common these days to speak in terms of "grand challenges." No challenge is grander than feeding the 9 billion or more people with whom we will share the Earth in a few decades.

Of course, those people weren't supposed to exist. Just a few decades back, "experts" were winning "genius" prizes for pontificating that "the battle to feed all of humanity is over" and forecasting that hundreds of millions were going to die and that there was nothing anyone could do about it. (Q: If that's genius, what does ignorance look like? Aren't the prize givers entitled to a refund?)

Instead of mass starvation and depopulation, the intervening years saw the most explosive improvements in living standards, food security, poverty reduction, and life expectancy in human history. Credit Deng Xiaoping's unshackling of the capitalist spirit in China for much of the gain, but it was the likes of the plant pathologist Norman Borlaug and wheat breeder Orville Vogel, whose green revolution, powered by modern plant science, saved the most lives and set the stage for the next grand challenge.

Today, their scientific successors are giving birth to a new set of miracles in plant production and animal husbandry that cannot only feed the world's growing billions but do so in far more sustainable, environmentally friendly ways. And though the new technologies are awe-inspiring, they are just refinements of cruder techniques that have been used for centuries.

Given the emphatic or, as some like to say, "settled" nature of the science, one would expect a united effort to spread these lifesaving, planet-sparing technologies as fast as possible to the poorer nations who will need them so urgently. Instead, we hear demands that developing countries forgo the products that offer them the best hope of joining the well-fed, affluent world. In the words of a gullible former Zambian president, "We would rather starve than get something toxic." Marie Antoinette couldn't have said it better.

It's not that the legitimate scientific community doesn't understand the seriousness of the problem or the distortions of the naysayers. But too many keep what they know to themselves or, when they engage, observe the Marquis of Queensbury rules in what is essentially a street brawl. One can understand their reticence, facing an aggressive, often self-interested anti-GMO lobby that is indifferent to the facts and quick with ad hominem attacks.

If you're an academic, you can tell yourself that, sooner or later, the science will prevail. If you're from the world of commerce, you justify your silence (or complicity) by saying that you aren't in business to argue with customers. If you're a regulatory bureaucrat, you worry that you will be drawn and quartered for any mistake, whereas no one is ever held accountable for the miracle that never makes it to the marketplace.

It's time to move the argument to a new plane. For the rich and well-fed to deny Africans, Asians, or South Americans the benefits of modern technology is not merely anti-scientific. It's cruel, it's heartless, it's inhumane—and it ought to be confronted on moral grounds that ordinary citizens, including those who have been conned into preferring non-GMO Cheerios, can understand.

Travel to Africa with any of Purdue University's three recent World Food Prize winners, and you won't find the conversation dominated by anti-GMO protesters. There, where more than half of the coming population increase will occur, consumers and farmers alike are eager to share in the lifesaving and life-enhancing advances that modern science alone can bring. Efforts to persuade them otherwise, or simply block their access to the next round of breakthroughs, are worse than anti-scientific. They're immoral.

PART III

Presidential Lecture Series

AS MENTIONED, ONE PREEXISTING ASSET I FELT OBLIGATED TO EXPLOIT TO PURDUE'S advantage was the ability to bring to campus noteworthy individuals who could enrich our students' educational experience, while enlivening the general intellectual environment for our faculty, staff, and neighbors in the community. Looking back over the catalog of those who graciously accepted the invitation to visit us reveals a list impressive in its quality and notoriety, and I think reflective of the interests of the Purdue family.

From the scientific disciplines highly popular on campus, we welcomed people like Akin Adesina, Anant Agarwal, Bjorn Lomborg, and Steven Koonin, and a host of experts on space technology. We had best-selling novelists like Harlan Coben and J. D. Vance; nationally renowned journalists and commentators in Mara Liasson, George Will, and Frank Bruni, and world-famous historians Joseph Ellis, Douglas Brinkley, and Walter Isaacson. Experts in world affairs were prominent on the list: George Shultz, Garry Kasparov, Condoleezza Rice, and Francis Fukuyama.

Although our goal in recruiting these presenters was internal enrichment rather than external exposure, their fame did frequently create a degree of outside attention. It could have been much more. We realized belatedly the potential of even a modest amount of advertising and promotion to multiply the same-day attendance, in person and virtual.

In 2022, after hosting victim compensation expert Ken Feinberg before a typical combined audience of some 800, a promotion campaign led to an eventual Internet viewership of more than 33,000, all across the country. As of this writing, the event with chess grandmaster and democracy champion Garry Kasparov has attracted more than 61,000 viewers. If only we had attempted this with the likes of more of those listed above, we no doubt could have boosted not just Purdue's recognition around the country, but its deserved reputation as a genuine center of intellectual exchange.

The excerpts that follow give a sense of the wealth of topics covered by the series and the tremendous contributions made by our speakers to American science and culture. I hope you'll enjoy listening to the full lectures by following the QR codes.

NO GREATER HONOR — PUBLIC SERVICE AT ITS FINEST

Condoleezza Rice, PhD
Sixty-sixth U.S. secretary of state; national security advisor;
current director of the Hoover Institution at
Stanford University
October 2019

In 1954, the year of *Brown v. Board of Education*, a young girl
was born in Birmingham, Alabama, possibly one of the epi-
centers of racism and segregation in this country at that time.
A few years later, in one of the most notorious and heinous ra-
cially based crimes we can remember, a friend of hers was lost.
From those beginnings, our guest tonight has gone on to com-
pile a spectacular life that could have led her in a variety of directions. She's an athlete, she's a musician, and she has become,
of course, a scholar and author, but America knows and remembers her best for a spectacular career in public service that led
her ultimately to the third highest office in the federal government. Won't you please join me in welcoming and thanking
Dr. Condoleezza Rice?

MITCH: Feel free to use the lightning round technique and just say a word or
two about China.

SECRETARY RICE: In lightning round fashion, there were two narratives about
China. One was China as a security threat—South China Sea, cybersecurity,
trying to build military forces to force the United States out of the Asia
Pacific, anti-satellite weapons, China as threat adversary. But there was, let's
call it, the CEO narrative. It's a big market. I can assemble there. I can
manufacture there. I know it's trouble, but it's a big market. I can't ignore
1.4 billion people.

What's happened is that second narrative has collapsed. Intellectual property theft, joint ventures that are fronts for intellectual property theft, privi-
leging national champions over foreign competition, whole segments of the
economy that are still closed. So now we just have one narrative: China as
adversary.

But the big issue is what's going to happen in technology. We are going to have two Internets. There's not going to be a single Internet anymore because our views of what the Internet is for are 180 degrees apart. Ours is, it's an open portal. You and I can, within some limits, look at anything we want to. We can say anything we want to. We can talk to anybody we want to. We can read anybody we want to. The Chinese believe it is a means of social and political control to the point that they're actually going into citizens' websites and Tencent pages and looking and seeing, "Who are you talking to?" "What have you said?" You get a social patriotism score. If it's not high enough, you might not be able to buy a train ticket.

These are two very different views of the Internet. The question is, How much of the other technology are we going to completely split? So, when you look at the Chinese claiming that they want to lead in AI and quantum computing, and the United States saying, "Wait a minute, you're not going to do that," it's going to affect places like Purdue, and Stanford, and MIT because there are people who are saying you shouldn't have Chinese students in your high technology labs. That, to me, would be a big mistake for universities. We are places that are open. It just gives you a sense of the feelings about the Chinese rise.

Just one other thing: we can't out-Chinese the Chinese. My view is the way that we win this technology competition, this arms race, is the same way we beat the Soviet Union in Sputnik, the same way we beat the Japanese on industrial policy. We out-innovate them. So why not increase the National Science Foundation funding by 25% and let's see what we get from places like this?

MITCH: At a time when you and I were working together, the president that employed us both gave some really pretty thrilling, certainly idealistic speeches about the universality of yearning for freedom, for democracy, and so forth. It was said that it was cultural condescension to say that this or that society wasn't really ready yet for free institutions. It was waiting to be unleashed. We wanted to believe it. Looking back, the things we've seen and maybe learned over the past ten or fifteen years, should we view that slightly differently?

SECRETARY RICE: I don't think so. I'll make three quick points. First is, I don't think anybody wants to live in tyranny. Most of the people who say, "Well, those people aren't ready for democracy, or those people don't want democracy," are people who actually are lucky enough to live in democracies. Because people who aren't know what it's like not to be able to say what you think, to worry about the knock of the secret police at night, and to have no say in who's going to govern you. I do believe those desires are universal.

Now, is it hard? Absolutely. It is hard to move people from relying on clan, and family, and violence to relying on these abstractions like constitutions, and elections, and rule of law. That's hard. But I don't believe there is any culture ... I don't believe there are any people in the world who don't have the DNA for it.

The Asians were too Confucian, but of course we have Asian democracies. Africans were too tribal, but we've got African democracies. Germans were too martial. They've done fine with democracy. Latin Americans, well, they liked men on horseback, caudillos. They've done fine with it. So, this cultural stuff? I always say to my political science colleagues, "You know what culture is? Culture is the explanation we use when we can't explain anything. We say it must be culture." That's what happens here.

The final point I would make is if any country in the world ought to be patient with people trying to build democracies, that'd be the United States of America. You mentioned where I came from—segregated Birmingham, Alabama. Not only that, but the birth defect of slavery in the United States. The American Constitution initially counted my ancestors as three-fifths of a man in order to found the United States of America. I stood in front of a portrait of Benjamin Franklin, took an oath of allegiance to that Constitution as secretary of state, sworn in by a Jewish woman Supreme Court Justice named Ruth Bader Ginsburg. It took a couple hundred years, but we got there.

I'll tell you just a little story about growing up in Birmingham. I was about six. It was Election Day, and George Wallace was up for election to governor. I knew in my own six-year-old way that he wasn't good for Black people. My uncle and I were coming home from school, and there's long, long lines of Black people. I said to my uncle, "Well, if all of those people vote, that Wallace man can't possibly win." My uncle said, "No, we're a minority. He's going to win." I said, "So why did they bother?" My uncle said, "Because they know that one day that vote's going to matter." We have to remember that people are standing in lines in Afghanistan, and Iraq, and Sudan, and places facing down terrorists to vote because they believe that one day that vote will matter. So, we have to speak for them and stand with them, even if it takes time.

George Shultz, PhD (1920–2021)
Sixtieth U.S. secretary of state; sixty-second U.S. secretary
of the treasury; first director of the Office of Management
and Budget; eleventh U.S. secretary of labor
April 2016

I try to avoid those words that too quickly become clichés. One of the recent ones is "icon." But because it applies tonight, I'm going to announce that we're in the presence of one. You're in the presence of a lot of history tonight. Purdue University is so very, very proud to welcome George Shultz—soldier, professor, businessman. We're so fortunate and grateful that he's come to share this next hour with us.

MITCH: Mr. Secretary, you served in four cabinet posts. I'm not aware of anyone else whose life matched that, but the one that most Americans may associate with you most closely was secretary of state. You led our foreign policy through some of the most eventful and successful years.

Let's start there. Take us on what they call a lightning round of the world here. Tell us what you see and what your take is. What about the Middle East?

SECRETARY SHULTZ: The preoccupation with ISIS, which is understandable, is leading people not to be aware of what Iran is doing. Iran is trying to develop a Shiite Middle East. They now have lots more money than they had before and access to weaponry. They're bad news. They are stirring up the Shiite population in Bahrain, where we have a naval base. The Shiite population of the Eastern Province of Saudi Arabia—there's a big problem there to be confronted. Let alone the weaponry they will be putting in Southern Lebanon on behalf of the Hezbollah.

There's explosive problems in the Middle East. I think we have to recognize that for centuries, since the Treaty of Westphalia way back then, we have kept religion and war separated. Now, they're joined. What that means is, there's a different kind of war.

MITCH: Let me ask a question about how you think about foreign policy. How should any of us think about foreign policy? What does that term even mean? There are a lot of times when one couldn't answer the question in any succinct fashion, what the policy of this country is. And that sometimes it's very obscure to us. You have shaped it in some of the most important eras of our history. How did you approach it and how would you now?

SECRETARY SHULTZ: Well, first of all, you have to establish the fact that you mean what you say, and you can carry out what you say you're going to carry out. Ronald Reagan had something happen early in his presidency that made a big impact. You remember the air traffic controller strike? People kept running into the Oval Office, "Mr. President! Mr. President! This is very complicated." He said, "It's not complicated. It's simple. They took an oath of office, and they violated it. They're out."

All over the world, people said, "Are those men crazy? These are the air controllers." But one of the things he learned as governor of California is you've got to pay a lot of attention to execution. He had his secretary of transportation, a man named Drew Lewis, who had been chief executive of a major transportation company. Drew understood the problem, and he also knew how to get something to happen, and he kept the planes flying.

All over the world, people had to say, "Watch your step. The guy plays for keeps." So he established early on, and he established as he went along, the credibility of "We mean what we say, and we can execute."

Earlier, I told you I was a Marine, and I am a Marine, but I can remember at the start of World War II, and I'm in Marine Corps boot camp. The sergeant hands me my rifle and he says, "Take good care of this rifle. This is your best friend. And remember one thing: never point this rifle at anybody unless you're willing to pull a trigger." No empty threats, boot camp wisdom. We've got empty threats littering the landscape. Boot camp wisdom: Mean what you say. Execute.

Second, be realistic. No rose-colored glasses. Describe the situation as it is. You describe Saudi Arabia realistically. That's where you've got to start, realistically. That doesn't mean you don't see opportunities when they're there, but you're realistic.

And then third, you need to be strong, and you're not going to be really strong militarily unless you have a strong economy. There are a lot of things we can do about our economy, I think.

But you have to be strong not only militarily, not only economically, but strength of purpose and self-confidence. And then you have to say to yourself, What is our agenda? What is it we're trying to achieve? Don't start thinking about the other guy's agenda or you'll start negotiating with yourself.

What's my agenda? And then on the basis of that, I'll engage. That's the way to go about it.

MITCH: How big an issue is our growing national debt, first economically and then in terms of the fiscal capacity of the country to do things that we ought to do?

SECRETARY SHULTZ: Well, I think that's a problem, but only part of it. The debt is very high, but we don't feel the burden of it because the Federal Reserve has kept interest rates practically at zero. But if interest rates get to even a semi-normal level, like 3% or 4%, the burden of that debt is a significant portion of the federal budget.

And then you've got deficits continuing as a result of the entitlement programs. We have to get hold of the entitlement programs in order to have any money left at the federal government to do anything except pay off the debt and do entitlements. It's a thing that's necessary to do. Conceptually, it's not hard, but politically it's very difficult.

 Bob Kerrey
U.S. senator
February 2018

> We were really grateful to have Senator Bob Kerrey, Governor Bob Kerrey, former university president Bob Kerrey, who has led one of the great American lives of our time. He's been a public figure of course, but also a successful businessperson, small and large, and is still very, very active on a host of issues that are very topical in our community and across our country. And among other things, he was trained as a pharmacist and finished in four years. I knew our students would want to know how he did that and all else he has achieved in his remarkable life.

MITCH: Among the other services you provided to the country was your leadership, your membership and leadership on the 9/11 commission. And looking back now with the benefit of fifteen years or so, are we safer or less safe? And in what ways?

SENATOR KERREY: I think we're unarguably safer. The Congress responded and made lots of changes, as did the executive branch. I don't think that anybody that was there at the time says anything other than we made some mistakes. And the problem is it doesn't take much to let guys like this get through safety precautions—all nineteen hijackers were unrecognizable if we saw them on the street. And in the old days, two years earlier, we were watching mainland Soviet forces. So even after the Soviet Union ended, we were still worried about large-scale military forces that were out there.

And that's how we had organized ourselves. There was lots of instability in the world when the Soviet Union collapsed, and we were paying attention to that, and we just missed something. Mohamed Atta was in a café in Hamburg, Germany, shopping for flight schools in the United States on the Internet. And that was a vulnerability, but we've tightened up security in the United States. The collaboration with the rest of the world has improved, particularly with European countries, but also with Arab countries, that now understand that this is an existential threat. So, I think the answer is yes. It's not possible to get the risk to zero, and it's not possible to operate without making mistakes. But I think we are unquestionably safer today than we were prior to 9/11.

MITCH: We're now in five decades after the Vietnam era, with all the changes that it brought to the country. It was obviously a major part of your life. And many of us have been watching the recent Ken Burns documentary . . .

SENATOR KERREY: The war itself was awful. What war isn't? And rather than getting into the whole debate, I told Burns, "The Civil War was easier for you to do because all the guys that were in that one are dead, and we're not yet. So you're going to provoke another argument about the world, which is fine." What it's done though, is provoked a big debate inside of Vietnam itself, because perhaps the most moving thing in that whole seventeen-hour series was a North Vietnamese soldier—and those guys were good. They were really good. And he said, "I used to think that the protesting in the United States of America was a sign of weakness. And I now realize it's a sign of strength. We couldn't then and we can't now protest this war."

Facebook is wide open in Vietnam. And I know that because in 1991 when the Soviet Union collapsed, the Vietnamese got interested in a hurry, as did we, in normalizing relations. George Herbert Walker Bush and Dick Solomon[17] were leading that effort. It was a difficult process. But we got money through a State Department program called the Fulbright Program to start a graduate school. And we've graduated 1,200 students since that time. About half of them are in the government. And now we're trying to do an undergraduate program. So, we have a pretty regular conversation with the people of Vietnam.

Other than the fact that they have clung to communism ... which I say to them, "If you're trying to figure out whether that's a good idea or bad idea, just answer this question. How have the 2 million Vietnamese who came to the United States of America done relative to the 2 million who didn't come?" By the way, one of the great things about 1975 was that the Congress at that time made an effort to change the immigration law and let all the Vietnamese who were in trouble come to the United States of America. And they've added enormous economic and social and political value to the country—an enormous amount of value. The reason is that freedom is not phony. They can do whatever they want. And they've created a lot of wealth and they've opened businesses, and so forth. So, the key current conversation with the Vietnamese political officials is to say, "If you want your country to prosper, maybe you're going to have protests against your own government as we do, but there's nothing better than emulating the economic system of the United States."

HOW WE GOT HERE—GREAT HISTORIANS OF OUR TIME

Walter Isaacson
New York Times best-selling author; fourteenth editor of *Time* magazine; television commentator; Tulane University professor of history
September 2019

When we decided that the best way to commemorate Purdue's 150th would be to try to build a continuous stream of brilliant and talented and knowledgeable people who would bring fresh ideas, the newest technology, newest insights to us, we couldn't have done better than Walter Isaacson. An eminent journalist, an author, obviously a scholar, a media executive, a CEO at the Aspen Institute, an investment banker, and, when called upon, he's been a public servant too.

It was clear that the audience who came to hear from Professor Isaacson hung on his every word, and we all left with a greater understanding of what it means to reconstruct a life through history, and a better appreciation for the nature of genius. It was a real treat to welcome my good friend and distinguished American scholar Walter Isaacson to the stage.

MITCH: Walter, I'll bet everyone in the audience has read some if not all of your books. And in our audience . . . including faculty and I hope many of our students . . . I'll guess a number either have written or aspire to write books themselves. Would you just take a minute or two and talk about the process, the meticulous research that you do, and how that may have changed over the decades in which you've been writing best seller after best seller?

PROFESSOR ISAACSON: Well, one of the things I do is I tend to write narrative biographies, which means there's a central character, and it starts at the beginning, and it goes to the end. It's chronological. And that makes it kind of simple because you're not having to make it a complex sort of formula. So, what I do—whether the person's alive as in the case of Steve Jobs, or has been gone a long time like Leonardo—is I start with the primary research. The person's notes. The person's memos. If I can, the interviews. And I just put it all chronologically.

There are two things that happened to the study of history when I was a student, and don't take this wrong, members of the academy, but what happened was biography fell out of favor. It was sort of, Oh, we're telling the story through powerful people. Instead, we had to have a "people's history" of everything.

I had a wonderful history teacher who has probably been on this stage, but back then, her name was Doris Kearns. She hadn't yet married Dick Goodwin and she was not tenured. This shows how old I am. She taught me American history. And for her dissertation and her first publication, she wrote a biography, *Lyndon Johnson and the American Dream*, and they didn't give her tenure because it was considered beneath the dignity of the academy to do so.

So, for a long time, for twenty or thirty years, until academics went back into the field of biography, it was people like me, David McCullough, Jon Meacham, Doris Kearns Goodwin, Bob Caro—people who were not academics got to write narrative biography. And to me it's good, because the Bible does it this way. We tell our lessons through people and their stories, and when I start a book, I just say, Okay. Let's start with where this person was born and let's move and let's figure out how they learn. Because that's what happens when you do it chronologically. Somebody who's 20 knows a little bit less than when they're 30, and you show how they accumulate the creativity that allows them to be innovative.

MITCH: One thing that's plainly common in these people is genius, whatever that term is taken to mean. Talk a little about the nature of genius. I was reading, particularly, your book about da Vinci. It got me thinking, because other authors writing about other people try to pin this elusive quality down and have said it has to do with the ability to concentrate with great fixity on a goal and exclude other things. In fact, that may be why it borders up on various things, mental disorders, or obsessive-compulsive behavior, or things like that, and there seem to be examples of people whose brilliance and breakthroughs came from that. I was thinking, I hope our students don't all read this book as twenty life lessons of da Vinci. It's got things like "procrastinate" and "get distracted"...

PROFESSOR ISAACSON: Yeah. He has more unfinished paintings than finished paintings. He's always putting things aside. Sort of a perfectionist. Well, a couple things about genius. First of all, I don't think there's one particular formula. Secondly, we think of genius as being really, really smart. There are students here—here's what we forgot to tell you. It ain't about being smart. Smart people are dime a dozen. You've met a lot of them in various parts of your career. They don't usually amount to much, right? It's creative people, imaginative people who amount to something. People who "can think different," as Steve Jobs would say.

Steve Jobs...I don't know if we're being recorded, and I don't know if he would care. He was not nearly as smart at mental processing as Bill Gates. You'd watch the two of them. Bill Gates is "Larry Summers smart," but Bill Gates creates the Zune. I don't know if anybody remembers the Zune, but it was the MP3 player that looked like it was made in Uzbekistan in a basement. And Steve at the same time creates the iPod, which looks gorgeous. Why? Because he was creative. He was imaginative.

So, to me, that's an element of genius. Genius means thinking out of the box. It means being able to make a leap that's not just smart but creative and imaginative. That often comes from seeing the patterns across different disciplines. Right before Einstein can get the theory of general relativity, the most beautiful theory in the history of science, he's totally stumped. Things aren't quite working. He pulls out his violin every day and plays Mozart and says it connects him to the harmonies of the spheres, and he eventually gets it.

Leonardo, likewise, can't do *Saint Jerome in the Wilderness*. If you go to New York, it's at the Met—they brought it from the Vatican for the next couple of months. He ends up dissecting the human body until he can have an understanding of muscles, and he goes back to work on it again. Jumping from discipline to discipline tends to help.

Douglas Brinkley, PhD
New York Times best-selling author;
Rice University professor of history
March 2017

Doug Brinkley is undoubtedly one of America's preeminent historians, and the descriptor "prolific" doesn't begin to do him justice. I quipped to our audience that evening in March 2017 that I wanted to start by saying I didn't know where to start. Jack Kerouac, Ken Kesey, Hunter Thompson, Norman Mailer, Dean Acheson, Gerald Ford, Walter Cronkite. What were all these people doing in the same sentence, much less the same body of biographical works? No one else I can think of has encountered as many, known as many, studied as many, and written about as many figures, historical and contemporary, as Doug Brinkley has.

Brinkley's career as a historian started at age eight, when he wrote "an encyclopedia" about the Americans he admired most— both factual and folkloric. Since that auspicious beginning, he has written more than a dozen books chronicling nearly every aspect of American history and culture since Teddy Roosevelt. He even leveraged his long passion for jazz into a Grammy Award for an innovative collaborative effort with Wynton Marsalis and Ted Nash. If you've missed his books—and that would be hard to do—you've likely seen Doug on CNN or read his commentary in some of our nation's best-known newspapers and periodicals.

It was a great pleasure to welcome Doug Brinkley to campus.

MITCH: I don't think anyone among us in America today has thought more deeply and studied more closely the American presidents, particularly in the last century. What I'm curious to know is, if we were starting Mount Rushmore today, and you were the designer, who would be on it?

DR. BRINKLEY: Interesting question. The two figures who are dominant that aren't on it are, in my mind, Franklin Roosevelt and Ronald Reagan. We've just worked on a C-SPAN poll—these polls come out every four years—and this year we had a polling of ninety-one scholars. Number one is always Lincoln, number two is always Washington, and number three is always FDR.

FDR is so giant, not just because he won in '32 and '36 and '40 and '44, which is big enough. Not only did he guide us through the Great Depression with the New Deal programs, but he won World War II—he put all the right people in place. And we have Social Security and the rest. But we lived in the "age of FDR" from 1932, all the way to 1980 with Ronald Reagan. Because up until '80, people believed the federal government is your friend. That's the shadow of FDR.

Truman will create the CIA, Joint Chiefs of Staff, Air Force . . . on and on. Eisenhower creates the interstate highway system and the St. Lawrence Seaway. And with Kennedy, we're going to put man on the moon—it's the government. Lyndon Johnson's whole Great Society is like the New Deal, with Medicaid, Medicare, and so on. Nixon creates the EPA and the Endangered Species Act. Jimmy Carter creates FEMA, the Departments of Energy and Education.

And then Reagan. Reagan was the rollback of saying that was way too much federal government. The federal government's not there to save you. You're being overtaxed. You need to stop wasting taxpayers' money. Suspicion of the federal government.

So, if you want to say political history, the giants are FDR and Reagan. In many ways, we're living in the age of Reagan right now, where we're a center/center-right country. And if you want to operate in a center-left fashion, you've got to triangulate like Bill Clinton, or be so unbelievably charismatic like Barack Obama was.

MITCH: How important is character or virtue in a president? Can you be a great president without them, or with bad character?

PROFESSOR BRINKLEY: I think about that question a lot. Mainly because I'm a teacher at heart—I'm a professor at Rice University. I always tell students the best presidents are the ones who don't lie. They tell the American people the truth, because we're a tough lot and we can handle it. And character matters the most in presidents. But then I studied FDR, and he used to make things up all the time. He was a masterful, deceitful liar, and yet I rank him as one of the great presidents. He had a great character, but he could be very, very deceptive. So, I think by and large character matters tremendously. I would still put it first with the caveat that if you're a really great Machiavellian politician, sometimes you'll do things for the larger public interest that might be deceptive. But in the long run it was what the country needed to be done at that time.

MITCH: I want to ask you something about your craft because you've done two big projects, *The Reagan Diaries* and *The Nixon Tapes*, in which instead of doing all the writing originally, you're editing and pouring through mountainous preexisting material, trying to decide what to keep, maybe what to say about it. Is that harder or easier than sitting down and writing your own material?

PROFESSOR BRINKLEY: It's a lot more work. Ronald Reagan kept a regular diary while he was in the White House. I knew he kept a sporadic one, but I didn't realize he did one every single day except for a few days after he was shot in the attempted assassination. For eight years all the time.

I got a random phone call from Governor Pete Wilson of California, who I knew a little, and he said, "Doug, your name's come up. You might be good to be the one who edits Reagan's diaries."

I said, "Count me in." He said, "Well, you have to meet Mrs. Reagan, and she has to agree that you're the person. You've got to go to the Beverly Hills Hotel and meet her." The advice he gave me was, "If you're in a lull, talk about Hollywood movies. She loves to talk about movies, current movies, not just when she was in film, but what's going on now. And if she mentions the historian Edmund Morris, pivot and don't even talk about it."

Edmund Morris had written a biography of Ronald Reagan called *Dutch*, where he fictionalized her husband. Mrs. Reagan had chosen him to be the biographer and she felt deeply burned. The problem the Reagan people were having in letting loose Reagan's diaries was Mrs. Reagan wasn't trustful. The thought was maybe I could build a relationship with her.

So, I sat in the "Nancy Reagan booth," it was called, and ordered the "Nancy Reagan cobb salad." And we were getting along splendidly until at one point I said, "Well, Mrs. Reagan, if you give me the project, you're going to have some rock-ribbed conservatives angry because I'm seen more as a centrist, and you might get some flack. She just glared at me and said, "What's your point? My son is more liberal than you'll ever be!"

I thought, Good point. All right. And then she was great. I moved out to Simi Valley and did this project, *The Reagan Diaries*. It was a lot of work, a different kind of work. I would put header notes on all of them and then had to cut it down and boil it into a volume. It became a popular book.

The Nixon Tapes. I don't know if you all realize Richard Nixon taped. Yes, presidents tape their phone calls, but Nixon voice activated the whole place. There are tapes of plates clinking, glasses tinkling, and people eating, and it's

unedited all the time. We have 3,800 hours of tapes. The reason we were able
to do it is there are new audio experts who have been able to work through
that sound. And secondly, the guy that I worked with, Luke Nichter, was a
genius transcriber. So, I had this pile of this stuff to edit through and make
sense out of. Both of those projects were much more time-consuming than I
had originally anticipated.

MITCH: I want to ask one more question about the *Diaries*. Inside the cover front
and back, in Reagan's handwriting, there's a replication of just one entry out
of all those thousands of pages you were talking about, and I was struck by it.
I was curious if you chose that particular one and if so, why? The entry is in
the president's writing. It might have been one of the first entries after he's
out of the hospital after being shot, and he says that he had sought God's
help there in the room where he is coughing up blood and so forth. But he
realized he couldn't do that while hating the "mixed up young man who just
shot me." That's a moving thing to read. I was just curious why you chose that.

PROFESSOR BRINKLEY: We picked it because it was so moving. We forget that
Ronald Reagan was inaugurated in late January and he was shot in March. He
wasn't president very long and he really almost died. But right before they're
going to surgery, he had consciousness and he would remember looking at
the ceiling; and then he went under, and they operated. When he woke up,
he really had almost a religious epiphany after nearly losing his life.

He was never a man of malice. Talk about Lincoln's famous "with malice
towards none"—that is Ronald Reagan. He never had malice toward people.
He didn't like enemies. He tried to befriend everybody. But I do believe after
that near death experience he became more determined to rid the world of
nuclear weapons. I don't want to say it softened him—it actually strengthened
him. It made him realize life is short: "My time is short, and I really want to
do something positive for humanity." One of the reasons Reagan gets ranked
quite high now is because of the diplomacy with Mikhail Gorbachev and
eventually the breakup of the Soviet Union.

MITCH: Clare Boothe Luce once told him . . . this is widely reported . . . she
said, "Mr. President, every president gets one sentence in history and yours
will be, 'He won the Cold War without firing a shot.'" I always say no, he
was a two-sentence president, because it could also be said that he restored
the American economy and spirit. Do you think every president finally gets
reduced in history to a sentence?

PROFESSOR BRINKLEY: Well, first of all, some get forgotten. If I honestly ask
people, "Tell me what you remember of Rutherford B. Hayes," most people

don't know. But we remember the big things that people do. I'm afraid now we live in a soundbite culture since the advent of television.

John F. Kennedy forever is known for, "Ask not what your country can do for you, but what you can do for your country." Everybody here knows that line, and you think of that as Kennedy. Ronald Reagan got, "Mr. Gorbachev, tear down that wall." And it lives on. Bill Clinton had, "I did not have . . ." And he was really a very good two term president—balanced the budget—and you can really argue the case of Bill Clinton's presidency. But in the public imagination, it becomes the Lewinsky scandal or the Clinton scandal. Sometimes now it's not just the line, but it's that image, the soundbite you're remembered for.

MITCH: There's a lot of interesting things in those diaries. I love, though, maybe more than any, the notation he put in when he was watching the Jerry Lewis telethon for muscular dystrophy. He called in and he tried to make a pledge, and the operators didn't believe it was him.

PROFESSOR BRINKLEY: The other thing about Reagan that I thought is very true, and FDR did this. They would tell people, "I want to see letters from everyday people." Both FDR and Reagan would grab the mail—they would get letters from anyone who wrote—and they would personally respond to them, not just a form letter. They took the interest to stay in tune with the American people in that way. There's a lot of similarities between Reagan and FDR. They both were very sunny optimists. I tried to find times when FDR, having polio, was unable to walk and was really bitter, and angry, and negative. It's tough. He was always making everybody else feel good around him. And Reagan was that way. And that's a reason why they both are so successful, I think. Optimism is an oxygen in this country. People want to feel good.

Joseph Ellis, PhD
New York Times best-selling author;
winner of the Pulitzer Prize
September 2017

Washington Crossing the Delaware is one of the most iconic paintings ever created, and there is no more fitting an emblem of America's battle for independence. So, it's no surprise that when the remarkable Kate Hutton Tweedy, her family, and the Washington Crossing Foundation contacted me seeking a long-term home for an authorized exact copy,[18] I jumped at the chance to bring it to Purdue.

We officially welcomed the painting to our campus twice. We installed the work temporarily in the Class of 1950 Lecture Hall on a very snowy afternoon in February 2014. Two of our esteemed faculty colleagues, art history professor David Parrish and history professor Franklin Lambert, gave us wonderful lessons on how to "read" the painting and the historical context of its subject. The painting did the lecture hall proud, but we had even bigger plans for it.

At the time, we were in the conceptual stages of what became the Wilmeth Active Learning Center—a new focus of twenty-first-century learning on the site of a defunct power plant squarely at the heart of campus. I tried to stay out of the way of the architects and active learning specialists, but I insisted on one feature for the new building—a Great Library with soaring ceilings and a wall designed specifically to accommodate *Washington Crossing the Delaware*.

The WALC, as it is now fondly called, opened in time for the fall 2017 semester, and the first grand event to be held there was the second official welcome of the great work of art. We were honored to have the distinguished historian Joseph Ellis keynote the occasion.

Dr. Ellis is a household name for anyone interested in America's founding. He earned the Pulitzer Prize for *Founding Brothers: The Revolutionary Generation* and the National Book Award for his biography of Thomas Jefferson, *American Sphinx*. Dr. Ellis's *His Excellency: George Washington* was a *New York Times* best seller.

MITCH: The illustrious speaker we're gathered to hear has written that "historical illiteracy is the new normal." How dismal yet true. The list of basic facts that many of today's Americans don't know is too embarrassing and discouraging to repeat. The basic civics concepts and principles of which a majority of Americans young and old are ignorant is equally appalling. Arriving college students, if they've been taught much at all, have often been fed a false and vacuous version of the epic saga that is America. Such knowledge gaps unaddressed will render a nation lacking in morale and vulnerable to harmful, even fatal, divisions.

Accompanying the loss of memory and enabled by it is the frequency with which midgets of today attack the giants of the past. The denial or even denigration of greatness is a sure sign of a small mind and small character, but the historically uninformed have no way to detect nonsense when it is peddled to them.

At the first meeting of a class I teach, I admonish the students to guard against the now prevalent tendency of presentism—the fallacy through which the values, mores, and conventions of the current day are used to judge our predecessors. Those who engage in this arrogant practice can rest assured that a century from now we will be looked on by our successors as hopelessly ignorant and morally backward in ways we cannot now foresee. The truth is that the storyline of America, with all its imperfections, past and continuing, is about the steady expansion of human freedom and unprecedented widespread material prosperity. That journey took its longest single step forward in the events evoked by this magnificent painting and in the life work of the man at its center.

A final danger of this age is that we may lose sight of a fundamental lesson of all the human past—that government by consent of the governed is not the natural way of the world. That on the contrary, history has almost always belonged to the kings, the warlords, the autocrats, the totalitarians. From the very day when the United States won its freedom, the victors worried about the durability of their breakthrough. They feared that the virtues of republicanism would fade with distance from the sacrifices they had made. That the ease and luxury they knew awaited the new land would leave their progeny open to the blandishments of demagogues and the return of tyranny.

No student of Washington or reader of Joseph Ellis will succumb to these errors. Dr. Ellis has labeled Washington *the* Founding Father, and that is certainly so. In biblical terms one can think of this creator as a Trinity—the three-in-one. First, the general who won the opportunity for free institutions to take root in this country.

As one learns from Dr. Ellis's most recent work, *The Quartet*, he was next the indispensable figure in giving those institutions a sustainable lasting structure. By substitution one could say the repeal and replacement of the unworkable Articles of Confederation with the world's original written Constitution.

And I would submit that Washington completed the trifecta of nation founding by relinquishing power when he could have ruled for life, thus teaching posterity the ethic of citizen service.

I hope you will join me in imagining that decades of Purdue students, as they study and commune beneath this magnificent canvas, will be reminded of the facts and the characteristics of true greatness; be reminded of the long and hazardous march of the freedoms we too often take for granted; be reminded of the fragility of government of, by, and for the people and the duty of its beneficiaries to be vigilant against the world of so many predators, foreign and domestic. If those students, and Purdue University, and the society around us are fortunate, they will glance at the painting having already read the works of our honored guest and speaker.

His has been a lifetime of extraordinary scholarship, historic in its own right, through which he has informed and enlightened millions of us. We look forward to continuing our study under his tutelage tonight. Please welcome Dr. Joseph Ellis.

DR. ELLIS: It's really splendid to be not flying over Indiana, but landing. My wife and I have come to you from western New England. We live in Amherst, which some people call the "People's Republic of Amherst." She is a southerner from Mississippi; I am a southerner from Virginia; and we're here today as Americans. I want to talk to you about what that means and how this painting helps us think about what that means. We happen to be at a moment in our history when that conversation is difficult, and this painting helps us make it possible.

The saying goes, "A picture is worth a thousand words." The deeper truth is that pictures don't speak words, they generate thoughts and feelings, some of which defy logic or reason. And then viewers give words to these thoughts and feelings. An iconic or classic portrait or picture, like da Vinci's *Mona Lisa*, somehow manages to generate thoughts and feelings, and then the obligatory words of interpretation. Across several decades or even centuries, every generation gets to decide for itself, Is she smiling?

The picture hanging in this grand room at Purdue University and projected behind me as I speak has become an iconic image indeed. Some historians believe it is the most famous and familiar image in American history. More Americans have viewed it, reacted to it, and then put words to their reactions for the last century and a half than any other American painting.

Though many art historians have found it aesthetically flawed, and several historians have described it as grossly inaccurate, it somehow managed to defy scholarly opinion to earn a permanent place in the popular imagination. It is the most viewed item in the Metropolitan Museum of Art, which has currently spent a small fortune of several hundred thousand dollars to renovate and replace just the frame. It is ubiquitous on the Internet, and cartoon versions are now available of Donald Trump at the prow being hurled headlong into the ice, thereby joining previous satirical descriptions of Richard Nixon crossing the Potomac toward a landing at Watergate, feminists crossing the Rubicon, and multiculturalists rocking the boat.

Our intentions this evening are less satirical and more serious. President Daniels has asked me to meditate on the meaning of *Washington Crossing the Delaware* for us today. What thoughts and feelings does it provoke or inspire? And what words do we give to our responses?

Obviously, the question before us is not, Was Washington smiling? Just as obvious, this is a picture designed to conjure up deep-felt emotions about a dramatic moment in the American Revolution. And that moment somehow captures the essence of American patriotism, or it has for several generations.

The larger and more urgent question at least as I see it goes like this: At a time when the American people are deeply divided, when political correctness has reached epidemic levels in our colleges and universities, when political partisanship reigns supreme in Washington, when traditional codes of civility have virtually disappeared in our public discourse, what does American patriotism now mean? What sense of common purpose do these thirteen figures and that boat symbolize? What if anything can we learn from them?

Responsible answers to these questions require us to go back to recover the context of two discrete moments. First when the picture was conceived and then painted by Emanuel Leutze in 1850; and second, when the scene it depicted occurred, which was on Christmas night 1776.

Our first destination places us within an electromagnetic field of ironies, where we encounter the awkward fact that America's most iconic picture was not painted by an American and was not aimed at an American audience. Emanuel Leutze was a Prussian immigrant to America who returned to his native land in 1841 with a vision much like Alexis de Tocqueville's a decade earlier. Leutze believed that America was Europe's crystal ball—the place where a more egalitarian and democratic future had made its initial appearance in the world and was destined to sweep Europe and the rest of the world over time.

For Leutze, that meant that the American Revolution provided a preview of revolutions destined, he believed, to unite the Germanic principalities into a single German Republic, modeled on the United States. It's part of what's called the revolution of 1848, you might say. Leutze was almost exactly a century ahead of his time in foreseeing the creation of the West German republic and now, of course, Germany.

He painted several large canvases on this theme he had in his head, about America as the crystal ball, to include three historical studies of Columbus and the discovery of America. But his masterpiece was *Washington Crossing the Delaware*, which he regarded as an inspirational recovery of the precise moment when what was simply and self-evidently called "The Cause," against all odds, snatched victory from the jaws of defeat. Leutze worked on his enormous painting, which was twelve feet by twenty-one feet, in his study in Dusseldorf for over a year, 1849–1850. American tourists and art students at Dusseldorf served as models for the characters in the boat. Some guy walks past him, he says, "Hey, would you be willing to come in to ..."

Even before he finished, all hope for a Germanic revolution along American lines collapsed, thereby undermining his original intention for the work. Six months after its completion, a fire in his studio damaged the painting he had just finished. So, he quickly painted an exact replica, which is the only one we have, and that's the version shipped over to America in 1851, where it immediately became a sensation. This is a funny story. The damaged original remained on display in the Dusseldorf Museum until 1942, when it was destroyed in a bombing raid by the Royal Air Force. Though late to the game, the British finally stopped Washington from crossing the Delaware.

Fortunately, the Royal Air Force was unavailable on Christmas night 1776, when 2,400 American soldiers rode across the ice-choked Delaware amid the sleet, hail, and snow of a classic nor'easter. About 300 horses and 20 heavy cannon came across on flatbed ferries. Three other regiment-sized attack groups were supposed to join the assault upstream and downstream of Washington's main force, but the combination of ice and river currents blocked their advance.

This was really the first offensive operation conducted by the Continental Army since the war officially started, and Washington's tactical plan proved more complicated than the weather conditions and the amateur status of the officer corps permitted. When his boat reached the New Jersey side of the river, Washington was forced to make a mid-battle decision to go forward or turn back, since only a third of the putative attack force had made it across. Not only that, but he was also an hour behind schedule, and because sunrise on that day was due at 4:41 a.m., his attack on the Hessian regiment at Trenton would now have to happen in daylight, another logistical liability.

Prudence dictated caution, and caution dictated withdrawal back to the safe shores of Pennsylvania. Washington decided instead to risk everything. That the fact that the cannon had made it across meant that despite the fewer troops, he would enjoy superior firepower at the point of attack, plus the hard weather probably meant that he would catch the Hessians off guard since no commander in his right mind would stage an assault in such conditions.

The Hessian garrison of 1,500 troops was not surprised, and the claim that they were all drunk or asleep when Washington attacked, which became a fixture in the early histories of the battle, is a total myth. The Hessians, however, were greatly fatigued because they had been kept on around-the-clock alert for several days expecting the attack. They fought bravely and with conspicuous discipline, like the veteran professionals they were, but they were outnumbered and outgunned. For the fullest and far and away the best account of the battle as well as the crossing itself, do read David Hackett Fischer's book *Washington's Crossing*, which won the Pulitzer in the year 2004. . . .

What about the historical accuracy of Leutze's depiction of the crossing itself? Art historians over the years have enjoyed a field day exposing Leutze's romanticized distortions. . . . I believe that Leutze's painting is historically correct in its larger message about that dramatic moment. And second, its more mythical message, which has *always* been the seminal source of its enduring significance, remains relevant and speaks quite directly to our current condition.

On the first score, historically, you need to know the political and military context in December of 1776 to appreciate the full meaning of the scene Leutze has captured so dramatically. No less than Tom Paine, author of *Common Sense*, came out with a new series called *The Crisis* at just this moment. The first line of *The Crisis* is a line all journalists throughout American history have wanted to be able to write, and very few of them have managed: "These are the times that try men's souls." And they really were.

If you think we have a crisis now, this is nothing compared to what they were facing. The American Revolution was on the verge of collapse. This was a final fling, a roll of the dice. More specifically, the Continental Army had just experienced a series of costly and humiliating defeats on Long Island and Manhattan. They should've been annihilated. If General Howe and Admiral Howe had decided to do that, they could have done it. They decided not to do it.

The patriotic presumption that ordinary farmers and artisans fighting for what they devoutly believe could defeat a professional army of veterans had been exposed as a grand illusion. The British high command believed that the spirit of the Continental Army had been broken, the American rebellion had been killed in the cradle, and all that was left amounted to little more than a mopping up campaign. Washington's army, which numbered 30,000 in August, was now down to less than 10,000, and that would dwindle to 2,000 on January 1, when most of the enlistments were up.

Even more significantly, the war for hearts and minds was being lost, and that was the crucial part of the war. On Long Island, recruits were signing up for the British Army in droves. In New Jersey, 3,000 colonists signed a pledge repudiating American independence, to include one signer of the Declaration itself. Continental currency had become worthless pieces of paper, as European bankers anticipated an imminent British victory. All the Indian tribes of the Six Nations, except for the Oneidas, had gone over to the British side and were now raiding American settlements on the frontier with impunity. Requests by the Continental Congress for money and men fell on deaf ears as each state legislature was stepping back from the larger conflict to protect its own population and will invest in militia, not the Continental Army. Militias stayed within the borders of the state.

I could go on, but you get the point. The movement for American independence was on the verge of extinction. As Washington himself put it, the cause would "probably expire over the winter unless we are able to strike some stroke."

The sense of drama and desperation that Leutze captured on canvas was utterly accurate. This was the portentous moment when the fate of the American Revolution hovered on the edge of the abyss. From this pivotal point, American history was poised to flow forward one way or another. Regardless of the rather rarefied source of the inspiration, Leutze's historical instincts were impeccable.

The larger and more mythical meaning of *Washington Crossing the Delaware* is based on the knowledge that all viewers of the painting, like us now, possessed, but Washington and the passengers in the boat did not. Namely, they would make it across. They would win victory at Trenton. The American Revolution would succeed. The first nation-sized republic in modern history would become the fountainhead for a global movement based on liberal principles—popular sovereignty, the rule of law, human rights, and free markets. And that political model would vanquish the European monarchies in the nineteenth century and then the totalitarian threats posed by Germany and Japan in the twentieth. Finally, with the collapse of the Soviet Union at the end of the twentieth century, the United States would become the undisputed and wholly triumphant world power. This is a picture that could have been entitled not just *Birth of a Nation*, but *Birth of The Nation*.

In the nineteenth century, the name given to this more mythical meaning was Manifest Destiny. Leutze actually painted another epic-sized portrait of this vision titled *Westward the Course of Empire Takes Its Way*, 1861. The original currently hangs in the U.S. Capitol. Historically, not just mythically, westward expansion could never have happened if the war for independence had failed. Indeed, the Treaty of Paris in 1783 transferred the entire British Empire south of Canada and east of the Mississippi to the emerging American republic.

Washington himself insisted that while independence was the great principle in the war, the land to the west, Indiana included, was the great prize, but an empire was something we hadn't even thought about. While the Mississippi was the initial western border, there was always a vague and unspoken assumption that all borders short of the Pacific were temporary, as the very terms "Continental Army" and "Continental Congress" seemed to suggest, though these more expansive definitions obviously were dependent on the Louisiana Purchase in 1803 and then the war with Mexico in 1846.

This is simultaneously a triumphant and tragic story. While Leutze emphasizes the former, we cannot avoid giving equal attention to the latter, most tragically the Indian removal under Andrew Jackson and the genocide in slow motion across the continent. A recent book by Robert Kaplan, which I recommend, called *Earning the Rockies*, has framed the moral dilemma nicely. As he puts it, "The American narrative is morally irresolvable because the society that saved humanity in the twentieth century was also a society built on enormous crimes—slavery and the extinction of the native inhabitants."

Kaplan's mention of the society that saved humanity in the great wars of the twentieth century is obviously a reference to America's role in vanquishing Hitler's Germany and then Soviet-style communism. The name often applied to this twentieth-century version of the original Leutze vision is "American exceptionalism," a term that turns out to be more elusive and multidimensional than "Manifest Destiny." In its quasi-religious variation, it suggests that the United States enjoys some providential place in the mind of God, who is predisposed to protect women, children, and the United States of America. You have to read this evangelical meaning into Leutze's painting, since he did not depict the ice and water of the Delaware parting in Moses-like fashion as the boats were going across.

It is true, however, that Washington himself frequently used the term "providential" to describe several moments in the war, Christmas night in 1776 among them, when events could have easily gone the other way if some higher power had not put his or her finger on the scales of history. But Washington never used the word "God."

Another more messianic version of American exceptionalism suggests the United States is fated to carry its national values to all the nations of the world, and that doing so is our distinctive historical mission. Woodrow Wilson provided the classic formulation of this doctrine in 1917 when he justified American entry into World War I with the words, "To make the world safe for democracy." John Kennedy echoed the Wilsonian message in his inaugural address in 1961 when he declared that "we shall pay any price, bear any burden, meet any hardship, support any friend, oppose any foe, in order to assure the survival and success of liberty." The crusading spirit of this version of the vision is still alive in some circles, though for Wilson's generation it died in the trenches of the war to end all wars; and for Kennedy's generation, among some at least, it died in the rice paddies of Vietnam.

Washington, you need to know, never used the words "American exceptionalism," but argued quite forcefully in the Farewell Address that, precisely because the conditions responsible for American success were truly unique, they could not easily be transferred to other nations. He was thinking of France at the time, correctly predicting that the French Revolution would become a bloodbath that ended with the dictatorship of Napoleon. One can only speculate what he would say about bringing democracy to Iraq and Afghanistan. People always ask, "Professor Ellis, what would Washington do about Iraq?" And I say, "He's busy being dead." Second, he doesn't know where Iraq is—it didn't exist. But if you really press me and you get into this time machine stuff, I think he'd say, "How did we become the British? I don't like that role."

The final variation on the "exceptional" theme does not require you to believe in divine intervention and does not urge you to go abroad. This is what John Quincy Adams said: "The United States does not go abroad in search of monsters to destroy." George Kennan loved to quote that. The two main spokesmen for this vision, which I also believe is what Leutze most had in mind, are both Republican presidents—Abraham Lincoln and Ronald Reagan. Lincoln's words, uttered at Gettysburg to justify his defense of the Union that the North was fighting to preserve: "...whether this nation or any nation so conceived and so dedicated can long endure." And Reagan's words, uttered on multiple occasions, that "shining city on a hill."

And in fact, this Reagan/Lincoln version of exceptionalism claims that the core values of the American Revolution, the ones that we win, declared to the world by Jefferson in the Declaration of Independence then institutionalized in the Constitution and the Bill of Rights, embodied the fullest and finest articulation of the political principles toward which western civilization has been headed for the past 2,000 years. They might very well be improved upon at some point in the future by another nation, but thus far, no other nation has done it. These principles cannot by definition be imposed on other nations and peoples, who must discover them on their own, because the principles make consensus, not coercion, a principal priority. Brandishing them in flamboyant fashion is unnecessary and even counterproductive, since self-evident truths, again by definition, need not be shouted. Doing so only diminishes their luster.

So, we gather together in this citadel of learning within the American heartland, all looking at this iconic picture of the American spirit, and where are our thoughts and our feelings? What words do we find ourselves uttering to express them? As a biographer of Washington, the words "courage," "self-confidence," "bottomless conviction" come to mind. Though as a historian, I need to remind you that once this existential threat of '76 passed, there were five long years of war remaining—a rollercoaster ride for Washington—that continued to threaten the very survival of the Continental Army and the Revolution itself. So, "resilience" comes to mind—in history and life, I believe, perhaps one of the most underappreciated virtues imaginable. Resilience.

As a fellow citizen living through a deeply divisive and partisan moment in our nation's history, what do I see? Well, this is where you get to ask me questions and I will answer as honestly as I possibly can. I see a diverse cross section of human beings, all gathered in the same boat, rowing together. At this moment, they are not men or women, they are not Blacks or whites, they are not New Englanders or Westerners, they are Americans, and they all assume that their common future lies ahead of them on the New Jersey shore, not behind them in America. (There's no such thing as let's make America great again. Again is in the past.) Though the winds of the moment are in their faces, they all fervently believe that the winds of history are at their backs and the looming events are about to confirm that they are right. The dawn is about to break, and as someone once said, "It is always morning in America," and I think it still is.

Thank you very much.

THE GRAND EXPERIMENT—THE FUTURE OF DEMOCRACY

Garry Kasparov

Chess grandmaster; world chess champion; founder of the Renew Democracy Initiative
September 2021

Well beyond the world of chess aficionados, Soviet-born Garry Kasparov's name is nearly synonymous with the game. He spent twenty years as the world's top-rated chess player, finding international fame in 1985 when, at the age of 22 he became the youngest world chess champion in history. During his career, Mr. Kasparov held the top chess ranking longer than anyone, and that phenomenal record holds to this day.

That achievement alone would have made for a memorable appearance, but it really wasn't the reason I invited Mr. Kasparov to Purdue.

His chess career was well established when Kasparov joined the vanguard of the Russian pro-democracy movement in 2005 and he was among the first notable Soviets to call for democratic and market reforms. In 2012 he succeeded Václav Havel as chairman of the New York–based Human Rights Foundation and in 2017 founded the Renew Democracy Initiative, dedicated to promoting the principles of the free world. For his courage in confronting totalitarianism, Mr. Kasparov has suffered brutality, imminent arrest, and continual threats to his life and safety. His tireless work to support civics education, integrity in public office, and the vital importance of engaged citizenry in a democracy offers us a lesson in what it means to live in freedom.

It was a great honor to host Garry Kasparov at Purdue, and after his opening remarks, we shared a fascinating conversation.

MR. KASPAROV: . . . Blindly supporting a political party or politician is very dangerous. The path to hell may be paved with good intentions, but compromises on principles are the streetlights. Like so many of my compatriots in the unfree world on the other side of the Iron Curtain, I greatly admired and envied the United States and what it stood for. I was fortunate to be able to travel for my chess career, if only escorted by KGB agents, just like the Soviet players in *The Queen's Gambit*.[19] (By the way, it was my advice to Scott Frank to incorporate KGB guys that were not in the original book—sometimes your experience helps.)

I peered around the Iron Curtain and saw the American republic as a proverbial "shining city on the hill." I admit that my view of the West and the U.S. was more than a little rose-colored. I was young and a little naive, but even today, *even today*, I would like Americans to appreciate what they have. The true beauty of American democracy is that it recognizes it is not perfect. It adapts. The people have a voice in their own system, as unhappy as they might be with it at any moment, especially when the other party is in power.

Real elections are a privilege. When I organized the Other Russia coalition in 2005, my fellow democracy advocates and I organized party primaries because we wanted the Russian people to have a chance at participating in free and fair elections, unknown in the Putin era. Today, some would-be American authoritarians are passing laws to suppress voting, gerrymander elections, and allow partisan functionaries to overrule the vote.

America's freedom of speech is a privilege. Even as a young world chess champion I had to guard my actions, my words, even my thoughts in the USSR. Everyone in the Soviet Union, from children to grandmasters, had to censor themselves. In Putin's Russia, even the smallest amount of protest, even just a tweet, just a tweet or retweet, can land you in jail. As the saying goes, we do have freedom of speech in Russia, but in America you also have freedom after speech.

Now that I live in America, I thought I'd never again have to look over my shoulder when speaking my mind, but today far too many people want to constrain public discourse to what is socially acceptable at the moment. This isn't the heavy hand of the state, but any, any chilling effect is a threat to democratic discourse. Democracy may or may not die in darkness, but it certainly dies in silence. Extremists on both political sides are pushing the same dangerous message: American democracy is broken. "Well, the other guys are doing it so we have to do it, too." It is a downward spiral. You cannot fight illiberalism with more illiberalism. . . .

MITCH: Your predecessor in this series of programs, the author and scholar Francis Fukuyama, wrote a book just twenty years ago or so proclaiming the end of history. The final triumph of individual freedom, of values, of free exchange. And yet here in a historical blink later we see a very different pattern, not just in your home country, but in so many other places. Freedom House, for the fifteenth straight year, just found a decline in freedom—fewer than 20% of the world's population now, they say, is living in free societies. What happened?

MR. KASPAROV: Going back to 1992/1993 when the book was written and released, I have to say that we all shared this sentiment. I remember celebrating the collapse of the Soviet Union and before that the collapse of the Berlin Wall. Country after country abolished communism, and you know we all thought it would be the end of history.

It's easy to be a Monday-morning quarterback, you know, saying, "Oh, you have to look at this and that, and you know there were already some seeds of future failure." But I think what we missed—and this is the hard lesson for us to learn—is that evil doesn't die. It can be buried temporarily under the rubble of the Berlin Wall, but the moment we lose our vigilance, the moment we turn to be complacent, it sprouts out.

In Russia, it took nine years. But it's not that Putin came out of the blue. We already saw many moments, turning points, that prepared Putin's appearance, even before we even knew his name. I wouldn't call him the right man, in the right place, at the right time, because it's exactly the opposite. But it was the right time to set up dictatorship because the seeds of dictatorship had been planted by many actions that we supported. Yeltsin confronted the Russian parliament, and I supported him in 1996. We believed that democracy had been protected because we were afraid of the return of communism.

What we didn't understand is that democracy is a process, not a result. The moment you go against the process, the moment you accept that your guy, who with the best intentions in this world, can violate the rules, can rig the results, a little bit of a tweak—it started with a little tweak here and there—that's it.

And the other problem was on the side of the free world, because ironically at the end of the Cold War America lost its vision of the future. From 1946 to 1991 it was easy. The Soviet Union was there, communism. America had to stay as the force for good, defending the free world against communism and against all sorts of dictators. And in 1991, what's next?

American democracy: Where do we go from here?
A conversation with former Speaker of the
U.S. House of Representatives Paul Ryan
and former U.S. senator Heidi Heitkamp
February 2021

A mark of Boilermaker pride is sustaining more than 1,000 student clubs and organizations, one of which came to my attention for the first time during the fall semester of 2020. The Purdue University Political Discourse Club is a unique enterprise in our times—a nonpartisan student organization that gives its members the chance to have civil discussions on wide-ranging topics across the political spectrum. The students' self-governed exercises in free expression and rancor-free debate stand to offer the older adults among us a genuine lesson in what it means to practice good citizenship.

So, when the club approached me with a request—to invite two of America's most prominent and well-reasoned public servants for a Presidential Leadership Series event—I jumped at the chance. But I set one condition. The Discourse Club and its members would help me with the interview.

Speaker of the House Paul Ryan and United States senator Heidi Heitkamp,[20] both in retirement from elected office and each representing a different political party, were game. The timing—the end of the first year of the COVID pandemic—meant a virtual event was called for. With the help of some of our university's top technologists, we pulled it off, and the result was an example of civil discourse which met even the high standards of Purdue's Political Discourse Club.

MITCH: I want to ask if you can identify areas, issues, topics that might serve to bring Americans together. Let's recognize that there's very little overlap in

Congress anymore, or very few of either party finding it in their conscience to vote with the other party. So, this will be harder than it maybe has ever been. But are there issues that you can think of where this division might be bridged and the country might be given a couple of examples of how compromise and cooperation can effectively work? Paul, can you go first?

SPEAKER RYAN: . . . A vital issue like immigration, if disagreement can be overcome, would be a real confidence builder for the country. And then things that we're already in sync on—infrastructure, China policy—there are a lot of things. When I was in my last term as Speaker, we passed 1,172 bills out of the House. That's about double the production of a session in the legislature. Usually, you pass about 600. We did almost 1,200. About 600 of them made it into law. Over 80% of those bills were bipartisan bills. Opioid is a big issue, criminal justice reform, the Cancer Moonshot/Cures Act. I can go on and on and on. The point I'm making, Mitch, is the system still actually does work, but all those bipartisan reforms, which were generational changing reforms, passed without much notice in the media, without any great notice because we all got along and we got together. We got stuff done.

SENATOR HEITKAMP: . . . I think that when we look at economic justice, and it's something that I know Paul has worked really hard on, we approach it from a different standpoint, but I will tell you I think both sides realize that you cannot have this level of economic inequality, whether it is income inequality or wealth inequality, and really maintain a balanced economy moving forward.

How do you address that? Now that's the problem. The problem is that, if you sat down with Americans and asked, "What kind of America do you want to live in?" it wouldn't matter if they're Democrats, Republicans, Independents, Green Party, they would all give you the same answer. The question is how do you get there? And that takes political leadership skills, and you've got to want to lead the institution of the Senate and the House. And I think Paul is a great example of this. You go to lead the institution and not be a political leader. Way too often, our leaders of this great Congress and this great institution, Article One branch of government, are political leaders. . . . Joe Biden is a creature of the Senate. He has a lot of friends there. He understands the legislature. But I will tell you that if you want unity in this country and you want to move things forward, get out of Washington, D.C., and start talking to the people of this country because we're less divided. And when the motivation is power and winning, you aren't going to get anything other than fear and division.

Francis Fukuyama, PhD
Mosbacher director of the Center on Democracy,
Development and the Rule of Law; director of the Ford
Dorsey Master's in International Policy, Stanford University
April 2019

Dr. Francis Fukuyama is one of the most erudite, essential, and thought-provoking intellectual leaders of our day. A prolific scholar of international politics, he first got the world's attention with a 1989 article and subsequent book, *The End of History and the Last Man* (1992), which has since been published in more than twenty foreign editions. In it, Dr. Fukuyama asserted that the fall of Soviet Russia and the Berlin Wall marked the triumph of liberal democracy and predicted that the last great stage of human development had finally arrived. Although humanity has ultimately proven Dr. Fukuyama's prognostication to be premature, the book clearly and carefully described the finishing line, perhaps for the first time, to which every society should aspire.

Dr. Fukuyama has followed his first master stroke with a series of works that get us all thinking about how humanity can and should organize itself, as well as the great challenges that continue to confront us. It was an honor to welcome him to Purdue.

MITCH: There are not very many essays or books or theories which capture the public imagination, are debated, and thought of, and remembered for a very long time, but you created one about a quarter century ago. When you said "the end of history" it was understood by some to mean that free institutions, liberalism in politics, free market capitalism, and economics had triumphed, then and forever. You've clarified that a little bit recently, but for those who haven't read it, talk a little bit about what you did mean and what it means today.

DR. FUKUYAMA: The question about the "end of history" is one I've been asked before on a few occasions. I guess the starting point is to understand what I meant by the end of history. It was not my phrase. It was the philosopher Hegel and then Karl Marx who used it. "History" in their sense could have a synonym of "modernization" or "development." And so the question is, You have this big, long-term evolution of human societies. Where is it heading?

The Marxists had one particular answer, which is that it would be heading toward a communist utopia. That was the end of history for them.

In 1988/89, when I wrote the original article, Gorbachev was in power in the Soviet Union. There was ferment all over the world. A lot of democratic revolutions were happening in Latin America and other parts of the world. And I said, hey, it doesn't look like we're going to get there. It doesn't look like we're going to get to communism. It looks like the terminal point is going to be some form of liberal democracy connected to a market economy. I still think that question is, Is there a higher form of human political/social/economic organization that's going to supersede liberal democracy? And that I really don't see in the world right now. China, I think, is really the only alternative system that looks like it's a contender because they can master high levels of technology. They're growing very fast. But in the end, nobody wants to move to China, really. They don't have an attractive society in many ways. So, I still think that there's something to the thesis.

MITCH: I may be reading him superficially, but if there's been another essay in the last several years that seems to have caught the attention of people in much the way that your original work did, it's one that seems to take an almost polar view. Robert Kagan recently wrote a piece called "The Strongmen Strike Back," which I understood to suggest that liberalism as we've known it now is in danger of eclipse from both the left and the right. He even suggests that authoritarians of the left and right might be coming together in various ways. What do you make of his theory? Is it completely inconsistent with yours or not?

DR. FUKUYAMA: Bob Kagan is an old friend of mine. We've been sparring for a long time, and he's been writing that article for the last twenty-five years. Even in the '90s when Bill Clinton was president and the United States was on top of the world, he was still worried that the world was much more conflictual. I think now he is closer to being right than at any time since then.

I do think that now there is this unique combination of challenges where you do have these external actors like China and Russia that are authoritarian. They're very assertive. Quite self-confident. I think that's a geopolitical situation that we've not had to deal with. And so in that sense he is quite right. And then the other big development is this upsurge of populist nationalism, which is hitting not just externally the security of democracies, but it's happening from within.

MITCH: There are tools available to tyrants now, or would-be tyrants, that weren't there before. Tools that George Orwell never imagined, I don't think. Does that change the possibility that Kagan is right in the long term?

DR. FUKUYAMA: It's very worrisome. This Chinese social credit system where, basically, every bit of information that Google and Facebook have about you is owned by the government, and they can use that to control your political behavior—not just what you eat for breakfast. It's quite scary. A friend of mine was going through an airport terminal in China and walks up to a camera. It says, "Hello, Mr. So and So. Your flight is on time. Go to gate such and such." He didn't have to say anything. It simply recognized his face. That's just over the horizon. I think that we've not yet seen an attempt by an authoritarian political government that is trying to control its citizens using that degree of technology. I think we should be very worried about it.

MITCH: Lots of carrots and potentially sticks for those who misbehave as the government sees it.

DR. FUKUYAMA: And the thing is, it could be for something very minor. You write some slightly critical thing on the *Washington Post* or the Chinese social media and, all of a sudden, you can't buy a train ticket to see your parents. That sort of thing.

MITCH: Some assert that liberalism as we've known it is incompatible with tradition and culture as we've understood those terms and that this may explain some of the friction in various societies today. You treat with this a little bit in some of your work, but could you explain your views?

DR. FUKUYAMA: Well, liberalism is basically about the liberty of individuals. The whole premise of our political system is that we're rights-bearing individuals who worry about the government taking those rights away and we want to defend a sphere of individual liberty. I think, though, that the way liberal societies have always worked is by being embedded in communities in which people are not just selfish individuals, but they're in families. They're in neighborhoods. They're in workplaces. And they are political creatures who have a sense of obligation toward public virtue. That they have an obligation to look to public interest and not just to their narrow self-interest.

I think that there's always been this tension between the emphasis on the individual, which can either be me as a proud member of a democratic system who participates in thinking with my fellow citizens about the public good, or it can just be me, me, me, and I'm going to use the system to get what I want.

That tension, that balance has shifted to the second version over the last few decades, so that the idea of public virtue, the idea that we should be thinking about communities and the way we relate to people, has been atrophied. This makes people very uncomfortable because, in fact, we are not just selfish individuals. We're social creatures and we feel intensely uncomfortable if we're not related to people. If we don't have a sense of belonging. And quite frankly, I think some of the very negative forms of belonging—white nationalism or some of the populist movements that you see—are a direct response to the atomization of a society, where we don't have structures that hold us together in communities. We're desperately seeking that and we go find it in some form of extremism.

A WAY WITH WORDS—JOURNALISTS, WRITERS, AND COMMENTATORS

 George Will, PhD
Pulitzer Prize–winning author, journalist, and commentator
December 2015

The credentials of Dr. George Will are impeccable. Among the very finest of our nation's thinkers and writers, Dr. Will has written widely on topics in politics, domestic and foreign affairs, American history, American culture, and, notably, baseball. The *Washington Journalism Review* once deemed him "the finest writer in any category," and he has won the Pulitzer Prize, the National Magazine Award, the Silurian Award, and every other distinction imaginable. Now, what the *Review* meant was of the various categories they were honoring, he was first among equals. Some of us would prefer he be named the best writer on any subject he chooses. Having Dr. Will join us for a Presidential Lecture was a true highlight of the series.

MITCH: Dr. Will, George, this being higher ed, we'll give precedence to process over substance. And so, I would like to ask a first question about your craft. You met today, very kindly, with hundreds of our students, many of whom want to become writers, or journalists, or pursue other such professions. What's your MO? You've generated by now somewhere in the mid–four

digits of columns, two a week for four and a half decades in the *Post* syndi-
cate and in the magazine formerly known as *Newsweek*. How do you work?

DR. WILL: The most frequently asked question of a columnist is the one I asked
my friend and colleague Bill Buckley when I started [in journalism]. I said,
"Bill, how do you come up with things to write about?" And he said, "The
world irritates me three times a week."

I would modify it and say it irritates me, piques my curiosity, amuses me,
something. I've never had a day in which I didn't have five topics I wanted to
write about. In fact, I have in my wallet—I can actually show it to you—I always carry a card with the coming topics I want to write about. And there they
are. It's my next column, that will go out tomorrow and it'll be in Thursday's
paper, on the hundredth anniversary of the birth of Frank Sinatra, the Great
American Songbook, and all that.

I think if I don't write a third of my columns, not only on subjects that are
not above the fold in the *New York Times*, but on subjects that are not on the
front page of the *New York Times*, or even in the *New York Times*, I'm not doing my job right. Because you're neglecting, among other things, culture. And
those of us who have sat at the feet of my former best friend, Pat Moynihan,
know that culture drives politics, and that politics can improve culture. But
culture is primary, and politics is, in some sense, an epiphenomenon.

So, my method of operating is to be open to the stimuli of this endlessly
stimulating country and to understand that there's an awful lot more going
on in the world than the Iowa caucuses.

MITCH: A common lament these days has to do with the dysfunction of particularly the federal government. People come at that from different directions.
You remind your readers every so often that our Constitution wasn't really
written for smooth, well-oiled efficiency. Mr. Madison had something different
in mind. Maybe this is the system he contemplated or the sorts of outcomes,
or have we really fallen into a state that we should worry about?

DR. WILL: This is what he had in mind with an important asterisk. When those
fifty-five extraordinary people gathered in Philadelphia in the sweltering
summer of 1787, they did not go there to devise an efficient government.
The idea would've horrified them. They went to devise a government strong
enough to secure our rights, but not too strong to threaten them. By the way,
the most important word in the Declaration of Independence is "secure." We
hold these truths to be self-evident, that all men are created equal, endowed by
their creator with certain unalienable rights, and governments are instituted *to*

secure those rights. Preexisting rights. Not given to us by government, they're given to us by our nature. They're called "natural rights." And the government exists to secure them. So, it is in the language of the first two paragraphs of the Declaration that limited government is written in. It has the limited function of securing our rights, including facilitating our pursuit of happiness.

So in Philadelphia they designed a government full of blocking mechanisms: three branches of government, two branches of the legislative branch, the Senate with its own constituencies and electoral rhythms, the House with different constituencies, different electoral rhythms, super majorities, veto, veto overrides, judicial review. All kinds of ways of slowing the beast down and making things go slowly so people can have temperate judgments. George Washington famously defined the Senate as the "saucer into which we pour our tea so that it will cool."

I've been in Washington for forty-six years, a not inconsiderable portion of the life of this republic, and I can think of nothing the American people have wanted intensely and protracted that they didn't get. Sooner or later, the government delivers.

Now for the asterisk over this. I so far have said it's working the way Madison designed it. It's supposed to be slow. It's supposed to be difficult. Get over it. The asterisk is this: Madison said in Federalist 45, "The proposed Constitution ..." (the Federalist Papers, of course, were newspaper columns designed to get New York to ratify the Constitution); he said, "The proposed Constitution delegates powers to the federal government that are few and specific."

They envisioned a federal government that did not tell us what kind of light bulbs we were going to have, how much water could come through our shower heads. Both of these are recent government policies. The government was to do a few things and try to do them well.

When you have a government that is into every form of national life, every nook and cranny, it begins to coagulate, and you begin to get these veto groups. And then what you get is government grows by the very negotiation of government. Someone says, "Well, there are no limits on what government does. I want it to do A, B, and C." And someone says, "Well, I want to do D, E, and F. So I'll support your three, if you'll support my three." And the very process of bickering, and brokering, and negotiating inexorably makes the government bigger, which makes it all the more hard to move and all the easier to bring to a halt. In that sense, it's Madison's basic framework, but without Madison's sense of limitation on government.

If I could add one more thing. We've just reauthorized No Child Left Behind. No Child Left Behind was the sixth, I believe, iteration of the Elementary and Secondary Education Act of 1965. I mention this bit of ancient history because until about 1965, there was what was called the "legitimacy barrier" to Congress. Before Congress did something, it asked the question, Where in the Constitution is the enumerated power that gives us the right to do this?

James Q. Wilson, the smartest social scientist of his generation, said that that really ended in 1965 after the anti-Goldwater landslide in 1964. (I was one of the 27 million Goldwater voters, but never mind.) The Democrats had this enormous majority in Congress; they could do whatever they wanted, and they passed, among other things, the first Elementary and Secondary Education Act. And James Q. Wilson said that was the end of the legitimacy barrier. If the government could casually intrude itself into the quintessentially state and local responsibility, there were no more limits on the purview of the federal government. And I think he was probably right.

MITCH: Pursuing that question of limits, you and many others have written in the last few years out of concern that extralegal executive actions were being taken, that things were being done by the executive branch of government that it did not have the delegated powers to do and/or were the rightful prerogative of the legislative branch. Unlike many folks who would agree with you most of the time, you have argued that it's a more activist judiciary which should be stepping up to these issues where they arise. Could you say a word or two about that?

DR. WILL: Yes. Conservatives alarmed by what they took to be the activism of the Warren court in creating new rights, not enforcing traditional rights, adopted the language that there should be less judicial activism, a more deferential judiciary to the popular elected branches, celebrating majority rule. In doing this, conservatives were doing the work of progressivism. It was the progressives who came along and said, "Well, the judiciary must proceed. We must allow the government to legislate and regulate where it will out of respect for majoritarianism."

My view is that it is a dereliction of judicial duty not to enforce the boundaries of government, because if it doesn't, no one will. To that end, there's now a real growing movement among conservatives to say the United States is not about majority rule. The United States is about liberty, and liberty can be threatened by majority rule. Our founder's catechism was roughly this: What is the worst outcome of politics? Tyranny. To what form of tyranny is democracy prey? Tyranny of the majority.

Now, Madison's answer to this wasn't, first of all, judicial; it was a new sociology of democracy. The Madisonian revolution and democratic theory was this: hitherto, everyone who had said democracy was possible—and it was few people who had said it—they said it is possible if, but only if, you have democracy in a small face-to-face society. Russo's Geneva, Pericles's Athens. Because the larger the society, the more factions you will have, and factions were thought to be the enemy of democracy.

Madison turned that on its head, saying that the way you will prevent majority tyranny is to not have majorities, by which he meant don't have stable, tyrannical majorities. Hence, he said famously in Federalist 10, have an extensive republic—not a small republic, an extensive republic. The larger the republic, the more factions you will have. And he said in Federalist 51, "The first job of government is to protect the different and unequal capacities of acquiring property." Because those would generate different factions. You would have this maelstrom of factions forming temporary, unstable majorities that would not be durable enough to be tyrannical. And that is roughly the interest group liberalism that we have in this country. Now, it gets out of hand, particularly when the government doesn't recognize Madisonian limits on its proper scope and actual competence, but beyond that, it's again Madison's great contribution to world democratic theory.

J. D. Vance, JD
New York Times best-selling author
January 2017

There are probably very few folks who aren't well aware of J. D. Vance and his sensational book, *Hillbilly Elegy*. Reviewers once in a while will use words only reviewers use, like "theorying." But having read J. D.'s book, I now know what they're talking about, and I think the term qualifies. I had been fortunate enough to strike up some modest acquaintance with J. D. over the course of the previous year, and he is as interesting a person, as authentic and insightful, as the book he has written.

It was a pleasure to welcome J. D. Vance.

MITCH: I'd like for you to paint verbally the picture you paint so impressively in *Hillbilly Elegy*. Let me just try to introduce the topic by asking you to comment on a couple of searing comments you made. You said early in the book that you wrote it to let people know what it feels like to nearly give up on yourself and why you might do it. What made you feel that way? And how close did you come to giving up?

MR. VANCE: The background with which I'll frame this is that the book is really a multigenerational family portrait, and it starts with my grandparents in very impoverished circumstances in eastern Kentucky. They moved to southwestern Ohio. My grandfather worked in a steel mill. It's sort of the land of opportunity. They do very well for themselves materially and earn a stable middle-class life. By the time I come around, all the family income they had generated had evaporated, and we were in pretty rough circumstances.

The argument I make in the book—why I almost gave up on myself—is that in a lot of ways I didn't see a path forward that made much sense. It seemed like all of the options that were out there were either way too hard or even actively foreclosed to people like us. There was a certain sense of hopelessness that I had about my own life and doubts whether people who were like me were the type who made successful lives. I really try to unpack that in the book through my own experiences, but also some data, and try to explain what is really going on in the mind of a kid who obviously has some external barriers, but at the same time is struggling with other things that aren't quite as easy to quantify.

MITCH: What makes me so excited about your book is it is all about social mobility. It is all about what has been the heart of this country. It's not only been the engine that drove the greatest prosperity in human history, but it's the glue that has kept us together as a functioning republic, as a functioning government by consent of the governed. It's the most important topic in the country. And you have some very pointed things that you've said to folks in situations much like yours. You say social mobility isn't about money or economics, it's about a lifestyle change. And yet you said you didn't do it all by yourself. So where do we look? You told us where not to look—government at the fringes. Where do we look if we would love to see in America millions of J. D.s?

MR. VANCE: Well, I definitely think government has a role, and an important role, to play in this. I wouldn't say that I'm a complete skeptic. My fear is that we tend to think in very technocratic terms about this stuff. And if we presume that the entire solution is going to come from government, I think we're going to be disappointed because a lot of the things that went right in my life, those twenty factors I mentioned, aren't totally amenable to being created by a public policy solution.

And I also think it's important, I say this in the very beginning of the book, that there is a strong economic element to this. I don't think we should ignore that if we were a little bit better at training a modern workforce, if there were better jobs available in some of these geographic areas, that would obviously help. Again, I just don't think that's a whole solution.

My sense is that if we're looking to create answers or looking to really figure this stuff out, we've got to think about the space in our society that exists between the individual and the state. I think folks on the left are really good at talking about the state, and folks on the right are very good at talking about the individual and the self. But there are so many things that exist in the middle—churches, unions, civic institutions—things that are really important for creating social cohesion, for creating values, for creating support, and that are very, very important and often get neglected in our conversation, I think partially because the conversation is overly technocratic, like I mentioned.

But I think that it really starts with a recognition of the real nature of the challenge. If the biggest driver is concentrated poverty; the biggest driver is too many single-parent families; the biggest driver is low social capital, which is another big thing that came out of that study, something I certainly believe I see. How do we build social capital? How do we create more stable families in our country? Or when families break down, how do we put kids in more stable backup situations? How do we break that cycle of concentrated poverty? I'm not a pessimist about this. I don't think there's nothing we can do, and there's no solution to that problem. I just think we have to really appreciate the scale of what's happening if we're going design solutions at the policy level or at every other level that are actually going to work.

Mara Liasson
Award-winning journalist and commentator;
National Public Radio political correspondent
October 2014

It was such a treat and thrill to welcome Mara Liasson, whom I
had admired for a long time and known personally for most of
that time. Mara is someone all of America knows as one of our
premier public journalists. She has earned the rare, nearly unique
esteem in which she is held. Mara has for the better part of three
decades been one of the premier reporters covering the most important events in our public life, on the Hill, at the White House,
and everywhere in between. Governmental activities, politics, and
the rest. Through it all she has maintained and built a reputation
for fairness, for insight, for savvy, that is certainly not surpassed
by anybody I can think of.

I have to say that Mara represents increasingly unusual traits
that were maybe once a little more common. She has a healthy
skepticism for people in public life, and for their claims, and for
their pretensions. But she maintains some sense of empathy for
those people who do enter the arena and in her or his own way
try to make our national life better. Mara has maintained a scru-
pulous objectivity, and never once has anyone suspected her of
any sort of agenda of her own. And sad to say, that's not always
so true anymore. Mara occupies important reportorial positions
simultaneously, and for sixteen years or so has been at National
Public Radio and Fox News. Only someone who is understood
to be truly impartial and truly interested only in the public interest is likely to bring off that sort of double duty.

MITCH: Let me ask you about one of those changes that you never succumbed
to or engaged in. Starting somewhere in the last couple of decades, and at
first it was a startling or noteworthy exception, then it became more common,
now it's entirely commonplace, for people in journalism to go through a
revolving door into active political activity. Then sometimes they come
back, and we're supposed to accept them as though they're fair, balanced,

and impartial, even though they may have just come out of a highly partisan activity. Is that a healthy trend? Is that an acceptable trend? How do
you look at that?

MS. LIASSON: Well, first of all, I don't think we should accept them as fair,
balanced, and impartial because usually they're not. Now, I think it's one
model to be a William Safire who wrote speeches for Nixon, and then became
a conservative columnist. That's okay. You know where he was coming from
before and you know where he's coming from afterward. That's okay. One of
the reasons people do this now is there's a huge explosion in the "punditocracy,"
where there's a market for people who have strong opinions and are parti-
sans on either side. That's one thing.

But the model you are talking about is a little bit different—where you literally go back and forth across the line as if you can be impartial as a journalist.
I really don't think you can. Maybe one 180-degree revolution we'll accept, but
the 360 I think is just too much. It's funny because that's never, ever crossed
my mind. I mean, literally never crossed my mind, because it's just completely
different. There are people like David Axelrod, the president's former political guru. He was a journalist, but he got bitten by the bug of polling and politics and he left, and that was it, and he never came back. That's why I'll take
the 180 degrees. I just don't want the 360.

MITCH: You mentioned polarization, which bothers a lot of us in two ways.
One is just the simple harshness, and coarseness, and negativity that tends
to accompany it in our public debates and in our campaigns. But maybe
even more important is the way in which it may get in the way of addressing
major national issues that are not going away. How do you look at it? And
is it really worse, as we tell ourselves it is? Is it really worse than many periods in our history? As they say, politics was never beanbag.

MS. LIASSON: I think that the partisanship was ever thus, the gridlock is something new, and I'd make a distinction. I mean, people have always had brutal,
nasty campaigns, and at least now, they're not beating each other up with
canes on the Senate floor. That's one thing. There always was extreme partisanship and divisions, but now we're not getting anything done. I think that's
something that's completely different. It's fine to have very different opinions, different beliefs about government. But at some point, you've got to
come together and make a compromise to do basic things that need to get
done in the country.

I'm not talking about one side capitulating to the other; I'm talking about making a hard-fought, principled compromise. I think that's what upsets people the most. It's not just that politics is mean and vicious, it's that nothing is happening in Washington. Academics who study this say this current Congress has been the least productive Congress ever. You see the most basic functions going undone—passing a budget, confirming nominees, increasing the debt limit, keeping the government open. I mean, these are basic, basic functions. That's what I think is different.

MITCH: We've all seen studies that show decreasing overlap in terms of viewpoints or votes cast. There was once a rather extensive overlap, where members of the Democratic party would often vote with certain members of the Republican party and vice versa. Statistically it is now demonstrable that there has never in recent memory been this kind of separation.

MS. LIASSON: There's no doubt. Based on the voting records of the current United States Senate, there is not a single Democrat with a more moderate or conservative voting record than a single Republican. As you explained, there used to be plenty of moderate or liberal Republicans—Jacob Javits—people like that. On the Democratic side, there were lots of moderate-to-conservative Democrats. The overlap between those two wings of the parties made the center of the political spectrum. And that's where deals got made and compromises got made. There's a whole lot of reasons why there is now just a big black abyss between the parties. In the House, part of it is how district lines are drawn. I think right now, 93% of Republicans in the House of Representatives represent a district that Mitt Romney won, and 96% of the Democrats in the House represent a district that Barack Obama won.

There's absolutely no overlap at all. The tragedy is that to the extent that there are any moderate-to-conservative Democrats left, a big handful of them are going to lose this year and we're going to be even more sorted out. In 2016, when you've got a lot of Republicans from blue states up for re-election, a lot of them are going to lose, too. I don't see anything reversing that trend.

There are other causes in addition to gerrymandering and the way district lines are drawn. Even the population is sorting itself out. Some of this is our fault. People tend to live near people who think like them. They listen to media that they agree with. The Pew Research Center took a poll and they found that 49% of Republicans and 33% of Democrats said they would be very unhappy if their child married someone of the opposite party. This polarization is one of the most important dynamics in American life today.

 Frank Bruni
New York Times best-selling author, journalist, and commentator
September 2015

When I think about all the people who joined us as Presidential Lecture Series guests, there was none as eclectic in his career and his writing as Frank Bruni. Anyone who appreciates fine journalism will be familiar with Frank's contributions over the more than twenty-five years he has been at the *New York Times*, as well has his frequent appearances as a television commentator. As a White House correspondent for the *Times*, its Rome bureau chief, and consummate restaurant critic, Frank developed a reputation for clearheaded, engaging journalism at its very finest. Most recently, Frank's decade's worth of weekly columns has brought thoughtful, insightful, and balanced views to his avid readers.

As the author of four *New York Times* best sellers, including his just-published volume on the way students and their parents make college choices, Frank has a wide audience that reaches well beyond newsprint. It was a real pleasure to share a conversation with him.

MITCH: You've written several books, but the recent one, of course, caught the eye of a lot of people here. It's a topic both generally and specifically of interest here at Purdue University, given that we're a land-grant school. I'm guessing a large number of attendees tonight have read *Where You'll Go Is Not Who You'll Be*. You have taken a critical look at the way parents and students choose colleges, the way colleges inveigle them to choose, and you've cautioned about some things not to look for—elite reputations, rankings, high sticker prices. What should today's students be looking for?

MR. BRUNI: I think college, if it's within your economic grasp . . . and I want to start out there, because I wish more kids had the ability to choose a college without worrying about the dollars and cents and whether that's all going to work out. But if you do have some economic freedom, agency, wiggle room,

I think the best way to choose a college, and the way I see far too few people choosing a college, is to think about how you're going to complete and grow yourself. I see far too many kids automatically going to a school close to home, or automatically going to a school because all his or her peers have gone there, and it offers that sense of the familiar and the sense of continuity.

I think college should be more disruptive. One of the reasons I'm a big fan of universities like Purdue is you have scale and an automatic socioeconomic diversity that no matter where you're coming from, if you want to use a school like this to become more fluent in diversity, to explore crannies and byways of your intellectual life or your social life that you haven't before, you can do it, because it's all here. But that's what I really think people—I mean, kids and their parents—need to have conversations about. "What of the world do I already know, and am I going to a college that's going to show me facets and sides of the world that I don't know." Because if college isn't going to make me a bigger person, why am I going in the first place?

... There's so much of life ahead where the price of mistakes gets a lot higher. It's hard to see this when you're in college, but the price of mistakes at that stage of the game is pretty low. If you're going to make mistakes, if you're going to go down dead ends, do it between the ages of 19 and 23. Do it in college.

But that requires some boldness. That requires some courage. To use a word our president [Obama] likes, some audacity. I feel too frequently people elect safety. They elect something that's going to be assured. They follow a script that's been laid out for them rather than inventing one themselves. I really wish they wouldn't, because I don't think you ever truly discover what you're capable of and your strengths unless you wander off script, unless you wander down tributaries that maybe don't look so welcoming at the start.

MITCH: Let me ask you about a really arresting column that you wrote not too long ago. It gets at a question that we wrestle with here. Is college about career preparation or about a larger, broader preparation for life? To the extent it's not all one or the other, how do you find that balance point? For those who missed the column, you said you were asked to name a transformative educational experience, and it took you a minute, and then it came to you, and it sort of informs that question that I posed.

MR. BRUNI: I was stumped, and so it was a very genuine answer. I was asked what was my most transformative education experience. For some reason, into my head popped the image of a professor I had. I went to the University of North Carolina at Chapel Hill, and I was an English major. I took a number of classes with an English professor there named Anne Hall. I remembered her in the instant when I was asked that question, just kind of seeing her in front of the class. She was so in love with Shakespeare, and this was a Shakespeare class, and she would be talking about one of the plays. This was, I think, a course that was entirely on the tragedies. She would occasionally recite a line, and her whole body would sway. I mean, it was sensual on the verge of erotic.

I heard her saying the phrase, "Cordelia, stay a little," from *King Lear*, which was her favorite play, and because I obviously had no independence, quickly became my favorite play. I just remember how, when she talked about that line and when she intoned that line, there was something I learned in that moment about just how much freight a few words could carry and about how closely you had to look at them to understand all the things they might mean. That moment, which was such a gift, struck to the very heart of what education could do. I learned that there was a reward to close attention, whether it be to a text, whether it be to a person, whether it be to a binge-watching experience on television.

I think that also spoke to what's so important about a liberal arts education. You can't say that spending an hour thinking about and dissecting the line "Stay a little" in *King Lear* has any direct professional application. But learning to pay close attention to what people say and how they say it, learning that the more attentive you are, the greater the rewards are, well, I can't think of a single career that doesn't translate into.

Interestingly, shortly after I wrote that column, two great things happened. One was Anne Hall, who didn't remember me, read the column. She's now at University of Pennsylvania, and she got in touch. I went down to Philadelphia on the train and took her out for dinner and got a second column out of it, so this is really good, when one column leads to another . . .

Harlan Coben
New York Times best-selling author of crime fiction and thrillers; winner of the Edgar Award, Shamus Award, and Anthony Award
April 2015

Harlan Coben is responsible for me reading Elmer Kelton. He's also responsible for me reading Ed McBain. And while I was at it, Stephen Crane, and George Orwell, and Tom Wolfe, and a lot of other people. And the reason is that until ten or fifteen years ago, I had a long period where I read nothing but nonfiction books. And I'd be lying there reading something of great substantive importance while my wife was breathlessly inhaling some book two feet away, which she kept thrusting on me, "You've got to read, you've got to read, you've got to read this guy Coben." And finally one day I did. And then I read everything else he'd ever written. And ever since that time, I now am always reading fiction along with the nonfiction. So, I owe Harlan my reintroduction to fiction. And clearly there are millions who have been just as captivated as I have.

Harlan is unquestionably one of America's most successful, closely followed fiction writers. He's won every award there is, including the Edgar Award, named for Edgar Allan Poe, the Shamus Award, and the Anthony Award—he's the first author to win all three. More to the point, Harlan's last six books all debuted at number one on the *New York Times* Best Seller list. Each has been a million copy seller. He's one of the most inventive, creative, and constantly delightful writers on the American scene today.

MITCH: I think people would like to hear about how you work at writing—what's the routine. And a question that's part of that, these unbelievably tangled and inventive plots, Do you map them all out to the end before you start? Occasionally I'll read somebody who claims that they let the plot take them along. Which are you?

MR. COBEN: Let me start with how I come up with ideas. And it's not a pretty process, but I'm going to really try to let you inside the brain. Normally it's from something in my real life. And I constantly ask, "What if?"

A few years ago, for example, I wrote a book called *Promise Me*. And the way that came to me is I overheard a couple of teenagers who I knew and loved. They were talking about drinking and driving. I overheard them. So, I pulled them aside. Maybe some of you have done something similar. And I said, promise me you won't do that. Here's my cell phone. I don't care if it's three in the morning. I don't care what you're doing, I'll drive you. I won't ask any questions, won't tell your parents. Promise me you won't get in a car with someone who's been drinking and driving.

Now in real life, that's it. Nothing else ever happened. But fiction writing's asking, "What if?" Well, what if a teenaged girl calls my house at 3:00 a.m. She's in New York City. He goes, he picks her up, he drops her off at what he thinks is a friend's house. The next day she's gone. No one knows where she is. What if?

Those are the ways. That's one example of how I come up with some kind of story. One time I was going to the photo shop, in the days when we used to go to MotoPhoto or photo shops to pick up your photos. And I'm picking up a roll of film. And as I'm going through it, for a second, just a split second, I thought there was a picture in there I didn't take. It turns out the picture was just upside down. But go with me on this.

And I said, "What if there was a picture in this roll I didn't take? What if that picture changed my life?" And I start asking, "What if, what if?" And I go through it like that until I start having the remnants of an idea.

The problem with this is it sounds like it takes about fifteen minutes to come up with. This is three months of work, ladies and gentlemen. This is three months of sitting on the couch going, "No, honey, I can't throw out the garbage, I'm working. Can't you see I'm working here?" The hardest part of my job is convincing my wife I have one.

So, that's the first part—the idea. I know the beginning when I start, and I know the end. And I compare it to driving from my hometown in New Jersey to LA. I may go Route 80. Chances are I'll go via the Suez Canal and stop in Tokyo. But I pretty much end up in LA.

One of my favorite quotes on writing comes from E. L. Doctorow, who said that writing is like driving at night in the fog with just your headlights on. You can only see a little bit ahead of you, but you can make the whole journey that way. I know a couple of spots maybe along the way—I can see a couple—but the rest of it, in my case, just happens. But if you ask writers their opinion, if you ask ten writers how he does it, you'll get eleven different answers. Every writer does it differently. Some books, I don't do it this way, but that's mostly my MO.

MITCH: I could be in a dead end here, but let me just venture a hypothesis. I haven't read all of your books, but a lot of them. To me, there's a couple of patterns: bad guys lose, they get what they deserve, there aren't these dark, black endings. There's an affection for small towns, suburbs, the kind that a lot of literary figures love to dump on. And your characters love their families. Sometimes it gets them into trouble, or tragedy, or something. But parents really love their children. And children, imagine this, love their parents. Are you a Midwesterner in disguise? I mean, am I misreading you?

MR. COBEN: Well, first of all, don't read the new book. I don't want to crush your spirits. Because every time I'm accused of being something, I almost intentionally write something that's the opposite. So, this new book has a pretty dark ending, and I really piss all over suburbia.

But normally, you're right. When I actually first created Myron Bolitar, not to get too corny, but I gave him something I always wanted. He has something I always wanted, and I have something he always wanted. Myron's dream in life is to get married, move to the burbs, and have kids. So, I can give him that.

On the other hand, my parents died fairly young. And Myron has this wonderful, warm, loving relationship with his parents that I have a tendency to overwrite and get sentimental on. Tough. Cut him if you don't like him. It's cheaper than therapy.

But part of that was also, I had not seen that really done in fiction. It's always like the father was abusive and the mother put out her cigarettes on the guy. I thought it would be interesting to represent more what I know, which is a loving relationship.

And also, when you're trying to write about what people want, if I were to ask everybody here, "Would you kill somebody?" the answer is no. But if I asked you, "Would you kill someone who's trying to kill your kid or to save your child's life?" Now the answer is yes. So where is that line? There's one, there's one. Where in the middle, if I bring it closer and closer on both sides, that's where I want to be. We all get that emotion. It's a universal emotion. And it's easy to be cynical, but it's more fun to be realistic.

GREAT CHALLENGES, GREAT COURAGE

Joe Lonsdale
Technology entrepreneur; managing partner
of 8VC; co-founder of Palantir
November 2022

Over the past decade or so, we've seen the emergence of a small but growing group of young tech wizards who combine their technical genius with a talent for entrepreneurship to create some of our nation's fastest-growing and most successful companies. Joe Lonsdale has certainly earned his membership in that august group.

After getting off to a fast start at PayPal, in 2003 Joe co-founded Palantir, which the *Wall Street Journal* regularly reminds us sells more AI software than AWS, Google, IBM, and Microsoft. He has founded or co-founded a host of other companies, including Addepar, a wealth management company with more than $4 trillion under management.

Joe's commitment to openness and transparency in the public sector led him to build a platform called OpenGov that is now used by more than 2,000 municipalities and state agencies. At the time of his visit, Joe was running a $5 billion venture capital firm called 8VC. And if that weren't enough, his latest project, which might end up being the most ambitious startup of all, is a brand-new university. And he achieved all that by the time he was only 40 years old.

It was a real treat to welcome Joe Lonsdale to Purdue.

MITCH: So Joe, what are you going to do when you grow up?

MR. LONSDALE: Still trying to figure that out, Mitch.

MITCH: Well, you have an astonishing track record. Do I have the chronology right? Did you really found Palantir at 21 or 22?

MR. LONSDALE: Yes, it was nineteen years ago. I was 21. My roommate and I at Stanford started it with Peter Thiel's backing and brought in Alex Karp. It wouldn't have worked without the older people, though. He was 36. He wasn't that old, but he was fifteen years my senior.

MITCH: How'd you get Peter Thiel's attention for this idea? A lot of people would be competing for it even then.

MR. LONSDALE: I was at PayPal for a couple of years while I was at Stanford. I grew up in Silicon Valley, and I guess I was lucky to have friends who taught me to program, so I was already building a lot of stuff. So, I was part of that whole ecosystem and learning from the guys at PayPal. And I was the editor of a newspaper Peter Thiel had started fifteen years before at the school. It was kind of a contrarian, liberty-oriented paper. And so we had a few things in common and got to know each other.

After people have a success like PayPal or anything big, they think they could do anything and they just try to start a lot of things. And usually it's too

many things because we all have egos and we're like, "I'm the best in the world and I'm going to be able to do this and this and this and this now, because I did the first one." You forget, of course, that the reason the first one worked was because you were really focused on it for a decade. We didn't know what we were doing at first, but thanks to his guidance and thanks to some amazing people around me, we figured it out after a while.

MITCH: The name of that company's kind of interesting.

MR. LONSDALE: Palantir. It was a warning we built into the name. Palantir is a seeing crystal in *Lord of the Rings*. And not to get too geeky, but the elves in the Uttermost West built this thing 2,000 years prior to the main story in order to see what's going on in the realm. They spread seven of them, and the men use these to see what the bad guys are doing, and they make the world peaceful and everything's really great for a very long time. Then you fast-forward and in comes Sauron, who's got one of them, and he's doing all sorts of bad things with it. And the whole point is this was a new technology we were creating that was very powerful and had a lot of ability to stop the bad guys and keep us safe, but we had to be really careful who gets ahold of it and what kind of restrictions and audit trails are built into it to make sure it's used in a way that's pro-liberty and not used for sketchy things.

MITCH: Take it right from there. We're all familiar with a brilliant software that makes people rich or gives us all fun games to play, but you had a different mission in mind, one that remains I think somewhat unique in the software industry. Tell us about it.

MR. LONSDALE: One of the things I have seen in a lot of software companies is that you can attract some of the very best and brightest and get them to work really hard on something if they really believe in the mission, because especially nowadays everyone's trying to hire software engineers. But if it's something they're really passionate about, then you're going to get the best out of them and you're going to get them to bring their friends. So, it's a bit chicken and egg.

Palantir came out of 9/11. After 9/11, we saw the government was spending about $36 billion to $37 billion a year at the time gathering information, but it was very incoherent. There were a million people whose job was some form of analyst in the defense and intelligence community. Most of them were not programmers. How could they see into thousands of databases to put the pieces together? And even about 9/11 itself we actually had all sorts of data that if one person had been able to see, they would've gone and looked into these guys and their pilot licenses and what they were doing.

And so the question was how to build a framework to make it so that we can share information while protecting civil liberties. How do you let people see what they're allowed to see between departments? How do you follow the rules? For example, there's some places where you're only allowed to see the data if you have a certain type of connection to it. And how do you build this into frameworks ahead of time? So it was about collaboration, knowledge management, data integration. How do you know that one person is the same as another between the databases? They are very complicated, very hard problems.

And then how do you expose that to a human mind in an intuitive way? How do you let a person see into all this information when obviously you can't have the 5,000 database in your mind—so how do you expose it to your mind so they can iterate and ask questions?

MITCH: All with the purpose of enhancing our national security, which a lot of very, very smart people weren't working on.

MR. LONSDALE: There were very few. This was something that was really surprising to me. When I was in Stanford's computer science program, we'd study things the NSA did in the 1970s. But that was no longer the case, unfortunately, in the late '90s. By the late '90s, a lot of what happened in Silicon Valley had actually gotten quite far ahead of things in the government, especially how to get the best engineers to build big systems. Washington, D.C., had fallen far behind Silicon Valley, and they were frankly wasting billions of dollars after 9/11 on stuff that broke, that they threw out, that wasn't scaling. Our mission was to take the best and brightest and go solve all these problems, because they weren't doing it in D.C.

MITCH: We've got some aspiring venture capitalists here and in the streaming audience, so a few words about your current ventures. What's in the portfolio? What are you looking for? What do you look for in new potential investments?

MR. LONSDALE: There's really two things you look for in venture capital. One is what's possible now that wasn't possible five years ago. So what's changed in the world? If you look at Silicon Valley, there have been five big waves over the last hundred years of new things. First it was the electronics and the semiconductors and the old original enterprise software. Then more recently in my career, it's obviously the Internet. There's web 1.0, web 2.0. There's mobile.

And all these new things are possible with mobile. And then there's the cloud, there's big data, there's AI.

So there are all these different things that became possible, and the question is, How should this industry be working? How should this part of logistics work differently based on what you can now do with the coordination with the cloud and AI or with IOT technology? For us it's logistics, it's various health care services, it's the revolution in biology with gene editing and cell therapy, and the list goes on. There's so many cool things.

And then the second question, which is probably just as hard and you have to spend just as much time on, is, Who are the top talent, what are they doing, and how do I partner with them? How do I attract them? Just like if you're going to run a university football team and you want to be the very best at that, you basically have to spend a lot of time finding those people and getting them in. So, we spend a lot of time on that question and we spend a lot of time on the first question. And then if you get those two things right, everything else is just details.

MITCH: One of the great joys of working here is that we're a very cosmopolitan campus. We have people from literally all over the world. You've been very outspoken about immigration from a couple of angles, but start with just your general thoughts about this subject, which is so topical and vexes Americans in more than one way.

MR. LONSDALE: I'm on the board of Ronald Reagan's library. His last speech as president was very clear that he thought the future of America would be bright as long as we could continue to be a place that attracted the best and the brightest. And that's been really core to our identity as a nation. And I very strongly agree with that. We do a lot in curing diseases, working on curing different forms of cancer. And a lot of my companies have already been saving lots of lives there, tens of thousands of lives.

And we have postdoc PhDs at Stanford that happen to be from China, and these guys were just the best in their field and they wanted to come help us with something that was very important to save people's lives. And we kept trying to get visas for them and there's just a slow process and we couldn't, so instead they went back and they worked with PLA [the People's Liberation Army] on bioweapons, and so you basically had people either going to be working on saving lives here or working on bioweapons. It's pretty frustrating.

I had dinner last night with a friend who started a yogurt company. He came here when he was 20 years old and couldn't speak the language at all.

Went to rural upstate New York. And it is amazing. He immigrated and became this very, very successful guy. And now one of his big causes is helping others, other refugees, and bringing refugees in. So I think it's important to bring the top skilled people here, but I think it's also important that America is a place that can continue to bring in those refugees and those immigrants.

And then the thing I think you're referencing is I wrote an op-ed in the *Wall Street Journal* last month on a related but different topic, which is that our visa system right now, it's just very disrespectful. There's no reason to make someone wait if they have a right to come here, hundreds and hundreds of days for a visa. Why are we doing that? We're making it harder to do business here. We have people who are already here, who are probably at Purdue and their parents or grandparents want to come visit. And it is literally an average wait in New Delhi of something like 400 days right now. And it's just incompetence and it's unaccountable and we shouldn't tolerate it.

There is a technology solution, but frankly it's leadership. You need leadership willing to hold people accountable.

MITCH: Well, say a little more about that. I bet we share the same frustration. On the one hand, I mean, we're the only country in the world that does it the way we do it, now including a fairly uncontrolled border. But we've had a policy unique in the world, as far as I know, that makes it hard to come here if you have the sort of talent that any modern country really wants, but easy to come here if you happen to be related to somebody, whether you bring any talent or not.

MR. LONSDALE: I think it's really silly. I generally am biased that it should be probably easier for people to bring their family. I think that's a good thing overall. But I think it's insane not to let entrepreneurs—not to let talented people—into our country. The data shows that each technology job created creates about four or five other jobs in the communities around it. So it actually creates prosperity. If you bring in a thousand great engineers who would've built a company in India, and instead they're building the company in the Midwest, there's a whole other prosperity going on in that area, thanks to those people. It's really silly not to allow them in.

MITCH: I said earlier that of all the fascinating things you have gotten started— businesses and other endeavors—arguably the most interesting and maybe the most difficult is the University of Austin. The U.S. has lost close to 500 colleges over the last couple of decades, and that rate is accelerating. So, some people will say the very last thing this nation needs is another university. Start there. Why?

MR. LONSDALE: And by the way, I'm a big fan of Purdue and what I've seen today, so I'm not speaking to Purdue when I talk about some of these issues. But in general, you've seen costs go up dramatically at our universities. You've seen the administrations double or triple in size over the last ten or twenty years, and these administrations tend to conquer things and tend to be more radical than the professors. So a lot of people complain, "Oh, the Sociology Department used to be three to one left to right. Now it's seventeen to one, and you're not allowed to say certain things or you get canceled, and it's really extreme." And that's true.

But the administrations are actually, by various studies, to the left of the Sociology Department. They're very, very radical. They're not there to minister. They're there to fight for societal change through these Foucault and neo-Marxist frameworks, which have kind of driven a lot of what they do. They don't believe in meritocracy. They don't believe in things like truth and beauty.

More importantly, they don't believe in Western civilization. And when I say Western civilization, I think this is something that's very misunderstood in our society today. If you go back two generations, people on all sides of our society had a really good understanding that there's been a discourse, a great conversation over the last 2,500 years that's built on itself, and it's formed something that's very unique about our civilization. And you had this sense that education was human excellence. The direction was a belief in excellence in both private life and public life. Because man's a political animal, and there was a belief that man is not a means to an end, but rather "man as man in a free society." The discussion was how to educate that citizen and how to learn to be part of that conversation—to apply these values—and how to use these shared values to run our society and confront and solve problems.

A lot of this has broken down. We don't have shared values; we don't learn about that conversation. I think both sides have gotten stupider, especially the left, by not having access to this conversation. You can be really smart, but if you're not basing it on these debates, if you're not aware of the debates that have gone on in the past, it's not coherent relative to what's been discussed and what's been understood, and it's just too easily dismissed right now.

In general, you want a more competent elite in our country that knows how to solve problems, that's virtuous, that understands what virtues even are, and that's able to be able to have intellectual courage, able to have free speech about controversial things, and able to work toward solutions in our society. And I don't think any of our universities are trending things that way. I think they're actually going in the opposite direction.

MITCH: Still in all, this is a very ambitious thing to try to do. What do you expect are the biggest obstacles that you'll face? And I'm guessing there's a category that's operational and there's a category that's more political.

MR. LONSDALE: Number one, it has to be a nonpartisan university, and we've done this very well so far. We have a lot of people from the moderate left and a lot of people on the moderate right. You choose people not by virtue of their politics but by virtue of the fact that they're not illiberal. We have a very illiberal extreme in this country. That means there's some people who are just against even being able to talk about ideas. . . . There are a lot of conversations of important topics we need to be able to talk about out in the open—need to be able to debate—rather than saying, "Oh, you can't even have this other view." It's illegal. I think it's very dangerous.

Kenneth R. Feinberg, JD
Attorney; special master of the 9/11 Victims Compensation Fund; chief of staff to former U.S. senator Ted Kennedy
February 2022

Ken Feinberg has overseen billions of dollars in compensation funds following some of our country's tragedies and financial disasters. In addition to serving as special master of the 2008 TARP Executive Compensation initiative and the BP Deepwater Horizon Disaster Victim Compensation Fund, Mr. Feinberg has overseen the compensation response systems for the Boeing 737 MAX crashes, Agent Orange victims, the Sandy Hook and Virginia Tech shootings, the Boston Marathon bombing, and perhaps most notably, the 9/11 Victims Compensation Fund.

Prior to founding his own law firm, Ken served as Senator Ted Kennedy's chief of staff and as a prosecutor for the U.S. Department of Justice. He is the subject of the major motion picture *Worth*, which was released at the Sundance Film Festival in January 2020.

As you will read below and hear in the video recording of our on-stage conversation, I met Ken for the first time within the compelling context of one of America's greatest challenges—the aftermath of 9/11. I've always considered it one of our nation's great fortunes that Ken took on the role of determining how the loved ones of the 9/11 victims should be compensated. And that Ken used that experience to decide the compensation for so many other families whose lives were upended in tragedies since then.

I've always considered Ken to be a man of the highest integrity. He approaches with deep compassion the unimaginably difficult job of assigning monetary value to human life. And he manages to do it while preserving the humanity of all those impacted, as well as his own. He is one of the finest public servants imaginable.

MITCH: We got a lot to cover but I want to start with the most important thing: did your family approve of Michael Keaton being cast as you in the movie?

MR. FEINBERG: My family said, especially my children, that Michael Keaton is a great actor and we marvel at his performances, "but Dad, in playing you he really ought to stick to Beetlejuice and Batman."

MITCH: I was fortunate enough to meet you, Ken, at a very interesting and memorable time in American history. I want to start with you reminiscing, especially for our students who are present, about that very unusual time. The circumstances you and I have each related are that you were suggested to me. I had certain responsibilities in the aftermath of 9/11, one of which was to organize and find someone to lead the compensation fund.

We come from different poles politically, you might say. But to me, what was always important was that what some saw as an improbable choice—you, a Ted Kennedy stalwart of his operations for so long, and an administration that I represented of different persuasion—was actually in the context of those times a rare moment of unity which we've really not seen replicated since. It was to me almost an inevitable sort of choice. Can you remember now, twenty years on, what that was like?

MR. FEINBERG: I can remember like it was yesterday. It was twenty years ago, thirteen days after the 9/11 attacks: the four airplanes—the World Trade Center; the Pentagon; Shanksville Pennsylvania. Congress passed a law, a federal statute—bipartisan, no roll call, voice vote, unanimous. Let's set up a fund to compensate the victims of the 9/11 attacks: World Trade Center, the airplanes, the Pentagon. And the law required the appointment of a special master, or administrator, who would have the responsibility for administering this very unique bipartisan statute.

And my former boss, Ted Kennedy, called John Ashcroft[21]; and John Ashcroft talked to Mitch; and Kennedy said what you better do is, you better at least interview Feinberg. He's done work like this. And that began the process.

When I went to be interviewed by Mitch Daniels, the head of the Bush administration Office of Management and Budget, I had in my mind that, well, I'll do the interview, but I don't know, this is going to be a tough sell—Ken Feinberg, Kennedy guy. But Mitch Daniels and I sat for forty-five minutes to an hour, agreeing on the statute, how to implement it, why it was probably a bad idea that some people would get all this money and everybody else, you're out of luck. And I left that meeting convinced that Mitch Daniels had my back if I got the job. He would have my back; he would make sure that the program from the perspective of the Bush Administration would work; and I got an inkling from Mitch, gee, you know, what better bipartisan symbol than Kennedy's chief of staff to take on this assignment. And to this day I'm in Mitch's debt forever with reverence. . . .

This will never be repeated quite this way. Mitch Daniels tried to do everything possible to make it bipartisan, apolitical, on the merits for the next thirty-three months. Anytime I had a problem we just worked it out. It worked well.

MITCH: Let me just correct one thing: the only debt that's owed is from the victims and their families, and the citizens of the country for the service he provided. And no one needed to have his back. He handled it beautifully.

MITCH: There are many questions of policy and philosophy that I want to ask you, but start at the human level. None of us will probably ever meet anyone who has been face-to-face with more people who have suffered in some cases the worst loss you can—the loss of a loved one, the loss of a child. You have made it a practice, when you didn't have to, to meet individually as with as many of those people as was practical. What do you have to tell us about what those experiences are like, and are there any generalizations you could make about the categories of people?

MR. FEINBERG: First of all, it's debilitating. It is the worst part of what I do. Calculating value is not that difficult. Courts do it every day in Lafayette, in Indiana, in every state in the country. Every court. Somebody gets injured by an automobile or whatever it is. What would that person have earned over a work life? What about pain and suffering? It equals dollars. That's the system. But that's not the part that Mitch is zeroing in on.

The real debilitating part of compensating victims of tragedy is the emotion. The emotion is debilitating. You don't sleep, you cry and weep in private, you try and be as professional as you can. An example:

A woman comes to see me after 9/11. She's crying. She's 26 years old. Sobbing in a private meeting with me, "Mr. Feinberg I lost my husband. He was a fireman at the World Trade Center, and he left me with my two children, 6 and 4. Now you have notified me that you're going to provide me $2.4 million, tax free from the 9/11 fund. I want it in thirty days."

I looked at her, "Mrs. Jones this is Treasury money. It's got to go through the U.S. Treasury bureaucracy. It's a government check. It might take sixty days, ninety days, but you'll get your money."

"No, thirty days."

"Why do you need the money in thirty days?" I asked her.

"Why? I'll tell you why, Mr. Feinberg. I have terminal cancer. I have ten weeks to live. My husband was gonna survive me and take care of our two little ones. Now they're going to be orphans. Now I only have a few weeks to get my life in order. I've got to find a guardian. I've got to make sure there's an estate. I've got to set up a trust. I don't have a lot of time—you've got to help me."

Well, we ran down to the Treasury and accelerated the check, got it to her. Eight weeks later she died.

One after another like that takes a toll . . .

Mary Lynne Dittmar, PhD, chief government relations officer for Axion; founder and former president and CEO of the Coalition for Deep Space Exploration
Bill Gerstenmaier, vice president, SpaceX; former NASA associate administrator for human exploration
Jonathan Lunine, PhD, David C. Duncan Professor in the Physical Sciences and chair of the Department of Astronomy, Cornell University
NASA's next moonshot.
April 2019

As part of our 150th anniversary celebration, we construed a series of events that addressed the question, What if? There was no better scenario to explore at the university dubbed the "cradle of astronauts" than the future of human spaceflight. To help us understand the when, the how, and the what of humankind's next moonshot, we were joined by three experts in the field—Dr. Mary Lynne Dittmar, Mr. Bill Gerstenmaier, and Dr. Jonathan Lunine—each of whom made brief introductory comments. Be sure to watch the video to see Dr. Lunine's spectacular photographic images.

The conversation kept the audience all on the edge of their seats, eager for what will be humanity's next foray beyond our own planet.

DR. LUNINE: Humans have been stuck in low Earth orbit for the last fifty years, and during that time, our robotic emissaries with scientific instruments and electronic eyes have wandered all over the solar system. And so, I wanted to set the context for our discussion tonight by showing very briefly some of the places that we have been through our electronic proxies.

The first of these slides shows Pluto, which is the farthest planet in the solar system. *New Horizons* shows that it has all of the processes that planets have—geology, glaciology, atmospheric weather—in spite of the fact that it's smaller than the Earth's moon. And in the lower corner of that picture, you see the next object that *New Horizons* went to, Ultima Thule, which is an example of some of the building blocks of the planets in our solar system. Two pieces stuck together for four and a half billion years. Early in the history of the solar system, that would've been the start of the planet-building process, but now it's a cosmic graveyard.

If we move from that graveyard to a place where life might exist, now we're at Saturn's moon Enceladus. The *Cassini* spacecraft, visiting Saturn for thirteen years, discovered that ice and organic molecules and gas are pouring out of the south pole of this small moon of Saturn. *Cassini* not only discovered this, but it actually flew through those jets of material that you see there, and it was able to make measurements that tell us that underneath the surface is an ocean that's supplying those salty ice particles, those organics, and that ocean very likely is habitable, it could support life. And so, the next step would be to go try to find life there. If we could find life, it might be independent of the origin of life on Earth, and that would be one of the greatest discoveries in the history of science.

If we move further still, we get to Jupiter. The *Juno* mission is not only exploring inside Jupiter, but it's taking some of the most remarkable pictures of this very turbulent, dynamic atmosphere, things that have not been seen with other spacecraft.

Then we move further in, we get to Mars, a place where it's quite possible we had our beginnings, that life might have started there and been transported to the Earth by the very process that this Lafayette meteorite was transported to the Earth.

Apollo 17 was the last human mission to the moon. The moon is the crossroad, it's the farthest point that humans have explored, and it's the starting point for planetary exploration in the late 1950s. And so, I think it's the touchstone, the tie point for connecting these remarkable robotic explorations with the future of remarkable human exploration on our nearest celestial neighbor, and it's a history that I think we'll hear a lot more about this evening.

MR. GERSTENMAIER: The vice president went to Huntsville, Alabama, to the place where all the human lunar activity occurred. In that great venue, he challenged us to go back to the moon in 2024. The good thing is, we've been planning for this all along. We've been talking about our gateway activity, we have the space launch system in work, we have Orion in work, we have all those pieces in work. And then we've been saying that they're adaptable and we can use those in new creative ways to meet these advantages or these challenges in front of us.

And now, we're putting all that together, maybe into a three-flight sequence. We'll do exploration mission one without any crew; we'll do exploration mission two and a flyby of the moon, similar to what we did on Apollo 8, just to check out the *Orion* spacecraft; and then we believe, on exploration mission three, using the *Gateway*, and pre-positioning some lunar landing hardware there, we should be able to land on the moon in '24. We've got that plan together. Technically, we've got lots of challenges in front of us. We're moving on procurements; we're moving on just trying to get a budget amendment this next year. So all those pieces are there, and as Jonathan laid out, this is this great intersection between where robotics and humans come together.

My job isn't just to go to the moon or help us go to the moon, it's how we move human presence into the solar system. And the moon is a great place to learn. And why do we want to go back to the moon? We talk about going back to the moon, but that's the wrong nomenclature. We want to go forward to the moon. And when we go forward to the moon, we go in a different way than we went before. We're going to go in a sustainable manner, with international partners, with the commercial sector. It's going to take every one of us, it's going to take every university, it's going to take all of us pulling together to go make this happen, and then we leave behind sustaining pieces that allow us to continue to do more and more dynamic things, and eventually head out to Mars with humans.

DR. DITTMAR: Part of what we spend a great deal of time talking about is the why of this, which some of you may also be wondering about. The technology is cool; this vision of going back to the moon is wonderful. I love the idea of the "crossroads" at the moon, but there are people who make decisions about policy in the United States, and they also write the checks, and those folks are sitting on Capitol Hill, and they have to interact with the White House. Ideally, what the White House wants to do and what Congress wants to do are aligned.

But Congress and the White House both have to figure out a whole lot of different priorities all the time. They've got the whole country they have to deal with, and these priorities are competing, and so the question is why. And I'm going to go ahead and answer the question from my point of view and the point of view of the companies that I represent. The answer as to why is really simple: it's about American leadership.

Leadership in space has been something that has been endemic to America for going on sixty years, beginning with space science and very early launches in response to Sputnik, and then the development of the human space flight program. And we dare not let that lapse.

That's my position, and it's a position of probably everybody on the stage. In terms of both science and exploration, it represents a place where nations have come together. We have many, many nations that came together to build the space station. We're up to 103 countries who have participated in some way in the space station program, either through science or exploration or both. That ability to bring people together, to bring nations together, and to demonstrate leadership is a gift that we have earned and dare not give away, and that's the why.

There's plenty of other whys—scientific achievement and discovery, expanding our knowledge, understanding better about who it is we are in the universe, what our place is there, going over the next hill. But the key for us is that drive for American leadership.

Akinwumi Adesina, PhD
President of the African Development Bank; former
Nigerian minister of agriculture and rural development
October 2017

Purdue proudly claims as alumni some of the most successful, bravest, and most impactful individuals of the past 150 years and counting. But there is none we are more proud of than Dr. Akinwumi "Akin" Adesina. After earning his master's and doctorate from Purdue, Dr. Adesina went on to a career dedicated to improving the well-being of the people of Africa. As Nigeria's minister of agriculture, Dr. Adesina worked to transform the country's system of subsistence agriculture into a viable agribusiness that has dramatically increased the country's crop production.

As a result of his vision, integrity, and commitment to serving the African people, Dr. Adesina was named the eighth president of the African Development Bank. Under his leadership, the bank has raised billions in capital to build Africa's value-added commercial sector and to reduce hunger by improving food production and distribution.

Dr. Adesina joined us days after receiving the World Food Prize, the "Nobel Prize" of agriculture. It was great to welcome him back to campus.

MITCH: Let's talk about [how to feed Africa]. You're the point person for this as much as anyone on the planet. Talk about the state of the effort to eliminate hunger and malnutrition in Africa, and in particular about the [African Development] Bank's so-called High 5s program to address it.

DR. ADESINA: It is actually quite mind-boggling that Africa is not able to feed itself. And for me, it's certainly not acceptable at all because I think God has given Africa all it needs. We've got lots of land, lots of cheap labor. We've got lots of water and we've got great sunshine. We don't have snow. It's just a fantastic place, but I think the problem has always been the way in which we looked at agriculture. So I'm starting from the point of, if we're going to do that, we have to change the lenses with which we look at agriculture. We were looking at agriculture as a primary sector. Even economic theory teaches you that agriculture is a primary sector; that you want to really focus on your industrial sector and move folks out of agriculture into that sector.

As a result of that, African governments wanted to start building planes, aircrafts, and they forgot all about agriculture. So, the first thing that I decided to do was to help African governments to understand that agriculture is a business. It's not a social sector; it's not a development activity. It is a business. It's a private enterprise. Every farmer you see is a private enterprise person, but the key is how do you unbound the constraints around them in terms of access to good technology, to information, to markets, to all the things that they need to be able to thrive.

And so, I think that a number of things are important. I really believe that the technologies to feed Africa are there right now. The problem in Africa is not a lack of technology; it's that those technologies need to be taken to the scale of millions of farmers.

So, at the African Development Bank, when I became president, we launched a strategy, which is to feed Africa, and we are going to be investing $24 billion U.S. dollars in the agriculture sector over the next ten years. And we're going to our board to consider an initiative that's called Technologies for African Agricultural Transformation. Essentially, we're going to take technologies that exist right here at Purdue—you have a great technology with the Purdue PICS.[22] You call it the improved storage systems. That technology, or the extruder[23] that is being worked on here, can go to a scale of millions of farmers.

What we're trying to do—the African Development Bank, the World Bank, the Bill and Melinda Gates Foundation, the Rockefeller Foundation, and the Alliance for a Green Revolution in Africa—is to take technologies to the scale of millions of farmers. That's the first part.

MITCH: In addition to the great reputation you have built as an economist and as an analyst of how to move your continent ahead economically, you've also built a reputation for integrity and for someone who is intolerant of corruption and has dealt with it effectively in many, many places where it has been a serious inhibitor of progress on the continent. Can you talk a little about this, and how can the bank, how can the tools you have in your new position enable you to help reduce the burden of corruption that's too often afflicted African countries?

DR. ADESINA: First, the monies of countries, all the resources of countries, don't belong to individuals. They belong to the collective. They belong to the country. And so probity, accountability, and transparency in the management of public resources is very critical for me. Africa is not a poor continent at all. Africa just happens to have a lot of poor people. That's because the resources aren't well managed. For example, when I was minister of agriculture in

Nigeria, I got in there and I found a really terribly corrupt fertilizer sector. For decades, more than forty years, the governments have been buying fertilizers and distributing fertilizers to farmers, but only 11% of the farmers ever got the fertilizers bought and sold by the government. And so there's a lot of rent-seeking behavior in it. I know what fertilizer is—you have nitrogen, phosphorus, and potassium—but in the case of Nigeria, at the time, the fertilizers actually had hands and legs. They could walk, just walk away.

And so, I figured, What was the way in which we use disruptive innovation to end corruption in this sector? And we began to use the power of the mobile phones. I started by saying, if you cannot register your farmers, you don't know your customer, and you're in a bad business. So, we started Africa's first major effort to have biometric information on farmers, register them, know who they are, know where they are. And I turned to the power of the mobile phones to send electronic vouchers of subsidies to the farmers directly. Why do I need an intermediary between the government and the farmer? And so, we began to send electronic vouchers, subsidized vouchers, to farmers via the mobile phones. And in four years we reach over 15 million of them directly via mobile phones.

It cut off all the middlemen. I woke up one morning and I told the whole country, effectively from now, the seed companies, fertilizer companies will not sell any longer to the government. If I can find Pepsi Cola and soda water in a village, and it's not sold by government, why can't I find seed and fertilizer in the same village not sold by the government? So, we inverted it completely. And I can tell you, it was a powerful thing . . .

Julie Wainwright
Business innovator; founder of The RealReal;
named to the *Forbes* 50 over 50
March, 2022

No one understands the challenges and deep satisfaction of starting large-scale businesses better than Purdue alumna Julie Wainwright. In 2011, Ms. Wainwright founded The RealReal, a luxury consignment business with a focus on sustainability that went public in 2019. Her success made Ms. Wainwright a Wall Street star, as one of just twenty-two women in history to found and see a company through an initial public offering. Named to both the *Forbes* 40 under 40 and *Forbes* 50 over 50, Ms. Wainwright has received wide recognition throughout the corporate world for her innovation, influence, and sharp business acumen.

We had looked forward to her return to Purdue for a very long time.

MITCH: I have to start in the obvious place. How's business? What's hot? What's selling?

MS. WAINWRIGHT: Well, let me just say we really did suffer during COVID because we don't make anything. We pick up things from others, we recirculate goods. We couldn't go into people's homes and pick up things, and people weren't willing to come to our stores and drop them off. We had a rough time, but we are back.

I would say everything sells within ninety days. There are some old favorites like Louis Vuitton, and Chanel, and Hermes. If these names sound expensive, we are a value play. The top brands continue to perform. Fine jewelry and watches are on fire right now. People are buying dresses and men are buying ties again. Believe it or not, we can't keep ties in stock.

MITCH: I knew I should have worn one tonight. It's the last bad decision I make today. I'm sure you probably have many customers or students who have studied the innovation that is your company. For the benefit of those who might not be completely clear, talk about the business model. You invented a better mousetrap.

MS. WAINWRIGHT: Right, yes. In about 2010, I had mapped out where I thought e-commerce was going and what position Amazon would play. I wanted to get back in that business. It was clear to me that if another person made it, and it wasn't high-end, because Amazon isn't a luxury destination, Amazon would resell it.

You really had to compete at a different level. The luxury space was interesting, but I knew I wasn't going to start a new luxury brand. There were other brands that I thought were going to start moving. I really thought "clean" cleaning products were going to be on the rise, and also organic makeup, which is really hard to do, but more natural products in every category.

Beauty has a low barrier to entry, a fragmented market, and not a high cost to run test. The same thing with cleaning products—a pretty low barrier to entry at the beginning, because there are always people willing to actually be your manufacturer, but I had no idea.

Then I'm shopping in a boutique with a friend who buys everything in the back of the store, which the woman called "the vault." It was consignment. I had never seen her buy consignment before, and when we walked out, I wanted to know what just happened. I asked, "Would you ever walk into a consignment store?" She said, "No, they're dirty and it's too hard to find things." I asked, "Would you ever shop on eBay?" She said, "No, too many fakes. I don't want to go back and forth with someone." I said, "But you will buy previously owned things?" She said, "Of course. Why not? That's a great deal."

By the way, this is one of the most successful venture capitalists in the Valley. She wasn't doing it to save money. She was doing it because she loves the deal, and everybody loves the deal. That was it. I researched the luxury market. I researched the value trapped in people's homes. I tested all the competition and decided there was only one way this was going to win....

It's a huge untapped market. There's about $200 billion worth of trapped products with value in people's homes now across the U.S. That's just a U.S. number—products that are 5 years or older, that people have in their home, that they're not recirculating. It's a $200 billion opportunity right there. I thought, How are we going to do this? How am I going to get into it?

I thought, Well, I'm going to have to go get the product. I'm going to have to operationalize it, so we authenticate it, because there are too many fakes in the market, and that'll ruin the business. I'm going to have to provide a full service, both on authentication and taking pictures. Then pick, pack, and ship, with customer service and a full sales team that goes to your house and gets the merchandise.

That's how we got started. We're still doing it. The model is almost exactly what I laid out at the beginning. What's different, and it's really changed the business, is we are using AI and machine learning in a way that I couldn't have imagined in 2010. The business launched in 2011, but I couldn't imagine where we'd be now. I would say we really understood the power of machine learning and AI about three years ago. It's revolutionizing our business and also providing a competitive moat.

The other thing I didn't know about the fashion industry is that it is the second largest polluter in the world. Every second, there is a truckload going into a landfill with unused fashion that's being discarded, mostly fast fashion. It's a really dirty industry. Recirculating goods is one of the easiest ways to do something good for the planet. I learned that about two years in.

MITCH: I've learned a new term. This may shock you, but I don't know a lot about fashion. "Fast fashion" is a new term to me. I'm pretty sure I'm a "slow fashion" type. I thought fast fashion is army surplus.

MS. WAINWRIGHT: At least that would be something that would recirculate. Fast fashion tends to be products that usually sell way under $50, and it's discarded regularly. It follows trends. They don't have innovation. They're copiers. There's a Chinese company that exploded during COVID and had sales of about $19 billion. You can probably wash their things twice or three times and they break down.

Just think of the economics. If you buy an item in the store or online for $20, and then let's say there's all the distribution costs, shipping costs. Consumers love when they throw in free shipping. If you just run the economics, that item probably costs less than a dollar to make. Now, think of the workforce. This is not an automated item. It's not machines that are making it. Think of what the workforce is making.

Then think about the products and think about the materials those things are made with. It's disposable fashion. It's meant for you to throw it away, so you keep giving them $20 every other month. It's a blight. It is absolutely a blight to the planet. That company in particular isn't under any pressure to change their manufacturing standards or to embrace any kind of climate change. The European companies are under pressure, because there are European laws to create better actors, but they still have a long way to go. It's really hard if the U.S. doesn't regulate fast fashion, because people throw it away. Literally, three wears and you throw it away.

MITCH: You told me something very interesting beforehand, which is the importance of data and analytics, which we are trying to make ubiquitous here at Purdue, no matter where a student's headed. You had an interesting observation that some young people don't understand exactly what the purpose is and what the real skill is.

MS. WAINWRIGHT: First of all, we're in complete agreement that everyone will benefit by understanding how to work with data and how to analyze that data. The people who win know it is harder to turn that data into information. I get presentations all the time from people who say, "Well, here's the data." I ask, "Well, what am I supposed to do with that? Where are we going? What problem are you solving? That's interesting—what does that mean?"

You can get into data overload. I would say it is critical to understand what information you want from the data and then either do the analytics yourself or work with people that can do it for you. When you're getting started, and I still do this, I download the raw data and look at it myself and cut it a different way to see if I'm missing something. Now, I could hand it off—we have a data analytics department—but that may take two hours and sometimes I want it now. Just having that ability to analyze the data to solve real problems and provide real information is a huge win. This is a data-driven world now.

The people who are going to win are the people that know how to create amazing algorithms and use data scientists. More importantly, the business-people are going to win by understanding what information they need from that data and how to put it into action. There's a gap right now. It's a real gap.

Anant Agarwal, PhD
Founder of edX; MIT professor of electrical
engineering and computer science
March 2014

In the spring of 2014, few of us had ever heard of a MOOC (massive open online course) or an OER (open educational resource), and a mention of online education recalled the old-fashioned correspondence courses, but in a new computerized format. So when I heard Anant Agarwal's name for the first time and read about his work in distributed education, I knew he was someone the Purdue community needed to hear from.

Dr. Agarwal was not one to pull punches. His claim, "There have been no innovations in learning since the printing press," was sure to raise eyebrows within the academy. His blatant ambitions to transform education—"I aspire to educate a billion people around the world"—rightfully caught the attention of universities whose freshman class ranged in the lower four digits.

Ascribing the title "founder of the global online education movement" to Dr. Agarwal is not hyperbole. But before founding his now legendary edX, he was already a superstar in the world of computer science and artificial intelligence. An academic "triple threat," Dr. Agarwal has won major awards for both research and teaching and is a serial entrepreneur. He is a member of the National Academy of Engineering, a fellow of the American Academy of Arts and Sciences, and a fellow of the Association for Computing Machinery.

As I noted to the audience, the disruptive threat that Dr. Agarwal, his protégés, and his imitators posed to traditional higher education might make it look a little like I had invited Alaric the Visigoth into the Roman Senate right before he sacked the place. But as it turned out, he gave us all a thrilling vision of the future.

After Dr. Agarwal's presentation, he and I sat down for a conversation.

DR. AGARWAL: A lot of the questions that I ask in terms of the future of the university are really meant to challenge us to think about a system that really hasn't changed in a long time. I've seen photographs from the earliest days of the classroom, with the teacher teaching and a whole bunch of students sitting in rows. I drove here from the Indianapolis Airport, and it reminded me—neat little rows like cornstalks right after a winter's thaw.

That system hasn't changed in hundreds of years. Everything around us has changed. Health care has completely changed. In the space of a few hundred years, look at surgery. A few hundred years ago, you'd be knocked on the head, and they would operate on you before you would come to, and that's the best that they did. Today, with laparoscopic surgery, it's in and out. Look at transportation, with jet engines and rockets.

It is absolutely shocking that at the same institutions where incredible research is done, changing the world around us, we haven't changed ourselves. So today, I want to give you a sense of what is possible. And really, the questions I ask are provocative questions.

Fundamentally, edX came out of universities. We're a nonprofit, and we're looking to transform ourselves from within, asking these questions to see how we can improve and reinvent education. Can we do a lot better on a number of fronts?

This [photograph of an enormous auditorium holding hundreds of students, with an instructor standing at the front] is actually a classroom at the Obafemi Awolowo University in Nigeria. All of you have heard of distance education, but if you look at the people [in the back of the auditorium], I would say they're undergoing long-distance education. And if you think that what we're doing in MOOCs and online education is new, talk to these people. When's the last time they've had any personal contact with the instructor? Our system is broken in terms of quality. And in large parts of the world, we don't have access to a good quality education either.

So, edX was formed with a $60 million investment by MIT and Harvard, and we came up with three parts to our mission. The first one is that we wanted to increase access to education for students all over the world. A second big part of our mission is to create research and learn about learning. And third is to improve campus education—really understand how we can improve campus education.

If you go to edX.org, you can take courses from some of the great universities of the world, such as a course on financial analysis and decision-making from Tsinghua. Tsinghua is among the top two universities in China. They are a partner of ours.

One reason why MOOCs, these massive open online courses, really caught the attention of the world was the sheer numbers in scale at which education could be offered. For example, in the first course on edX that my colleagues and I taught, we had 155,000 students sign up. That number, 155,000, is actually bigger than the total number of alumni of MIT in its 150-year history. This was an MIT hard course on circuits and electronics, and we advertised that fact—differential equations as a prerequisite. And 7,200 students passed the course, and these were from 162 countries.

At MIT I teach about a hundred students each semester and teach the course twice a semester, and I've been teaching at MIT for twenty-six years. To teach this many students, I would have to teach at MIT for forty years. In one fell swoop, you get a large number of students, so the access part is a really big aspect of these MOOCs.

To give you a quick sense of edX, we started about two years ago, and today we have 2.2 million students from all over the world. They come from 196 countries, and that is all the countries in the world. We have 4 million enrollments, which means that on average, students are taking two courses. We have courses in virtually all subjects—music, art, history, engineering, computer science, business, math—name it and there are courses in those areas.

We also work with a number of university partners. We have close to fifty university partners on our platform, and we also work with a lot of campuses where universities put up a course online and make it freely available to students around the world. It's completely online. And then they also bring it back to campus and create a blended model class where they combine in person with online. We have over 12,000 students that are taking these blended model classes across a number of campuses all over the world.

You can take these great courses for free. Students can audit the course, but they just audit the course for free. They can also sign up to take an honor code certificate where, if they pass the course, they get a nice little certificate. We've also launched verified certificates where we use a webcam to take [the student's] picture and a picture of their photo ID, and make sure that they are who they say they are. We charge a small fee for a verified certificate service, and that becomes a revenue source for edX.

We are a nonprofit, but nonprofit does not mean money-losing. A nonprofit does not mean slothful. Nonprofit does not mean big government. Nonprofit does not mean non-innovative. Nonprofit does not mean slow-moving. We are looking at various approaches to generating revenue, and our goal is to make sure that outflow matches input. We're not looking to do an IPO or get huge profits, but we want to break even.

One of the things that edX has done uniquely is we've made our platform available as open source software. In other words, anybody can take our software and they can go off and build their own MOOC platform or system. And if they want, they can compete with edX. As an example, Tsinghua and the Chinese Ministry of Education launched a Chinese national platform. France launched a national platform. Queen Rania from the Middle East launched Edraak, which is a Middle East Arabic platform using edX. We're also working with the World Economic Forum.

Recently there's been some angst about low completion rates. For the course that I taught, I showed you the numbers: 155,000 signed up, 7,200 passed the course. If you look the completion rate, it's about 5%. So people are saying, "Oh my God, this is terrible—a 5% completion rate—therefore MOOCs must be terrible." Looking at completion rates as a percentage of the people that sign up doesn't make any sense, and I'll give you a quick example why. We really need to put these certification rates in context.

Let's take, for example, a course from any selective university. I'll use my own example. At MIT, the course that I taught was of the same rigor as the campus course that I teach, and I noted that typically about 7% of learners pass these edX courses. For the course that I taught, 5% passed the course.

But remember, anybody can take an edX course. You can go to edX no matter what your background and you can sign up to take a course. There is no admissions test. Part of our goal is to democratize education. It doesn't matter if you have the background. It doesn't matter if you have the money. It doesn't matter what your race is, your color, your geography. Really, nothing matters. All you need is to have an Internet connection and be able to click and sign up to take a course for free.

So, 7% passed the course, but then if you look at the MIT admissions rate, you'll see that it is 7% of people that applied. So, 20,000 applied and they made admission offers to 1,400 students this year. Then why is the press surprised that 7% passed the course and 7% get admitted to MIT? It's not surprising that those numbers are similar. You just have to put this in perspective. About 70% to 75% of the people who sign up are auditors who say, "Look, I just want to listen. I'm not looking to get a certificate."

So, what does an online course look like? In a typical course on campus, you have a lecture. We replace lectures with what we call "learning sequences." A learning sequence is a sequence of short videos, five- to ten-minute videos, interwoven with interactive exercises. You may watch a video, and following a video, we may ask you a simple problem or a hard problem, and you go and answer the problem. So really, you interact with videos and then you do some exercises. This form of learning, where you watch a video and then interact and try to answer a question, is a form of learning that is called "active learning."

Education researchers have known this for a long time, so a lot of what MOOCs are doing is not new. We've just found a way to apply what learning researchers have known for decades. In a landmark 1972 paper, Craik and Lockhart found that learning and retention relates to how deeply you process the material. If you sit and just listen to a lecture, you're going to forget. But, if you use the Socratic method—you teach by asking questions, get the students to engage—studies have proven that the material lasts a much, much longer time. On edX, mechanically, by making sure that we have videos interleaved with exercises, it really promotes this form of learning.

I was in one of your blended classes today, where they've replaced a lecture with having students watch videos before they come to class, and then in class, they have discussions and projects. I asked the students what they like about the videos and the blended class vs. a traditional lecture class, and one thing they all said was the flexibility. That in a classroom, at the fifty-minute mark, they would lose the professor and would be sitting there scrambling, writing notes.

But here, you can pause the video of the professor. You can rewind it. Heck, you can even mute the professor. And in fact, in the blended model class that I taught at MIT, I took a poll. It turned out that two-thirds of the students were actually muting me and reading the transcript on the side. So, it's very flexible. Different people like to learn in different ways, and the video gives just a lot of flexibility to learning.

One question people ask is, "If you have a hundred thousand students in your class, how do you grade these students? There's no way you can sit down and do it on paper." We use computing technology to do all of that stuff. A student will enter an equation, have the computer check it, and give them instant feedback. Most of us remember in classes where you submit the homework, get something back a week later; but here you get quick instant feedback and you can fix things if something were slightly wrong. Students absolutely love this, and they're telling us that this little green check mark has become somewhat of a cult symbol at edX. The students are telling us that they go to bed at night dreaming of the green check mark.

We also have a social component, where students can ask questions on a discussion forum, and the students are answering each other's questions. And really, rather than getting rid of iPhones and iPads from the classroom, we embrace the social and bring the discussion into the online experience. That is also really engaging the students. In fact, there's a study by Lori Breslow, who's a researcher at MIT, and what she found was that the student success rate was very highly correlated with the student collaborating and working with somebody else....

Finally, I want to show you some fun results. At edX, we gather a lot of data to improve learning, and I like to call edX the particle accelerator for learning, just for that reason.

I'll give you one example. One question we've always asked is how long videos should be. Should videos be one hour long, like our lectures? Or heaven forbid, an hour and thirty minutes, like some lectures? Or should they be one minute long? Who knows what the right number is?

We did a study looking at all the video lengths over a number of courses, a number of subjects, a number of universities at edX, and here was the finding. Six minutes is the ideal video length. Students watched a six-minute video for almost six-minutes. But for a video that was an hour long, students watched it for barely three minutes. This really goes to show that after you show something to a student for about six minutes, it behooves you to have some exercises.

We can use this data to really understand how people learn, how students learn, and in a very short amount of time, maybe discover really new ways in which people learn, and really improve learning around the world.

Thank you.

MITCH: Update us on one thing. Some of the early reports I saw indicated that, of the completers or those who were earning the certificates, degrees, or at least passing the final, they tended to be people who were already well-educated. These were people pursuing continuing education to a greater extent. Has that begun to change as edX has continued to grow? Because for those of us who were thrilled at the idea of a democratization of education, it looked as though, at least earlier on, what you had was principally people who were already ahead of the education game getting further ahead.

DR. AGARWAL: Let me describe some of the statistics and the rationale. Right now on edX, if you look at the statistics for the course that I showed you, the circuits course, 5% of the learners were younger than 18. So, 5% were high schoolers, and our youngest learner is 8 years old—high schoolers and elementary schoolers; 45% are between the ages of 18 and 25, so you could think of them as college age or master's students; and 50% are above the age of 25. And so, what we've seen is around two-thirds of our students already have a degree, but one-third are in college or younger. So, if we have 2 million learners, a third of 2 million are college age or high school age. That's a big number. But that said, two-thirds, a significant fraction, already have a degree.

Now, is that a good thing or a bad thing? Certainly, in terms of democratizing education, I would like to see more students who do not necessarily have a degree. And there are two impediments to that. One is that universities are our partners, and our university partners and professors are used to creating courses in the spring and fall, and so that's what we did, spring and fall courses. And when the semester's running in the spring and fall, students are already taking six courses.

And so, many of the students who don't have a degree are already learning and studying, and they can't take on even more than they're doing. How are we fixing that? Well, we're encouraging our university partners to offer courses in summer. That's one example. The second is that we give certificates, but our universities need to come around to giving some campus credit for students who've taken a MOOC course.

SCIENCE AND SOUND THINKING

 Bjorn Lomborg, PhD
Author; president of Copenhagen Consensus Center
April 2017

A central ambition of the President's Lecture Series was to bring provocative thinkers and people who might offer insights that are not common, or that are different than those we hear most of the time. Dr. Bjorn Lomborg, prolific author, researcher, and founder and president of the Copenhagen Consensus Center, certainly satisfied that goal.

Before making his acquaintance, I had admired Dr. Lomborg for a long time, and I was not alone. He had recently appeared on some of the world's most noteworthy rankings, including *Foreign Policy*'s Top 100 Global Thinkers, *Time*'s 100 Most Influential People, *Esquire*'s 75 Most Influential People of the 21st Century, and the *Guardian*'s 50 People Who Could Save the Planet.

And moving on down to more exclusive territory, his organization was found in the top 20 think tanks in the world, among a universe of 7,000. But still more exclusively, he is the one person I can name who was able to gather over one hundred of the world's top economists, led by seven Nobel laureates, to assess in his book *The Nobel Laureates' Guide to the Smartest Targets for the World* those things that might be done through collective action to make this a better, safer, more humane, and sustainable planet. In so doing, Dr. Lomborg set forth some original insights and raised important challenges to conventional wisdom—exactly the kind of thinking that Purdue audiences appreciate the most.

Dr. Lomborg treated us to a remarkable presentation that is a must-watch for anyone interested in the human condition. At the end, we had time for just a few questions.

DR. LOMBORG: At the Copenhagen Consensus Center, we work on all the big problems in the world and how to fix them. I'm going to focus on three main points. First, to recognize that things are generally getting better, not worse. That's crucial because that's the only way we can get out of this panic mode

where we often are. It seems like everything is falling apart. If we can get
to a point where we realize things are getting better, not worse, we can start
asking rational questions about where can we do the most good to make an
even better world for the future.

Then I'm going to talk about climate change, partly because this is probably where there's the most interest here, and it's also one of the things that get
a lot of people excited and interested. But it's also a great example of how we
don't do the smartest things we could.

And then at the end, I'm going to talk about some things that you can
do to help.

First, things are getting better. Let me just take the three main points that
the UN talks about: welfare and economics and environment. If you look at
the economy, we've seen since 1820 a dramatic decline of poverty. We started
in a world where more than 90% of everyone was poor; today, for the first time,
we have less than 10% who are absolutely poor. That's a phenomenal outcome,
and we should be very, very thankful for it. Likewise, we live longer and longer. We used to live about thirty years on average; today that's about seventy.
We basically have two lifetimes.

The third one, environment, requires us to answer the question, What's the
deadliest environmental problem, or in some ways the biggest environmental problem, in the world? Almost everyone gets this wrong. People think it's
water or it's climate change. It's actually indoor air pollution. It kills 4.3 million people annually because about 2.8 billion people, almost half the world's
population, cook and keep warm with dirty fuels—wood, cardboard, dung, or
whatever they can get their hands on.

That means for 2.8 billion people the pollution inside their homes is typically ten times more polluted than the outdoor air in Beijing. The World
Health Organization estimates this is the equivalent of smoking two packs
of cigarettes every day. The second largest [environmental problem] is outdoor air pollution and lead, which is mostly a legacy issue, followed by water
and sanitation, then ozone, then global warming, and then radon. Of course,
people will then say, "But global warming surely gets worse in the future." Yes,
it does. By 2050, the World Health Organization estimates we'll see about
250,000 people die each year. So yes, it's a big problem, but it's important to
keep the scale.

So overall, things have gotten better. We live longer, we have many fewer
people who are poor, and we have less of the world's biggest environmental

problem. This is important, because if the world is getting better—and remember, this does not mean that there are no problems, there are lots of problems and I'll get to those—it means that we are moving in the right direction. Then we can stop being scared witless, start talking about of all the problems that remain, and ask what we should do.

I would like to spend a little bit of time talking about global warming, because it in many ways is the centerpiece for a lot of conversation in the rich world. I'll get to where it is for the rest of the world afterward. Fundamentally global warming, yes, absolutely, it's a problem. It's real. It's a significant and negative impact.

We estimate that the impact right now is probably about 0%. It's very little net impact if you measure it against GDP, but by the 2070s, the International Climate Panel estimates that the cost will be somewhere between 0.2% and 2% of GDP. That's a significant problem and something that we need to fix.

Unfortunately, it's often dramatically exaggerated. Everyone talks about how we are going to see more hurricanes, we're going to see more dramatic deaths, and all kinds of stuff. Everything you see in the news can, in some way or another, be connected to global warming.

Typhoon Haiyan in the Philippines is one of those very much talked about events when a hurricane hit and a lot of people died.[24] It was really seen as a flash point for arguments that we going to see more and more deaths because of global warming. But again, if you look at the numbers from the international disaster database for climate-related deaths, there has been a dramatic decline since 1930. Fundamentally, we've gone from a world where, on average, almost half a million people died each year, to much fewer than 50,000. Actually, this decade is the lowest on record.

This does not mean that global warming is not actually making this worse. That's possible. I don't think we have good strong data for it, but it's possible. But the argument here is that many, many other factors are countering that.

We need to start talking about why we are so bad at fixing global warming. A lot of people tend to think, Well, if CO_2 causes more warming and CO_2 comes from fossil fuels, why don't we just stop using fossil fuels? It seems like an obvious thing, but we burn fossil fuel because it powers everything we like about civilization. It gives us heat, cold, transport, food, electricity, everything we like. And so, unless we can find a way to get all these good things without fossil fuel, we are not in a place where we're going to be willing to give it up.

SCIENCE AND SOUND THINKING

The International Energy Agency is commonly regarded as having the best estimate, and their latest prognosis from late 2016 looks to 2040, basically a quarter of century out. If you look at what the energy consumption over a wide range of different things—coal, oil, gas, nuclear, hydro, biomass—will be, it's coal, oil, and gas, and then a little bit of nuclear, and a little bit of hydro, and a lot of biomass. This of course is, to a very large extent, exactly what drives all the indoor air pollution.

People believe that solar and wind are the future, but remember, wind makes up almost nothing—only about 0.5% of global energy today. And solar makes up nothing—0.1%. We believe that it's a huge number and it's not. We're seeing a lot of these beautiful pictures of wind and solar, but it's a trivial matter right now. But then we also believe that certainly in a quarter of a century, it'll be a huge impact. No, it will not.

If everyone does what we promised in the Paris Agreement,[25] the treaty that is supposed to solve global warming, this is what happens: We use more coal, we use more oil, we use more gas, more nuclear, more hydro, more biomass. Yes, more wind, and yes, more solar. But notice how small these numbers are. We go from 0.5% to 1.9%, and 0.1% to 1.0%, respectively. We still have less than 3% of our energy, in a quarter of a century, from solar and wind.

To put it differently, in 1800 we had 95% of our energy from renewables and we've spent two centuries getting away from that. Now, of course, we're actually trying to increase renewable energy, but we've been hovering at around 13% for the last forty years. Again, we'll see an increase in utilization—we're aiming to get up to 19% from our current 13.5%, but more realistically, we'll probably get up to about 16%. But let's just get a sense of proportion. We are not anywhere close to solving this problem in the next quarter of a century, and solar and wind will play an almost trivial part in this. I think by telling ourselves stories that are not true, we're not actually helping the world. . . .

Cutting CO_2 has real costs. There is a very strong correlation between GDP growth and CO_2 growth. You can have less CO_2 growth, but you also get lower GDP growth. That's the basic outcome of all these macroeconomic models. When you promise to cut carbon emissions, it has a real cost. . . . and if there's anything we know it is that climate policies are phenomenally ineffective. So, a cost of $1 trillion to $2 trillion per year for the rest of the century will buy you a reduction temperature of something that's almost immeasurable.

So which climate policies do work? ... Climate adaptation, double energy efficiency, supplying electricity to everyone will actually give you $5 back on the dollar. More energy research will provide $15. Modern cooking fuels, getting rid of some of the indoor air pollution is a phenomenal idea at $15. Phasing out fossil fuel subsidies would be an incredibly good investment at more than $50.

But remember, there's a lot of other things you can do. On infrastructure, for instance, get mobile broadband to developing countries. We estimate that it's going to be fairly expensive, but it's going to drive a little bit of economic growth. And that will probably mean for every dollar you spend, you'll do $17 of good. If you look at biodiversity, the best thing is to halve coral reef loss. If you do that, not only will you get better biodiversity, which is great, but you'll also, because the reefs act as hatchlings, you'll get higher fishery incomes and more tourism—about $24 worth of good.

Reducing child malnutrition is an incredibly good investment. We estimate it gives you $45 back on the dollar. In health, there are lots of great interventions. Halve malaria infections, $36. Cut tuberculosis death by 95%, $43. Immunization—we've gone from about 20% coverage to about 80%—but there's still more things that we can do. The Global Alliance for Vaccines estimates that if we spend about a billion dollars a year on extra vaccines, especially on cutting down diarrhea, we could possibly save about a million kids each year. So, every dollar spent would do about $60 of good.

This is not money you can take home. It would be wonderful if it were, but this is how much good you can do. It is, if you will, an ROI [return on investment] for philanthropy. The fundamental point here is to say, yes, there are smart things to do in climate and there are smart things to do in all these other areas. [The world] is not going in the wrong direction. It's generally going in the right direction. That doesn't mean that there are no problems. There are lots of problems still, and I've noted some of them. But let's focus on where we can do the smartest things.

MITCH: Bjorn, as your book makes plain, but the point may need clarification here, you're an economist. But these are not purely financial calculations. You're measuring social benefit as well as directly financial.

DR. LOMBORG: And environmental. That's very, very important. We're not just talking about financial benefits. We're also talking about social benefits and environmental benefits. We're measuring how much higher economic outcome will you have, how many fewer people will die, and how many more wetlands will you have. We try to estimate all that but make it in one-dollar estimates.

MITCH: Your book points out that seven times more people die from cold than heat, but I didn't see any reference to that in your presentation. Why not?

DR. LOMBORG: It's important to recognize that when we talk about global warming, there's a tendency to focus on all the bad things that will happen with warming. Back in the '70s, some people worried a lot about global cooling . . . a significant number of people. The *New York Times* and many others wrote about it, saying we'll actually have lower productivity in agriculture, and that's going to cause us a great deal of problems. These things are probably all true, but it's amazing that nobody said that at least there'll be less malaria.

We only focus on the things that are going to get worse. And to a certain extent, that's reasonable because remember, we have a civilization that's stabilized at exactly the temperature that we have right now. That's why people from Finland are not very concerned about it being cold and why people in Athens or in Florida would probably be terrified if it was really cold. A lot of our expenditures focus on specific temperature outcomes, and any deviation, colder or warmer, is likely to create more problems.

But we should also remember it's likely to lessen some problems. And cold is a good example. I'm always astounded that every year in Britain, official figures show that somewhere between 25,000 and 50,000 people die from cold. Why is that not in the news? Because it doesn't happen in one day. Whereas a heat wave happens in one day. These are mostly older people—and it is also true for heat deaths—and when it's cold for a long time, they simply expire sometime before they would otherwise have.

But that's still something that ought to outrage us. There was a point two years ago when morgues were about three months behind because there were so many people dying. Yet, I don't think anyone in this audience heard about that. Had this been because of global warming, that would've been a big story. But it's not. And in some ways you could argue that the global warming would probably slightly alleviate that. Now, again, that's not to say that global warming is good. I'm not making that argument. I'm simply pointing out that there are both negatives and positives to global warming, just like there is to pretty much everything else in the world. and we are not well served by only focusing on the negatives.

Steven E. Koonin, PhD
Theoretical physicist; New York University engineering
professor; author of *Unsettled: What Climate Science
Tells Us, What It Doesn't, and Why It Matters*
October 2021

One of the most fascinating books of 2021, and one of the most controversial, was penned by Dr. Steven Koonin. Theoretical physicist, public servant, academic, academic administrator, and prolific researcher and author. Dr. Koonin has established his credibility through wide-ranging posts, including governance roles at some of America's most well-known national laboratories; tenure as provost at Caltech; and service as President Obama's undersecretary for science in the U.S. Department of Energy, where he administered the climate research program and the country's energy technology strategy. A member of the National Academy of Sciences and the American Academy of Arts and Sciences, Dr. Koonin has published more than 200 peer-reviewed articles.

Dr. Koonin's 2021 book, *Unsettled: What Climate Science Tells Us, What It Doesn't, and Why It Matters*, deals, of course, with the issue of climate. But I really invited him to campus because of the broader issues it raises about the proper role of science, and the proper role of places of science like Purdue, in helping inform public decisions and in advancing knowledge generally. Dr. Koonin's message is that the scientists among us and we as consumers of scientific information must practice continuous vigilance. As the Royal Society's motto cautions us, *Nullius in verba* . . . take nobody's word for it.

MITCH: For those who haven't read the book, again I'm frankly more interested in the more general questions that the book illuminates, but to get there it's important to have your views on the record for those who haven't had a chance to read it, as I know many of your critics didn't get around to reading it. So, let's start with a lightning round of sorts. Is the world's climate changing?

DR. KOONIN: Of course. Is it getting warmer? Yes. It's gotten about one degree centigrade warmer in the last 120 years.

MITCH: And does humankind have a lot to do with that?

DR. KOONIN: Certainly, humans are influencing it. Exactly how much remains to be determined.

MITCH: Again, for those who haven't yet had the chance to read Dr. Koonin's book, he has not done original research for all of the assertions. The findings in the book come from the government's own reports, including the United Nations, and now they have issued a subsequent report. Is there anything about that new report that changes your views or causes you to modify them?

DR. KOONIN: I have of course looked very carefully at it. The report is 4,000 pages long, so it's taking some time for me and others to digest, but there isn't very much at all that I would change about what I've written.

MITCH: A number of people have taken strong exception to things you wrote. One of the most common criticisms is that you cherry-pick the data. From having read the book I know you found some instances of that happening among those who differ with you on the issue, but talk a little bit about it.

DR. KOONIN: As you mentioned, everything I've written in the book—95%—is not my words, not my science, but the official science is from the IPCC,[26] and I tried to stick with summary statements. The statement that there are no detectable trends in hurricanes over a century, I would say that's not a cherry-pick—that's a pretty important observation. . . .

MITCH: I do think that it's important to pay attention to the mission you thought you were on as a scientist, challenging the accepted wisdom of the time, and also the reaction to it—many people saying that's not appropriate or you should even be silenced. I'd like to hear you talk a little about that. You talk a lot in the book about whether science should be used to inform or to persuade. You say at one point that there's people who believe . . . and let's accept their sincerity . . . that have said, "No harm in a little misinformation if it helps save the planet." So, if it helps save the planet as they see it, can it possibly be justified?

DR. KOONIN: Well, I don't think so because these are complex decisions that society has to make. They will involve policies of one sort or another and those policies will express values and priorities, but they have to be founded on a clear picture of what the science says and what it doesn't say. And if the scientists, with the help of the media, spin the story one way or the other, we are usurping the right of the public to make fully informed decisions. We are distracting from other priorities or other threats that are more immediate, more obvious, and more tractable, and you can probably list them as well as I. We are tarnishing the reputation of science in other important matters like pandemics. And finally, we are really depressing young people, and I think that that is one of the most criminal things that has gone on—to give young people little hope for the future when the reality is we're going to do just fine. The world is not going to end in twelve years.

MITCH: The notion that at least many great scientists have espoused is that it is always incumbent on them to challenge, to be skeptical even of those things they believe to be accurate and true. I believe I'm right that Einstein used to write letters to Niels Bohr or somebody urging them to disprove the general theory if they could, to run experiments that might disprove it. He wanted it tested. He wasn't trying to silence those who disagreed. It turned out he was right, but he wasn't trying to silence those who might demonstrate that he was right by trying to prove he was wrong.

DR. KOONIN: A good scientist wants to be proven wrong. You have beliefs, but you want to keep testing them against different challengers. And you're always willing. All understanding is contingent, it's subject to revision, but if you try to revise some well-accepted principles, then you've got a much higher barrier to go through. So yes, skepticism, challenge is in the nature of the scientific enterprise, and if it weren't there, the enterprise would not be as powerful as it is.

PART IV

The Ten Commencements

O F PURDUE'S MANY WISE TRADITIONS, ONE I HAVE COME TO APPRECIATE IN PARTIC-
ular, is our approach to commencement ceremonies. The setting in ma-
jestic Elliott Hall, the musical selections, the way in which tight limits on nonessentials keeps the focus on the graduates, all these make for events
which, over and over, bring effusive compliments and favorable comparisons
from students and family members alike.

Most of all, I love Purdue's steadfast commitment to honor every graduate
individually. Most schools even half our size long ago abandoned that practice
in favor of mass degree conferral. But even as Purdue's student population has
grown far beyond its historic levels, it has preserved the opportunity for every
student to hear their name, walk across the stage, and be photographed at their
moment of accomplishment. It now takes seven sessions and a full three-day
weekend to fulfill this commitment, but the huge cast of participants—organizers, stagehands, deans and trustees, the band, the singing groups, and so many
others—do their jobs uncomplainingly. The joy on our students' faces is all the
motivation anyone needs.

One other aspect of our commencement ritual has a personal implication for
the occupant of my office. It is expected that the president, not some invited guest
speaker, will deliver the commencement address. This practice has a lot to recommend it, not least that it eliminates the problem of what guest speaker to invite, and the risk that anyone worth hearing is likely to generate griping or worse
from people who dislike the choice. It's a fine idea, as long as you're not the one
who has to write the speech.

I have always prepared all my own speeches. (The very first administrative
saving I remember effecting at Purdue was to thank those who had been writing speeches for my predecessor and redeploy them elsewhere in the university.)

I have delivered most talks over the years either from notes or completely extemporaneously. But there are some occasions which really require a written text, and commencements are in that category.

And, if you take them as seriously as I always have, they're hard. Having given a number at other schools before becoming a Boilermaker, I learned that, unless one is willing to merely spout platitudes, few assignments are more challenging. As I said in one such talk, commencements and eulogies are the very hardest speeches to do well. You're not the star of the show, not who people came to see. And what does one say that hasn't been said better by someone else a hundred times before?

So the commencement speech has always been near the top of my annual worry list, and my biggest homework assignment. I start stuffing ideas into a file literally as soon as one year's ceremonies were over and think constantly about alternative themes right up until Christmas break, which I used each year to finish an acceptable first draft.

Commencement speeches are all about the students, and trying to send them on their way with a useful, maybe memorable thought or two. But many of them, I found, did recirculate in a surprisingly wide fashion. Excerpts frequently appeared in national publications, and often I heard from people who had received them from friends or discovered the talk ricocheting around on social media. So I believe they played some role in the growth of Purdue's reputation. Here then, are what one wag in our office has labeled the Ten Commencements.

Ingenuity
May 2013

"Armed with a rounded education, rich in the liberal arts, they go into the world prepared to lead, and to teach, in a time of unprecedented complexity. Engineers and scientists who can distill, demystify, and communicate complex questions to their fellow citizens; liberal arts graduates who absorbed enough of the transformative science of the day to teach it to our children or help shape the sound choices and trade-offs that a free society must make together."

Greetings to all today's joyful graduates: those who are graduating from one of our remarkable academic colleges, those who are graduating from one of our exceptional professional schools, and especially those parents who are finally graduating from the School of Tuition Check-Writing. We salute and welcome you all.

Purdue is known for the pioneers and adventurers it produces, men and women whose sense of wonder has led them to frontiers of new knowledge, across our planet and beyond it. But even a Nobel laureate or an astronaut could not surpass by much the curiosity of a newly minted college graduate: I wonder what's next? Am I good enough? Were these the best days I'll ever know? Most of all, in what kind of world will I live my adult life?

Maybe you saw the following headlines: "Salary Rise for Graduates"; "More Jobs Ahead: Outlook for Graduates Is Better Than Usual"; "Thriving Economy Gives Grads Bright Prospects."

Okay, maybe you didn't. They were from 1956, 1985, and 2006, respectively. Most classes have departed this place in years like those, bound for an America of unquestioned economic promise, national confidence, and world leadership.

The headlines of your graduation year are different: "Class of 2013 Might Earn Less"; "Class of 2013 Faces Grim Job Prospects; "Without Jobs, College Grads Head for 'Debtors' Prison." About half of you will leave here with debts from a student loan. Averages are often deceiving, but on average those with loans will amount to around $28,000. As daunting as that burden may feel, the debt you chose to incur is small compared to the debt you are inheriting, through no decision of your own. Your elders have run up an enormous national tab for you to pay off. As matters stand, your lifetime share today looks to be some $710,000, and it's getting bigger all the time.

We just endured a cold, damp winter here in Indiana, and in a way that seems fitting. You can't miss the damp chill of pessimism in the national news and national mood these days. The last two years are the first on record in which more Americans believe today's youth will have a worse life than their parents.

An old story has the optimist saying, "This is the best of all possible worlds!" to which the pessimist replies "You're right." In a stagnant economy, with national debt weighing down the present and threatening the future, pessimism is hardly surprising. But then, the pessimists are with us in all eras, good and not so good. Consider a quick sample:

"The power of population is so superior to the power in the earth to produce subsistence for man that premature death must in some shape or other visit the human race." That was Thomas Malthus, whose predictions were so famously gloomy that we attach his name to their modern-day versions and the mentality that produces them. Or, more recently, this: "(E)ven with the optimistic assumption that all possible land is utilized, there will still be a desperate shortage before the year 2000.... Food prices will rise so high that some people will starve; others will be forced to shift to lower quality diets." That was the erudite consensus of the world's allegedly wisest people, in 1972, in the so-called Club of Rome report. Or, to take an extreme case, this gem, from 1968: "The battle to feed all of humanity is over. In the 1970s and '80s, hundreds of millions of people will starve to death in spite of any crash programs embarked upon now.... Nothing can prevent a substantial increase in the world death rate."

For the latter forecast and a career of equally comical errors, the author was granted a MacArthur "genius" prize as recently as 1990. After years in Purdue's laudably rigorous grading system, you're entitled to ask, "If that's genius, what would foolishness look like?"

Anything that titillates, that excites, that sends a shiver up the spine tends to sell, so there's always a market for doomsaying. Check any best-seller list, or the lines at the latest disaster film. But something keeps getting in the way of Armageddon. That something is human ingenuity.

That population "bomb" that was going to detonate and destroy the world? It was a dud. Rising incomes and education levels brought birthrates plummeting down, first in the developed world and now even in developing countries like Vietnam, Tunisia, and El Salvador. Now books with names like *The Birth Dearth* and *What to Expect When No One's Expecting* bring us data showing that the looming danger comes from aging societies with far too few young people.

Those global starvation scenarios are in the file of pseudoscientific embarrass-ments. Instead of global famine, the proportion living at subsistence income lev-els is smaller today than ever in human history. We harvest two and a half times more wheat, corn, and rice on just one-third more farmland than in 1960. The proportion of undernourished humans in developing countries has fallen a stun-ning 36% just during the lifetime of today's graduates.

Is world hunger still the largest challenge we face? Of course, but instead of the worldwide catastrophe we were told to expect, the last few decades have seen sensational improvements. And how proud we are that no place has contributed more to that improvement than our university.

Most recently, another set of models hit the wastebasket. Through new break-throughs in energy extraction, we now can see enormously larger supplies of af-fordable and cleaner energy than was believed even as you were entering Purdue a few short years ago. Old alarms about "peak oil supply" are being supplanted by new estimates of "peak oil demand," meaning supplies will outlast our need for them. A new era of rebuilt manufacturing close to home, lower living costs for homes and transportation, and lower CO_2 is unfolding. Best of all, the world's emerging peoples have suddenly much greater hopes for the energy supplies on which their ascent from poverty depends.

What happened? Why were all the sages and their sophisticated models so wildly wrong? Because they fell into the oldest of traps, the fallacy of extrapolation. They failed to imagine that human ingenuity, first and foremost scientific and tech-nological ingenuity, creates enormous and often sudden discontinuities that de-molish the old forecasts and reset in fundamental ways the path of mankind's prog-ress. The steam engine, the automobile, the green revolution, the silicon chip ... no matter how often history repeats, the doomsayers never see the next one coming.

And they fail to account for one more thing: great leadership, the kind that can bring to bear the power of reason, and the lessons of history, and the skills of persuasion, to change minds and hearts and therefore both private action and public policies. The most noteworthy passing of your senior year occurred just over a month ago, when Margaret Thatcher left us. If you doubt for a moment that leadership, sometimes that of a single person, can change history, study her life and the difference between the Britain she found and the one that she left when her work was through. Like the great scientists, and inventors, and busi-ness builders, she was a one-person inflection point who altered the arc of events and set it on a new and better trajectory.

That's what Boilermakers do. They imagine, conceive, devise, and finally engineer the breakthroughs that create the resets and the discontinuities.

Think of the countless lives saved from starvation by the work of our two World Food Prize winners alone. Or Ward Cunningham, whose inventions enabled a whole new mode of collaboration and eventually gave the world a new word: "wiki."

Year in, year out, Boilermaker innovations create new jobs, wealth, and life opportunities for innumerable others. Business builders like Allen Chao of Watson Pharmaceuticals, Dick Dauch at American Axle, Brian Lamb at C-SPAN, or just this year Akshay Kothari of Pulse News have given birth not only to better lives but in some cases to whole new industries.

There's something else Boilermakers do. Armed with a rounded education, rich in the liberal arts, they go into the world prepared to lead, and to teach, in a time of unprecedented complexity. Engineers and scientists who can distill, demystify, and communicate complex questions to their fellow citizens; liberal arts graduates who absorbed enough of the transformative science of the day to teach it to our children or help shape the sound choices and trade-offs that a free society must make together.

I make no pretense to special foresight, and I don't claim to know with certainty that humankind will yet again overcome the very real threats it faces. But I know this: in this audience, and in the graduating classes that preceded and will follow you, are people who will make huge differences, quite possibly the kind that reset all the forecasts and send the pessimists back to their gloomy little corners.

And I know that bright futures lie ahead for you as individuals. Armed with the special rigor and quality of a Purdue education, you are highly likely to lead happy and successful lives. The data tell us, and employers tell us all the time, that Purdue grads perform well and prosper accordingly. But that shouldn't be good enough for you.

In a few minutes, you will own for life one of the proudest emblems of achievement anywhere on the planet, a diploma from Purdue University. You will validate its worth as you move through lives of personal success and satisfaction. But you will fully honor it only as you invent, or start up, or build, or teach, or lead others in ways that alter and thereby continue the world's upward path.

A friend told me he rushed from work to his son's Little League game, which had already started by the time he got there. Spotting his boy in right field, he walked up to the fence, where the scoreboard told him the team was behind 14–0. Between pitches, he waved to his son, who responded with a huge grin and a

"Hi, Dad!" My friend said, "Billy, I'm glad to see you, too, but how can you be so happy with the score the way it is?" To which his son replied, "No problem, Dad, we haven't been to bat yet!"

Neither have you, but your turn at the plate has come. I know some of the nation's scoreboards don't look too good at the moment, but I know something the doubters don't: another team of Boilermakers is in the on-deck circle. Batters up. Or, better said, "Boilers up!"

You won't remember these last thirteen minutes, but I will. For an expectant graduate-to-be, these speeches are just a trailer to be endured while waiting for the real show to start, and I get that. But you're my first Purdue commencement. So no matter how many of these I am called on to officiate, I'll always recall the Class of '13. And if I live long enough for my memory to start slipping, I just know that you will supply plenty of reminders in the form of great achievements of the kind on which human progress depends, and for which Boilermakers have always been known.

Hail Purdue, and each of you.

Change
May 2014

"In 2014, we know for certain that massive change lies ahead. It is now the rule and not the exception it has historically been. There is no prospect that, like most generations before you, your world will look more or less the same in your older years as it does today. Rapid, unexpected, and often disruptive change, most of it driven by the accelerating advance of technology, is a constant fact of modern life."

Commencement week is an occasion for joy, as a new chapter in life opens, but simultaneously a time of wistfulness, as some things happen for the last time: the last class, the last exam, the last party. Of course, not all endings are sad; those parents who have now written their last tuition check are all smiles, and deservedly so. Can we salute all those family members who have played such a big role in the successes we are about to celebrate?

Here's something else for us all to celebrate. For much of history, these ceremonies, including speeches like this one, were conducted in Latin. I love tradition, but that's one you and I can both be glad has seen its day. Of course, there were ways to work around it. Andrew Jackson, the common man's president, was ambushed at Harvard by a pompous dean who challenged him to accept his honorary degree in Latin. Jackson was up to the moment: "E pluribus unum, my friends," he said. "Sine qua non."[27] And sat down.

I won't detain you much longer than that today. But I am thrilled at the chance to offer congratulations to the Class of 2014. The history students among us may already have noticed a small coincidence about the year of your graduation. In each of the last two centuries, this particular year ushered in a period of monumental and unforeseen change. In a world in which often life varied very little during centuries of time, both 1814 and 1914 happened to be rare hinges between one era and the next.[28]

In 1814, the allied powers defeated Napoleon and sent him into exile. Soon, French domination of Europe and decades of constant warfare came to an end. In North America, the Battle of New Orleans ended British pretensions to authority over their former colonies, solidifying the Louisiana Purchase and eventual American development of the frontier. Wisely constructed peace treaties ushered in an era of relative order and prosperity on both continents and, in one historian's phrase, gave "birth to the modern."[29]

Within the next fifteen years, more people acquired more land more cheaply than at any time in human history. Much of that was in the new state of Indiana, where the Ice Age's Wisconsin drift and its retreating glaciers had deposited topsoil of immense fertility. The population of the nineteenth U.S. state multiplied fourteen times between 1810 and 1830. Similar to the Moore's Law of our computer era, the number of travelers and the number of letters carried began doubling every five years.

The biggest leaps forward came, as they almost always do, from technology. An explosion of interest in science led to revolutionary, life-saving inventions like the coal mine safety lamp and the stethoscope. It was then that Charles Babbage designed the first mechanical calculating machine. In what some historians designate the single most important innovation of them all, the steam engine appeared shortly thereafter, bringing swiftly the sweeping transformation we now call the Industrial Revolution. Between 1814 and 1830, patents per million people doubled; in New England, they quadrupled.[30]

Unlike today, universities played no part in any of this progress. They were still principally in the business of preparing young men for the clergy, or educating the children of the elite. Innovation at the time, such as the first shoes made differently for left and right feet, was the output of what one writer called "clever young men," self-taught tinkerers out to make a buck and a name for themselves.

That, too, changed in the period after 1814, most importantly when Michael Faraday, approaching the matter of electricity from a scientific vantage point, insisting on experimental verification of his theories, provided "the first clear demonstration of the central relevance of scientific research to material progress."[31] His work laid the foundation for the telegraph, described now as "the first important invention based on the application of advanced scientific knowledge rather than the know-how of skilled mechanics."[32] It inaugurated the modern epoch of science-driven progress, in which Purdue and Boilermakers now occupy such a prominent place. There was no Purdue yet, so no commencement, but the fortunate young people who came of age in 1814 lived their adulthood in a time of revolutionary progress and positive change.

Fast-forward a century, halfway to today, and the year brought change of an equally profound but tragically different character. By then, Purdue was a well-established 45 years old. The Class of 1914 gathered in the first Fowler Hall, where Stewart Center is today, doubtless full of the hope that makes these occasions so inspiring. They had been born into an upbeat age of material progress, scientific achievement, and globalized trade and commerce that everyone believed would make armed conflict a thing of the past. From the evidence we have, they had no foreboding that, just eight weeks later, the world would plunge into the disastrous catastrophe we remember as World War I. It was arguably the most senseless and avoidable of all the atrocities that humankind has inflicted on itself over the centuries. Technologies like the tank and the machine gun had advanced ahead of men's capacity to manage them, with tragic results in stupidly wasted lives.

By 1918, the whole world was totally different, this time not for the better. Millions were dead and millions more maimed. Four members of that Purdue class had been killed serving their country. Six of every ten French men between the ages of 18 and 28 had perished, and with them the whole idea that history is a linear march upward. In the historian Paul Fussell's phrase, the war "reversed the Idea of Progress."[33] Compounded by an unwisely punitive peace treaty, World War I led more or less directly to a second global conflict just twenty years later, and to the totalitarian regimes, which, while they lasted, enslaved and murdered countless millions more.

So, in 1814, a great war ends and an era of marvelous improvement begins. 1914, a great war starts, and humanity takes a long step backward. Neither of these sharp turns could have been foreseen in those years; maybe life would drift on

without much change in any one lifetime, the way it had for most of our species' existence.

That possibility no longer exists. In 2014, we know for certain that massive
change lies ahead. It is now the rule and not the exception it has historically been.
There is no prospect that, like most generations before you, your world will look
more or less the same in your older years as it does today. Rapid, unexpected, and
often disruptive change, most of it driven by the accelerating advance of technology, is a constant fact of modern life.

The only questions for this century's fourteenth class are, what kind of changes
will you see? Will you manage them well and humanely, or recklessly? Will
their benefits be widely shared, or increasingly concentrated among the technically gifted?

It's easy, as it always is, to find things to worry about. Maybe the jobs lost to au-
tomation and robotics will not be replaced this time with new, family-supporting
occupations. Maybe a society with increasing numbers of chronically idle men and
women will fall prey to disorder and civil unrest. Maybe, as some now fear, the artificial intelligence now being devised will hit an inflection point at which the machines we have created take off beyond our control. I could name a dozen more.

When a new grandfather permits himself to worry about such things, it's
helpful to recall that, over the long haul, the pessimists have always been wrong.

Within the short lifetimes of you graduates, more people have been lifted out
of true, sub-subsistence poverty than in all of previous human history. In just
the last twenty years, global infant mortality rates and the percentage of humanity living on less than $1.25 per day were both cut in half. Life expectancy rose
five full years in that historical blink. We live in the safest, wealthiest society ever,
where average people routinely own things that the richest people on Earth did
not when you were born, because those things had not been invented yet.

But what keeps me on the optimist's side of all these questions is not the past
record, but the future promise, the promise I see before me right now. You have
successfully earned one of the most valued emblems of achievement available
anywhere, a degree from Purdue University. I say "earned" with emphasis, because as you know, this school has never joined the trend to softer curriculum
or lenient grading. You got these diplomas the old-fashioned way, and everyone
here is very proud of you for it.

By now I've met thousands of you, and I know you are ready for a world of
constant change. I know you will make much of it yourselves, through your innovations and creativity and initiative. But I know you'll also help your fellow
citizens adjust to and manage that change, through your leadership and active

citizenship. So I'm not fearful, I'm excited for my grandchildren; they'll get to grow up in a world that Boilermakers help build.

What to make of this little coincidence of the "'14s"? Only that there are no guarantees, that history presents opportunities and dangers. That the choices men and women make, the uses to which they put the products of their ingenuity, are what matters. That will be a test less of your content mastery, which you have now demonstrated, than of your character, which you will spend the rest of your lives demonstrating.

In a few minutes, it will be my honor to read the induction oath that confers your degrees. It's easy to zone out listening to somewhat arcane, stilted language like that the oath comprises. But I hope you'll pay some attention to the part near the end. It talks about the "rights, privileges, duties, and responsibilities" that come with your degree.

We live in an age when people are quick to demand what they think are their rights and privileges, but not always so ready to live up to the duties and responsibilities of life in a free, self-governing country. Citizens in full, highly productive, yes, but also dutiful, responsible leaders of others are what Purdue University and its land-grant counterparts were created to produce. Our nation never needed such citizens more than today; it's so uplifting to know that the Class of 2014 is chock full of them.

Hail Purdue, and each of you.

Duty
May 2015

"Universities like ours were created specifically to build a broader middle class and a more inclusive, unified society. When so many trends, and so many strident voices, operate to foster divisions among us, who better than Boilermakers to bring Americans together?"

Thanks to the foresight and taste of past trustees and presidents, ours is a campus of beautiful visual images: the Bell Tower, the Armstrong statue, the Mall Fountain. I love to gaze at them and think of the history each has seen and represents to us today.

But no sight I take in all year quite compares to this one: a sea of shining faces, wearing bright, hopeful smiles, all looking ahead to a new era of freedom and high promise. I'm referring, of course, to the parents, who have now made their last tuition payments. Can we take a moment and acknowledge them, and all those present who have enabled today's graduates to reach this wonderful moment of accomplishment?

We call these occasions "commencements," of course, to remind ourselves that they mark not an ending but the beginning, the commencement, of the next chapter of life. But I doubt any graduate here is thinking only ahead; a little nostalgia is natural, too. It's only human to reflect backward, after all, on a set of experiences that in most cases here comprise a healthy fraction of all the days these young people have spent on Earth.

We hope that you depart with memories of friendships, and fun, and at least a little frivolity. But this is Purdue, so in most cases the dominant recollection you will have is of work, hard work. These days, it has become clear, many colleges are less places of serious higher learning than a sort of summer camp or, as one writer put it, "four years of extended adolescence." A point of pride for every Boilermaker should be that you chose and succeeded in a serious university, a place where tough subjects are taught by a tough-minded faculty.

In every analysis of the national phenomenon called "grade inflation," through which many schools have come to hand out As like Halloween candy, Purdue stands apart. It may seem everything else has changed since your parents' generation went here, but the average GPA has barely budged. One report named Purdue a "number one seed" in its "Sweet Sixteen" of rigorous universities. Be proud.

This means, of course, that the diplomas you will soon take with you did not come easily. In the words of an old commercial your elders will recognize, you got your self-esteem the old-fashioned way. You earned it. And that is why, in survey after survey, employers rank Purdue near the top in the attractiveness and the job performance of our graduates. That is why, in the Gallup-Purdue Index launched last year to measure the life success of college grads, Boilermakers surpassed their peers in every category.

Later in these proceedings, we will pause to pay special tribute to those graduates who have served our nation in its armed services. For them, this is not the first such occasion. They took on, and passed, some previous, rigorous sets of tests. They left basic training, or boot camp, or flight school with the insignia that tells the world that they were skilled, they were equipped, they were fully ready for the duties ahead.

Those duties are, of course, extraordinary. They are the most arduous and often dangerous that a free society asks any citizen to undertake. Our veterans were prepared to endure blows and hardships without complaint. They had mastered equipment to help them succeed in the harshest situations or environments. They had demonstrated judgment, enough to be trusted with the lives of others who would rely on them.

I won't equate your Purdue education with the challenges of military training. But I will express the hope that, in a similar fashion, it has prepared you, readied you, equipped you for the lives of citizenship and leadership we expect you to lead.

I hope, for instance, you're taking with you some protective headgear. In addition to the content you have mastered, in education, the liberal arts, or engineering, were you issued your BS detector? (That stands for "bogus statistics," by the way.) I mean, did you learn to think critically, to know when you are being conned, or misled, or indoctrinated?

Did you acquire some body armor? Are you ready to take the blows that are sure to come? At a minimum, you should have learned that our freedom starts with free speech, and free speech means disagreement, and disagreement means that now and then you will be upset by things you hear and read. Or, as people like to say these days, "offended."

If you absorbed anything of our Constitution, you know that it contains no right not to be offended. If anything, by protecting speech of all kinds, it guarantees that you will be. As they say, "Deal with it." And if you are disturbed enough, then answer it, with superior facts and arguments. Your diplomas say that Purdue has equipped you for this.

But is that where the metaphor runs out? Or does all your training, all your new equipment, imply a set of duties for life after Purdue? Later, we'll hear a suggestion that it does.

This little talk, and everything else beforehand, are mere prelude to today's real highlight, the moment when we formally confer your degrees. To me, the core of that conferral is its declaration that along with your diploma come its "rights, privileges, duties, and responsibilities."

We live in an age when people are quick to demand what they claim are their rights or privileges, but far less often recognize any attendant duties or responsibilities. I earnestly hope that your Purdue years have invested, or strengthened, in you a strong sense of responsibility and duty. After all, those basic training graduates were all taught, and equipped, for a specific reason—to do a duty. One of yours is to be a productive, participatory citizen.

That means we expect you to be not just solid citizens but leading ones. And that means that you will occasionally "offend" someone else. Leaders conceive and bring change, and change always causes discomfort, and reaction. It was well stated that "no consequential idea ever failed to offend someone; no consequential person was ever spared great offense." Never with malicious intent, always with a respect for the views of others, in this sense, do your duty and "take the offensive."

Of course we anticipate that as individuals you will lead personally responsible lives. That at work and at home you will conduct yourselves with the discipline, character, and regard for others on which a free society depends. That you will transmit these values to the next generation as teachers, role models, and, I hope, for most of you as good and loving parents.

But these things are basic. There are other roles for which you are now unusually well equipped. In a world dominated and directed by technology beyond any extent humankind has ever known, you have a handle on things that baffle, confuse, and often scare your fellow citizens. A high percentage of you tackled the subject matter that gives birth to these technologies, so you comprehend them at a level known only to a small percentage of your countrymen. But even those of you who chose less technical disciplines or the humanities still have a grasp beyond that of most Americans—I include myself.

But the opportunity goes a lot deeper than explaining the benefits of biotechnology to a neighbor, or showing Mom and Dad how to use that smartphone.

A course I taught this year dealt with the horrible cataclysm of the Great War, or World War I as we came to call it. Among the intellectual confusions that helped condition the peoples of Europe to accept or even welcome the war was a gross misinterpretation of Darwin's theory of evolution.

Right after the war, Albert Einstein watched in dismay as his theory of relativity was misapplied to suggest that, just like time and space, human values and morals are totally relative and incapable of being determined.

A popular movie of your graduation year was welcomed for introducing elements of relativity and quantum mechanics to a wide audience. But it, too, caused some physicists to caution that casual analogies from complex scientific concepts can cause serious cultural misunderstandings. As Boilermakers, you are unusually equipped to share your insights with those less knowledgeable.

Let me cite one other duty that, paradoxically, your Purdue training has equipped you not to fulfill but to shirk. When our ceremony concludes, you will enter the ranks of a new societal elite. Unlike elites of the past, it's not based on an aristocratic name, or inherited wealth, or membership in the ruling political party of a totalitarian state. The elite of our age is a knowledge elite. It's made up of people like you who have acquired the skills and knowledge we are celebrating today.

In all of history, the marketplace has never rewarded cognitive skills as it does now. Where once what counted most was physical strength, or courage, or mechanical aptitude, today it's brains and smarts. The data say that you are destined to earn more money, work in safer occupations, and live longer and healthier lives than those without the kind of degrees you are about to receive.

Statistically, you are far more likely to take the actions that produce success in modern life. You are more likely to practice prudent preventive health. Most of you will choose spouses of similar intellectual readiness. You are far more likely to get married and stay that way. That in turn means your children will have greatly increased chances of their own success.

Social scientists have begun to document the extent to which our new knowledge elite congregates together, cozily insulated at work and at home from much contact with those less academically prepared. It's a dangerous development. As one scholar summarized it, "It's not a problem if truck drivers cannot empathize with the priorities of college professors. It is a problem if college professors, or producers of network news programs, or CEOs of great corporations, or presidential advisors, cannot empathize with the priorities of truck drivers."

Starting today, life will invite you to separate—professionally, socially, residentially, and attitudinally—from those without your educational equipment. Please don't.

Universities like ours were created specifically to build a broader middle class and a more inclusive, unified society. When so many trends, and so many strident voices, operate to foster divisions among us, who better than Boilermakers to bring Americans together? The businesses you form or grow, and the active civic and charitable lives I hope you will lead, will be a start. But don't stop there. Somewhere there's a softball league, an adult education class, a church on the other side of town, where you can make the human connections that keep a society healthy. For your own sake as much as theirs, seek out and connect with those who are making their way through life without the same equipment you've acquired. It's not just a right thing to do; one could say, it's your duty.

And of those of you who have come to study with us from other nations, we express a similar pride, and wish. Whether you choose to make a life here in the U.S., as we hope many of you will, or take your talents and learning back to your homeland, use your new equipment to know, understand, and lift up those around you.

At the battle of Trafalgar, on the day that would cost him his life, the British hero Admiral Horatio Nelson signaled his fleet, "England expects that every man will do his duty." We hope earnestly that you will live in peaceful times. We pray that none of you will ever be summoned to a duty that threatens your very life. But we do expect that you will employ your Purdue training, and the equipment this place has provided you, to perform the essential duties of citizenship and leadership, in the interest of all people, in particular those who were not so fortunate as to be with you here today.

Hail Purdue, and each of you.

 Intention
May 2016

"There's more value to all your hard work than just getting your money's worth. Scholars on the topic of human happiness have proven that the single strongest key to a satisfying, fulfilling life is 'earned success,' the kind that can come only from sustained effort, overcoming difficulties, dealing with setbacks."

I've often observed that the two most difficult assignments in public speaking are eulogies and commencements. They share two daunting characteristics. First, you are not the star of the show; no one is there to hear you talk. And second, it's tough to come up with thoughts that haven't been expressed more eloquently by others a hundred times before.

Still, the Purdue tradition that assigns this task to the occupant of my current job is a welcome one, in large part because it regularly provides me this inspiring view: a sea of bright, shining faces, full of hope and expectation as they look forward to a new era of freedom and promise. I'm looking, of course, at the parents, who have finally paid that last tuition check. Can we pause for a moment of appreciation for the parents and family members who have played such large roles in the achievements we celebrate today?

Around the country this weekend, ceremonies like this one are dispensing diplomas. They all read about the same—bachelor of this, master of that. But they will not be equal in meaning. Repeated studies reveal that the seriousness of subject matter and the rigor with which student mastery is evaluated vary widely. As employers have come to learn, many diplomas tell little or nothing about the holder's readiness for work or for life. At most, they are a proxy for the intelligence that got the student admitted to college in the first place.

Your diplomas are different. You chose a school where, by and large, serious subjects are taught seriously. Where high grades are still provably hard to come by. No participation trophies here. You got your diplomas and your self-esteem the old-fashioned way. You earned them.

There's more value to all your hard work than just getting your money's worth. Scholars on the topic of human happiness have proven that the single strongest key to a satisfying, fulfilling life is earned success, the kind that can come only from sustained effort, overcoming difficulties, dealing with setbacks.

And yet, among many pernicious notions of our time, perhaps the most dangerous is the idea, sometimes implied and sometimes express, that life is more or less a lottery. That we are less masters of our fate than corks floating in a sea of luck. Or, even more absurd, that most of us are victims of some kind, and therefore in desperate need of others to protect us against a world of predators and against our own gullibility.

I doubt you or your parents believe such nonsense. If you did, you wouldn't have come to Purdue. You wouldn't have invested the time, money, or hard work that brought you to this moment. And I hope you will tune out anyone who, from this day on, tries to tell you that your achievements are not your own.

Oh, sure, we all get important help along the way. I hope you will never lose sight of those parents, teachers, coaches, and others who nurtured and assisted the growth of your intellect, skills, and character. But in the end, your successes, and your failures for that matter, are, like your diplomas today, really up to you.

I used to like that clever metaphor about the turtle on the fence post. You know, the one that ends "What you know for sure is he didn't get there on his own." It's cute, but I don't use it anymore. It dawned on me that it sends just the wrong message. Because the fictional turtle on a post did nothing to lift himself to that height; he just got lucky, when someone else put him there. Life's achievements are never like that.

I'm not saying that luck never plays a part; of course it can. But, unless it's the tragic kind of luck, it almost never decides a life's outcome. Like the referees' calls in a basketball game, the good and bad breaks are likely to even out over the course of a season. What counts in the long run is the quality of your play.

Here's the deal: You can't take luck completely out of the equation, but you can tilt the odds in your favor. Decisions you make, and effort you either do or don't put in, will either increase or reduce the chances that life's breaks break in your favor.

Some of these choices are pretty obvious. Practicing basic preventive health, like exercise, a prudent diet, and avoiding things you should avoid, raises radically the odds that you will live a longer and more vigorous life span. Getting married and staying that way is powerfully correlated with all kinds of positive outcomes: better health, economic security, and career success, and best of all, higher levels of long-term happiness.

But nothing will improve your odds more than the characteristic that got you into this auditorium today. Ask the great achievers of history, like our greatest inventor, Thomas Edison: "Opportunity is missed by most people because it is dressed in overalls and looks like work." Or the incomparable champion of freedom Frederick Douglass, who taught: "We may explain success mainly by one word and that word is work . . . enduring, honest, unremitting, indefatigable work, into which the whole heart is put." Or movie pioneer Samuel Goldwyn, who said, "The harder I work, the luckier I get."

Baseball fans here will remember Eddie Murray, a Hall of Famer and one of the great clutch hitters of all time. Once, after his wrong-field bloop double had scored a winning run, Murray was yelled at by an opposing fan who shouted, "You must be the luckiest hitter in baseball." To which Murray politely replied, "You must not watch batting practice."

A few years ago, an intriguing case came before the Indiana Supreme Court. A man who had trained and disciplined himself to count the cards at a blackjack table had been banned from Indiana casinos because he was winning too much. He hadn't cheated, and he wasn't just getting abnormally lucky. He was just winning by way of his hard work. The judges said the case pitted his right of access to a public space against the casinos' right to decide who came on their property.

The court decided for the casinos. I can't second-guess their reading of the law, but I admit I was rooting for the customer. All he had done was to tilt the odds in his favor, and he did it through his own effort, the kind Douglass called "honest, unremitting, and indefatigable." That's the formula I recommend to you; far more important, that's the formula history recommends. Follow it, and you'll minimize the role of luck; practice it, and you'll never be anybody's "victim."

At these ceremonies, I have started drawing particular attention to a few words in the conferral language we are about to recite. They refer to the "rights, privileges, duties, and responsibilities" of your new degrees. I cite them because today's world abounds in people who are quick to demand what they claim are their rights and privileges without recognizing any concomitant duties and responsibilities.

Not Boilermakers. Not today, not ever. The history of this university is one of people who came from modest circumstances, accepted the responsibility to work hard, and went on, through good luck and bad, to achieve great things and to be great citizens. Who accepted the duty to lead others in lives of similar character. Who knew, with George Washington, that "we cannot ensure success, but we can deserve it."

You're going to see, and I believe make, a lot of history. Maybe more than you may have thought about.

A few years ago, I took up with two new lady friends. It's okay. My wife, Cheri, knew and approved. You see, for a few months in 2007, the two oldest people anywhere on Earth lived in Indiana, just thirty or so miles apart, and I found that, and them, just fascinating. Bertha Fry was 113, Edna Parker 114, two Hoosier farm girls who had been 18 when the *Titanic* sank, your age when the U.S. entered World War I. When I brought them together to celebrate Edna's 114th, the *Guinness Book of World Records* declared it the oldest combined age of any two humans who ever met. Try to imagine all the history, and changes, they witnessed.

I bring it up because, during your lives, 114 will cease being incredible. It may in fact become routine. In just the historical blink since Bertha and Edna were your age, life expectancy has increased by thirty years in the U.S., thirty-six years worldwide. With the advance of medical science, the trend is sure to continue.

So your life expectancy is headed for three digits, to levels humanity has never known or imagined. You will be called on to rewrite the rules about what a career is, what "old age" is, what "'til death do us part" means. And you will have tons of time to shift the odds and take luck out of the equation.

But that is not the sort of life expectancy that matters this morning. Purdue expects much more of you than longevity. We expect that you will do great and important things with all those years you are so likely to have. That you will produce new knowledge, great companies, innovative breakthroughs, sound families, and, most important, build lives of character and virtue. When you do, luck won't have had much to do with it.

I will always have a unique memory of and affinity for the class that leaves us today. We were freshmen together. You arrived at Purdue the same year I did, a semester before me, officially. But my first speech in this job was to you, at Boiler Gold Rush, in August of 2012. I called you my classmates that night, and I think of you that way today. I'll be watching with the pride of association all your future growth and accomplishments.

I know with certainty they will come. That you will continue to do the hard work, and make the choices, and develop the kind of character that the world associates with Boilermakers. The kind that tilts the odds of life steadily, and decisively, in your favor. I wish you good luck in the firm belief that you won't need it. Hail Purdue, and each of you.

Humility
May 2017

> "... will you recognize that your degree doesn't mean that you know what's best for those without one? Or that, even if you did, it's not your right to make the decisions of life for them? A lot of damage has been done by people who, in their well-educated superiority, saw those around them not as creatures of dignity but as objects of therapy."

The intimidating challenge for every commencement speaker is to say something even remotely interesting or original. The sobering reality is that, even if you do, no one will remember it for very long.

But there are some words that, however overused, are appropriate and even essential on these occasions. Phrases like "Is this hat on straight?" and "Say cheese!" And one more that is probably the most common of all: "We're so proud of you."

You'll be hearing those words all day long, and rightly so.

In a few minutes, you will be a recipient of one of the proudest emblems of achievement possible at this stage of your life: a degree from Purdue University. In a way not all college degrees connote, the world will know you earned it. As you know, here we aren't into participation trophies. Year in, year out, good grades are hard to earn at Purdue. Year in, year out, our graduates surpass those of other institutions in the eyes of employers, graduate schools, and their future colleagues in life.

So a Purdue commencement, this day of great pride, may seem an odd place to talk about humility. But that's the word that kept coming to mind as I reflected ahead to this event; because if there is a single quality that one associates with your university and one quality that will assist you in earning other emblems of achievement later in life, it is the inverse of pride. It's the trait we call humility.

I know I'm not the first person to bring this to your attention. You may have first heard it at church. Almost all the religious traditions admonish their adherents to guard against excessive pride. The Proverbs are full of warnings about it: "Pride goeth before destruction, a haughty spirit before a fall." Confucius taught: "A wise man has dignity without pride; a fool has pride without dignity." The Buddha cautioned against letting praise affect "the poise of the mind. Follow the calmness, the absence of pride."

The ancients came to similar conclusions. In mythology, one of the most powerful images is that of Icarus, whose pride led him, fatally, to believe he could fly near the sun. Marcus Aurelius wrote, "Short-lived are both the praiser and the praised."

These days, advice like that is out of fashion. Everywhere one looks, it's a showboat, look-at-me, dance-in-the-end-zone world. The age of the pseudo-celebrity, where people of no apparent talent or character, famous only for being famous, people who never could have passed English 106 or Math 153, let alone a course in thermodynamics or microbiology, preen and strut and spout off on subjects they know little or nothing about. So maybe all those ancient admonitions just don't apply anymore.

Or maybe they apply more than ever. Maybe humility, the awareness that one's own ideas, values, and attitudes may just not be superior or perfect, is the quality that makes a person wiser and more effective, a better learner in an era of unending education, a better teammate in a project team world.

Drafting history's first constitution restricting a government to the consent of its people, Ben Franklin suggested to his fellow delegates that they all resolve to doubt just a little their own infallibility. The modern world is full of self-styled experts, not nearly as smart as Old Ben, for whom a little self-doubt might have come in handy.

On the first Earth Day, confident scholars from places like Harvard and Stanford predicted worldwide famine and starvation, a universal need for gas masks in urban areas, the complete exhaustion of crude oil and a host of other raw materials, and the coming of a new ice age, all well before now. Your first years of life were filled with predictions of collapsed electric grids, planes falling from the sky, and revolutions worldwide, from the failure of software programs to handle the change of centuries. The economic forecasters of our federal government just completed what one could call a perfect season. Eight years out of eight, they predicted substantially faster economic growth than the nation experienced.

You'd think that the election year just past would have boosted the National Humility Index a little. We discovered that most talking heads were talking nonsense. Highly paid pundits wrote reams of what turned out to be rubbish. An entire industry, public opinion surveying, is in crisis after its readings turned out to be grossly inaccurate and based more on flawed assumptions than statistically valid methodology.

There are worse forms of hubris than overconfident forecasting. History is replete with the cruel arrogance of those who believed they had the genius to reorder society and the lives of their fellow humans. In their most benign and well-intentioned form, they produced short-lived failures like the New Harmony colony here in Indiana. But this same proud presumption also gave rise to the worst monsters of history, the totalitarians of the last century who murdered millions in the unshakable belief that it was their right to tell others how to live, even to reshape human nature itself.

I bother you with all this because life will soon invite you to overindulge the pride you justifiably feel today. Few, if any of you, were raised to see yourselves as an aristocrat, but in a real sense that is what you now are. Today's aristocracy is of a new and very different type. It's based not on title or land or inherited wealth, but on intellect and learning. The kind that claims almost all the best jobs in our economy; the kind that, in fact, puts less-educated folks out of work. The kind that made a handful of kids at Snapchat richer in their 20s than George Eastman was when Eastman Kodak dominated the photographic world and employed a quarter million workers.

Some of you will invent the next round of productive tools that will eliminate somebody's job. That's progress, and it's inevitable. But will others of you create new businesses with new opportunities for those displaced? Or new ways of learning that enable them to find new work, and with it the dignity that comes only from earning one's own success?

Just as important, will you recognize that your degree doesn't mean that you know what's best for those without one? Or that, even if you did, it's not your right to make the decisions of life for them? A lot of damage has been done by people who, in their well-educated superiority, saw those around them not as creatures of dignity but as objects of therapy.

Too much pride may annoy those around you, but what's worse is the growth it can prevent within you. When you're too self-assured to accept the greater wisdom of others, you deny yourself a lot of continuing education. Lord Maynard

Keynes's economic theories haven't worked out too well, but I've always admired his rule: "When I find I'm wrong, I change my mind. What do you do?" The stubborn refusal to admit a mistake and absorb its lessons can be the biggest mistake of all. I have never found "oops" a difficult word to say, and what follows saying it is often a great learning opportunity.

At one especially low moment, when I felt I had let down a cause and in fact a president of the United States, then secretary of commerce Malcolm Baldrige snapped me out of it with some simple but sage advice: "Good judgment comes from experience; experience comes from bad judgment." Don't be too proud to face up to your goofs and improve your future judgment.

Starting when you leave campus today, it will become all too natural for you to slip into your new status in the knowledge elite and to drift away from the millions of your contemporaries who didn't make it to Purdue or someplace of comparable opportunity. You'll likely work with people much like yourself; socialize with them; one day probably marry someone similarly well-educated. Without meaning to or even thinking about it, you may find yourself living in a social class apart from far too many of your fellow citizens. That will disserve them and limit you. Try not to let it happen.

There's one good reason I doubt that you will. It's because you attended this particular university. Because, just as high achievement is a Purdue hallmark, so is humility. Maybe it's in the DNA so many Boilermakers arrive with, from families that taught them all this years ago. Or maybe, as our biologists might say, it's epigenetic, a trait their time at Purdue helped embed in their characters.

All I know is that, over and over, your greatest predecessors have been as authentically humble as they were accomplished. Captain Chesley Sullenberger, awash in adulation for his piloting skills that saved 155 lives, subject of a movie bearing his name, has yet to utter a conceited word. Neil Armstrong, in an elevator with an oblivious, starstruck matron who was telling everyone around her that the famous astronaut was staying in their hotel, got off without ever identifying himself. The father of Purdue computer science, Dr. Alan Perlis, famous for his "Perlisisms," used to say, "In programming, as in everything else, to be in error is to be reborn."

It's not just the old-timers. The ethic of humility is alive today. Akshay Kothari, who created the news scan company Pulse and sold it to LinkedIn for $90 million, now runs LinkedIn's 750-person affiliate in India, at the ripe old age of 30. When asked by our Indian alumni newsletter for one piece of advice for today's students, he said—can you guess?—"Stay humble." Maybe I should have just quoted Akshay and sat down.

Class of 2017, I've been waiting for you and this day. You were the first class I welcomed to campus after taking up my official duties at Purdue. I hope you don't mind that I think of you as my classmates. I just know you are bound for exciting places, great achievements, thrilling moments. And that, when those moments come, you will meet them with the quiet grace the world has come to associate with the word "Boilermaker."

Oh, in case I forgot to mention it: we're so very, very proud of you.

Hail Purdue, and each of you.

 Tribalism
May 2018

"Life in a tribe is easy, in all the wrong ways. You don't have to think. Whatever the tribe thinks is right; whatever the other side thinks is wrong. There's no real responsibility; just follow what the tribe, and whoever speaks for it, says to do. Boilermakers aren't made for tribes."

I look forward all year to this moment and this view. No sight all year comes close. All these excited, beaming faces, each realizing that a new world of freedom and opportunity is about to open. Congratulations, parents, on that last tuition check.

And to our graduates to be, the stars of our show today, we extend the same, on this day of validation. Around the nation today, too many diplomas are being handed to your peers by institutions where, studies tell us, little was expected or demanded of them. Soon many of those graduates will be "mugged by reality" as employers inform them that they are not adequately prepared for the roles and the jobs they expected to take up.

Not here. Each year's data, and the constant feedback from the enterprises who welcome Boilers into their ranks, confirms that the hard work of a Purdue education is worth all the effort. That you are more than ready for the challenges ahead.

"Challenges" is one of those commencement clichés, but that doesn't mean it doesn't fit the occasion. In great research centers like Purdue we talk a lot about "grand challenges," and properly so. Conquering disease, world hunger; managing whatever climatic changes are on their way; continuing the breathtaking ascent from poverty that the world has achieved even in your short lifetimes—all these will provide many of you thrilling careers and opportunities for deeply rewarding service. And that's just the beginning of the challenges you'll confront.

Beyond these material hurdles lie moral and ethical questions the likes of which, and the rapid onset of which, humanity has never had to deal with. When we can genetically engineer perfect children, should we? When wealthy adults can radically enhance their own mental abilities and life spans well beyond those less fortunate, should we let them? If and when robots, and a dwindling fraction of technologically gifted workers, are producing the majority of all the value and wealth in society, what will become of those who appear unnecessary? Will they be treated with respect, or as helpless dependents? If the latter, will the productive minority decide, as some have already begun to speculate, that the others no longer deserve an equal say in the society's decisions? There will be dozens more such mind-bending dilemmas.

I don't fear the inability of a world led by new leaders like you to overcome even our most daunting scientific and material problems. Again and again, the pessimists and doomsayers have been proven wrong by the unexpected, unpredictable power of human ingenuity.

I don't even doubt your generation's capacity to work through the tortuous ethical issues that astonishing technological breakthroughs are forcing on the world. Every day I see in Purdue students the innate decency and the ability to wrestle with complexity that it will take to work through these problems.

Instead, I believe the biggest challenge you may face lies elsewhere. It will involve the repair and renewal of trust among ourselves as a people, and trust in the free institutions that alone can protect and nurture individual human dignity. If ever a challenge was grand, this one is.

The last few Mays, I've found myself issuing the same caution to each departing class. I've pointed out that, although you don't think of yourselves this way and I hope never will, you are now aristocrats, members of a privileged elite. It's not the kind we've known through history. It's not based on a family name, or inherited wealth, or a father's position in some ruling totalitarian party. It's the new aristocracy of a knowledge economy, with membership conferred by unusual cognitive skills, augmented by a superior education like Purdue's.

I've noted that the people I'm describing have begun to cluster together—to work with each other, live near each other, socialize with each other, marry each other, have children just like each other's children, starting the cycle over again. And unintentionally to segregate from their less blessed, less well-educated fellow citizens. I've urged each set of graduates to resist this tendency, to make special efforts to connect with those who never made it to Purdue or a place like it. It's a shame to go through life with a narrow range of human interactions, and all one can learn from those who are different.

But over these last few years this new self-segregation has taken on a much more worrisome dimension. It's no longer just a matter of Americans not knowing and understanding each other. We've seen these clusters deepen, and harden, until separation has led to anger, misunderstanding turned into hostility. At the individual level, it's a formula for bitterness and negativity. For a self-governing people, it's poison. The grandest challenge for your leadership years may well be to reverse and surmount this threat.

Over your final year with us, people have begun to use the word "tribalism" to describe this phenomenon. To people who have only known freedom and self-government, it's easy to forget that tribalism was the way of the world for most of history. Anthropologists long ago discovered that our humanoid ancestors formed tribes for survival and responded violently to the presence of outsiders. As one essayist wrote, "Tribalism . . . is the default human experience. . . . The notion of living alongside people who do not look like us and treating them as our fellows was meaningless for most of human history."

Suddenly, or so it seems, this nation has divided into tribes, made up of people with very different views of true and false, right and wrong. They seem deeply alienated from each other, and deeply distrustful.

Pollsters have even begun to use the term "hatred" to describe the degree of estrangement. They tell us that members of both tribes tend to belong mostly because of their animosity to the other side. In almost reciprocal numbers, they describe the other side as "closed-minded," "dishonest," "unintelligent," even "immoral."

As we trust each other less, trust in the institutions of our society has eroded in parallel. Almost no sector—government, business, the media, higher education—has escaped a steep drop in public confidence. Some constant vigilance and skepticism about centers of authority is a healthy, all-American instinct. But ultimately, to function effectively as a free and self-governing people, we must maintain some degree of faith that our institutions and those leading them have our best interests at heart and are performing their duties with sincerity and integrity. And today, we plainly lack such faith.

There are plenty of culprits here, starting with too many who have misused positions of authority. The so-called social media—I have come to think of it as "antisocial media"—enables and encourages hostility from the insulated enclave of a smartphone or a laptop. People say things to and about each other that they would never say face-to-face, or maybe even think, if they knew each other personally.

Our various modern media lead us to, and feed us from, information sources that reinforce our existing biases. They put us in contact with other tribe members, but rarely those who see things differently. We're starting to resemble ominously our primitive forbearers, trusting no one outside the tribe.

That's a very dangerous development. The freedoms we take for granted, the "blessings of liberty" of which our Constitution speaks, are the gross exception in history. Almost all of history has belonged to the tyrants, the warlords, the autocrats, the totalitarians. And tribes always gravitate toward tyrants.

Here's why I'm still an optimist, and here's where you come in. In addition to all the professional and career achievements I know await you, and the great personal and family lives I'm confident you will build, Boilermakers as a group are exactly the kind of citizens this fractured, hostile, tribal country needs to heal and repair itself. The best way to do it is to take a piece of Purdue with you.

Here, you have lived in daily close contact with people of all faces, races, and places. If you kept your ears open, you heard viewpoints very different from your own, in an environment that safeguards the right for every such viewpoint to be heard. You heard arguments that made sense, and some that were absurd. And you became better at telling which was which. And, no matter how addicted you were to your smartphone, you experienced the fulfillment that only life in a genuine community can furnish.

Before you know it, you'll be a big part of one of those institutions people today say they can't trust. You'll be running a business, writing the news stories, maybe making public decisions that have a big effect on the lives of others. We look to you to do so with the integrity of the Purdue Honor Code you created during your years here. To set examples that promote confidence, not cynicism. To excel not only in your competence but even more so in your character. And to live your personal and vocational lives without becoming trapped in any echo chamber, drifting into any tribe. To not merely sympathize but to actively empathize with your fellow citizens, and the values they hold dear. Just the way I have witnessed you treating each other during your time in this special community.

Wherever you're headed, you can be a part of reawakening that sense of community among those you meet and live among. It's not just our civil engineers we need to be bridge builders; every Boilermaker can build bridges to those who lead different lives. Bridges between those who today reside on opposite banks of our cultural ravine.

Barring a man-made cataclysm, you are destined to live to an age unimaginable until the last couple of decades. Medical science and unprecedented wealth will see to that. I'm excited for you. But when I bring up your life expectancy, I'm not referring to longevity. I'm talking about what we expect of you as citizens.

Just as Purdue has expected more from you than another school might have, so does democracy. To survive and succeed, it requires its members to know its workings; participate in its operations; accept the reality of each other's different outlooks, and the need to reconcile them by meeting in the middle.

Life in a tribe is easy, in all the wrong ways. You don't have to think. Whatever the tribe thinks is right; whatever the other side thinks is wrong. There's no real responsibility; just follow what the tribe, and whoever speaks for it, says to do. Boilermakers aren't made for tribes.

Renewing the covenants and the confidence of a free society is a lot to load on you on the first day of your new life. I recognize that you have a few things to attend to first. But, if our democracy is to be rejuvenated, I believe it is the younger generations who will pull it off. Your elders have had their chance, and most are too dug in to change.

Like Purdue grads before you, you won't be just talkers, you'll be makers—of new products, services, companies, opportunity for others. Look for chances to be peacemakers now and then along the way.

A friend once told me about watching his 8-year-old son play a Little League game. When he arrived, the scoreboard behind him in right field read 14–0 against his team, but Robbie had the biggest smile on his face. He yelled, "Robbie, how can you look so happy?" The boy hollered back, "No worries, Dad, we haven't been up to bat yet!"

You haven't been to life's home plate yet, but you're in the on-deck circle. The bases are loaded with opportunities. To continue the stunning growth of knowledge and global wealth; to tackle successfully the grand challenges facing our nation and world; and to breathe new life into the greatest system ever devised for promoting human dignity, prosperity, and happiness.

Our first wish, of course, is for your own happiness. It's been said we are given memory so we can have roses in December. I trust your years here were full of memorable roses. But I hope they are just the first of many more you will plant—for yourselves and your loved ones, and for an American society in need

of Boilermakers to make the wealth, the moral choices, and the rebuilt civic life
this great nation deserves.

Hail Purdue, and each of you.

Grit
May 2019

"... in the world you're about to enter, emotional strength, in the
form people are now terming 'resilience' or 'grit,' will be essential for
you to realize the enormous potential we see in you. For those who
possess and display it, it will be a competitive advantage in any endeavor they pursue."

Here we are again. My favorite moment of the year. It's a genuine day of dreams:
In the student section, dreams of new careers, marriage, children, new adventures.
In the parents' seating, dreams of what to do with that disposable income they're
no longer sending to West Lafayette. All in all, a day like no other.

My own dreams about today are more like nightmares. What to say that's fitting—that's meaningful but still concise enough to get us on to the main event
quickly? Hardest of all, What to say that's the least bit original?

While dreaming, or daydreaming, about today, I found myself thinking about
Purdue Pete. Again this year, Pete was ranked among the most identified college
mascots in the country, and the favorite in our Big Ten Conference.

A few years before your class arrived on campus, someone tried to redo Pete
and turn him into some new symbol of our school. I wasn't here, either, but as
told to me, the idea started an immediate backlash, a near-riot, and died within
days. I got to thinking about why.

Maybe part of it was his uniqueness. At last count, there were sixty-four ea-
gles, forty-six tigers, and thirty-three wildcats among college mascots. There's
only one set of Boilermakers.

But I think our attachment to Pete stems mainly from the way he personifies
our self-image of strength. When our up-and-coming football program chose
its slogan for this year, it was "Only the Strong." One of the year's YouTube sen-
sations featured a five-foot-nine Purdue player squatting 600 pounds.

Strength is a big part of the Boilermaker mystique. And it comes in forms
even more important than the physical strength of our terrific athletes or those of

you I see at the CoRec and our intramural fields. Purdue has always been known for sending into the world young men and women who are strong and ready in all the ways that matter in adult life. That's never been more important, or a bigger advantage, than right now.

By making it to this hall today, you have proven that you are strong intellectually. Your university has never believed in participation trophies. Your parents can rest assured that, in the words of a long-ago commercial they will remember, you got your diploma the old-fashioned way. You earned it.

I can testify that you are strong in character. In each of your years here, our campus was rated among the safest in the country, in large part because of fewer incidents of student misconduct. Each year on our big event weekends, police calls here are a small fraction of those at nearby universities of similar size. Naming no names.

You have not just behaved well yourselves, you have demanded it of others. Bystander actions and reports that prevent harm to other students have risen sharply in recent years.

And your heart for others is truly inspiring. We watch with admiration your dance marathons and countless other charity projects demonstrating the ethic of service and selflessness that we associate with great character.

But there's even more to strength than muscle, smarts, and character. For the last few years, the air has been filled with studies, surveys, and books reporting a growing "fragility" among American young people, a decreasing capability to handle even modest stress or setbacks without seeking some sort of adult assistance. The number of college students requesting counseling or therapy has doubled in just four or five years.

Experts offer various explanations for this surge. Clearly more perceptive diagnosis of real mental illness is a factor, and a highly positive one. It seems just yesterday when, working in the business that brought the world the first highly safe and effective antidepressant, I took part in a huge worldwide effort to destigmatize depression, schizophrenia, and related illnesses. We must and will do all we can to find those among us who suffer from these soul-searing, treatable diseases and bring them effective help.

But, the data say, something broader is going on. As one scholar has written, there has been an increase in diagnosable mental health problems, but also a decrease in the ability of many young people to manage the everyday bumps in the road of life.

At other places, but I'm happy to say not yet at Purdue, students have demanded to be kept "safe" from speech—that is, mere words—that challenges or discomfits them. At one large university, one "study" purported to find a quarter of the student body suffering from PTSD because of an election outcome. Referring to such young people, someone has coined the distasteful but descriptive term "snowflakes."

Some find a cause in the social media, which have reduced personal interaction among your younger contemporaries. Easier grading in high schools can lead to an unexpected jolt when a student arrives at college, at least if it's a place like Purdue where top grades are still hard to come by. Another diagnosis points to overprotective parenting that limits children's opportunities to play and explore in unsupervised ways that require them to solve problems and resolve conflicts on their own.

I don't pretend to know what's causing the phenomenon. I do know that in the world you're about to enter, emotional strength, in the form people are now terming "resilience" or "grit," will be essential for you to realize the enormous potential we see in you. For those who possess and display it, it will be a competitive advantage in any endeavor they pursue. After watching you these last few years, I'm betting you'll be in that category.

You're about to hear a fine student response at the end of today's program. (I know that because I get a sneak peek at those remarks.) But I wish you could also have heard the two talks given at last December's winter commencements.

Jordan Cebulla told of being a poor student in high school here locally who almost abandoned any idea of higher education. But, told by a family friend that Lafayette is "a gritty town full of gritty people," he gave Ivy Tech a try. Four years later, he is a Purdue alum. He told his classmates, "In the end, if we quit on ourselves, everyone else will quit on us, too."

In his response speech, Seon Shoopman confided that, out of the sixteen schools he applied to, Purdue was the only one to admit him, provided he attend our summer boot camp. Three and a half years later, he, too, earned his Purdue degree, with honors, becoming the first in his family to graduate from college. Seon said that, more than any other motive, he wanted to do it for the mother who had pushed him all the way: "When I wanted to quit, she told me not to. When I wanted to leave school, she told me not to. She told me to fight, be strong, and make something of myself."

Some in today's world think they have discovered something new in the concept of grit. A Harvard Business School article just last fall was titled "Organizational Grit" and reported that "high achievers have extraordinary stamina.... When easier paths beckon, their commitment is steadfast. Grit predicts who will accomplish challenging goals." So that's why a Harvard MBA costs $200 grand.

Maybe this is all revelatory at Harvard. In our part of the country, it's not news. The slogan of the Whiteland (Indiana) High School Class of 1930 was "Grit Wins." It could be a slogan at Purdue every year. I'm tempted to call *Roget's Thesaurus* and let them know the antonym of "snowflake" is "Boilermaker."

Just as physical strength is built through hard exercise, emotional fortitude is enhanced by adversity and conflict. Every great achievement requires a confrontation with stress, a conquest of fear. Our engineers know: there is no traction without friction. Wilbur Wright, the father of the aviation world Purdue now leads, wrote, "No bird soars in a calm." Your strength of intellect and character will give you opportunities to lead, but it will be your strength of purpose, your resilience, your grit that will enable you to lead successfully, and by your example to give new heart and strength to those around you.

There's one sure way to minimize stress and difficulty in life: attempt nothing that's bold, challenge nothing that's wrong, risk nothing that's dangerous. Those endeavors always bring disappointment, frustration, criticism, setbacks. But they also are the source of the achievements that make life fulfilling, and the even greater grit that will get you ready for the next challenge.

From opposite ends of life's continuum, I offer you two closing examples of the qualities I hope you have built here at this institution. Both stories involve Purdue students even younger than you are today.

Last December, we said goodbye to a great man. A great man, but a typical Boilermaker. In his 94 years, Fred Fehsenfeld built a series of businesses that employed and enriched thousands of people around Indiana and the world. A model for what we now call lifelong learning, he was always on top of the latest technology, always conceiving large new projects and looking far into a future he could not possibly live to see. And modest about his achievements every step of the way.

He almost didn't get the chance to do any of that. On his 18th birthday, in 1942, he left his freshman dorm room in Cary Hall and enlisted in the Army. He flew eighty-six missions over Europe with a storied unit in which almost half his fellow pilots were killed in action.

In an oral history of his experiences, Fred told of his first close-air dogfight combat. He was low to the ground, with bullets everywhere, and death perhaps an instant away. The interviewer asked, "What were you thinking at a moment like that?" Fred answered, "I was thinking, I finally got a chance to make some German pay for yanking me out of Purdue University." He survived the war, came back, still younger than most of you, to finish his ME degree and lead a life of epic accomplishment.

Long after you leave us, your senior year will be remembered as the year of Tyler Trent. His is a story I need not recount; everyone here knows who he was, and how he faced a situation for which words like "adversity" and "stress" don't come close. He impacted more people, and left deeper footprints, than most who will enjoy lives several times longer than his. We'll never forget you, Tyler.

God willing, none of you will face at any age the kind of dangers and fears that Fred and Tyler did. But they, and so many others like them, have left us all a legacy that provides perspective and proportion for those inevitable moments when the pressures and disappointments of life get us down.

Don't misunderstand this, but I wish for you many such tough moments. You can easily avoid them. Just lead a safely inconsequential life: run no risks, confront no injustice, accept no roles of leadership. But that's not the path we expect you to choose. You are about to become graduates of Purdue University, which throughout its history has supplied leaders to a world that needs them now as rarely before.

Leaders with the academic preparation to solve mind-bending technological challenges. With the moral character to help society navigate times of blurringly fast change, in ways that are ethical, equitable, and humanistic. Most of all, with the inner strength to take on the burdens of high responsibility, and the heat, envy, and hostility that comes with them, and deliver the positive change that human progress requires.

You showed the quality of grit before you arrived here. That's why we admitted you. I hope that your days here, with a faculty that pushed and stretched you, and classmates like Jordan and Seon to inspire you, built your reserves of resilience.

Now take the strength you brought here, and the new strength I trust you built here, into a world where the need and, therefore, the opportunities, for real leadership are enormous. Seek out the hard jobs and the toughest problems. When you find them, or they find you, think of Fred and Tyler, maybe even Pete. And you'll make yourself, your family, and your university proud of you, as Boilermakers have for a century and a half.

Hail Purdue, and each of you.

Connection
Delivered virtually, May 2020

 Commencement preparation

 Commencement address

"For most of human history, personal contact was hard to avoid.
Suddenly, our digital age can mean it requires extra effort."

Introduction

I never expected this. To be addressing you with me in an empty hall, and you far away. Wherever you're viewing this virtual ceremony, I hope you are surrounded by people you love, people who helped you reach this moment of achievement.

As is my practice, I wrote a commencement speech over last Christmas, at a time when COVID-19 had only recently gotten its name. I chose a theme without any clue what was coming. In a different year, I might have felt obliged to start over. But as things have unfolded, the events of recent months have in some ways made my chosen topic seem at least as relevant as the day I wrote it.

Our thoughts today should not be dominated and consumed by temporary troubles. Like all such things, this too shall pass. Today is about what you've accomplished these last few years, and all you'll do in the decades ahead. So here are some thoughts about that future; I hope you find they fit the occasion.

Commencement remarks

Welcome, graduates and friends, to this day of celebration. Those of you in the caps and gowns are gathered to celebrate the great accomplishment that is a degree from Purdue University. Meanwhile, your parents are, I know, quietly celebrating the clearing of the final tuition check. Congratulations to you all.

Purdue celebrated its own landmark this year, our 150th anniversary. Since it coincided with the 50th anniversary of the moon landing, by our most famous alumnus, Neil Armstrong, stories were abundant. My favorite claim is that, later in life, Commander Armstrong took to telling corny, lame jokes about the moon, and when nobody laughed he would say, "Well, I guess you had to be there."

A year or so ago, a major national journalist visited our campus and later wrote a gracious, complimentary article about what he saw here. While I enjoyed his accounts of the progress and successful results he thought he had witnessed, my favorite part of the column was a single phrase, basically a throwaway line. He described Purdue as "a happy place."

That got me wondering how many college campuses these days would strike a visitor quite that way. I hope it's been that kind of place for you. We know you've worked hard and fought through a lot of pressure. You'll probably remember that; just wait for those scary dreams where you haven't studied for the test or can't find the exam room. But I hope that, among your memories of these years, "I was happy there" is prominent among them.

I've reflected on that more and more during your last couple of years with us.

Your parents love you and are proud of you, but from time to time they also must worry about you. That's what we parents do. I hope it's okay if I worry about you and your futures a little also. I've sometimes used these commencements to fret out loud about trends that trouble me in that big wide world you're about to enter.

In recent years, I've spoken about the tribalism that now divides Americans. I've talked about the seeming shortage of emotional resilience and grit in your peer group. Twice, I've found myself urging graduates to guard against the so-called Big Sort, the tendency for young people of your quality and educational attainment to cluster together professionally and socially and to drift apart from those of different backgrounds.

But one thing I never expected to worry about, but now do a little, is your being lonely. I have known you and met thousands of you personally in an environment that, despite our size, does a pretty good job of getting people together, creating bonds among them. A thousand clubs. Dozens of faith-based organizations. Our Greek system. And, maybe our best examples of true communities, our co-op residential houses, where students not only live but cook, clean, and do repairs together. And, most recently, the learning communities, where thousands of Boilermakers live in mutual support with others who are studying the same subject matter.

But elsewhere, the academic journals and lay periodicals are now filled with research about the epidemic of loneliness in our society. Surveys report record numbers of Americans living alone and suffering from strong feelings of isolation. Many view it as a new public health crisis, linked to rising rates of depression, anxiety, even suicide. A lack of strong social relationships has been found to raise the risk of premature death by 50%. That's as bad for you as smoking fifteen cigarettes a day. It's not just an American phenomenon. The government of

Britain has appointed a minister for loneliness. All this was before anyone heard of COVID-19.

Most startling, and alarming, are studies finding that the worst loneliness today is not among adults or the elderly but in your age group. Astonishing percentages of today's young people say they have few if any close friends. Dating and other traditional forms of youthful interaction have declined sharply. The University of Southern California recently named a director of belonging and, while the title may be unique, I'm sure the idea is not.

Humans are social creatures or, as is sometimes said, relational beings. The ability to interact, communicate, and collaborate is what defines us and what assured our evolution as the dominant, civilizing species on this planet. We thrive on contact with others; we suffer severely from its absence. The worst punishment we impose on a heinous criminal is solitary confinement; much of our literature and religious tradition thinks of hell as a state of total, permanent aloneness.

So an outbreak of loneliness is worth worrying about, especially where those with the longest to live are a big part of it. In the case of your elders, sociologists can identify some obvious causes. Plummeting birthrates play a role: having fewer children and fewer siblings limits the opportunity for caring contact. In a short two decades, the percentage of retirement-age citizens living within ten miles of their children, in the same neighborhood with any relative, or having a good friend living nearby dropped by double digits. It's easy to see how that leads to greater loneliness.

But particularly in the case of your age cohort, there is no doubt that the sudden eruption and dominance of what we call social media—I often think "anti-social media" would be a better term—has played a huge role. Some scholars put all the blame there. One major article was titled "Have Smartphones Destroyed a Generation?"

It wasn't supposed to be this way. The original promise of all the Facebooks and Twitters was that they would connect us in wonderful new ways. But connection over a text message or what is often a glamorized presentation of one's daily life just isn't the same as in person contact. In fact, it often turns out to separate and alienate its users more than it brings them together.

I remain concerned that, as members of the new knowledge aristocracy, absent a little special effort you will rarely make friends different from yourselves. Now, studying the growing evidence about isolation, I'm concerned that you, the first age group raised entirely in the iPhone era, won't make many friends at all.

In my own college days, a briefly famous Harvard professor offered probably the worst advice ever given to a younger generation. Encouraging both drug
use and a nonproductive lifestyle, Dr. Timothy Leary suggested, "Turn on, tune
in, drop out." Lately, I've been thinking the best advice one could give you, tomorrow's leaders, might be the exact opposite: "Turn off, tune out, drop in." As
in turn off the phone more often, tune out the video screen, drop in personally
on friends old and new.

For most of human history, personal contact was hard to avoid. Suddenly, our
digital age can mean it requires extra effort.

Confession being good for the soul, it's only right that I make one here. I am
not a good role model for the advice I am foisting on you. I have not devoted the
time I should have to deepen acquaintances into true friendships, or to stay in
closer touch with the old friends I do have.

I've let the call of work get in the way. I've told myself that jobs of broad responsibility mean that one can't get too close to co-workers and colleagues. I've
procrastinated and rationalized, and skipped too many chances to spend meaningful time with people I admire and even love. I regret it, and I'm the worse for it.

You can do better. The same research that is documenting the loneliness epidemic reveals ways to immunize oneself against it. Geographic rootedness makes
a difference; people who live in the same community for extended periods are
far less likely to be lonely. The great C. S. Lewis wrote, "Friendship is the greatest of worldly goods ... the chief happiness of life. If I had to give a piece of advice to a young person about where to live, I think I should say, 'Sacrifice almost
everything to live near your friends.'"

Having a religious affiliation also correlates strongly with feelings of connect-
edness. And nothing statistically reduces the chance of loneliness more than marriage, especially marriage with children. It's a sermon for another Sunday, but I
do hope most of you will not miss the joy, and the lifelong education, of raising
children. I promise, it's life's greatest reward and the best graduate school you'll
ever attend.

I heard about one wise guy commencement speaker who instructed his audience, "Remember, in life it's not who you know. It's whom." I've thought of
that as just a joke, but in our new situation it takes on a more serious tone: a lot
of your success, and happiness, will depend on whom you know, and know well.

The author Gore Vidal once said, "We never know when we are happy, only
when we were." I hope in your case that proves way too cynical, that there will be

countless moments when you are truly happy and know it. But I also hope that, when you reflect back on times when you were happy, your days at this university will rank high among them. And when people ask you, "What was it about Purdue that made it such a great place for you?" you can just answer, "Well, I guess you had to be there."

I know great achievements lie ahead for you. My wish for you is that so do great friendships.

Hail Purdue, and each of you.

 Risk
May 2021

"...the biggest risk of all is that we stop taking risks at all."

This year, when I say I am happy to be here, I'm not just making small talk. If you're like me, you're happy to be anywhere after the year we've all been through. I wish we were over in Elliott Hall, celebrating your achievements individually as only Purdue does among schools our size. But this beats the virtual version we were forced to in 2020 and marks a long step back on the path to fully normal life.

As we've never done an outdoor commencement before, we may have gotten a few things wrong. For one thing, way out here on the fifty-yard line, it feels like we've carried that social distance thing a little far. However well it goes, like everything about your senior year, it will be one for the history books. For all the trouble and downsides, there can be some real value in living through a time like that.

For decades to come, scholars and ordinary citizens alike will look back on your senior year, trying to identify its consequences and imagine what lives so disrupted were like. As they do so, they will know more than we can now about the results of the choices today's leaders made. They will reach judgments, with the benefit of hindsight, about the wisdom and maturity with which our nation handled the challenge of this particular pandemic. Odds are, not all those judgments will be favorable. Time will tell.

An ability to comprehend and work with complex facts and data has always been part of a Purdue education. At least since the industrial age, that's been an essential tool for a useful life of the kind at which Boilermakers excel.

But that's never been nearly so true as today. Massive amounts of information are being collected, intentionally by us and silently by the machines we invent and use in daily life. Interpreting its meaning, and discovering patterns within it, is perhaps the most important skill in the economy of 2021. Our faculty has determined that data analysis, as we now call it, should be as universal a part of a Boilermaker education as English composition.

You'll leave this stadium able to evaluate statistics and whether they are significant or meaningless. You'll know better than to confuse correlation with causation. You'll look at decisions critically, and holistically, understanding that any objective pursued too far eventually yields diminishing returns not worth their cost. That, just as medicines have side effects, almost all actions produce collateral consequences, often collateral damage.

It doesn't stretch a point to say that we wouldn't be meeting here today without those skills. Keeping Purdue open last fall, so that you could stay on schedule and graduate today, required the daily examination of COVID-19 infection rates and patterns of its spread on and around campus. Prior to that, the decision to reopen at all involved a reading of the available data, which showed that people your age were at far less risk from the virus than from a host of other dangers.

Starting soon, the decisions will be yours to make. In businesses you start or join, in causes in which you feel called to enlist, or in that most important of all organizations, the families I hope you will form. Wherever they are, the very essence of your coming leadership roles will lie in making hard choices. After weighing all the options, the competing priorities, and the uncertainties that even the biggest databases cannot totally eliminate, others will look to you to choose.

The risk of failure, of a hit to one's reputation, or just that the gains don't outweigh the costs, all these can deter or even paralyze a person out of fulfilling the responsibility someone has entrusted to them. Should I make this investment, or husband my cash? Take that job offer, or stay where I'm comfortable? Engage in this debate, or sit silently? Choose this life partner, or play it safe?

This last year, many of your elders failed this fundamental test of leadership. They let their understandable human fear of uncertainty overcome their duty to balance all the interests for which they were responsible. They hid behind the advice of experts in one field but ignored the warnings of experts in other realms that they might do harm beyond the good they hoped to accomplish.

Sometimes they let what might be termed the mad pursuit of zero, in this case zero risk of anyone contracting the virus, block out other competing concerns, like the protection of mental health, the educational needs of small children, or the survival of small businesses. Pursuing one goal to the utter exclusion of all others is not to make a choice but to run from it. It's not leadership; it's abdication. I feel confident your Purdue preparation won't let you fall prey to it.

But there's a companion quality you'll need to be the leaders you can be. That's the willingness to take risks. Not reckless ones, but the risks that still remain after all the evidence has been considered.

Great societies before us tended to look backward for their inspiration, to locate their golden ages in the past. Here our eyes have always been forward. Now signs abound of Americans losing that eagerness to move ahead boldly.

Before the virus visited us, there were already troubling signs that fearfulness was beginning to erode the spirit of adventure, the willingness to take considered risks, on which this nation's greatness was built and from which all progress originates. Rates of business startups, moving in pursuit of a better job, or the strongest of all bets on the future, having children, all have fallen sharply in recent years. And now there are warnings that the year 2020 may have weakened that spirit further.

As early as April of last year, researchers at the Federal Reserve of St. Louis documented the "belief-scarring effects" of COVID-19. Psychologists proved a long time ago that we humans tend to overestimate how common terrible events are. Because they are terrible, we are more sure to hear about them, and we trick ourselves into believing that they are far more likely than they really are.

Now we learn that such misconceptions can be long-lasting. The scarring effect is, the Fed's economists tell us, "a persistent change in beliefs about the probability of an extreme, negative shock producing . . . long-lived responses to transitory events, especially extreme, unlikely ones."

Fortunately, Boilermakers don't scar easily. If Amelia Earhart had been intimidated by uncertainty, we wouldn't know her name. If our recent board chair Keith Krach had stayed within the safe confines of a giant corporation's career ladder, the world would not enjoy the huge efficiency breakthroughs of Ariba and Docusign. If Neil Armstrong, Gus Grissom, and more than a score more Purdue astronauts had run from risk, humanity's knowledge of its universe would be far short of its current boundaries.

In the most jarring book of recent years, the Israeli philosopher Yuval Harari predicts that humans your age will live to see the "last days of death," when the species we call *Homo sapiens* becomes "godlings" and immortal. He sees this happening through one of the same technologies at which this university ex-cels: either biological engineering, or cyborg engineering, of our organic beings, or simply the complete replacement of humans by super-intelligent machines.

Immortality sounds good, until Harari points out the implications. One of them would be a total aversion to risk. As the author explains it, if you believe you can live forever, why would you ever take a chance of any kind?

I hope that the experiences of 2020 left you with an attitude not of fearfulness but of confidence. Confidence that we can tackle hard problems, and that hiding from them is rarely the best course. That given a careful examination of the avail-able facts and a thoughtful calculation of relative risks, we can overcome even the biggest obstacles and be the masters of our fates and our futures.

As school started again at her campus, the provost of the University of Kansas sent a message to her students and colleagues that is relevant far beyond the present day or the recent pandemic. "In times of high anxiety," she wrote, "it is human nature to crave certainty for the safety it provides. The problem with craving certainty is that it is a false hope; it is a craving that can never fully be met." She quoted the astronomer Carl Sagan: "The history of science teaches us that the most we can hope for is successive improvement in our understand-ing, learning from our mistakes . . . with the proviso that absolute certainty will always elude us."

Maybe the great historian Jacques Barzun summed it up best: "The last de-gree of caution is cowardice."

Certainty is an illusion. Perfect safety is a mirage. Zero is always unattain-able, except in the case of absolute zero where, as you remember, all motion and life itself stop.

You are leaving here ready for leadership. Your academic records say so. The history of Purdue graduates says so. The character you demonstrated this last year, when your embrace of the Purdue Pledge enabled this place to stay open at all, clearly says so.

We expect—no, we know—that you will tackle leadership's challenges as they present themselves to you. You're taking with you the tools to weigh alternatives, balance priorities, assess relative risks. All you'll need is the courage to act on the conclusions you reach.

Now take that readiness into a fearful, timid world crying for direction and boldness, where the biggest risk of all is that we stop taking risks at all.

Hail Purdue, and each of you.

You

May 2022

"Someone attempting to herd you into a group is someone with an agenda, and your personal well-being is not its main purpose."

Greetings, friends, and welcome. I should say welcome back. We are back in Elliott Hall, where Purdue spring commencements belong, for the first time in three years. And as I'll tell you in a few minutes, to me that matters beyond just the pleasure of returning to this beautiful, traditional venue.

Starting with my first delivery of these remarks a decade ago, I have ended them with the same signoff: "Hail Purdue, and each of you." It was just meant to be a little signature, a rhetorical device chosen as much for its cadence as for any deep meaning. But reflecting on this year's ceremony got me thinking that maybe there's more to it than what I've intended all these years.

Many talks on these occasions address themselves to "all you graduates" or "the Class of 20xx." I guess I've approached it that way some years. Today, I'm thinking more like those movie tough guys who ask, "You talkin' to me? You talkin' to me?" Today, I'll be talking to you, each of you, individually, or at least I'll be trying to.

A friend told me of a commencement he attended where the speaker, to inject a little levity, advised the graduates, "In life it's not who you know that counts. It's *whom*." (I assume at least the English majors in the crowd get it.) A funny line, but bad advice. It is *who* that counts. Not who you know, but who you *are*.

The further I go, the less I'm sure how to answer the question, "Who are you?" Where to start? I'm a Purdue employee, a happy husband, a father of four, a businessman, a former elected official, a Presbyterian elder, a history buff, and a mediocre golfer. Ancestry.com informs me that genetically I'm more Syrian and Lebanese than anything else, but I've got high percentages of Scotch, Welsh, and a dash of Italian mixed in.

And I'm a dog lover. I grew up in a family of them. We got all ours from the Humane Society, every one some sort of mixture. And every one was great: loyal, loving, a full member of the family. During those years, I adopted my mother's opinion that mutts are the best.

We'd all better hope Mom was right. Because we're all mutts here today. Hybrids, amalgams, crossbreeds, mongrels. Mutts. If you doubt that, go check with Ancestry.com.

There are no one-dimensional "yous." Every one of you, when you pause to think about it, can already name a list of qualities that make up "you." That list will keep growing as you leave here and launch into the fascinating and varied lives you are destined to lead. You'll keep learning, and growing, and adding new elements to your individuality. The more facets a diamond has, I'm told, the more brilliant it is; the same will be true for an ever more interesting and differentiated you. The one certainty is that there will be no exact copies, no one just like you, and therefore no one box anyone can stick you in.

But there will be people who want to take away your you. There always have been. The pharaohs, monarchs, and warlords of old, to whom other people were mere tools, to be used and discarded. In recent times, the proponents of all the "isms" that viewed people as helpless ciphers in some predetermined historical trend, or valueless instruments of an all-powerful state. In the worst cases, some people were grouped together and treated as subhuman, not deserving to exist at all.

These days, your individuality is challenged by some who seek to slap a label on you, to lump you into one category or another, and to assert that whatever you are, your choices have little to do with it. What matters is not what you think or do, they claim, but what group they have assigned you to. You're a prisoner of your genes, or of circumstance, or of some societal forces against which you are defenseless.

Such views may be cloaked in caring, sympathetic terms, but they are deeply disrespectful of those they affect to be supporting. They are a denial of your personal dignity, and ability, and willpower. Someone attempting to herd you into a group is someone with an agenda, and your personal well-being is not its main purpose.

Your experience, and success, at this institution should convince you not to listen to such disrespect. In a few moments, when you walk up here, it will be your individual achievement we are honoring, and only you know how much individual effort it took to get here.

He eventually gave Colts fans like me a thousand great memories, but never one I admired more than Peyton Manning's first action as a professional athlete. At the news conference announcing his multimillion-dollar contract, the 22-year-old Manning was asked, "What are you going to do with all that money?" He answered, "Earn it."

The degree you are about to receive is not being conferred on a group. We aren't awarding it to any club, team, or fraternity you happen to belong to. It's not because of your hairstyle, eye color, or because your parents went to Purdue. Nothing entitled you to it. It is yours, and yours alone, because the work that justifies it was yours. You earned it. You.

The years ahead will bring new, even more difficult threats to your "you-ness." The onrushing technologies of artificial intelligence will, some believe, supersede and devalue human intelligence and judgment. When the machines we have made, which can already beat any human in chess, or at reading x-rays, or at discovering new drugs, race vastly past our ability to reason or to perceive reality, where will that leave us—actuarially, I probably mean leave you—as individuals?

In an emergency, will tomorrow's pilots take the controls or defer to the computer? Will the surgeon trust her eyes and judgment or allow the robot to make the incision the algorithm has chosen? Will the president yield to the sensors that tell him to launch the missiles right now, before it's too late? At least one recent author asked if AI will be a tool, a partner, or a rival.

In everyday life, when you have all around you gizmos that make Alexa look like a kindergartener, will you still be using the intelligence and reasoning skills that got you here today? Or will you turn over your you to a dazzling device that, experts predict, will know you and your preferences before and better than you do. In other words, as the machines become more and more autonomous, will *you* still be?

One of today's eminent philosophers thinks not. He writes that when twenty-first-century technology "know[s] me far better than I know myself . . . individualism will collapse and authority will shift from individual humans to networked algorithms." Call me old-fashioned, but I don't like the sound of that.

Many of you are already contributing to the advance of these technological miracles, and thus to the problems they will bring with them. Heaven knows where your future innovations will take us. All of you will be involved in the answers because these changes and their challenges will be part of literally everyone's life.

The answers start with you. Somewhere I came across another commencement speech, given at another university by Purdue's own Neil Armstrong, less than a year after he walked on the moon. He quoted Aldous Huxley: "There's only one corner of the universe you can be sure of improving, and that's yourself." That chore will only get tougher in a world where the machines are smarter than their owners, where it becomes easy to let the machines make the decisions. Quoting the same book I just mentioned, "Reason alone may come to seem archaic." Some people may "let their capacities for independent reason and judgment atrophy."

Due to other technological miracles, your life expectancy will be decades greater than ours from earlier generations. But that's not the life expectancy that I think about at these commencements. Purdue expects more of you than a long life span. Purdue expects that you will take the best of what you absorbed here into a world that becomes better for your being in it. That you will prove that you are in charge of our technologies and not the other way around. That you will, with Commander Armstrong, constantly improve that little corner of the world that is you. That you will politely but resolutely decline to be labeled, stereotyped, or reduced to any one-dimensional version of the true you.

At the outset I said there was a larger reason I was so happy to be back in Elliott Hall. That's because, in here, over six separate ceremonies, Purdue still honors every graduate one by one. Most schools our size long ago went to batch processing, where degrees are conferred on groups, sometimes the entire class at once.

Here, we take a different view. No matter how big Purdue gets, we value each Boilermaker as an individual. That diploma we're about to hand you is yours and yours alone. Sure, you had help, and support, and I hope some valuable mentoring, but fundamentally you will be crossing this stage because of what you have accomplished. You.

So walk proudly. You are about to add another facet to the diamond that is you: graduate of Purdue University. It will be far from your last distinction, but I hope it will always be one that you value as highly as your university values you today.

Hail Purdue, and each of you.

PART V

Selected Media Interviews and Articles from the Daniels Decade

M Y PREVIOUS LIVES HAD INVOLVED MY FREQUENTLY BEING INTERVIEWED ON A WIDE range of national television programs, and many of those same reporters and programs continued to invite my comments on a variety of topics over my Purdue years.

The opportunity to capture millions of exposures for Purdue was too attractive to pass up, so I accepted most such offers. I often had to duck or demur when interviewers tried to lure me into areas I thought would cross the line into politics. I knew they were simply pursuing their professional duties, and almost always I think they understood that I was just trying to be equally faithful to mine.

C-SPAN's *Washington Journal*
September 2014

One of a series of interviews with university officials during a bus tour of the Big Ten Conference. Topics include the cost and value of higher education, Purdue's tuition freeze, and measuring the impact of college on career and life well-being.

PBS NewsHour
May 2014

An interview with PBS's Judy Woodruff on the measurement of college outcomes and the creation of the Gallup-Purdue Index.

National Public Radio
One university president's candid take on the future of higher ed.
July 2017

An interview with NPR's Anya Kamenetz on the creation of Purdue Global as a new and vital addition to Purdue's land-grant mission—serving adult learners who did not complete a degree in their first college enrollment.

Forbes
Mitch Daniels and the Purdue miracle: Lessons for the rest of us.
October 2017

Columnist Tom Lindsay examines Purdue's focus on affordability and the impact on student debt.

Bloomberg
Can Mitchonomics fix the broken business of higher ed?
December 2017

Columnist Romesh Ratnesar looks at how a focus on affordability has led Purdue to enrollment growth, a dramatic decrease in student debt, and increased graduation rates.

Fox News Channel's *Special Report with Bret Baier*
Mitch Daniels on big data and your privacy.
March 2018

An interview with Bret Baier on growing concerns about data privacy, the national debt, and opportunities for reforms in intercollegiate athletics

Wall Street Journal
College bloat meets "the blade."
December 2018

An interview with the *Journal*'s Tunku Varadarajan on reining in costs while expanding access to highest quality higher education.

PBS's *Firing Line*
December 2018

Margaret Hoover conducts a wide-ranging interview that includes topics of fiscal conservatism, entitlement reform, the tough choices facing our nation, and the road ahead for higher education.

Reason
Mitch Daniels is the president America should've had.
July 2018

An article by Peter Suderman on fiscal conservatism, the demands of national leadership, and accountability for results.

Forbes
Mitch Daniels: Revolutionizing Purdue's affordability while keeping a commitment to quality.
April 2019

A podcast with chairman and editor-in-chief Steve Forbes on the impact of the national crisis in high student debt, low graduation rates, and the impact on upward mobility.

Freakonomics Radio
The $1.5 trillion question: How to fix student loan debt?
May 2019

An interview with Stephen J. Dubner, co-author of the 2009 widely acclaimed book *Freakonomics*. Topics include the nation's burgeoning student loan debt, Purdue's solutions for its students, and what it all means for the future of higher education.

 CNN's *Smerconish*
Lessons to be learned? Purdue U.'s response to COVID-19.
December 2020

An interview with Michael Smerconish on the Protect Purdue measures that allowed students to study on campus safely and with low COVID transmission during the fall 2020 term.

 Fox Business's *Cavuto Coast to Coast with Neil Cavuto*
August 2021

An interview with Neil Cavuto to discuss COVID preparations for the fall 2021 semester, including voluntary vaccinations and the indoor mask mandate.

 Independent Institute
One of our few great college presidents retires.
July 2022

Richard Vedder, institute senior fellow and author of *Restoring the Promise: Higher Education in America*, writes a retrospective of the Daniels administration at Purdue.

Forbes
Nation's best college president is calling it quits.
June 2022

Fred Hess looks back fondly on the Daniels Decade at Purdue.

National Public Radio
Purdue's reputation for affordability results
in substantial growth for the school.
September 2022

An interview with NPR's Steve Inskeep on how Purdue bucked the national trend of declining college enrollments through its reputation for affordability.

Acknowledgments

FOR ANY PROJECT, GRATITUDE SHOULD BEGIN WITH THE ORIGINATOR OF THE IDEA. BUT in the case of this book, that credit must be shared with a number of people, including those mentioned below, who in one way or another suggested gathering the written and spoken pronouncements of the last ten years into some sort of accessible compilation.

So in addition to thanks for encouraging the endeavor, let me extend profound appreciation to:

Spencer Deery, who helped conceive topics for many of the speeches and columns, provided research and factual quality control, and critiqued near-final products.

Robin French, my executive assistant who, overhearing a discussion of the clumsiness and excessive length of reprinting the Lecture Series transcripts, produced the ingenious idea of presenting the actual videos in QR code form.

My old pals Neil Pickett and Mark Lubbers, who along with Spencer and Gina DelSanto, served as critical pre-readers of the newspaper columns, commencement speeches, and others of the written products.

Ethan Braden and the remarkably talented, national award-winning Purdue Marketing and Media team, who took charge of the design and packaging of the volume.

Director Justin Race; editorial, design, and production manager Katherine Purple; senior production editor Kelley Kimm; and all the good folks at Purdue University Press, who found merit in the idea and brought the work to reality.

I save for last the indispensable Gina, our office's chief of staff for a decade, who did all the heavy lifting: editing, selecting the accompanying foreword, cover notes, and other ancillary features, along with innumerable creative contributions. This book is one of the smaller of the thousands of invaluable actions Gina DelSanto performed over these years; Purdue would not be the strong, noteworthy university it is without her.

Okay, next to last. I should reserve the final thanks for the people of Purdue—the faculty, alumni, administrative colleagues, and always, always the nation's most purposeful and principled students, who gave me the opportunity to work with them for the ten most fulfilling years of my life. I'm ever grateful.

Notes

1. As I mentioned previously, in 2021 and 2022, Purdue University was named one of *Fast Company* magazine's inaugural "Brands That Matter." According to *Fast Company*'s editors, the list honors companies and organizations that give people compelling reasons to care about them and offer inspiration for others to buy in. *Fast Company* editors judged each brand on relevancy, cultural impact, ingenuity, and business impact. The only university named a Brand That Matters, and the only entity selected from the state of Indiana, Purdue joins ninety-five internationally recognized brands, including Ford, McDonald's, Nike, 3M and other large multinational corporations. You can read more about the recognition at https://www.purdue.edu/newsroom/releases/2021/Q4/purdue-only-university-in-fast-company-magazines-inaugural-list-of-brands-that-matter.html.

   In 2022, Purdue University was voted America's No. 4 most trusted public university, and No. 21 overall, in Morning Consult's "Most Trusted Universities." The study measured how deeply the public trusts universities "to do the right thing." You can read more about this at https://www.purdue.edu/newsroom/releases/2022/Q3/purdue-ranked-no.-4-most-trusted-public-university-in-the-u.s..html.

   As of this writing, Purdue has been ranked as one of U.S. News and World Report's top ten most innovative universities in America for five years in a row. You can read more at https://www.purdue.edu/newsroom/releases/2022/Q3/purdues-most-innovative-status-reaches-5-years-in-u.s.-news-38-world-report-rankings.html#:~:text=Purdue%2C%20whose%20graduates%20earn%20an,World%20Report%20Best%20Colleges%20rankings.

2. In 2005, Norm Augustine, former CEO of the Lockheed Martin Corporation, former undersecretary of the U.S. Army, and recipient of the National Medal of Technology, responded to a bipartisan congressional call for a study of our nation's competitiveness in engineering and technology. Sponsored by the National Academies, the committee under Chairman Augustine's leadership produced the

seminal report *Rising Above the Gathering Storm, Revisited: Rapidly Approaching Category 5*. In the report, all twenty members of the committee agreed that the U.S. would soon lose its global technological edge unless science education and research became the focus of our country's educational and research enterprise. In June 2011, President Barack Obama, following recommendations from his Jobs and Competitiveness Council, called for the U.S. to increase by 10,000 annually the number of graduating engineers and computer scientists.

3. Ultimately during my tenure at Purdue, we extended the tuition freeze for eleven years, one year past the end of my presidency. Over time, I heard from thousands of parents how much it meant that we worked to make a Purdue degree affordable for their children and families.

4. Dr. Gebisa Ejeta (1950–), Purdue alumnus and distinguished professor of plant breeding and genetics, earned the World Food Prize in 2009. To read more about Dr. Ejeta's remarkable achievements in crop storage, see https://www .worldfoodprize.org/en/laureates/20002009_laureates/2009_ejeta/.

5. Nobel laureate Norman Borlaug (1914–2009) is known as the father of the green revolution for his work to increase the world's food supply. For additional information, see https://www.nobelprize.org/prizes/peace/1970/borlaug /biographical/.

6. In September 2014, General Mills shareholders voted overwhelmingly against a proposal by the company to eliminate the use of genetically modified/bioengineered ingredients in its products. In April 2015, Chipotle announced it would become the first national restaurant to ban the use of GMO products from its menu. Later that year, the company suffered significant reputational hits, as customers were sickened in multistate incidents involving *E. coli* and norovirus contaminations. Both fecal-borne bacteria, *E. coli* normally derives from the slaughtering process, while norovirus usually results from unsanitary conditions among food workers. Neither is a result of genetic modification.

7. Since 2016, the total debt of U.S. students has only increased, with current estimates between $1.6 trillion and $1.75 trillion.

8. Applications for Purdue's 2022 entering class exceeded 66,000.

9. Sullivan's article "America Wasn't Built for Humans" carries the lede, "Tribalism was an urge our Founding Fathers assumed we could overcome. And so it has become our greatest vulnerability." See https://nymag.com/intelligencer/2017/09 /can-democracy-survive-tribalism.html.

10. When we created the Indiana Economic Development Corporation, we made sure that its leader would also be a cabinet member. So, we asked the General

Assembly to codify a dual assignment, making a single individual both the secretary of commerce and the CEO of the Indiana Economic Development Corporation. The public law passed in 2002 was IC 5-28-3-4.

11. Passed into law on February 1, 2012, and codified at IC 22-6-6, the Indiana Right-to-Work law provides that no employer, labor organization, or any person may require an individual to become or remain a member of a labor organization, or pay dues, fees, or assessments (or charitable donation substitutes) as a condition of employment, new or continued. The law gives individuals a private right of action that can be brought in civil court, and it provides for an administrative remedy by the Indiana Department of Labor. It also criminalizes violations of the statute and gives prosecutors discretion to charge people or organizations criminally for violations. The law does not apply to collective bargaining agreements that were in place on or before March 14, 2012, and it does not prohibit exclusive pre-hire agreements with labor unions in the building and construction trades.

12. On June 14, 2010, Western Governors University Indiana, familiarly known as WGU Indiana, was established by executive order as the state's eighth public university. WGU Indiana's mission is to expand access to affordable higher education for Indiana residents through online degree programs in in-demand fields.

13. On April 2, 2018, Purdue University completed the acquisition and announced the launch of Purdue Global, a public, online nonprofit university designed to serve the postsecondary educational needs for working adults and others seeking a high-quality remote learning option.

14. Tippecanoe County, Indiana, is the state's seventh largest by population and the home of Purdue University.

15. Except where noted, all columns appeared in the *Washington Post*.

16. Sadly, our nation lost President George Herbert Walker Bush on November 30, 2018.

17. Richard H. Solomon, PhD, was a scholar and diplomat who was nominated by President George H. W. Bush to the position of assistant secretary of state for East Asian and Pacific affairs. During his tenure in that role (June 1989 to July 1992), Solomon helped to negotiate the Paris Peace Agreements, which transferred control of Cambodia to the United Nations and ultimately resulted in Cambodia gaining independence in 1995. He subsequently led the formation of Asia-Pacific Economic Cooperation initiative, which helped normalize relations. He also participated in bilateral negotiations with Vietnam, Mongolia, and Japan.

18. For those less familiar with *Washington Crossing the Delaware*, it was painted by German-born, American-raised artist Emanuel Gottlieb Leutze in 1851. Leutz had returned to his country of birth, where he created the painting in hopes that its theme and spirit would inspire Germans, and Europeans broadly, to adopt the liberal democratic reforms of the American Revolution. The original painting did not fare well—it was nearly destroyed by a fire in Leutze's Bremen studio shortly after he completed it; and the restored work was completely lost during a World War II bombing raid.

Fortunately for us all, Leutze had created two replicas. The first, an original scale replica, was placed on display in New York in 1951 and ultimately found a permanent home in the Metropolitan Museum of Art. The second, a smaller scale replica, was displayed in the White House until 2014, when it was purchased for display at the Minnesota Marine Art Museum.

The painting that now hangs proudly at Purdue was created by Robert Bruce Williams and is an exact copy authorized by the Metropolitan Museum. The work was commissioned by Mrs. Ann Hawkes Hutton in memory of her husband Leon "Jack" Hutton, a 1929 Purdue graduate. Mrs. Hawkes Hutton subsequently donated the painting to the Washington Crossing Foundation in Bristol, Pennsylvania.

It is to Mrs. Kate Hutton Tweedy, daughter of Mr. and Mrs. Hutton, and the Washington Crossing Foundation that Purdue owes a debt of thanks for a twenty-five-year loan of the painting. We were delighted to have Mrs. Hutton Tweedy, members of her extended family, and a delegation from the Washington Crossing Foundation on hand to dedicate the installation in the Great Library of the Wilmeth Active Learning Center.

19. *The Queen's Gambit* is a 2020 Netflix miniseries written by Scott Frank. Despite being offered a starring role in the series, Garry Kasparov chose instead to serve as a consultant, noting that his travel schedule would not permit a more extensive engagement.

20. Paul Ryan, a Republican, represented Wisconsin in Congress from 1999 to 2019. During his tenure, he chaired the two most prominent House committees—Ways and Means and Budget. He served as the fifty-fourth Speaker of the House from 2015 to 2019. Ryan was the 2012 Republican vice presidential nominee.

In 2019, he founded the American Idea Foundation to connect local community organizations to expand economic opportunity through the application of evidence-based public policy.

Heidi Heitkamp, a Democrat, represented North Dakota in the U.S. Senate from 2013 to 2019. In addition to Senate committee assignments in agriculture and banking, she sat on the Committee on Homeland Security and Governmental Affairs. Prior to her election to the Senate, Heitkamp served as North Dakota's attorney general from 1992 to 2000.

   In 2019, in collaboration with former Indiana senator Joe Donnelly, Heitkamp formed the One Country Project, an organization helping Democrats connect with rural voters. Heitkamp also is a visiting Pritzker fellow at the University of Chicago Institute of Politics and a contributor to both ABC News and CNBC.

21. Senator Edward "Ted" Kennedy, a Democrat, represented Massachusetts in the U.S. Senate from 1962 until his death in 2009. Former Missouri governor and U.S. senator John Ashcroft, a Republican, served as the seventy-ninth U.S. attorney general from 2001 to 2005.

22. The Purdue Improved Crop Storage technology is a triple layer sealed plastic bag that dramatically reduces insect damage to dry grain by creating a hermetic storage condition. Designed as a low-cost technology for small farmers in Africa, distribution of the PICS has expanded from ten countries in West and Central Africa to wide distribution across Africa. Although PICS was originally targeted for cowpea storage, it has since proven effective for all types of grain.

23. Although the NASA-commissioned extruder was originally intended to provide a scaled-down way for astronauts to process grain during missions to Mars, Purdue scientists have worked to modify the device to help African farmers reduce the highly labor-intensive work of refining grain at scale.

24. Typhoon Haiyan, one of the most powerful storms ever recorded, had winds gusting up to 230 mph. The typhoon made landfall in Southeast Asia, particularly the Philippines, in November 2013, killing in more than 6,300 individuals.

25. The United Nations Paris Agreement was adopted by 196 governmental entities (countries, territories, city-states) in 2015, effective November 2016. The goal of the agreement is to limit global warming to two degrees Celsius compared to preindustrial levels.

26. The Intergovernmental Panel on Climate Change (IPCC) is the United Nations body for assessing the science related to climate change.

27. H. W. Brands, *Andrew Jackson: His Life and Times* (New York: Anchor Books, 2006).

28. I hope the reader will indulge as permissible three minor licenses I took in order to maintain the parallelism of the "14s": (1) I recognize that, after his defeat and exile in 1814, Napoleon escaped and had to be defeated again at Waterloo the next year; (2) similarly, that the War of 1812 ended in late 1814 with the Treaty of Ghent but, the news not yet having reached the American continent, the Battle of New Orleans occurred in the first days of 1815; and (3) that the majority view

would take the year 2000 as the first of a new century and therefore count this year's class as the fifteenth and not the fourteenth.

29. Paul Johnson, *The Birth of the Modern: World Society, 1815–1830* (New York: HarperCollins, 1992).

30. Johnson, *The Birth of the Modern*.

31. Johnson, *The Birth of the Modern*.

32. Daniel Walker Howe, *What Hath God Wrought: The Transformation of America, 1815–1848* (New York: Oxford University Press, 2007).

33. Paul Fussell, *The Great War and Modern Memory* (New York: Oxford University Press, 1975).

Index

Note: The photo insert pages are indexed as *p1, p2, p3,* and so forth.

World Bank, 288
World Food Prize, 8, 43, 222, 287, 314
World Health Organization, 301
World Trade Center, 281
World Values Survey, 209
World War I, 186, 248, 317, 322
World War II, 236
Wright, Wilbur, 340
writing skills, 130–32

X
Xi Jinping, 181

Y
Yale University, 38; Grand Strategy
   program, 115, 116
Yeltsin, Boris, 191
Young, Todd, *p8*
You've Got Mail (film), 19

Z
Zimmer, 102
Zimmer, Robert, 63, 67

About the Author

MITCHELL E. DANIELS, JR., IS ONE OF THE FEW INDIVIDUALS IN AMERICAN HISTORY to excel as a leader in the private, public, and education sectors. Within the span of a decade, he was called both "America's best governor" and its "best university president."

Elected Indiana's governor in 2004 in his first bid for public office, Daniels was reelected in 2008 with more votes than any candidate in the state's history. During his tenure, Indiana went from an $800 million deficit to its first AAA credit rating, and passed sweeping education and health care reforms. By the time Daniels exited office, Indiana was rated a top five state for business climate, and number one state for infrastructure and effectiveness of state government.

During a decade of service as Purdue's president, Daniels exemplified the role of public intellectual and thought leader in poignant speeches, provocative opinion pieces, and national interviews on topics of great currency to American society. He captured the country's attention by prioritizing student affordability and investment in faculty and research. After thirty-six years of consecutive increases, Daniels took the unprecedented step of freezing tuition at 2012 levels, with student borrowing falling 37%.

In 2015, he was named to *Fortune* magazine's World's 50 Greatest Leaders, and in 2019, he was elected to the American Academy of Arts and Sciences. In 2023, Purdue University named its business school the Mitchell E. Daniels, Jr. School of Business.

Daniels served as chief of staff to Senator Richard Lugar, senior advisor to President Ronald Reagan, and director of the Office of Management and Budget under President George W. Bush. He was the CEO of the Hudson Institute, and he held top executive posts at Eli Lilly and Company.

Daniels earned a baccalaureate from Princeton and a law degree from Georgetown. He is the author of three books and a contributing columnist to the *Washington Post*.

He and his wife, Cheri, have four daughters and seven grandchildren.